TEAM LOTUS

THE INDIANAPOLIS YEARS

TEAM LOTUS
THE INDIANAPOLIS YEARS

Andrew Ferguson
Foreword by Mario Andretti

PSL

Patrick Stephens Limited

For my daughter, Alice

First published in October 1996

British Library Cataloguing in Publication Data:
A catalogue record for this book is
available from the British Library

ISBN 1 85260 491 3

Library of Congress catalog card no. 95 79118

Patrick Stephens Limited is an imprint of Haynes Publishing, Sparkford, Nr Yeovil, Somerset, BA22 7JJ.

Designed & typeset by G&M,
Raunds, Northamptonshire, England
Printed in Hong Kong

CONVERSION TABLES

£ sterling/$ dollar exchange rates:

1963	$2.80
1964	$2.79
1965	$2.80
1966	$2.79
1967	$2.80
1968	$2.39
1969	$2.40

To convert …	*… into …*	*… multiply by*
Imperial pints	Litres	0.5682
Imperial quarts	Litres	2.5400
Imperial gallons	US gallons	1.2009
Imperial gallons	Litres	4.5460
Inches	Centimetres	2.5400
Feet	Metres	0.3048
Cubic inches	Cubic centimetres	16.39
Cubic centimetres	Cubic inches	0.06102
Pounds	Kilograms	0.4536
Centigrade or Celsius	Fahrenheit	9/5ths and add 32
Fahrenheit	Centigrade or Celsius	Subtract 32 and multiply by 5/9ths

Liquid weights:

Gasoline	Imperial gallon	7.015 lbs
	US gallon	5.84 lbs
Oil	Imperial gallon	9.222 lbs
	US gallon	7.677 lbs
Water	Imperial gallon	10.022 lbs
	US gallon	8.345 lbs

Contents

Core of the Lotus Indianapolis years – Colin Chapman and Jimmy Clark with the victorious Lotus 38 of 1965. (Indianapolis Motor Speedway)

Acknowledgements

Sadly, Andrew Ferguson died on 31 October 1994, shortly after completing this book but before it could be published.

The publishers and his widow Jackie Ferguson are grateful to Doug Nye for editing Andrew's manuscript and preparing it for publication. They would also like to thank Mike Underwood, Jim Endruweit, Arthur Birchall, Graham Clode, David Lazenby, Noel Chiappa, Roy Franks, Bob Dance, Chris Mann, Tom Candlish and Walter Goodwin, who helped Andrew with his original research.

In turn, Doug Nye would like to thank the following:

Dan Gurney, creator of the whole Lotus-Ford Indy project in the first place, who spent long hours looking backward when he's only ever been really interested in looking forward. Noel Chiappa, prominent Indy Lotus car collector and tireless researcher, whose endeavours have unearthed a vast number of important photographs; photographers Bob Tronolone and Dave Friedman, who have also given valuable assistance, Dave in particular filling in a great deal of background information, especially about Bobby Marshman, who led Indy in 1964 with one of the ex-Team cars; Jack Beckley, past crew chief for Lindsey Hopkins; Vince Granatelli, STP crew chief; Martin Flower whose personal Lotus Indy car research has been so deep and painstaking; Team Lotus members Jim Endruweit, Dave Lazenby, Dick Scammell and Ron Chappell; David Phipps, Jabby Crombac, and Richard Spelberg, who have all been more than willing to help with photographs and information; the staff of the Indianapolis Motor Speedway, its Museum and photo archive; John Miles, Lotus past Formula 1 Team driver and engineer; Jim Allington, great cutaway artist; and Patrick Stephens, who encouraged Andrew to write the book in the first place and who has provided support throughout.

Finally, Jackie Ferguson, whose quite remarkable strength and determination to see her late husband's project through to completion has ensured that this book has seen the light of day.

Author Andrew Ferguson was Competitions Manager of Team Lotus from 1961 to 1969, returned to them in the 1970s, was founding organiser of the Formula One Constructors' Association and was one of the best-liked men in international motor racing. Here in Team Lotus's garage on 'Gasoline Alley' at Indianapolis in 1965 he tries his hand – as described later in these pages – at applying the winning car's race numbers. Andrew died in 1994 before this book, into which he put so very much, could be finalised for publication.

Foreword
by Mario Andretti

I first met Colin Chapman and Jim Clark at Trenton's 1 mile oval in September 1964. Team Lotus was there for testing and a race in which I was driving for my good friend and sponsor, Al Dean. I was already well aware of their achievements; Jimmy was then the reigning Formula 1 World Champion, a title that was still a dream to a 'rookie' like myself; but 14 years later Colin and I were to win World Championship crowns together.

At Trenton, Colin's rear-engined lightweight creations were still regarded by the Indy establishment as 'funny cars', but their influence, stemming from Cooper's assault on the famous Brickyard in 1961, was to have a profound effect on chassis design throughout the American auto racing world.

In 1965, just two years after his debut at the Brickyard, Colin was to see 27 rear-engined cars out of the 33 on the starting grid. He offered me a drive the same year and I was to be associated with him, on and off, for the next 15 years.

A race car is like a thoroughbred; you can't always analyse it by studying its blood lines, but I always figured that a Lotus out of Chapman should be a winner, and more often than not I was right.

The Indy 500 of 1965, which this book celebrates in particular, provided an important milestone for at least three of those present. Jim Clark won the race at just his third attempt, much to the delight of his mentor and close friend, Colin Chapman. For myself, as a rookie, it would have been memorable just to take part, but I was fortunate to finish third, just 6 seconds adrift of second-man Parnelli Jones; in 1969 I won the classic.

Team Lotus's participation was also notable for another reason. It focused even more attention on the event around the world and triggered an influx of European drivers; this might not have gone down too well with Indy's regulars, who could see large sums of money going overseas, but it certainly brought a healthy injection of new faces.

The international exploits of the tall, rugged Californian Dan Gurney were already well known, but it is important to remember that it was Dan who first brought Colin to Indy, and who engineered the link with Ford of America's immense involvement.

There was also the shy and sensitive Jim Clark, an incredible race driver who was the prototype of the complete gentleman on the track. He seldom made a mistake and never made a dangerous or foolish move. I think he took great pride in giving other drivers every possible advantage and still beating them. He wasn't the eager, angry type who went around spouting opinions. He kept to himself, and when somebody asked a question, he gave an honest, forthright answer. I didn't race against him often, and for this I'm sorry.

Graham Hill I always reckoned was the cartoon Englishman, with his snappy moustache, a look of complete disdain, a finely tuned sense of humour and a tongue that could cut through stone. An announcer once asked him, 'What is your biggest problem here, Graham?', to which he replied, testily, 'At the moment, my biggest problem is you.' Invited to comment on the importance of the main straight, he squelched the hapless interviewer with, 'I think it's very important – since it connects two turns.' And Graham also brought progress to the Speedway. He was offended by the primitive rest-room facilities in the garage area, so that every time he was attacked by Mother Nature, he had to fight this very private if necessary war in view of anybody who wandered past. When asked by track-owner Tony Hulman how he liked the track, Graham cut loose.

'It's barbaric, degrading, uncivilised, and downright embarrassing to go into the men's convenience and find there are no doors.'

That very same night, doors were fitted to all the stalls.

The off-track personalities are here too. The literally larger-than-life Andy Granatelli, 'Mr STP', he of the constantly grinding propaganda mills. Andy has been called 'the last of the snake oil salesman', a huge man with excess energy coming out of his ears. He brought the first efficient turbine to the track, a concept that I disagreed with, and said so. It's ironic that for all my criticism of his attempted revolution, I was to drive his only Indy-winning car after his 20 years of trying. For this he kissed me.

All these characters are in Andrew Ferguson's remarkable book, so too are the hard-working, unsung heroes of mechanics, designers and engineers who then, as now, make the whole extravaganza possible.

Nazareth, Pennsylvania, 1996

The Guv'nor, the Old Man, the Boss – Colin Chapman, creator of Team Lotus and all that it achieved, on the pit counter at Indianapolis, 1965.

CHAPTER ONE

The Contestants and the Track

The story of Lotus's Indianapolis years involves automobile people from both sides of the Atlantic, many of whom – largely unknown to the spectators and public at large – were responsible for remarkable events. They created countless media headlines, initially in America, then around the world. To onlookers the drivers played the glamorous role; some had already achieved star status, some were on their way towards achieving it.

Of the three companies that combined to conquer 'Indy', two were motor manufacturers, one major, one very minor. One was the giant corporation, Ford of America, the other Colin Chapman's minuscule British organisation, Lotus.

Ford's history reached back to the turn of the century, that of Lotus to the early 1950s, a mere ten years or so before this tale opens. Ford's story is too well known to bear repetition here, and the stories of Chapman and Lotus have also been well told, several times. When these two companies assumed converging paths, Ford was the world's second largest motor manufacturer, employing well over a third of a million people, while Lotus employed barely one hundred, fewer than ten of them on the 'Team Lotus' competition department payroll.

The third major player in our story, the STP Corporation, does not make its entrance until Act 3, when it will provide invaluable financial support to see Team Lotus return annually to the Speedway for a further four years after the close association with Ford had ended. STP's primary driving force was the remarkable Anthony 'Andy' Granatelli, born in 1923, 5 ft 10 ins tall and weighing between 274 and 300 pounds (20–21 stones). 'I defy all medical science,' he sometimes commented. Andy combined his lifelong passion to win the 500-mile classic with promoting the sale of literally millions and millions of cans of 'Scientifically Treated Petroleum', merging these two ambitions perfectly.

Centre of attraction for these organisations and personalities was the 2½-mile Indianapolis Speedway in America's Midwest. Other works detail Indy's background, but suffice here to recall that it was founded by Carl G. Fisher, who led a consortium (one of whom was James A. Allison, the future aircraft engine magnate) that purchased a 539-acre site 6 miles west from 'downtown' Indianapolis. The track, initially surfaced with crushed stone and tar, opened in August 1909.

Louis Schwitzer won the first race over 5 miles, and Bob Bowman in a Buick won the 250-mile event at 53.7 mph; accidents claimed the lives of one driver and two spectators. An improved track surface was required, and the rebuilding was a perfect example of enthusiastic American enterprise; over 3,200,000 bricks were laid in just four months, and the track reopened for business just before Christmas 1909. A contemporary review of the work reported the largest number of bricks (each weighing fractionally under 10 lbs) laid in 9 hours as 140,000. A portable conveyer belt driven by an automobile engine enabled one bricklayer to lay an average of 11.4 tons every 9 hours.

In 1911 the track's owners decided to hold an all-day festival of speed and chose America's Memorial Day of 30 May as the date. To enable spectators from the outlying countryside to travel to and from the event in daylight, they chose a race distance of 500 miles, which would last around 7 hours.

A fact of some interest, considering the unreliability of cars in those far-off days, was that 26 cars were still running at the end of this inaugural Indianapolis 500-mile race. Winner Ray Harroun, in his Marmon Wasp, averaged 74.59 mph for a fraction over 6 hrs 42 mins. His was the only one-man car in the race, the others carrying riding mechanics, one of whom became the only fatality. Prize money totalled $27,550, of which Harroun's share was an impressive $14,000. More importantly, spectator attendance totalled over 75,000, guaranteeing the future of both the venue and the 500-mile race, each to become enshrined in all-American legend.

The first crash helmet seen at the track was reputedly a British Cromwell worn by Louis Chiron in 1929; American Wilbur Shaw was later presented with a Cromwell on a tour of Europe, and by 1935 most Indy drivers wore helmets, although they were not mandatory.

In 1926 Carl Fisher became involved in another business venture, developing the swamplands in Florida that would become Miami Beach, so the following year the Track Presidency passed to James A. Allison, who then sold out to Captain 'Eddie' Rickenbacker, racing driver-cum-First World War American flying ace. Modernisation of its facilities included resurfacing all but the main straight with asphalt in 1935.

The Second World War brought the event to a close after the 1941 race. Then, when peace returned, Rickenbacker, by then President of Eastern Airlines, wanted to sell. Three-time Indy race-winner, Wilbur Shaw, was adamant that the now ramshackle track and its buildings should not become mere folklore, and he turned for help to a local Hoosier living in nearby Terre Haute, Anton (Tony) Hulman Jr. An outstanding athlete in his youth, Hulman was a millionaire, controlling the fortune generated by his grandfather, and he acquired the facility in October 1945 for a reputed $750,000. He installed Shaw as President and General Manager and the two proved an excellent combination, despite the immense tasks they set themselves.

The numerous buildings and grandstands built of wood needed extensive refurbishment to allow the event to continue before further plans could be brought to fruition. Hulman and

Indy tradition – the American Mid-West's historic Speedway was nicknamed 'The Brickyard' after the brick sett re-surfacing that had made it viable from 1909. By 1962, when Colin Chapman saw it for the first time, only this final yard of bricks remained, beyond the start/finish line.

Shaw brought a new level of professionalism to the Speedway in race organisation, promotion and provision of modern facilities. By 1952 five of the nine enormous wooden grandstands had been demolished and modern concrete and steel constructions erected to a size and standard unheard of in Europe.

Shaw was killed in a private plane crash in 1954, and from then on Hulman assumed overall control, and modernisation continued. The track required overall re-surfacing, which was completed in 1955, leaving just a yard-wide strip of the original bricks on the start/finish line, with a superb new museum-cum-office centre built beside the main entrance in 1956.

Constructed in the early 1920s, the famed pagoda building, which had come to symbolise the track for over 30 years and which housed the timekeepers and other race officials by the start/finish line, was to remain a landmark until it was replaced in 1957 by a new control tower, tower terrace and pit area. With these additions came a new road tunnel under the back stretch.

In 1959 the well-known electric scoreboard pylon displaying all 33 race positions on each of its four sides was erected, followed in 1963 by a luxurious clubhouse and the 96-unit Speedway Motel adjoining the Speedway Golf Course, which enjoyed its own 'Festival' golf tournament during the month of May.

Beside the control tower, a 14,000-seat spectator tower terrace containing a large restaurant was built parallel to the open 'pits', with a walkway alongside a retaining wire fence where onlookers could gather to watch the drivers or their crews working on the cars. Similar wire fences around the garage area allowed fans to watch work behind the scenes.

In the early 1960s the two attractive but aged garage blocks with their clapboard walls still remained. Known as 'Gasoline Alley', the garage area contained over 80 units, of which 62 were allocated to race cars on a first-come-first-served basis. Provided free of charge when the entry fee had been processed, they offered space only, entrants being responsible for supplying their own equipment. A number of 'vendors' or supporting organisations offered technical co-operation and use of their equipment free of charge for such work as wheel alignment, ignition servicing, fuel mixture checks, shock absorber servicing and much more, including the Magnaflux and Zyglo certification sections, both concerned with the safety of race car components in detecting cracks or other signs of sub-standard materials or manufacture that might cause failure.

The provision of the fuel tanks situated in the pits for re-fuelling the race cars was also the responsibility of each entrant; fortunately the manufacturer of these large items was situated in Indianapolis, and able to work quickly to its customers' individual specifications.

The qualifying procedure to secure a place on the 33-strong rolling-start grid for the annual '500' provided three attempts to attain sufficient speed over four allotted days, scheduled over two weekends preceding the race. Each attempt of four consecutive laps (10 miles) saw the car running solo and being timed to

The Indianapolis Motor Speedway – self-styled 'World Capitol of Auto Racing' – becomes just that on every American Memorial Day. Here in 1965, before a quarter of a million spectators, Lotus lead the pack into Turn One with 500 miles to go; Jimmy Clark's works Lotus-Ford 38 leads from A. J. Foyt's Sheraton Thompson Special *uprated Lotus 34, Dan Gurney's Yamaha Lotus 38 and Parnelli Jones's Agajanian-Hurst Lotus 34. Clark and Jones would finish first and second . . . (Indianapolis Motor Speedway)*

one-hundredth of a second. The emphasis was on the first day's running, as those that qualified on that day took the relevant positions at the front of the grid; those qualifying on the second day were allotted positions according to their times, but behind those that had qualified on the first day and so on. In other words, the final grid layout would be composed of four sections, or subgrids, reflecting the qualifying on each of the four days.

The fastest man at the end of Day One sat on the coveted pole position, and no one could dislodge him even if a faster time was recorded on Days Two, Three or Four; such a procedure could produce the odd situation, to European eyes, of having one or even several cars faster than pole having to start some way to the rear.

On Day Four of qualifying came the 'bumping' of some cars by others qualifying faster. As anyone familiar with the vicissitudes of motor racing can guess, 'bumping' involved heartache and misery, ecstasy, almost delirium, dependent upon results. Anybody

could be in danger – much-loved veterans, supporters and novices alike.

Drivers new to the Speedway also had to pass a 'rookie' test, regardless of their experience elsewhere. This consisted of solo runs, 10 laps at a time, at ever-increasing speeds under the watchful eye of the track's Chief Steward, prior to any attempt at qualifying. Apart from some cases when a driver was told he needed more experience and would have to wait a year before making another attempt, there were also occasions when car failure, with insufficient time remaining to rectify the problems, could prevent a driver completing this test procedure, so a frustrating year would pass before another attempt could be made.

As the Ford histories relate, it was in 1932 that the Model A Ford became available with the company's first V8 engine, a 3.6-litre side-valve unit developing 70 bhp. This was soon found in competition; in fact, a modified Ford roadster powered by the V8 won the 1933 Elgin 200-mile stock car race, averaging

Hallowed ground – the track entrance view to 'Gasoline Alley', the Indianapolis Motor Speedway's paddock workshop area. The open bleacher stands on each side back the similarly open and unprotected pit row. Here throughout the month of May – in often intolerable working conditions – the Team Lotus crew slaved through seven assaults upon the 500 Mile American classic.

80.22 mph, driven by the previous year's Indy 500 winner, Fred Frame. That race was the first of countless competition events in which Ford cars or power units would compete in the future, and the stock car category would lead eventually to the formation of the National Association for Stock Car Auto Racing (NASCAR) in 1947.

Production of the millionth V8 came in 1935, just three years after its introduction, and the milestone coincided with Ford's only official participation at Indianapolis between the wars. This involvement by proxy with Miller-designed cars powered by modified Ford V8 stock engines – producing some 150 bhp at 5,000 rpm – was a disaster, albeit not Ford's fault. The project involved building no fewer than ten all-new, front-wheel-drive all-independently-suspended chassis. It started late and ran later; the last of the cars arrived at the Brickyard only two days before the race. An inherent steering design fault saw several drivers turning their backs on the cars during practice. Only four qualified, then retired due to steering problems, while five other Ford-engined cars failed to make the grid. It was, in fact, commendable that any of the cars had even made the start, but in the eyes of the public this was an enormous loss of face for Ford. Those with most to lose were Ford dealerships. Funding for the project had come indirectly from their allocated funds, and they screamed! Ford would not return to Indianapolis until its partnership with Lotus 28 years later.

Over the years there was a wide variety of cars in competition using what were basically Ford V8 engines, from hot-rods running on dry lakes, the Bonneville Salt Flats and drag strips, to out-and-out racing and sports cars.

In 1956 a small offshoot of Ford was quietly engrossed in a racing version of a V8 32-valve engine. Situated in California, the facility was part of a special projects department headed by Joe MacKay, responsible for Ford's stock car engine programme. The project had come about thanks to a senior Ford executive, Harley Copp, who had long harboured a desire to see his company back in contention at Indianapolis. Years later, Copp was to play an instrumental part in Ford of Britain's decision to provide the launch capital for Keith Duckworth's Formula 1 Cosworth DFV V8 engine, which became the most successful Grand Prix power unit ever.

Working on the American Ford V8 were two well-respected engineers, Jim Travers and Frank Coon, who were even to travel to Germany to investigate the desmodromic valve operation employed by Mercedes-Benz in its 1955 Formula 1 engine. Both engineers had, before the war, modified and experimented with 1932 Ford V8 hot-rod engines.

After the Second World War Travers had worked with Stuart Hilborn to perfect the Hilborn-Travers fuel injection system, and he joined forces with Coon in 1946, preparing midget racing cars. By 1948 they were at Indy, later building and preparing cars for the legendary Bill Vukovitch from 1952 to 1955, winner in 1953 and 1954.

In 1958 Lance Reventlow contracted them to prepare the Chevrolet engines for his new Scarab sports cars. Later Travers and Coon formed their Traco organisation, a name that became a byword in big sports car events through their connection with the Bruce McLaren-owned Zerex 4-litre V8 Oldsmobile unit. Later they were to help to build McLaren's first 3-litre Formula 1 engine using the quad-cam Ford engines as a basis.

But meanwhile the competition programmes of America's motor industry had been set back. In 1957 inter-company politics brought what most believed to be a mutual cessation of competition involvement by the manufacturing giants. The AMA (Automobile Manufacturers' Association), prompted by General Motors, declared that competition activities should cease in favour of providing 'safe, reliable and comfortable transportation'. Although GM had cited the rapidly escalating costs of competition, the opposition felt that the company was more concerned at Ford's rapidly growing list of race successes and had merely used the safety lobby as a lever.

With the ban's official announcement, all Ford competition projects, including work on the V8 in California, came to a stop, frustrating and disappointing those executives throughout the industry who firmly believed in the value of competition in terms of sales and technical spin-off.

Meanwhile, engineer Jacque Passino had joined Ford from Willys Overland, where he had been Vice-President. Originally of French extraction, Jacque (his mother forgot the final 's' at his christening) suffered similar pangs, and although unknown to him at the time, the ban was to provide a huge boost to his career. Thirty-six years old, tall, thin and prematurely grey, this bespectacled executive had joined Ford's sales promotion department. Aware that race success spelled car sales, when he heard of Joe MacKay's resignation from special projects he applied for the post and won it.

Regardless of Ford's official withdrawal from motor sport, he continued to keep a watchful eye on the competition world, convinced that it would not be long before everyone re-entered the fray. When his intuition proved correct, Jacque assumed supremo status within Ford's racing fraternity, his quietly spoken, sometimes blunt opinions expressed with authority. His essentially pragmatic approach was to provide an invaluable contribution to the cause.

By late 1958 it was clear that the AMA decree was being flouted by other manufacturers. Robert McNamara, General Manager of Ford Division and hardly an advocate of racing, had held firm until a decline in sales forced him to shift his stance. The problem he faced was where to find the finance required for a return to competition – Ford had only just been able to fund a shareholders' dividend. Fortunately, business revived the following year, as did Chevrolet racing activity, and almost simultaneously Ford made its U-turn on racing.

One of McNamara's aides was Donald Frey, who had joined Ford in 1951. A former university professor, now promoted to Executive Engineer of Product Planning, Frey was given the task in 1959 of planning the company's re-entry to competition. One of his first moves was to install a long-serving Ford man, Dave Evans, as head of a three-man consortium; Dave had been part of Ford's first stock car support group.

Responsibility for engines fell to Don Sullivan, an 'old-timer' from Ford's last Indianapolis foray in 1935 and renowned for extracting additional horsepower from any unit committed to his care. Leo Levine, author of *Ford: The Dust and the Glory*, recorded that money was so short that Sullivan was reduced to working on a new intake manifold on his kitchen table. Lacking approval to use a company dynamometer, the group was forced to rely on Sullivan's expertise in gauging an engine's efficiency by its sound ...

Destined to take charge of the engine project was William (Bill) H. Gay. Steadily ascending the corporate ladder, Gay was an accomplished engineer within Ford's engine and foundry division and had worked with George Stirrat in the design and development of the original 221 cu in Fairlane engine. Hardly a motor racing enthusiast, Gay was acknowledged to be an expert on engines, and from executive engineer of his department it would not be long before he would advance. Now assisted by Tom Landis and Ed Pinkerton, Gay would oversee construction on the initial push-rod V8 racing engine and follow on into the initial design and construction of the replacement quad-cam unit.

Another important cog in the wheel was Bill Innes of the same division. Innes was soon made aware of the group's intentions and saw to it that his department provided the special components they required.

Frey's small band, devoid of sufficient funding, was forced to beg, borrow or 'steal' components and even complete cars from the prototype production test section to ensure that their so far confidential development programme progressed. Then came major benefits from two sources.

First was the emergence of possibly the most influential player in the developing scenario, Lee Iacocca. Switching from an engineering career to one in sales, Lee had risen some years earlier to automobile marketing manager of Ford Division. He supported the promotion of safety, but instinct told him that competitive activities should not suffer as a result. A year after the ban had been signed, Chevrolet was found to be stocking and selling go-faster components, and Iacocca had circulated a memo pressing Ford to follow suit. They had not.

As 1960 approached there came Iacocca's golden opportunity to wield a far more influential stick. Ford Division General Manager Robert Tallowy was invited to join President John F. Kennedy's administration, and the 36-year-old Iacocca was suddenly promoted over more senior candidates into the vacant seat. From then on there would be a champion of racing in a seat of real power at Ford. He wasted no time in making vital decisions. He chopped Ford's soon-to-be-announced version of the Volkswagen and plumped for a model being nurtured by Frey, conceived as outwardly a saloon car but with sports car qualities, and still four years away from its launch date in 1964. By then Ford's new and aggressive competition image had been broadcast far and wide and the car would become an enormous marketing success. Its name? Mustang ...

Another major boost came from the opening of new tracks for the NASCAR circus in 1960, complete with increased media attention and TV coverage. This gave invaluable impetus to the small group's pleas for extra funding, and with Iacocca at the helm they had the man to help them.

At the time of Iacocca's accession, he knew full well that Ford desperately needed 'youth market' support to guarantee future sales, and the company's staid, conservative image was less than acceptable to him. As someone who had learned the value of competitive successes in previous years, he decided to go all out on all fronts and received Henry Ford II's approval to do just that.

The first item on the agenda was the NASCAR stock car category. High priority was given to establishing the degree of support required, the engineering time scales and systems needed, securing the drivers and crews and integrating the new approach to competition within the company. Ford's field of activity in other categories of racing was often touched upon in management meetings, and several times Indianapolis was discussed ...

Then in 1961 came the British Cooper Car Company's entry in the all-American classic, an event Jack Brabham was to describe as a 'month-long Girl Guide camp'. Rodger Ward, star of USAC (United States Automobile Club) racing, had run a midget car in the 1959 United States Grand Prix at Sebring. He had been outclassed there, but immediately recognised the potential of the winning Grand Prix Coopers.

Rodger impressed John Cooper and his driver Jack Brabham with his talk of Indy, so much so that the following year (1960) they took a Formula 1 car to the Speedway, where its performance stunned the track's 'establishment'. Right from its first laps, on 5 October, the knowledgeable onlookers were agog. That year's pole had been taken at 146.952 mph, and the race-winning average was 138.767 mph, yet here was a 'foreigner', new to the track, driving a 'funny car' (the contemporary American term for a rear-engined car) with an undersized engine 1,700 cc below the regulation limit, yet lapping at 144.834 mph!

I worked for Cooper's at the time and recently found my itinerary and budget scribbled on Cooper envelopes. We studied three ways of freighting the car: by Pan-Am (with 350 lbs of spares) the cost was £212 single, by sea (RMS *Queen Mary* or *Queen Elizabeth*) to New York was £110, or £80 on the SS *United States*, the on-going flight to Indy costing a further £55. In the end we flew it over. John Cooper and chief mechanic 'Noddy' Grohmann had the option of going turbo-prop or jet, the latter costing £199 return, £13 more than the droning propellers!

After that test, events moved quickly. Jim Kimberly, millionaire owner of the Kleenex Corporation, provided the sponsorship, engine makers Coventry Climax provided an engine with the slightly enlarged capacity of 2,750 cc (still almost 1½ litres less than the standard 4.2-litre Offenhauser-powered American cars), Cooper built a car more suited to the track, and so the stage was set for an entry in the 1961 '500'.

In qualifying, Brabham was 13th fastest amongst the 69 entries (fifth row of the grid) at 145.144 mph. On race day, the car finished a highly creditable ninth, recording the fastest time of the day through Turn One, a whole 8 mph quicker than the fastest American roadster. The performances of both Jack Brabham and the Cooper thoroughly deserved the plaudits of the enormous crowd and the entire motoring fraternity.

Memorial Day 1962 found Don Frey and Dave Evans of Ford spectating at Indy. After Rodger Ward's win they made their way home, chewing over what they had seen. Back at the factory each made contact with those whose financial and engineering support they would need; Bill Innes, Chief Engineer of the Engine and Foundry Division, had been conducting research and development on an aluminium Fairlane-based power unit, and he supported Frey's interest in Indy. Frey talked to Iacocca; no positive decision emerged, but like most over-sized corporations everyone carried on along the same routes as before, awaiting an official decision one way or the other.

Work on the engine continued, albeit slowly. Those in Ford's advance engine department knew full well that if and when a decision came it was more than likely that they would be faced with the 1963 Indy race as the ultimate deadline. They compared data from other racing engines such as the Offenhauser, the Ferrari V6 and Climax four-cylinder and V8-cylinder, evaluating these for both push-rod and overhead-cam purposes. Although it was obvious that time would not be on their side, they chose to pursue not one but two engine configurations, one push-rod, the other a double overhead camshaft version, known as the 'quad-cam'. Their choice of basic unit was the 260 cu in production engine then powering their Falcon, Fairline and Comet models. Its capacity came closest to the Indianapolis displacement limit, only a slight reduction being required. The possibility of building a pure race engine had also been discussed, but, as time was of the essence, the idea was put to one side and the most sensible route was taken of developing a proven and established unit.

While the talking continued, someone had posed the obvious question: who should build the chassis? Initially, attention focused naturally on the established Indy chassis men, but then veteran Indy entrant, the wealthy banker Lindsey Hopkins, was invited along to state his views. Hopkins, a soft-spoken Southerner, had owned racing cars since the late 1930s; Henry Banks drove Hopkins midgets in 1938, eventually landing the AAA National Championship for his entrant in 1950. Hopkins had entered cars at the Speedway for the past 12 years (Banks drove his first championship car), and was regarded as second only to entrant J. C. Agajanian. His cars had come close to winning the '500' on two occasions, but bad luck, or as some said a jinx, had stepped in before the big win, although he had taken two second places. He had employed a galaxy of star drivers in his time and was an avowed rear-engine man . . . Like Rodger Ward, he had been convinced by Cooper that a rear-engined layout was the way forward. Although the Indy Cooper had been well underpowered and the team had miscalculated tyre wear, thereby making an unplanned stop and losing yet more time, Hopkins had in fact been so impressed by the concept that he had even tried to purchase the car.

Meanwhile, the men from Ford continued to keep a close watch on the USAC scene and, unknowingly as yet, were coming to the conclusion that they were looking at an establishment that might not have the inspiration required to cope with the image they were seeking to attain. Then, one day in July, just a few weeks after the 1962 race had been run, an elevator in Ford's executive building in Dearborn hummed towards the topmost level. Inside it stood driver Dan Gurney and an expectant, hopeful Colin Chapman . . .

• • •

Indianapolis would not have been uppermost in Colin Chapman's mind as he sketched out the new Type 25 'monocoque' Formula 1 car in 1961. The story goes that the concept of a frameless chassis came to him as he tried to solve the recurring problem of installing aluminium fuel tanks in the tubular frames of that period; such rigid tanks were a constant source of trouble, both to fit and to prevent them leaking. The same story also suggests that Colin's brainwave came to him as he lunched with his top aides, scribbling his ideas on a scrap of paper or serviette in a restaurant in Waltham Abbey, a short drive from the Lotus factory in Cheshunt.

More cafe than restaurant, 'The Trough', as it was known, was popular with Lotus personnel. Boasting only seven or eight tables in what had once been a shop, Colin's group had a reserved table in the corner furthest from the door. Other senior Lotus staff such as sales personnel, the chief draughtsman and fellow 'pencils', project engineers and myself favoured a longer table by the door, principally to eye and assess any females walking past the window. Whatever was going through our boss's energetic and fertile brain as he ate lunch, he never once used the opportunity to involve his managers on the other table with matters of urgent business. The only time that silence would descend on both groups simultaneously was when a particularly attractive fellow diner would eat her dessert of a fresh banana.

Whether it was Colin's sketch that crystallised into the Type 25, or his design work on the Elan chassis that led to what the media described as a 'monocoque' is not important. What does matter is that Team Lotus was about to produce a world-beating racing car that, together with its successor, the Type 33, would win both the 1963 and 1965 World Championships and 19 Grands Prix, and whose derivatives would take Indianapolis by storm and change for ever the constructional concepts of race car builders on both sides of the Atlantic.

As, in great secrecy, Colin pencilled the general arrangement drawings of the Type 25, Lotus progressed its already designated tube-frame Formula 1 car for 1962, the Type 24. In those still formative years of Team Lotus, the staff totalled just nine and a half; myself as manager, a secretary, chief mechanic Jim Endruweit, and six mechanics. The 'half' was a teenage book-keeper, Trevor Whitford, who divided his days between Team and production car accounts. While Lotus Components Ltd built the customer racing and sports car, Team's engineering, orchestrated by Lotus Developments Ltd under director Mike Costin and two of his staff, John Lambert and Colin Knight, constructed the chassis frames for Team Lotus.

Chief draughtsman Alan Styman headed a group of five in the drawing office. Among them was Ian Jones, Lotus's first full-time draughtsman, who as an employee of Vanwall (the first British team to win the Formula 1 World Constructors' Championship in 1958) had first worked with Colin in 1955. Already acknowledged as an authority in chassis and suspension design, Chapman had been invited by millionaire Vanwall owner, Tony Vandervell, to solve the handling problems of his cars; later Ian was himself invited to work for Chapman, which initially he did on a part-time basis working in the evenings and weekends at Colin's home. His first tasks were drawings of the five-speed Lotus gearbox (later known as the 'queerbox'), the first single-seater Lotus (the Type 12), and the Elite road car. Alongside Ian were Bill Wells, Mike Wardle, David Shuttle and Paul Wright, and under Styman's leadership this group produced all the drawings for the projects Chapman dreamed up, from sports and racing cars to road vehicles plus countless additional schemes and ideas.

Alan Styman recalls, 'I don't think any of us considered ourselves as Team Lotus *designers* in the current sense. Colin had the dominant influence; he would do the "schematic" layout of a new design to one-fifth scale showing wheelbase, track, suspension geometries, engine, gearbox and driver, plus a few cryptic notes. He would give us a short briefing, then we would detail the overall concept. Producing work for both race and road cars caused unhappiness between Colin and Design Engineer Ron Hickman (later to achieve fame and fortune as the inventor of the 'Workmate'); each wanted his work done first, but Colin nearly always won because his cars were more exciting!

'Contrary to other people's opinions since, I always found him relaxed and sympathetic to our problems when he was in the drawing office. His comment "Let's lean on the board" would incite a response of togetherness. Knobs in the ear would also be handed out, but always with a whimsical smile. He would remind us that "A man who never made a mistake never made anything", and "Let's rather have something wrong than not at all"! I still clearly remember him trying to explain to me a rack-and-pinion modification; I usually got the drift quickly, but this time I had a mental blockage. He was very patient and tried three different explanations. Eventually he quietly gave up and walked away, muttering that he couldn't put it across in any other way. My impression was that he was never happier than when he was involved directly with racing cars – anything else for him was a complete pain in the arse ...'

There were few perks for this group as it struggled to keep pace with Chapman's fertile brain. One of Costin's project engineers, Brian Luff, still remembers the rare occasion when Mike told him what a stupendous effort he had maintained in conquering a particular problem.

'I'm going to take you out for a dinner on the company,' said his boss with obvious gratitude, and he took Brian to a transport cafe on London's North Circular Road. 'The knives and forks were chained to the tables,' Brian recalled.

The first Type 24s were for Team, and they appeared at the Brussels Grand Prix at the beginning of April 1962. Customer cars were soon in production and began racing early in May, while back in Team's small race shop everyone available was busy working round the clock building the first stressed-skin fuselage Type 25. As Team had no fabricators on its staff, the 'skinning' of the car, using aluminium panels produced by Williams & Pritchard, was undertaken by a group from Lotus Components, referred to by Chapman as 'those communists'. I never discovered why Colin was decidedly off-hand when dealing with sheet-metal workers; perhaps this particular group's solidarity over working practices and in negotiating wages smacked too much of union attitudes, which Colin despised. His attitude improved some time later, after he had personally fired them, by which time we had our own Team fabricators, but his feelings of old were to re-surface on occasions in years to come.

Mike Costin personally led the riveting. Like a number of Chapman's early associates, Mike was an ex-de Havilland Aircraft man. His engineering expertise and commonsense approach to everything he tackled and his ability to maintain an 18-hour working day made an invaluable contribution to Lotus's survival in those early years.

The prototype Type 25 was completed in May 1962. That it was still a secret was quite an achievement bearing in mind the cramped working conditions within the race shop area, which measured barely 75 by 25 feet, with only roof-high sliding doors separating it from the outside world. A few steps away was both the customer road car service department and Lotus Components' race car production area, their frequent and inquisitive visitors always anxious to catch any glimpse of Team's racing activities.

When the new car appeared in public for the first time as it rolled down our transporter's ramps at the Zandvoort circuit ready to practice for the first 1962 World Championship race, it created a sensation, with journalists, photographers and anyone else able to get within close proximity absolutely agog at this obviously radical change in chassis design. Equally so were the recent purchasers of the 24s, who felt that they had drawn short straws, but Colin placated them by saying that he did not want them to suffer a car that might not work.

There was no exotic, outlandishly expensive fanfare to herald the new car; the Type 25 had to make do with the sand-blown race paddock situated just a few hundred yards from the North Sea. Even official press releases were still then far in the future. In those days we would wait until a description appeared in a motoring magazine, then 'Roneo' it through inky masters on to company notepaper.

One of those showing more than enthusiastic interest at Zandvoort was 31-year-old Californian driver Dan Gurney, son of opera singer John and at that time No 1 for the Porsche Formula 1 team, whose own new flat-eight-engined car was being unveiled at the same time. A latecomer to circuit racing, with military service in Korea having intervened, Dan had been 24 in 1955 when he first raced a Triumph TR2 in events near his home town of Riverside, although he had been well known for some years to the local Highway Patrol for his drag racing on public roads.

His first major competitive event had in fact been at the Bonneville Salt Flats in 1950. Graduating through various Porsches to a 4.9-litre Ferrari, his driving had impressed Ferrari's American importer, Luigi Chinetti, who recommended Dan to Ferrari team manager Romolo Tavoni; this subsequently secured him a seat in the Scuderia's sports car team for 1959, and shortly afterwards he was promoted to single-seaters. His switch to the BRM team for 1960 was dogged by mechanical unreliability. So were his appearances in Lucky Casner's Camoradi 'Birdcage' Maserati although, partnered by Stirling Moss, he won the Nurburgring 1,000 kms. In 1961 he joined the Porsche team and finished every Championship race, taking a joint-third place with Moss at season's end. His Formula 1 contract with Porsche continued into 1962, but in April that year he drove the ex-Louise Bryden-Brown Type 18 F1 Lotus at the Louisiana Hilltop Raceway event, setting a course lap record and winning both heats of the 200-mile race. No doubt this experience was uppermost in his mind as he surveyed the new Lotus.

At Zandvoort, Dan was into a period of Atlantic-hopping that was soon to become a familiar way of life at Team Lotus. Entered in Mickey Thompson's rear-engined Buick V8-engined *Thompson Enterprises Special* for the Indy 500, he passed his 'rookie' test on 29 April (lapping at 141 mph). He then left America for Sicily where he was to practice his new 'works' 2-litre flat-eight-engined Porsche for the Targa Florio sports car classic the following Sunday, from which he retired after hitting a wall. Back at Indianapolis for qualifying the following weekend, he successfully put his car on the third row (eighth quickest), an impressive performance considering that his was the only non-Offenhauser-engined car to qualify out of 65 entries. Parnelli Jones, a future adversary of ours in Team Lotus, took pole.

From Indy Dan took another transatlantic flight back to the Formula 1 world at Zandvoort. He qualified eighth (third row of the grid), but gearbox trouble took him out of the race just after half-distance. Jim Clark started from the front row (third fastest) with the new Lotus 25, and led until lap 12, after which clutch mechanism problems dropped him to tenth at the finish.

Dan had been fascinated by the Memorial Day classic for ten years or more, and the ways and means of getting together people capable of leading a competitive assault on the race had in his own words 'been fermenting in my mind ever since'. Chapman was at the top of his list; Dan regarded him as the finest designer in the business, renowned for wasting no time in taking up a new challenge. Now as Gurney surveyed Colin's new car, his mind was made up. He engineered a quiet chat and summarised for Colin the 500's most pertinent aspects. He was so enthused, he invited Colin along to the race, just ten days hence, going so far as to offer a free round-trip air ticket. Legend has it that Colin waited for the ticket to arrive in his office before accepting Dan's invitation ...

This was the race at which Frey and Evans of Ford would also be spectating along with a crowd of 200,000. Chapman's opinion of what he saw that Wednesday in May has been well chronicled since. He could barely believe his eyes as he inspected the outmoded chassis construction of the traditional 'roadsters'; for a moment he thought he had been transported back to the pre-war days of motor racing. In the race Dan ran no lower than tenth until his first pit stop, finally retiring on lap 93 (of 200) with transmission trouble.

Dan Gurney recalls the inception of the Lotus-Ford assault on Indianapolis: 'I had first gone to Indianapolis in 1962, at the invitation of an entrant named John Zink. I took the obligatory driver's test in his traditional front-engined Offy roadster, but what he was hoping to qualify for the race was a rear-engined frame – I'm sure it was actually an old Lotus chassis – powered by a Boeing gas turbine ...

'He had some Boeing engineers who were keen to promote these things as high-reliability, cheap-to-run engines powering Kenworth trucks. One of the engineers was running one on the street in a '32 Ford roadster, which must have been quite exciting.

'But when Jack Zink appeared at Indy with his turbine car he was stiff and sore and his face and arms covered in scabs and grazes, because while testing the car back at some place in Oklahoma he'd flipped it during a test run. And when I got out on to the Speedway in the car it was plain that its 350 horse-power wasn't enough. A gas turbine develops maximum torque at stall, like a steam engine, so the faster you ran it the less it delivered.

'In those days we were still having to brake into the turns at Indy, so when you went back on the gas that turbine could set very competitive corner speeds, and came off the turns with good acceleration. But part way down the straight it would be all over for the day. It just ran out of power and stopped accelerating.

'I was really having to hustle it in the effort to set competitive lap times, and it became clear that it just didn't have enough power. So I told Zink that if he could find anyone who could drive it faster he shouldn't worry about hurting my feelings – he should go right ahead and try them . . . and then Mickey Thompson asked if I'd like to drive one of his new rear-engined Buick V8-powered cars.

'They were somewhat like the rear-engined 2.7 Cooper-Climax that Jack Brabham had both pioneered and driven at Indy the previous year, making such an impact. Mickey was the great West Coast hot-rodder and lake car builder who knew all about tuning Detroit V8s, and he'd brought over an English design engineer named John Crosthwaite to build him these Indy Thompson-Buick cars with the engine in the back.

'It was a hell of a car. It really worked well, and for qualifying we used Mickey's quarter-mile drag-race engines. They were built for him by Fred Voight, and they just barely survived the four laps – 10 miles – for qualifying. But they were quick – no question. And so I found myself driving in my first oval-track race – the Indianapolis "500" . . .

'I'd been interested by Indy racing and the disparity between the technology involved and that which I was more used to in European-style road racing. I'd been to Monza in '58 for the Indycar race they ran and had seen the Ecurie Ecosse D-Type Jaguars, with a fraction of the American roadsters' power, still pulling at a great tall gear and just about hanging on to them thanks to their better shape. Now I was trying to deduce from that kind of real-life experience how good – or bad – rear-engined road-racing-type chassis might be around an oval compared to the big-time traditional roadsters. I concluded that it was going to happen, and with that thought in mind I went out to see if I could help it happen – to be in there early with good equipment.

'At that time, with that kind of technical racing challenge – plus a clear requirement for a dash of salesmanship and, um, bravado – there was only one guy to approach: Colin Chapman.

'So I approached Colin. I told him that I was running at Indy – we'd both lived through the rear-engined revolution when it came to Formula 1 and it was plain to me that someone was

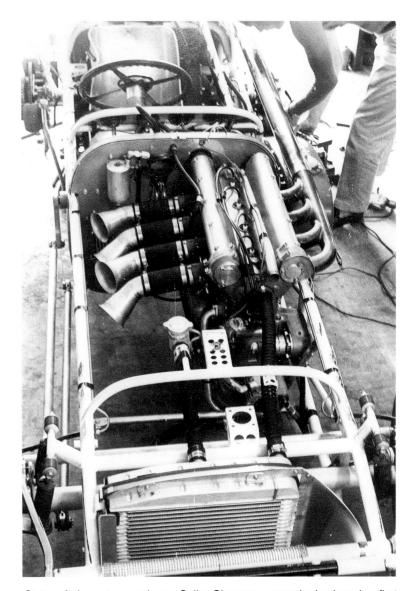

State of the art – and, as Colin Chapman remarked when he first encountered it in 1962, 'What a state'. This is the sparse tube-frame chassis of Rodger Ward's 1962 Indy-winning Leader Card Special *as built by specialist A. J. Watson and powered by the offset-mounted 4.2-litre Offenhauser four-cylinder dohc engine with Hilborn fuel injection. Watson had built 12 such roadsters new for 1962, and a total of 17 Watson-Offies took the start that year. 'I couldn't believe it,' Colin recalled. 'I felt as if I'd been transported back to pre-war, seeing all these great monsters heaving and wallowing around . . .' But even he would admit that the best of them, such as this, were fast.*

going to do the same to Indianapolis. That challenge really appealed to Colin, and I thought it would also appeal to Ford . . .

'When I grew up in racing through the '50s you tended to become either a Ford guy or a Chevrolet guy. I was from the generation that learned about speed with the flat-head Ford. Until 1955, when they brought out the overhead-valve range, Chevy had always been second-best. We talked about them dismissively as "Stovebolts". To us Ford was king.

'So I had this natural affinity with Ford. I'd always enjoyed driving different cars, a different challenge, and I'd just driven a Holman & Moody Ford stock car at Daytona, so I had fresh contact with Ford people. This encouraged me to say to Colin that I would buy him an air ticket to that year's race at Indy to see what it was like, and if he agreed that there was potential for a programme there, then I could introduce him to people at Ford who might be persuaded to fund the thing.

'And that's how it happened. We went to Ford and they recognised it as a great challenge, and appreciated that a Ford win at Indy could be of immense promotional value. But they remained sceptical and reserved. They didn't want to get involved in building a pure racing engine. They kept asking, "Just what would we have to do?" – and we were asking them, "Do you have anything current that could produce our target horsepower – and survive 500 miles?"'

Colin's presence at the Brickyard did not go un-noticed, and photographs of him talking to Mickey Thompson, Rodger Ward and various race officials appeared in numerous magazines. Rodger had been a top-flight midget driver on the West Coast before first qualifying for the '500' in 1951. He had qualified every year since then, achieving his first win in 1959, the year he took the coveted USAC National Championship crown. The following year he very nearly won again at Indy, losing by just 12 seconds when he backed off to save a tyre close to failure. In 1962, in the race watched by Colin, Rodger won again by just 11½ seconds.

Ward, as an enthusiastic advocate of rear-engined cars, did his best to persuade Colin that he had everything to gain by building an Indy car, and no doubt Rodger's winning share of $125,000 from the $426,000 race purse was not lost on Chapman!

Monaco Grand Prix practice opened the day after the '500', and Colin, his appetite now whetted at the prospect of an assault on Indy, discussed the next stage with Dan as they flew through the night back to Europe. Dan need not have suffered his exhausting schedule on this occasion; he was shunted out of his second row starting slot just seconds after the starter's flag dropped. Jim Clark was on pole in only his second race with the new Lotus 25, but he was also caught up in this start-line mêlée, completing the opening lap sixth. He was to break the lap record in catching and passing the cars in front, but as he manoeuvred to pass the race leader on lap 39, a gearbox problem intervened. Having lost two gears he struggled on, but retired on lap 56 of the 100.

Back in England, Chapman began scouring all the material he could find relating to the Brickyard, reading reports of the races of recent years, writing and re-writing specifications and sketching the outlines of the car he had in mind. He pored over the drawings of the track given him on his visit, particularly those detailing the four corners, each one unique. Additionally he called for an imaginative budget detailing all the costs entailed in such an American project.

Dan had already established useful contacts within Ford, so it

was left to him to pave the way to what was hoped would be a constructive meeting, Colin no doubt keeping a weather eye on proceedings through his contacts at Ford of Britain. Earlier in the year, in what was possibly a prophetic fluke, Dan had accepted that last-minute invitation to fill a Ford seat at Daytona. Although the race result was inconsequential, he had met Jacque Passino there, establishing a relationship which was to prove most useful.

In July a meeting of the various parties was arranged at Ford's HQ in Dearborn, and Dan remembered later that both he and Chapman left for America after the French GP at Rouen on 8 July. Dan was in excellent spirits, for the race had marked his and Porsche's first Formula 1 World Championship race victory. Team Lotus had seen Jim Clark on pole again, but the Scotsman retired from the lead when a front suspension component unscrewed itself. The No 2 car had been written off in a quite frightening accident right on the finishing line, its driver, Trevor Taylor, emerging with nothing worse than shock. By way of consolation, Team's Formula Junior section had finished 1–2–3 in their supporting event.

Colin agreed with Dan that an engine producing 350 hp would be adequate for the Indy project. The modified stock Buick V8 in Dan's Mickey Thompson car had produced 330 hp in peak form, less in the race, but he had remained in contention until transmission problems intervened. Colin had calculated the total time spent on fuel stops and recognised that there was an advantage to be gained by using an economical power unit. The winning margins of the last three races were at best 12.6 seconds, the least just 8 seconds. 'Something for nothing' was a Chapman ideal that featured throughout his life.

Of course, as the two took the elevator to the top of the plush Ford executive building they had no way of knowing if their approach would bear fruit. Author Leo Levine recorded that Chapman's primary characteristic was his arrogance, an opinion he could only have derived from the people at Ford who had known and worked with Colin, but at this meeting Gurney's all-American-boy image would have done much to offset that. Six feet 2 inches tall, lean, tanned and with, as someone described them, 'shoulders like a coal-heaver', the crew-cut Gurney had come fresh from a stimulating World Championship race win. Outwardly a charming and modest individual, he had reputedly become fascinated by the subject of psychology at college and still applied its principles to everyday life. Presumably the meeting at Ford provided an ideal opportunity for him to utilise these acquired skills.

Those on the Ford side of the table were taken aback by Chapman's simplistic requirements. They were confident that they could muster an engine with more than adequate power, but he would be content with less. They inclined towards methanol fuel, but he plumped for gasoline. They could supply a double-overhead-camshaft unit, but all he wanted was a push-rod. Dan agreed with Colin in going for the push-rod engine; as he pointed out, if the job could be done with a push-rod unit that had been running reliably for donkey's years, it was logical to use it. According to Levine, the two visitors met Passino and Frey initially, then the engineers Gay and Innes. Gay knew little about the Englishman and doubted that a man with no experience of the Brickyard could succeed. However many doubts he inwardly harboured, Gay recorded the objectives of those around the table. These were:

1. Complete the race in only one pit stop.
2. Carry and consume a total of only 400 lbs (57 Imperial gallons) of fuel (this precluded the use of exotic fuels involving a penalty of 800 lbs fuel load).
3. Carry only 24 lbs of oil instead of the normal 80.
4. Use carburation in place of fuel injection.
5. Limit the complete installed engine weight to 350 lbs.
6. Use automotive battery ignition and a distributor instead of a magneto.
7. Develop a minimum of 325 dependable horsepower from 255 cu ins.

The meeting also agreed the following time schedule for the engine, car, track, and various other aspects of the project, covering the period to April 1963 as follows:

1. Survey the Indianapolis track during August.
2. Investigate the maximum horsepower capabilities of the production 260 engine by September, and compare the performance with the measured output of a purchased Offenhauser engine.
3. Compare vehicle performance of a Lotus 25 with a known Coventry Climax engine during October.
4. Duplicate the production 260 engine in aluminum and resolve any basic weight or high-speed durability problems by 1 November.
5. Obtain competitive vehicle data to verify performance calculations and supply analytical results for final engine design and car concept by November.
6. Complete basic engine tests at Daytona by December.
7. Design, build and test a new engine and car concept prior to the April 'upset date'.

Although these 'minutes' of the meeting appear to confirm that Ford would go with Lotus, this was not so. Colin returned to England with no more than an informal nod to progress further; there was no contract and Ford continued to assess the American Indy car builders.

A report by Ford on the contemporary scene was circulated to the executives concerned and the following extracts show the company's awareness of the Indy establishment's general stagnation in design and concept. The liquid capacities are given in US gallons, and for ease of comparison the [bracketed] data gives the Chapman estimates:

DESIGN: The design of today's Indianapolis vehicle is the result of over 50 years of trial-and-error development .., only minor changes being cautiously applied each year.

DESIGNERS AND BUILDERS: . . . mainly highly skilled craftsmen with small establishments. They have little or no technical facilities that would allow them to develop advanced concepts.

PACKAGE CONFIGURATION: . . . forward engine, rear drive; with offset weight of 1,600–1,700 lbs dry. [1,130 lbs with oil and water]

ENGINE: Meyer-Drake 255 cu in, twin OHV, water cooled, four-cylinder in line producing 415 hp at 6,800 rpm with fuel injection using methanol (a 10% nitro-methanol fuel is usually used in the race). The unit weighs 480 lbs [350 lbs] and was designed some 30 years ago.

DRIVELINE AND CHASSIS: Two-speed transmission used only for accelerating away from the pits. Solid rear axle (independent) with either disc or drum brakes [disc]. Independent or solid axle front suspension [independent]. 72-gallon gas tank [57 gallons] with 7-gallon oil tank [4.8 gallons].

PERFORMANCE: . . . cars require three or four tire changes during race [one] . . . almost every year a few cars of unconventional design show up. Few of these have qualified and not since pre-war years has a non-Offenhauser (Meyer-Drake) engined vehicle been successful in the race.

SELECTING A DESIGN APPROACH: Although conventional cars have been predominant at Indianapolis in modern history, two unconventional entries have demonstrated great potential . . . the midship-engined Cooper finished ninth . . . dry weight 1,055 lbs with engine capacity of only 156 cu ins . . . burning comparatively low-grade fuel . . . 2 miles an hour quicker through the corners than any previous recording . . . the driver could apparently follow any course around the corners with equal ease. The Mickey Thompson car in the 1962 race gas-powered by a high-performance version of the small Buick V8 . . . it gave a good account of what can be achieved with a modified family car engine in this vehicle configuration . . . the evolution of the midship-engined race car started with the Auto-Unions of the mid-1930s . . . although successful, they were difficult to handle . . . post-war European race cars have corrected the shortcomings and have capitalised on the package, weight distribution and traction advantages inherent in a midship-engined race car . . . the midship-engined car has reached a high state of evolution . . . it is the most suitable for a V8 installation . . . it is suggested this is the most feasible design approach to pursue at this time.

Ford had by then acquired an Offenhauser engine evaluation and had also commissioned a survey of the speedway. As a Ford report stated, 'no accurate information on the track has ever been compiled, except that there is a 10-inch drop from north to south for the length of the 3,300-foot straights. There is also a slant toward the infield on both straights of 5 inches to 50 feet.' The report commented that the surveyors were 'quite busy but would take on the work only as a favour to Mr Cagle' (the track superintendent). Ford even noted the cost of the survey, which was for four men at $1,000 a day, the total cost including drawings being $1,500–1,800 for the 10-day project.

An in-depth account of the construction of the track published in 1909 was also made available, and an accompanying note commented that no one had ever checked either the original configuration or the two re-surface jobs. The surveyors in 1962 described how the later re-surfacing had been undertaken, and took 'readings at 10-foot increments to give the most accurate set of gradients as to transition into and out of the turns'. It was interesting to note the concluding comment of the 1909 report: '. . . as to accidents, there should be none'.

Modification of the 260 cu in engine continued as the Offenhauser was dyno-tested. As Gay later wrote, 'The "Awful Offy" proved awfully good.' The four-cylinder, twin ohc 16-valve unit featured an exceptionally large induction system specifically designed for fuel injection of methanol and nitro-methane, and with a compression ratio of 14.95:1 it returned 401 bhp at 6,000 rpm; it was run on the methanol fuel for which it had been calibrated. Data required for Ford's computer programme, including volumetric efficiency, were extracted from the tests and a comprehensive survey compiled.

Meanwhile, Ford's 260 engine was undergoing tests and subsequent modifications which Gay summarised as follows:

1. Four dual-throat 46 mm Weber carburettors installed.
2. Intake and exhaust ports and valves modified on the basis of static bench air-flow studies.
3. Combustion chamber revised by relocating the plug and providing a domed piston with provisions for a three-path flame travel. The resultant compression ratio was 12.5:1.
4. Valve train revised by adding lightweight mechanical tappets, Teflon push-rod guide, dual valve springs, an aluminium valve spring retainer, a screwed-in rocker arm stud, hollow valves and a camshaft with a jerk factor of .00038 in/deg (squared).

Running on gasoline, the engine surpassed Ford's objective of 325 bhp, but as the Offy had used methanol, the engineers then became engrossed in a detailed survey of fuels. As Gay reported, 'It is probably safe to say that every blend of fuel capable of being ignited by a spark has been used.' Included amongst these were aviation gasoline, benzol acetone, methyl alcohol, ethyl alcohol, isopropyl alcohol and butyl alcohol. To these were added nitro-compounds, water, organic nitrates, peroxides, tetraethyl lead, ether, and explosive elements. The engineers also ran their own experimental unit on methanol, plus additives, so as to draw comparisons with the Offy; the improved torque of the latter showed its advantage, particularly over the two smaller straights, known as 'short chutes', but finally the increased weight of fuel carried by the car, coupled with the additional fuel stops that would be necessary if exotic fuel was used, provided the answer. They would follow Chapman's initial recommendation and go

gasoline. Arrogant he might be, but right he certainly was . . .

What may have provided a crucial factor in helping Ford to make its final choice of chassis constructor followed completion of the track survey. Bill Gay's men wanted a 'live' interpretation of the study, and they enlisted the services of renowned American car builder A. J. Watson together with double-Indy-winning driver Rodger Ward.

Watson was a dyed-in-the-wool member of the Speedway 'establishment', building the famed roadsters that had epitomised the track for many, many years and about which Ford was just beginning to think twice. It was with Watson that Ford had talked at around the time Chapman had visited Dearborn, and A. J. had been totally against the Englishman's concept.

Watson had first come to the speedway in 1948 as a mechanic, after completing his war service as a navigator with the American 8th Air Force. Two years later he built his first car for the '500'; its driver, Dick Rathmann, qualified 18th, but an oil line breakage took him out early on. Despondent and short of funds, Watson tried to forget racing, but the following year he was back for good. Subsequently numerous National Championship race successes fell to Watson cars; in 1955 they won both the Indy 500 and the Championship title. In '56 a Watson achieved record speeds for both one and four laps around the Speedway, starting from pole and winning the race. In 1959 Watsons took first and second places, and the following year he built four cars and again took first and second. He took a third in 1961, but now in 1962 his cars again took first and second for the third time. Parnelli Jones, driving an older 1960 Watson chassis, had set new one- and four-lap records, and of the six cars starting the race in the front two rows, four had been Watson-built. A. J. was definitely a constructor to be reckoned with at the Brickyard.

But perhaps he was now to experience a change of fortune, as his car provided printed data that would soon be compared with Jim Clark's Speedway laps in a Lotus. Rodger Ward was shutting off two-thirds of the way down each of the long straights, his engine peaking at 6,600 rpm, then slowing to 5,200 rpm in the middle of the turns. It was back up to 5,600 rpm by the end of the 'short chutes', back to 5,200 rpm in the middle of the next corner, reaching 5,600 rpm as it exited on to the next long straight and back to 6,600 two-thirds of the way back into the recurring cycle. As Ward's Watson-Offenhauser bowled around the track time and time again, so the Ford engineers recorded every minute detail, calculating wind resistance, drag coefficient, engine friction, overall gross weight, driveline efficiency factor, tyre rolling resistance, and previous race speeds. Every factor was carefully noted, then taken back to the engineers' offices for detailed analysis.

Colin had already obtained the financial gist of Indy 1963 from both Ford and the Speedway; we went through it in detail, and Chapman asked me to try out a scheme whereby our preferred driver, Jim Clark, would be paying his own expenses. On Saturday 8 September I phoned Jimmy about these financial arrangements for what we were all calling 'the American excursion', and he asked me to put it in writing. This I did on Wednesday 12 September before he left for Monza, pointing out that from his retainer of $5,000 he would be responsible for paying all his out-of-pocket expenses for air travel and hotels for the April testing as well as the month of May, but that if we managed to get the prototype finished by January and testing followed during that month we hoped to be able to reimburse these particular expenses.

Jimmy took Colin to one side at Monza and explained that the $5,000 was insufficient to cover expenses as well, and immediately after the race I sent him another letter confirming that we would pay his expenses on top of the retainer.

It is amusing in retrospect that when mentioning the 45 per cent of the $10,000 qualifying money he would receive, I wrote, 'As the starting grid is composed of 33 cars it will be impossible for you not to qualify', which really demonstrates how little we knew about Indy!

All prize bonus and race leader monies, as well as those sums paid by Ford, would be split 45 per cent to the driver, 45 per cent to the team and 10 per cent to the mechanics. However, there were two stings in the tail: all such monies due to the drivers would be pooled between them, and all trophies were automatically the property of Ford. Although again in retrospect it may seem strange that the two drivers, one a relative stranger to our camp, should share the monies, it must be remembered that at this juncture Dan was attributed No 1 status for the part he had played in the programme's conception.

Team Lotus duly arrived at the Speedway to fulfil part three of the rubber-stamped Ford schedule.

Meanwhile Jim Clark continued his fight for the 1962 Formula 1 World Championship in exemplary fashion, but the ever present 'ifs and buts' that make motor racing the fascinating business it has always been, sometimes saw him take one step forward, only to slip back two . . .

The German Grand Prix in August 1962 was where, in retrospect, he lost that year's title. Heavy rain at the start caused his goggles to mist up, and in keeping them clear of his face he lost concentration as the starter raised his flag. As a result he forgot to switch on his fuel pumps, and his engine died as the grid roared off around the 14.2-mile Eifel mountains circuit. He had got away 14 seconds late, and skilfully threading his way through the rain-obscured field round the 83 left-hand and 84 right-hand corners of each lap, he finished fourth.

In the following title round in Italy, a gearbox failure took him out on lap 1. Now there were two races left. If he could win both the title was his, and in October Team was at Watkins Glen in America for the first. Here Jimmy fully revived his Championship chances. From pole position he put up a record fastest lap and won, despite being without a clutch for half of the 100-lap distance. Now there was only one race to win to secure the World Championship crown, the South African Grand Prix on 29 December.

Meanwhile, after Watkins Glen his team-mate Trevor Taylor's

When Jim Endruweit (right) and Dick Scammell (left) took Team Lotus's second-string Formula 1 Lotus 25 to Indianapolis immediately after the 1962 United States Grand Prix, it was well over 30 years since a 1½-litre – 91 cu in – car had last run there with serious intent. Here Dick and Jim are fettling the car by the pit lane entrance to Gasoline Alley just before Jim Clark's historic first fact-finding run. (Indianapolis Motor Speedway)

car, chassis 25/R2, was taken to the Speedway. Chief mechanic Jim Endruweit recalls that 'the car was loaded into one of Ford America's trucks and taken the 100 miles to Indy. The old man only told us about the trip a short time before, saying, "Oh yes, I'd like you and Dick [Scammell] to go to Indy tomorrow and I'll see you there." My reaction was "Where?", but we got a map and the two of us trundled off in a hire car. I remember that, knowing the old man, I had said to him, "You know we won't be there tomorrow?" He was a bit reluctant to accept this, but eventually said, "I'll see you the day after then".'

The car left Watkins Glen on the Sunday evening and, after a thorough post-race check, Wednesday morning saw Jimmy quickly circulating the Brickyard. The engine used in the race remained in the car (even though Trevor had dropped back to 12th place with a faltering oil pressure gauge that was put down to oil surge), and the spare engine they took with them remained unused.

The Ford engineers returned with their notebooks and recording devices and were impressed beyond their wildest expecta-

Just unloaded, the 'bathtub'-chassised stressed-skin car's Coventry-Climax V8 engine awaits refitting of its long twin megaphone tail pipes. (Indianapolis Motor Speedway)

tions. In comparison with Brabham's 2.7-litre Cooper, Jimmy's car, with its 1.5 litres, was almost half the capacity, yet almost as quick! Jimmy took umbrage at the Speedway 'rookie' procedure. He later wrote: 'Everyone was very interested in our ploy. After all, it was not every day that someone arrived with a puny little 1.5-litre racing car that produced only 175 bhp on their sacred track, and just to see that I was a good little boy the officials had invited a number of drivers along just to watch me go round and see that I did the correct thing at the correct time. This is one thing that really annoyed me. They treated me like a kid who had never raced before. On this first occasion I took things easily and tried to get the hang of driving around left-hand corners all the time. Remember, the car had come straight from Watkins Glen so it was running on normal racing tyres and was not set up for left-hand turns only and the banking.

'I did about 100 laps on that occasion and I remember thinking that it was a bit dull. My fastest lap of 143 mph average made most people sit up and take notice, but what made them even more interested was the speed at which I was taking the turns. The Indy cars rely on their acceleration between the bends to give them their high lap times, and the fastest times an Indy car had recorded in the turn was something like 138 mph. Our Lotus was doing over 140 on the corners . . .'

As was the norm in those days, Jim Endruweit made typically brief notes. The ZF gearbox with the 9.37 'Glen ratio' was

replaced by a 9.35; carburettor settings were altered; Dunlop D12 tyres remained on the car for the first day, but their individual pressures were changed to suit the conditions of the oval; and the second day both D9s and D12s were compared. From 30 psi front and 32 psi rear for the Glen, they were finally pressured to 38 (left front) and 44 (right front), 40 (left rear) and 46 (right rear).

The test over, Jim and Dick Scammell set off for Dearborn with the car, where it was carefully examined by Ford's engineers. The story goes that they wanted to purchase a Type 25 for extended evaluation and Colin was happy to provide one, but without a home-grown driver experienced in driving such a car the idea was abandoned. Jim and Dick re-assembled 'R2' and continued on their way to Mexico, scene of a non-Championship race just ten days later.

Ford now went to item four of its time schedule. As they wanted to verify various objectives not associated with lap speeds, they built a second 260 cu in engine to the slightly reduced capacity (bore size –0.04 in) required by Speedway regulations, but this time with aluminium block and heads. Virtually every item of the standard unit required design changes, although these would be barely discernible when completed; Ford was after all faced with the challenge of producing twice the power from a unit three-quarters of the weight. The cylinder block (with cast-iron dry liners) and heads were of sand-cast aluminium produced from modified production engine patterns. The engine was set up to run with either fuel injection using methanol, or with carburettors and gasoline, and it immediately duplicated the power output of the original cast iron unit.

Bill Gay reported that by November the engine was installed in a Galaxie and taken to Daytona to assess such variables as transient control problems during acceleration, engine crankcase breathing, cooling, starting, battery size and ignition. Driver Nelson Stacy was soon circulating at high speeds, registering 146.7 mph on gasoline and 159.8 mph on methanol. After four days and 435 miles the engineers studied the data. The two speed bands had been achieved with appreciable differences in fuel consumption, the carburettor version running on gasoline giving 6.41 mpg to the fuel-injected methanol's 2.22 mpg; for computer calculations they also had to build in an adjustment to cope with the fact they had been forced to use 46 mm twin-choke Weber carburettors while awaiting delivery of 48 mm and 58 mm units from Italy. Gay summed up: 'The fuel economy thus obtained would bear out our initial analytical study.' On this basis, the decision to 'go gasoline' was emphatically reaffirmed for the second time.

Another negative factor to be allowed for was the high banking angle at Daytona, which produced considerably lower G-forces than those encountered at the Speedway. On the positive side, previous problems concerning crankcase breathing and cooling had been resolved, and generator and battery sizes finalised. Ignition problems encountered on the prototype engine were also solved; a new breakerless transistorised system was tested and signed off. Bill Gay later wrote of how the Ford engineers had eradicated the head gasket failures that had affected the engine, both on the dynamometer and the track: '. . . the problem was solved by separating the cylinder head from the block with an air gap of approximately .012 and using a mechanical joint for sealing. Rubber 'O' rings transferred the water through the dry head deck from the cylinder block to the cylinder head. One interesting aspect of this design is that, should a cylinder head joint fail at high speeds and the resulting leakage rate be no greater than the piston ring gap, the failure would not affect horsepower and vehicle performance.'

At Dearborn the computer calculations continued. They knew the power output of the Formula 1 Coventry Climax V8 engine in Jimmy's Type 25, as well as the extensive data derived from Rodger Ward's roadster test. Now they substituted their own engine performance figures for those of the Climax and fed into their computers the Lotus's drag coefficient data, turn speeds, overall efficiency and dynamic weight transfer information. The estimated gross weight of a Ford V8-powered Indy Lotus – the car complete with driver, fuel, oil and water – was assumed to be 1,600 pounds, and they were thus able to calculate acceleration times and corner speeds. For the latter they accepted an average range of 137.5 to 141 mph and a minimum of 132.5 mph, but increased the speed of entry into turns to 143 mph.

Minimum cross-section – 25 'R2' on the Indy pit lane, reminiscent of those classical head-on shots of that other 1½-litre eight-cylinder Indy classic, the mid-1920s Miller 91. (Indianapolis Motor Speedway)

Jimmy picks up a gear before the high-speed runs whose cornering pace put the writing plainly upon the wall . . .

Gay wrote: 'A number of variables were introduced into the computer programme in order to develop an ideal driver programme from the track data. Once the desired engine speeds and

Stunner in the Autumn sun – the exploratory Indianapolis test session of October 1962 in which Jimmy Clark's corner speeds in his team-mate Trevor Taylor's 1½-litre Formula 1 Lotus 25, fresh from the United States Grand Prix at Watkins Glen, staggered the regular Indy 'railbirds'. Team mechanics Jim Endruweit (left) and Dick Scammell look on as Jim leaves the pit lane for another run.

shut-off points were developed for the Ford engine we arrived at the following lap speeds:

Calculated Lotus Ford lap speeds

Fuel	Hp	Notional value	Average turn speed (mph)	Rpm	Lap speed (mph)
Gas	395•	39.7	140	7,200	146
Gas	350	40	141	7,500	149
Gas	365	39	141	7,500	150.5
Methanol	400	38	141	7,200	153
Gas	425	42	142	8,000	155

• programme objective

As Gay concluded, 'we now had a driver pattern and horsepower rating that indicated we should go at least 150 mph. The accuracy of this last figure would be proven later in the programme when validation of our calculations would be sought in March 1963 at Kingman, Arizona, and Indianapolis.'

Despite all this, Dan Gurney considered that 'Looking back on the way Ford tackled the engine programme, I guess I was actually more disappointed than impressed. The first time we were taken to Detroit to see what they were doing for us, we arrived expecting some kind of NASA-type facility teeming with white-coated technicians and high-tech equipment. In fact we were shown to an old, poky, dark, dank building that appeared to be inhabited by just one elderly guy who we judged to be somewhere in his early 70s. He was Czech or Hungarian or something – he spoke with this real thick accent – and he seemed to be the only guy at Ford drawing our new parts. That was truly amazing to us. I'd had more people designing my cars at Porsche and BRM!'

Although there was still merely a tentative on-going arrangement with Ford America to pursue an association for Indy, when Colin returned from the Mexican race to Cheshunt in November he told me that Team Lotus would be running in the 1963 Indy classic. There was no mention that a contract did not exist; to Colin's way of thinking, such a revelation would merely diminish the importance of the project in everyone's eyes and introduce an element of doubt. But Colin made no great fanfare about our association with such an important corporation and their reliance upon our capability to deliver the goods. The Indy programme was merely another section added to Team, similar to the Ford of Britain/Lotus-Cortina development section that had been formed earlier that year.

I had joined Team Lotus as Competition Manager in February 1961; towards the end of that season Colin told me that he wanted a more up-to-the-minute accounting system that would be only a week or ten days in arrears. Although he did not mention the fact, the minimal numbers of book-keeping staff and qualified accountants employed for the whole of the expanding Lotus empire of racing, sports car and road vehicle production and sales (one), plus our own race programme (our half-day teenager) were always exceedingly busy, and had more than enough to do coping with their everyday tasks. However, Colin wanted weekly summaries under the headings, ranging from race engine, gearbox and chassis repair and refurbishment costs to company car, van and transporter expenditure, race meeting expenses, driver earnings, wages and salaries, company aircraft maintenance and journey costs.

Our accounting year end was October, and Colin wanted the year just closed to be summarised within two weeks; it took a lot of persuasion talking the accountant, Geoff Page, into handing over all the Team Lotus invoices, following which I worked at home around the clock trying to introduce some semblance of order and scribbling down the results. It took ten days, at the end of which, having had no previous experience of accounting, I was thoroughly dismayed with the whole affair. After all, I reasoned, Fred Bushell was the accounting wizard and head of finance – surely it was up to him to provide a system to suit Colin.

It was clear that Colin had two primary objectives in mind; one was to have a comparative set of figures to throw at the accountants to keep them up on their toes, and the other was to instil in me the need to keep a close eye upon expenditure. The latter was, however, irrelevant, as Colin was responsible for most of it and no one could ever control his natural profligacy.

After he had briefly announced that we were 'going to Indy', he asked me to add another column to my 'pencil ledger', as I called it. 'Head it "Indy bucket",' he said. 'Anything that comes through that you are not clear about, or it doesn't relate to any-

thing else we are doing, put it under "Indy bucket" and I'll explain it for you later.'

July 1962 had seen the departure of Mike Costin to Cosworth. I regarded this as a stunning blow to every department within Lotus, as Mike was a highly skilled engineer whose talents were combined with a good straightforward approach to everything he tackled. A senior engineer with such enormous quantities of common sense, I considered him to be essential to the cause and the perfect foil for the 'Old Man' and his more outlandish schemes ...

In September, Len Terry joined Team Lotus for the second time, having first joined the company at Hornsey in March 1955. He had left a church school in South Tottenham, London, in 1938 at the age of 14. Although interested in cars from the age of eight, constantly reading about them in books from the local library, with a scarcity of jobs available and his parents opposed to him entering the motor trade, he joined theatrical producer Tom Arnold's organisation in London, starting as office boy and working his way up the ladder until National Service in the RAF intervened in 1944.

Len had enjoyed an aptitude for drawing from an early age, and with Arnold he had become involved in designing theatre programmes and posters. In the RAF he had qualified as an aircraft instrument repairer, which also saw him undertaking work as a draughtsman. When he returned to civilian life he joined Ever-Ready, the battery manufacturers, and within three months was in charge of its drawing office. In 1952 he joined a contract drawing office as a technical illustrator (he spent his spare time producing cutaway drawings for *Autosport* magazine, going around to shows with Technical Editor John Bolster), and around the same time purchased his first car, an Austin Seven. After replacing the body with an aluminium structure and christening the result the 'Boot Brad Special' (after the shoe-repairing nails used to attach the body), he found that it was not competitive in club racing.

Meanwhile John Teychenne, an early associate of Colin Chapman, had built a Ford-engined special called the 'JVT'. Shortage of free time had meant that he could not race it, and Len acquired it in 1954, cannibalising it to his own requirements when he found that Lotus Mark IX and Eleven sports cars were quicker. The overall dimensions of the tubular chassis he designed, of tetrahedron shape, were dictated by the size of the sash window in the front room of his small terraced house, so that when it was completed his friends in the 750 Motor Club could help him lift it out. His wife Iris went off to evening classes to learn welding and car mechanics while Len personally cut and mitred the chassis tubes, marking each end with a number to facilitate final assembly. At the welding shop in Hornsey that he had used, he checked the torsional stiffness by hanging on to the end of a 10-foot bar fastened to the chassis.

'I was delighted by the result,' Len reflected years later. 'It was completely solid. While I was hanging there, Frank Coltman of Progress Chassis, the company building chassis for Chapman, walked in, and he couldn't believe how strong it was.'

The frame then returned to Len's front room where its panels, steering gear, suspension and brackets were added. His 750 MC friends then lifted it through the window and on to soap boxes in the street to fit the braking system, wheels and install the engine. The chassis was a complex structure and Len was therefore satisfied when it was found to weigh only 59 lbs.

That car was Len's 'Terrier Mark I'. It earned enough successes for his name to be talked about, but he was still short of cash to progress further. Then another 750 MC member, Brian Hart (still designing and building racing engines in the mid-1990s), advertised an engine for sale. As they negotiated the price, Brian told Len that he was looking for a new car; as a result Len set to work on a 'Terrier Mark 2' financed by Brian. That the car was a success was proved by Brian taking 18 first places in 21 races entered.

It was now 1959 and Len had become Chief Designer at Lotus, but Colin did not like what he suspected might be cross-fertilisation. Len was also spokesman for staff not happy with revised contracts, and was asked to leave. He went on to work for Gilbey Engineering, where he conceived two monocoque structures for an 1,100 cc sports car and a 1½-litre Formula 1 car, but lack of finance saw these concepts set aside. In 1960, while Len was building a Formula Junior car for Brian, another 750 MC member was doing the same. His name? Maurice Phillippe ...

In 1962 Len was freelancing, his main task being the design of a French Alpine Le Mans sports car. He also accepted work for Colin Chapman, which included production drawings for the Harry Mundy and Richard Ansdale Lotus Twin-cam engine, which would power the Lotus Elan and Lotus Cortina road cars. At a meeting with Len, Colin talked of his plans for the immediate future; the Type 25 had structural troubles that needed to be solved, the Lotus-Cortina prototypes were encountering rear suspension problems and, last but certainly not least, Colin was going to Indy and wanted a car designed for the '500'.

Many years later, Len described how enticing the Indy project was. 'I clearly remember being fascinated by the magic of Indianapolis as far back as 1932 when I was eight years of age, and when Colin announced his plans I was hooked immediately.'

A month after Len was introduced to his new but minute office within the asbestos-roofed first floor above the Team Lotus race shop at Cheshunt, Bill Gay arrived to discuss with him and Colin detail layout and exterior dimensions of the Ford V8. There was no need for extended discussion, and from Cheshunt Gay went on to Bologna to discuss carburettors with Carburatori Weber.

When he returned to Dearborn the whole atmosphere had changed. Animated discussions had ensued during his absence over the fuel to be used, types of ignition, horsepower limits, and push-rod or overhead valve layout. The allocated budget had also been exhausted. Then came news guaranteed to shock. The project was terminated, full stop. At Cheshunt, however, the Lotus programme continued. How much Colin knew of the eruptions in Dearborn, none of us knew ...

The first item on Len Terry's agenda was the Cortina's rear suspension. All Lotus senior staff joining the company were given a whistle-stop tour of the factory by Colin himself, and Len was no exception. He recalled later, 'When we got to the Lotus-Cortina he showed me its newly finished rear end. I looked at it and said, "Cor, that's going to oversteer like a pig, isn't it?" You can imagine his reaction to that sort of comment! Two days later they went testing at Snetterton with Jimmy; sure enough, as soon as it looked at a corner the back-end wanted to come out. When they got back to Cheshunt I asked Colin how the day had gone. "It oversteered badly," he said. "Just like the man said," was my response, to which Colin retorted, "Hell, if you're so bloody clever, *you* sort it out," which I did.

'I had seen from the start that Colin had copied the live rear axle layout of my Terrier Mark 2, but had missed out the important bit, so it was relatively easy to put right. The alterations converted the car from a gross oversteer to considerable understeer; pictures of Jimmy racing the car show the inside front wheel 9 inches off the deck; prior to this it had been the rear wheel clear of the ground.'

Quite soon Len started drawing the Type 29 Indy car; by early October the drawings were being discussed with the engineers, fabricators and mechanics responsible for building the car. With the essential dimensions of the power unit available, Len produced installation drawings, and followed with the left- and right-hand longitudinal diaphragms, and front and rear side-members. Colin and engineer Steve Sanville had already visited Valerio Colotti at his establishment in Italy to discuss gearbox requirements, and alterations to the Italian's Type 37A four-speed unit were soon being drawn at Team Lotus. Colotti's partner was Alf Francis; they had met at Maserati in 1954 when Alf was looking after Stirling Moss's 250F, and Francis had later been responsible for Stirling's double-Monaco GP-winning Rob Walker Team Lotus 18s.

As the days and nights passed, so the car slowly took shape, albeit only on paper at this early stage. By November the drawings were fairly flowing, an indication of the long hours Len was committing, no doubt with pleasure, to a project of which he had long dreamed. The rear frame was drawn, and the centre bulkhead complete with six-element instrument panel, top and bottom channels, the chassis jig for construction, the steering rack, undertray and engine bulkhead were all completed and signed off in November '62.

In compiling a list of the cars he designed for the book *Racing Car Design and Development*, written by Len and his friend Alan Baker, Len omitted the first two Lotus Indy cars, Types 29 and 34, as he regarded them merely as off-shoots of the Team's Type 25 Formula 1 car. Nor, strictly speaking, did Colin Chapman ever use the description 'monocoque' for these vehicles. Although the word had been used in the magazine write-ups and therefore transposed on to the press release draft of the Type 29 given to Colin to approve, he had replaced it with his own 'twin-tube ladder frame' description. Len agreed that this was how Colin had described the concept to him, adding the even shorter term

What a team – Dan Gurney, Jimmy Clark and Colin Chapman pose with Dan's intended race car – chassis '29/2' – during the May running before their first assault upon the world's most lucrative single motor race – the 1963 Indianapolis 500 Miles.

'bath-tub'. 'It was, in fact, just that,' Len continued. 'Those early cars were not monocoques in the true sense of the word, and Colin, as usual, hit the nail on the head correctly with "bath-tub" because that exactly describes the shape the driver lay in. It is where the word "tub" came from that is still used today, but now incorrectly!'

Team Lotus was now approaching the end of a long and tiring season in which it had competed with ten cars of three different Types, totalling 25 Formula 1 and Tasman races, with 47 car starts. Then in October came the shattering announcement that Coventry Climax was withdrawing from racing, but after earnest pleas from the constructors they changed their minds and engine prices, and continued for another three years.

Returning to the final stages of the 1962 Grand Prix season, all Team's activities were now centred upon that crucial South African Grand Prix on 29 December. If Jimmy could win he would take the World Championship from Graham Hill of BRM; their points totals would be equal, but Jimmy's greater number of wins would prevail. Of the three races leading up to the final, Jimmy had started from pole in all three, set fastest race lap in two, won two and finished a happy second (after a spin) in the third behind his friend and team-mate Trevor Taylor. Then in practice in East London, Jimmy had tried two new Type 25s and had problems with both, following which Colin discarded the fuel-injected Climax V8, settling for the carburettor version.

At flag-fall Jimmy led away from pole position, setting a record fastest lap on lap 3! Twenty-three laps from the end of the 82-lap race he was 30 seconds ahead of Hill when smoke began to trail from his car and he was out. A fitter at Climax had omitted a star washer on an engine bolt hidden from view, a painfully disappointing end to what could have been Jimmy's and the Team's first World title.

CHAPTER TWO

1963:
The Road to Indy

I had first met Jim Clark in February 1961 a few days after joining Lotus on the 13th. My office, recently vacated by Colin's father Stan, was exactly the same dimension as the one women's toilet across the minute corridor: 9 feet long by 5 ft 8 in wide. It contained two steel filing cabinets, a small desk and two chairs. That was it. However, its diminutive scale never bothered me. When I had first arrived I had met Ron Richardson, then Export Sales Manager, with whom I had dealt when working for the Cooper Car Company over the previous three years. Ron's opening gambit was, 'What are you doing here?' When I told him I had now joined Lotus, he looked surprised.

'Good heavens,' he replied. 'This lot will be gone inside a month – we've just sacked half the employees – it's going down the pan ...'

After that inauspicious start I began a savings plan in earnest. It did not matter how big or small my office was, as I was convinced it would be merely a matter of weeks until I would be unemployed.

When I had left Cooper the previous year and told my friends I was joining Lucky Casner's American Camoradi team they had looked askance. 'The man's gone mad,' they were saying to themselves. After all, Cooper had won three World Championships (two Formula 1 and one Formula 2) and I was joining an unknown American outfit with outlandish plans to run in both the Formula 1 and Sports Car World Championship series. Soon after, I had gone to Lotus to collect our first Formula 1 car, and as I was standing beside the white Type 18 with Lucky and our Commercial Manager, Tony Mawe, Colin's father had sidled up to me and said, 'Mr Colin would like to talk to you.'

Within half an hour I had made a tentative agreement with Colin and had gone away to talk to Lucky about the possibility of leaving Camoradi. When I told the same friends I had left they showed relief.

'Going back to Cooper's are you?' they asked.

'No, I'm joining Lotus.'

This time they were convinced I was mad. Lotus? They only got a longer than average mention when they lost wheels!

Just a week later I was ensconced in my small office, wondering 'What next?'

The amusing aftermath to that rather fraught day when I had gone to collect the Type 18 came 18 months later when I was called to Fred Bushell's office.

'Did you hand a cheque over that day?' he demanded.

I simply couldn't remember. It transpired that amidst all the shenanigans, Camoradi's trailer had left with the new Formula 1 car on board without payment being made, and by the time Lotus had tumbled it, Camoradi was no more.

Although to all intents and purposes Innes Ireland was Team Lotus's No 1, or team leader, this never came into play. Jimmy was his own man, and Innes his, and the suggestion of No 1 or 2 never became relevant. When Jimmy became No 1 in 1962, the same applied. He was never known as such, or his team-mate as 'No 2'. It was just accepted without any formal ruling.

Jimmy arrived during my first week, back from his first Tasman trip. My office door opened a few inches, and his head appeared with a simple 'Hallo, I'm Jim Clark' in a soft Scottish voice. He stood holding the half-open door and I invited him to sit in the one spare chair. Understandably it never occurred to me that I was face to face with a driver who would before long dominate his profession and about whose magical qualities millions of words would be spoken and written. His bright brown eyes had the customary sparkle of any other racing driver I had met, but were in the same mould as Jack Brabham and Bruce McLaren, with whom I had worked at Cooper - people I classified as 'normal' with few pretensions.

The day before, I had met Innes Ireland for the first time. I had left my office briefly and returned to find him calmly flicking though the papers in my desk drawers. When I suddenly appeared he continued to sit in my chair completely unabashed.

'I always have a look through things,' he said, 'as there are usually cheques for me knocking about.'

At the end of that season Innes had departed and Jimmy had assumed the mantle of No 1, but his manner would change not at all until the final years of his life when he became more outwardly a man of the world with a more relaxed manner and with his hair growing sufficiently long to creep over his collar.

The agenda at that first meeting was to go through his Tasman accounts, establishing who owed what to the other. Jimmy handed over an envelope full of bills all neatly clipped together; like most racing drivers he preferred using other people's money to pay expenses for the Team and himself, and had secured cash advances from the race organisers, which I would deduct from his income a month or two later.

When he visited the factory after that desperately disappointing South African Grand Prix of 1962 I recall him showing no hint of any frustration. All the time that I knew him he acted in a thoroughly professional manner, and I can remember no more than a few rare grumbles about anything to do with racing or indeed with life in general. Genuine grievances that he might have about my management of his affairs or finances were always drawn attention to in a matter-of-fact way, and once resolved were never mentioned again. To me, having previously worked with Jack Brabham and Bruce McLaren, Jimmy merely fitted the same pattern. He really was completely normal.

It is on reflection easy to understand how well he fitted Colin's requirements for a driver. In comparison with Innes, at this stage in his life Jimmy was decidedly prim and proper. To go for a drink with Innes was a more relaxing affair and much more to my liking; with him you could enjoy a smoke and some hard drinks, and you would almost certainly be the first to put the cork back in your own bottle as Innes outstripped the rest of the party. This is of course no personal criticism of Jim Clark. He was an extremely easy personality to get along with, but he was not the sort of person you enjoyed having an 'eff and a blind' with.

As to his much-reported dislike of Indianapolis and the way that officialdom treated him in his 'rookie' test, the reference he made in his book is the only pithy comment I am aware of. In fact, later in the same book there appears another passage extolling the virtues of racing in America, which is often overlooked.

After the New Year celebrations of 1963 there came a change of Dearborn policy. Suddenly Indy was back on their calendar. While Team Lotus prepared for the start of the new season that March, they tested their Formula 1 and Formula Junior cars and the new racing Lotus Cortinas, although the latter would not be entered in a race until the end of the season; standard production of the car (as well as the new sports Elan) had been delayed, and so had the model's required homologation.

January saw the various component parts of the new Indy car, the Type 29, slowly coming together. Although Jim Endruweit was officially titled Chief Mechanic, he was by this time acting more as manager of all the technical aspects undertaken by the racing section, and the Indy project was just another item on his agenda. Jim's senior Indy mechanic was David Lazenby, who along with Colin Riley had switched from Formula 1.

Jim Endruweit had joined Lotus upon leaving the Fleet Air Arm in 1958 after 12 years service on aircraft, learning a trade that stood him in good stead at Lotus; just 18 months later Colin promoted him to Chief Mechanic. I first set eyes on Jim in a bar in Stavelot, Belgium, accompanying his boss late on a Saturday night after Belgian Grand Prix practice in 1960. They were not there for relaxation; just hours previously two privately owned Lotus Type 18s had been involved in serious accidents. One had badly injured Stirling Moss, the other Michael Taylor. I was then with Cooper and had heard a great deal about 'that crazy lot at Hornsey'. Jim's workload of never-ending hours tending his cars as well as his ability to keep Colin happy was already a legend amongst the other teams, so I viewed him with much interest.

Sadly the following day would bring more tragedy to Team Lotus. Their driver, Alan Stacey, would be killed (as would Chris Bristow in his Cooper); Innes would also have a big accident; and Jimmy, although finishing a creditable fifth in only his second Formula 1 World Championship race, would from then on never be happy at Spa, even though he would win there four times in Formula 1 Lotuses.

As well as being a tireless worker, Jim Endruweit was one of the most laid-back characters I ever worked with. Lacking any pretensions, and the first to admit that he was not a dyed-in-the-wool motor racing devotee, he was more interested in the engineering aspects of his job. When he interviewed mechanics he concentrated more on their ability to 'muck in' and live happily with other people than on their professed skills. In those days mechanics spent long periods of time crammed together in minute spaces within often unreliable transporters travelling the length and breadth of Europe, so his thinking was entirely correct. The luxury of air travel, so common today, came only for events held on other continents.

On one occasion I was filling in a new mechanic's 'background file' when I discovered he was actually a master butcher by trade. Jim's reaction was that his pre-war Citroën was so mechanically sound that he must be a worthy addition to our ranks, and so it proved. He would make it clear from the outset that if a chap seeking a job was an enthusiast for motor racing, he would be better to remain a spectator. 'Too much enthusiasm can get in the way,' he once wrote. He had come to cars rather later in life than his colleagues, professing not to have ridden in one until he was 15; his father was a bus-driver, so the family had gone everywhere by bus.

He was also proud of his aircraft recognition abilities, and reckoned that he could identify an aircraft at 10,000 feet. 'But park a car outside my house and it's odds-on I won't know what make it is,' he once said. He was, in fact, far more interested in racing bicycles, and the reason that he bought his first car when he was 25 years old was to carry his bike around.

Jim could and still does keep anyone entertained for hours with stories of the Navy, most of them accounts of life below deck – he maintained that his work on an aircraft carrier was totally confined to the innermost depths of the vessel and that he had only once emerged into the sunlight on an overseas voyage. After 12 years, tired of Navy life, he had left without a clue what he wanted to do. It was then that he had joined Lotus, after seeing their stand at the London Motor Show. His first spell at Hornsey had been three days and two all-nighters preparing for a race. After the event someone asked him how his cars had got on, and it was then that he realised he didn't know the drivers' names. 'I knew the cars were green though,' he said later.

After a spell of quite extraordinarily long hours spent preparing cars for a meeting at Silverstone, one of them, driven by Innes, had won. It was too much for the exhausted Jim and, for once overstressed, he had broken down in tears. With all his colleagues seriously concerned at his apparent breakdown, Colin had put his arms round Jim's shoulder in consolation. Jim said later, 'I couldn't believe the Old Man had it in him. I was most impressed. I was incredulous when he told me to have the next day off – mind you, it was a Sunday!'

For those who might imagine this is a personally slanted eulogy of a colleague, I should add that we were still receiving letters from people around the world enquiring after Jim's health and whereabouts 17 years after he left us; to those and others may I say that in the 1990s he continues to live but a stone's throw from Team Lotus and is still in excellent shape.

As January neared its end, Len Terry was drawing the Lotus Type 29's various suspension components, the oil tank and its relevant system, water and oil radiator dimensions and driveshaft assembly, and everyone on the Team was now lending a hand with construction. Formula 1 section mechanics David Lazenby and Colin Riley were now on the new Indy section with F1

In Team's shop at the Lotus factory in Cheshunt, veteran mechanic Ted Woodley helps skin the so-called 'monocoque' chassis for the prototype Indianapolis Lotus-Ford Type 29. Its cockpit-section outer panels have been rolled to shape and are locked into the jig, pinned to the fabricated front bulkhead structure on the right, Ted just adding the folded footwell-area inner panels. Separate stressed-skin rear horns to accept the American V8 engine will unite this cockpit 'tub' to that fabricated steel rear hoop, with its suspension and gearbox pick-up holes, far left.

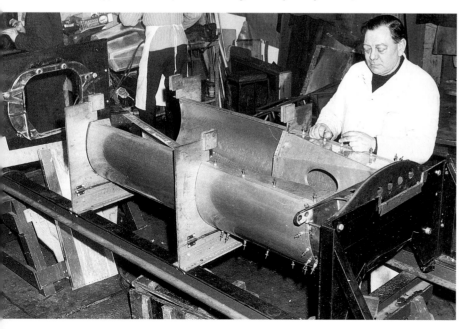

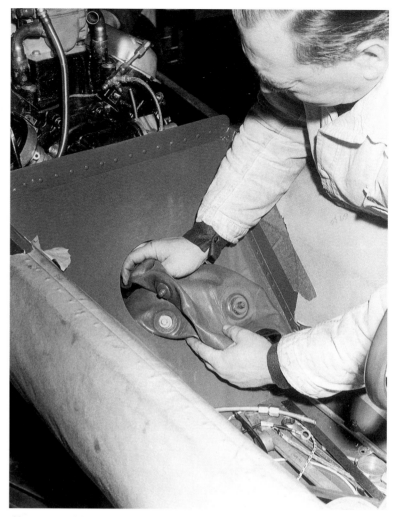

Almost complete – Ted Woodley feeds the central rubber bag tank through the access provided in the prototype Lotus 29's sloping seatback panel as '29/1' nears completion at Cheshunt in February 1963.

'regulars' Dick Scammell and Ted Woodley also helping. Bob Dance, who had joined Lotus in 1960 and had switched to Team in 1962, was part of the new Lotus Cortina section; his previous experience of Colotti gearboxes (he was known as 'Boblotti') saw him working with Formula 1 gearbox man Jim Bull.

The car contained four aircraft-style FPT rubberised rupture-proof bag tanks; we had received special dispensation from USAC for these, and the concept would soon be mandatory in American racing. There were two on either side, a fifth being situated behind the driver's seat and a sixth, of aluminium encased in glass-reinforced plastic (GRP), behind the instrument panel and over the driver's legs. Total fuel capacity was 42 Imperial gallons (50 US).

All the fuel compartments were inter-connected to allow pressure re-fuelling, but the system was fitted with non-return valves to prevent weight transfer caused by a surge of fuel from one

Lotus-powered-by-Ford – the Type 29. (James Allington)

side to the other through the constant left-hand cornering. Fuel surge to the rear, where the off-takes were positioned, was allowed under acceleration, but not a forward surge under braking. The scuttle tank incorporated a 'filler cap', which acted as an air vent when refuelling and as a shut-off valve when closed; refuelling was through a valve situated on the left-hand side, all tanks filling simultaneously, the scuttle tank last of all. For qualifying, the refuelling valve was replaced by a simple lightweight aluminium 'disc'. Three electric Bendix fuel pumps located under the driver's legs completed the system.

The torsional stiffness of the 'tub' due to its deeper side-members (they were also slightly wider) was even higher than on the Type 25. The engine, mounted solidly at eight points, added a further 50 per cent to the figure, which was estimated to be in excess of 1,500 lbs ft/degree, giving a total of well over 2,250 lbs ft/degree.

The front suspension consisted of welded-up cantilever top rocking arms operating inboard coil springs with Armstrong co-axial damper units. It used lower wishbones that were wider-based than those on the Type 25. In the interests of tyre wear, weight transfer through the corners was reduced by offsetting the chassis 2³/8 inches to the left of the centre-line of the car's

track. To achieve this the front suspension had longer links on the right-hand side; as Team's press release stated, 'the Type 25's sortie at Indy last year proved that even if built symmetrically the car would more than hold its own through the corners.'

The rear suspension employed a single top arm with reversed lower wishbone attached to the chassis with a single mounting; the coil springs with Armstrong dampers were mounted outboard, the unequal-length twin parallel radius arms of larger diameter than the Formula 1 car. Unlike the front suspension, both wishbones and top arms at the rear were of equal length, the pick-up points on the chassis being offset by the required amount. Also incorporated were additional suspension pick-up points so that the car would run in symmetrical configuration on normal road circuits. The vertical links, unlike the solely magnesium versions on the Formula 1 car, were now a mixture of magnesium and zirconium to provide increased strength. Roll centres were given as approximately 2 inches above ground level in the static position.

Rubber driveshaft couplings of sufficient size to cope with the torque delivered by the engine were found to be too large to be accommodated within the confines of the body, and conventional sliding spline shafts tended to lock up, bringing severe interference with suspension movement. These disadvantages were overcome by fitting Saginaw recirculating ball splines in the driveshafts, which had Hookes joints at either end.

Front and rear hubs were designed to accept Dunlop peg-drive, knock-off wheels of either 15 or 16 inches in diameter. Specially manufactured by Dunlop for the Type 29, the rims were of very wide section.

The bodywork, described in the press release as 'characteristically Lotus', was of GRP and incorporated aircraft-style ducts in each side of the detachable one-piece nose-cowling-cum-cockpit surround, feeding cooling air to the suspension units and cockpit. The engine cover was shaped at its leading edge to provide intakes on either side of the head fairing to feed cool air to the carburettors. A gearbox fairing completed the car. The windscreen was identical to that on the Type 25, and the seating position 5 degrees more upright than that of the Formula 1 car. Lotus rack-and-pinion steering was employed, with a collapsible column and the standard Lotus three-spoke, light-alloy, 12-inch steering wheel, its rim covered in the now traditional red leather. It provided $2^{1}/_{4}$ turns lock-to-lock. Initially an alloy nose panel was used.

Water, oil, brake and clutch plumbing was located in 'V'-shaped channels incorporated in the underside of the fuselage, but the scheme differed from the Formula 1 car in that the two oil pipes were concentric with one another in order to accommodate them in the limited space available. The radiator, positioned in the

Ford's prototype push-rod Indy V8 'live round' with its temporary stack-pipe exhaust system installed in '29/1' ready for press inspection at Cheshunt. The cranked rod beneath the exhaust stack is the right-side gear-change linkage. Note the steeply angled spark plug location 'outside' the vee, canted front-mounted distributor, transverse-mounted Weber carburettors and cooling system swirl-pot under the roll-over bar.

'Those Communists' in the Lotus body shop finishing the prototype top panel for '29/1', later to be moulded in glass fibre. They are, left to right, George Holdaway, Roy Kemp, George Farmer and Roger Tanner. Note the fuel filler neck ahead of the screen and what by modern standards would be an entirely inadequate, slender and solid brake disc. The side NACA duct will feed cooling air on to the inboard front damper units. At the rear the Ford V8 engine is already rigged with its prototype separate 'stack pipe' exhausts.

nose of the car and basically oval in shape, combined both oil and water sections, the water pipe lying on top of the left-hand pontoon insulated to protect the driver. The 4-gallon (4.8 US) aluminium oil tank was located behind the radiator, its forward-facing 'V' shape acting as a deflector to the air passing over it.

Provision was made for a separate oil tank for the four-speed Type 37A Colotti gearbox; this was of 1 gallon (1.2 US) capacity, and if required would be mounted on the left-hand side of the gearbox. The gear lever and its two-piece linkage was located on the right-hand side of the cockpit, the link being almost straight for its entire length. Girling disc brakes of $10^{1}/_{2}$-inch diameter front and rear were fitted, and provision was made for fitting $11^{1}/_{2}$-inch discs should initial testing indicate this necessity. The system incorporated independent front/rear operation.

The Team Lotus release quoted that the car, complete with its Ford V8 power unit, produced a power-to-weight ratio (dry) of 800 bhp/ton. 'This latest development built at the Cheshunt works,' it said, 'represents one of the most if not the most potent pieces of racing machinery ever built, surpassing even that of the pre-war Mercedes and Auto-Unions. All the outlined factors, coupled with renowned Lotus road holding, equip this car with the potential of being able to break almost every circuit lap record in the world!'

We would have used more conservative phrasing had we known of the trials and tribulations going on at Ford. With the confirmation in January that the company was going 'second class', which signified that a push-rod engine fuelled by gasoline

Massive Colotti transaxle, push-rod Ford V8 engine, 'bathtub'-type stressed-skin chassis and hub-height upper radius rods in the rear suspension identify this Type 29 under assembly in Team's workshop at the Cheshunt factory. (Autocar)

would run at Indy, the Ford engineers had resumed work on their V8. With a series of races scheduled at Daytona in February, one of these units was fitted into an AC Cobra entered for the 250-mile Daytona Continental on 17 February, to be driven by Dan Gurney.

Pre-race testing was hampered by numerous problems with the unit, and these carried on into official practice. Two hours before the start of the race, Dan discovered that an engine freeze plug had blown, and Carroll Shelby, in charge of the team, made the decision to change the engine. Some of the press people thought that it was all part of a major strategy. The Holman-Moody engine stock numbered 17 V8s, and there were ten mechanics on hand to do the work, but numbers do not guarantee success and work was still continuing as the flag fell. Dan got away two laps down, but in the panic of preparation the throttle linkages had not been installed correctly; the car soon developed a mis-fire and, although he tried hard, Dan eventually retired. As with most preliminary trials much had been learned, and more data was accumulated from a similar power unit in the Galaxie sedans that also competed.

Bill Gay was thoroughly depressed by the continuing problems. Back at Dearborn he talked to Bill Innes and together they went through the list of failures. Innes promised Gay that he would provide the answers.

Meanwhile, at Cheshunt the Lotus component fabricators were busy finishing the centre bulkheads and rear frames and suspension components; Williams & Pritchard were equally occupied producing the various 'skin' panels. Len Terry was still hard at work churning out drawings, many of them detail items but all essential to the projected early-March date for shakedown tests. He also had the task of designing the wheels to be produced by Dunlop, ironically including the rim detail to suit Firestone tyres! The original GRP-encased scuttle fuel tank was dimensionally declared obsolete on 22 February, and another drawing begun. A fuel tank pump had to be designed, it was time to fit gear-change linkages, and so it went on.

The various items made their own timetables – designing, making and fitting, and possible re-design, making and fitting, all followed each other in a logical process, but with the time left

Lotus-Ford '29/1' – 'The Mule' – extensively instrumented for rolling-road testing at Ford's vast facility. Note the bottle-screw lateral tensioner on the restraint tethers and 'fifth-wheel' acceleration and speed recorder outboard of that left-rear wheel. Here on the rolling road the car is wearing Dunlop racing tyres – American Firestones would quickly replace them once Speedway running began in earnest.

The completed prototype as shown to the press at Cheshunt in March 1963, demonstrating the Lotus style of stressed-skin 'bathtub' chassis construction, welded-aluminium scuttle fuel tank, rocker-arm front suspension with inboard spring/damper units, right-hand gearshift, copiously instrumented dash panel, roll-over bar mounted on the V8 engine, 'stack-pipe' exhaust and Colotti transaxle gearbox. The car is on symmetrical suspension and Dunlop racing tyres. (Geoffrey Goddard)

diminishing rapidly as each day passed. (It is also as well to remember that there were other projects and cars to build or modify for other categories of racing.) The concentric oil pipes for the Type 29 were not signed off until the end of February, and they still had to be made and fitted. The top and bottom radius arms, two sets of each for the prototype, had just been approved, made and fitted. Drawings for bearing housings and outboard driveshaft yokes had been sent to pattern-makers; soon would come the process of casting or forging, followed by machining and fitting to the car.

Ford's drawings of the V8 engine had arrived at Lotus the previous October, and as these detailed mounting points, overall dimensions and ancillary items, they had enabled Len Terry to produce three-dimensional sketches and primary chassis drawings. A mock-up engine had arrived early in December and a 'runner', one of Ford's test units, arrived in January for the car's initial shakedown. Such a chronological procedure would appear to be a matter of common sense and of much value to the design staff wanting to finalise general arrangement drawings as well as those people responsible for constructing the car, but in reality this is not always the case. The first mock-up can sometimes differ from the initial drawings, and the first 'runner' might not resemble either! Delivery of the first 'live' unit is therefore usually awaited with some anxiety in case major redesign work becomes necessary.

During one of Jim Clark's visits to Cheshunt he had climbed into the almost completed car for his cockpit fitting. With Len Terry and Jim Endruweit on hand, it was vitally important for Jimmy to make himself as comfortable as possible and to tell them the changes he needed for pedal layout, ease of gear-change operation and final positioning of the steering wheel. His seat in the car also needed to fit him perfectly to counteract the forces he would encounter when cornering the car at high speeds, so this demanded maximum attention.

In the second week of March the prototype was complete at last, and was taken to Snetterton for its shakedown run. The special Dunlop knock-off wheels were not available, so Lotus six-bolt 'wobbly webs' were fitted as a temporary measure; in addition, the exhaust system was still under scrutiny at Ford, so an eight-pipe smoke stack was employed, giving the car a dragster air. As the track was a normal road circuit, the 29 also ran in symmetrical suspension form.

It fell to Jim Endruweit to fire up the engine and, since the starter trolley was still in its design stage, the car was towed around the circuit with our chief mechanic in the cockpit. He remembers to this day how long it took. 'I completed a full lap with the engine coughing and spluttering, firing on two, then three, sometimes four or five cylinders, then dying out again. Then as I started my second lap all eight fired up – my goodness, that was an experience I haven't forgotten! Fortunately I had kept a close eye on the tow car, so I managed to avoid that . . .'

Several members of the press were on hand, all of them much impressed by the car's tremendous acceleration and the fact that

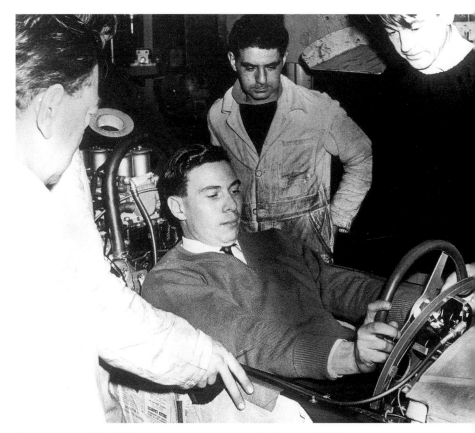

Fitting for the World Champion elect – Jimmy Clark tries '29/1' for size at Cheshunt, tended by (left to right) Ted Woodley, South African Cedric Selzer, and Chief Mechanic Jim Endruweit.

Jimmy promptly broke his 2½-litre circuit lap record without visibly trying. After all, it weighed 200 lbs less than a Mini!

Mechanic Derek Wild remembered the Snetterton test some years later: 'During the test Jimmy came in and reported a rattle coming from around the exhaust system primaries. It was a spare exhaust bolt that had become trapped between the monocoque and the primaries. We were always impressed by his feel and sense of all aspects of driving – it was truly amazing. He could come into the pits, and reel off revs into and out of any corner, brake balance, ratio requirements and many other details, including the nice-looking girl sitting by the hairpin!'

At this stage the prototype was not scheduled to go to Indianapolis for the 'month of May' being earmarked for test running only. With only minor faults revealed at Snetterton, the car was soon back at Cheshunt to be prepared for its journey to the Ford test track at Kingman, Arizona. It was then flown to Los Angeles where Dan saw it for the first time, his crew taking it on to Kingman. Ford had still not clinched the deal with Lotus, but with the opening of Indy practice fast approaching, construction of the two race cars continued at Cheshunt regardless. The decision to continue such work says a great deal for Colin Chapman's self-confidence.

First tests – Jimmy shaking-down the prototype Indianapolis Lotus-Ford first time out at Snetterton, the aluminium bodywork still unpainted, and soon after at Indianapolis with Dan Gurney discovering if his idea might be worthwhile in '29/1', now resplendent in British Racing Green. Quaint to relate, it was this colour that became perhaps the British invader's most detested feature! (David Phipps/Dave Friedman Photo Collection)

The Ford-owned 5-mile banked oval Kingman proving ground, with its two long 140 mph bends, could take various forms, and for this test part was marked out to duplicate one straight and corner of the Brickyard with entry speeds on to the straight regulated to correspond to that estimated at the Speedway using the data Ford had already accumulated. The whole venture at this time depended on the car being able to maintain a 150 mph average speed around Indy. Ford had all the data recording equipment on site at Kingman to make a detailed analysis, and the result was found to match earlier calculations; the car should lap the Speedway at 150.50 mph, its top speed around Kingman being clocked at 165 mph.

But all was not well. The engine proved somewhat troublesome, its problems attributed more to its method of assembly than basic design faults. The valve train was suspect (the studs holding the rockers in place were snapping), there was a carburettor deficiency, and other niggling problems. Like any trial of a new racing car and engine, such maladies were inevitable, but Colin and Dan suspected that the main problems lay not only with Ford's engine but in the organisation behind it, and after three days of running they flew to Dearborn to thrash out the matter. According to Ford, they both wanted out of the project; presumably this was a front they were putting up to get the programme moving along the lines both were more familiar with in Formula 1. After all, the race was fast approaching and the engine was still not sufficiently reliable.

Bill Gay accepted the criticisms and gave the assurance that a solution was just around the corner and that a revised engine would be ready for a further test at Indy the following weekend. Colin and Dan took Gay at his word, and as Dan was driving in the Sebring 12-Hour race on the weekend in question, with practice opening on the coming Wednesday, he left for the Florida circuit.

From Kingman, the Lotus chassis with its troublesome engine was shipped quickly to Dearborn, where both Ford engineers and Lotus crew set to work on their respective charges. Jim Endruweit and David Lazenby still clearly remember their introduction to Ford of America. Jim: 'I wasn't familiar with who was who namewise – I just gauged the importance by their office decor. The top guys had wooden furniture, the next down had metal and what I call the "workers" appeared to have no office at all.'

David 'Laz' Lazenby had joined Lotus in 1959 after his five years in the Royal Air Force. His first task had been to assemble Lotus Elites in Len Street's production area for 4s 6d an hour; he stayed there for three months before an equally short spell in the Service Department working on customer cars. At the beginning of 1960 he transferred to Team Lotus just before the new Formula 1 Type 18 made its sensational debut in the Argentine Grand Prix, and he remained in the Formula 1 section through the introduction of the Type 25 until the Type 29 Indy car had started to take shape, soon finding himself seconded to the new project on a permanent basis. Now in Detroit, he and Jim were busy sourcing

materials and additional tools required to prepare the car for the following week's test.

'I remember Jim and I working in this simply enormous engine research and development building getting the car ready. It wasn't the last time we would work there in the coming months and years – I had to make a new swirl pot from nothing, and I remember hunting about for materials and tools to get it done.'

Not very far away Ford's engine people were working round the clock fitting rapidly re-designed parts, but with the work completed and the unit running on the dynamometer, a camshaft broke. Another long work session followed, this time non-stop for two days and nights. When the engine went back on to the dyno it ran perfectly, and even gave a slight increase in horsepower.

The engine arrived at the Speedway on the Saturday of Sebring, with Colin and Jimmy already in attendance. However, in the rush to re-fit the engine in the chassis several ancillary items had been forgotten, but the initial panic subsided when someone recalled that they were standard Ford Fairlane components, and two similar cars were quickly rented and the required items removed. It was not quite this simple, however, as members of the press, learning of the historic event about to take place, had quickly gathered around 'Gasoline Alley', and the hijacked parts had to be smuggled into the garage area to maintain Ford's credibility.

It was Sunday when the car was finally rolled out into public view. Stories of what was rumoured to be a multi-million dollar

The Ford V8 stock-block push-rod-valvegear engine installed in the prototype '29/1' on test at Indianapolis in March 1963, showing the east-west-mounted 58 mm Weber twin-choke carburettors, which would subsequently prove such a handicap on the tighter ovals at Milwaukee and Trenton. The 'stack-pipe' exhaust system was speedily replaced by properly coupled 'snake-pit' manifolding exiting into twin megaphone tailpipes above the gearbox. (Indianapolis Motor Speedway)

Anglo-American assault on the Speedway had been circulating for some time, but no one in their wildest imagination could have guessed just how ramshackle the whole deal really was. According to Leo Levine's account, one of the media hacks poking about in the garage area asked Bill Gay where he was hiding his spare engines. Gay's reply went along the lines of, 'The car's got one driver and one engine – perhaps you can show me space for another?' The conversation ended there.

Dan was back from Sebring, and Jimmy was the first to drive the car late on the Sunday afternoon, running around the 140–144 mph mark as he went through the car's first shakedown on the 'establishment's' hallowed ground, initially trying various carburettor and suspension settings, the car still sporting its symmetrical suspension layout.

Jimmy drove again on the Monday, getting the car up to 146 mph-plus, but then came wind and rain and the track shut down. With the bad weather continuing through the Tuesday and into

Feverish activity characterised the Lotus 29 prototype's initial test session at Indianapolis. Here Colin Chapman takes notes while project initiator Dan Gurney makes some point about the dash panel array to Jimmy Clark and – hidden – Bill Gay of Ford. An additional perspex lip has been taped on to the windscreen to protect Dan, the taller driver, from buffeting, and the car is on Dunlop road-racing tyres. Perched on the pit counter in the background is a distinctive crash helmet – Graham Hill's. He would opt out of the '500' this year after deciding that he had little chance in one of Mickey Thompson's Harvey Aluminum Specials. Three years later he would deny Clark and Lotus a famous double and win the '500' for Lola. (Indianapolis Motor Speedway)

Wednesday morning, and Jimmy due to practice for Team's first European race at Snetterton two days later, he and Chapman departed leaving Laz and Colin Riley to look after Dan. It was the first of many occasions when the Ford hierarchy would be dismayed by the defection of their 'partner' to fulfil 'foreign' commitments.

On Wednesday the weather cleared and the track re-opened. Dan, still conducting carburettor trials while familiarising himself with the car around the Brickyard, worked up to more than 149 mph. Ford had its electronic recording devices on site, one charting throttle positions and oil and water temperature readings. An American scribe reported, 'Weber carburettors will confound the Indy regulars; they have become so enamoured of Stu Hilborn's lawn-sprinkler system that they ignore the fact there are carburettors that will do the job better than almost any currently available fuel-injection system.'

As the test continued, three different types of tyres were tried, and carburettors and gear ratios played with. Both Firestone and Dunlop tyres were tested, the latter being standard Grand Prix D9 compound; these proved faster, but the two types of Firestones tested were harder wearing, although not suited to the car. They had been developed for the heavier Indy 'roadsters' with their different suspension, and their contours meant that there was less rubber on the track. The fastest speed recorded through Turn One was over 142 mph; the best an American car had so far recorded was 138 mph. Jimmy's much smaller Formula 1 car had registered a touch over 140 mph, although its lap average of 143 mph was down on Dan's 149 mph-plus, the American driver clocking 175 mph along the straights.

Dan Gurney: 'To be honest, that first push-rod engine in '63 was not very impressive. We were told it had around 350 horsepower, but you never knew if it really had it. You just had to hustle the car around the Speedway to be competitive – I mean, you really had to drive it. And we also had to catch up on the specialised oval-track-racing technology and practices, which all the established roadster teams had been accumulating for years. They knew when the track would be quick, and when it would be slow. They knew how to read the weather conditions, and they knew all kinds of tweaks and tricks and strokes to pull with Firestone and the Firestone tyres which we had to learn and adapt to what were at that time after all very strange Speedway cars. A lot of that knowledge is not at all university text-book engineering, nor the kind of deductive reasoning Colin could apply . . . it was real fundamental hand-me-down folklore, and quite a high proportion of it really worked . . .

'Troy Ruttman once told me how, early in his career, he'd crashed his roadster badly and it was just slammed back together again in a real hurry but immediately ran faster than ever and won him a lot of money. Truth was they'd left a twist in the chassis that just set it up ideal.

'A lot of that set-up lore for left-hand-only racing is real rule-of-thumb stuff, and since the drivers are all pros, the winning guy who has the key to the best set-up isn't about to go around

Some novice – Jimmy Clark awaiting his mandatory 'Rookie Test' at the Speedway, perched on the Type 29's right-front wheel in conversation with David Lazenby (resting against the rear wheel) and Colin Riley (right). Colin Chapman's company-issue briefcase marks his presence, out of shot. The car's left-side offset upon its asymmetric suspension is very apparent, as is its USAC regulation 'nerf bar' bumper bolted to the gearbox tail-plate. Jimmy's 'Rookie stripes' are applied in tape on each side of the engine cowl, to be ceremonially peeled off once his observed laps have been completed. The driver of the roadster ahead in the Indy pit lane is in the same situation. (Indianapolis Motor Speedway)

telling everybody, "Hey, aren't I clever, I do this to my car and it wins. You do that to yours and you can win some too!" That just isn't going to happen – so a lot of that lore has always been closely guarded.'

That Wednesday evening the 29's final-drive ratio was changed from 3.295 to 3.477, and first running on the Thursday saw Dan trying the Firestones again. When the Dunlops were fitted, the lap times improved. There was a delay in running due to a film crew from Chevrolet making a promotional film of the pace car to be used in the forthcoming '500', and by the time the Lotus went out it was late in the afternoon. As a result Dan had to contend with a glistening pit straight reflecting the bright sunshine into his eyes, but shortly before the test ended he clocked 59.78

seconds, 150.501 mph – only the second time in the Speedway's history that the 150 mph barrier had been broken.

Parnelli Jones's four-lap average in taking pole the previous year had been 150.370 mph, including one lap at 150.729 mph. The Lotus was still on its 'wobbly web', Formula 1-style magnesium wheels, its Colotti gearbox employing four speeds rather than the two planned, the engine still sporting its 'dragster'-style exhausts. Dan was all in favour of retaining the four speeds for the race, as he thought acceleration away from the pits would be much improved while less strain would be placed on both transmission and engine.

After the test the car was returned to Cheshunt and its power unit to Dearborn, where it was taken apart for a thorough examination. It had covered over 450 miles at the Speedway, yet showed nothing amiss, its fuel consumption just under a remarkable 7 mpg. Re-assembled without renewing any components, and put back on the dyno, the Ford engineers then used the tape taken from their 'black box' at Indy and started running the engine to the same programme; after a number of hours it was still running strongly with no loss of power. Meanwhile, further running to cure a carburation fault was carried out with a similar engine in a Galaxie run over the Dearborn test track.

These results finally clinched the Ford-Lotus deal, and Ford's Special Vehicle Manager, Frank Zimmerman, flew to England to sign a contract with Chapman. Now Team Lotus was set to try and secure the first Indianapolis 500 Miles success by a European car since 1940; indeed, if Jimmy won he would be the first European to do so since 1915. Two cars were to run in the race; the third, or prototype, was also entered as a back-up.

It was now into April, the Speedway opening for the month of May just under four weeks away. If Colin Chapman had waited until now to start building the cars, the Indy Lotus-Ford project would never have got off the ground. But Ford's delay also left its own engine people in an unenviable position. The two cars in Cheshunt were awaiting the new V8s and additional units would be required during practice and the race, complete with a reliable back-up service of men and components. On 11 April Bill Gay issued a memo to his chief aides confirming that there had been 'no basic engine problems' at the Speedway, and that 'engine design AX-230-2' was now frozen. Gay added, 'It is fully recognised that no engine is ever completely developed, and improvements can always be made in performance, durability, reliability and fuel economy. However, this policy, and the deferment of the overhead-cam engine, have been implemented to eliminate the possibility of a major design change which could result in post-race-day hindsight.'

During April the Lotus factory was its usual scene of great activity. Team had five races, from Oulton Park in Cheshire to Pau in France and Imola in Italy. At the end of the month it would be back at Aintree, Liverpool, not far from Oulton Park. At Cheshunt, meanwhile, the two-storey 25,000 sq ft factory extension, built primarily for production of the new Lotus-Cortina, the styling department, and an improved drawing office with after-sales also rehoused, was about to open.

As the month progressed and Indy approached, so more people from other sections were seconded to building the new cars. Bob Dance, then with our newly formed Lotus-Cortina racing section and still with Lotus as I write, was one of these. Bob kept a diary of all the major events on each day he had spent in racing, and his entry for Monday 8 April 1963 records that all work on building the racing saloons had come to an end until homologation had been confirmed. The following evening he started work on the Indy cars, involved in the trial assembly of an engine and gearbox, then built up four right-front strut castings. By the following evening the gearbox mounting points had been repositioned, and fitting started again. Initial installation of the

bag tanks followed, and on the Friday he was to work from 10 am through to 5.30 am on Saturday fitting disc brakes to front hubs.

By the middle of April the engines had arrived and production of the throttle components was under way; this in turn led to modification of the throttle pedals (for all three cars), then assembly of the gear-change mechanism followed. With his Colotti gearbox experience Bob was given the task of preparing both those on the cars and the spare units that would be air-freighted out. On Thursday 25 April Bob completed a 24-hour session of Indy work, then answered a plea from the Formula 1 section, on their way to Aintree. They were also short of hands, so Friday afternoon found him working in the ash-surfaced Aintree race paddock. The race was on Saturday, and by 10 am Sunday he had returned to the Indy section at Cheshunt, fitting the rear crash (or 'nerf') bar and windscreen on Jimmy's Type 29.

On Tuesday 30 April, three days later than scheduled, Jimmy's car was due for dispatch from London Airport, and rather than risk a possible delay en route, Bob left for the airport in the early hours, quickly unloading the car into the cargo shed and continuing the work that still remained. He finished at 5 am and was back at work by 10.30 am Wednesday, helping to complete the spare car. By 3 pm Friday it was finished and was trucked to the airport.

For those who over the years have questioned the chassis numbers of the Type 29s when they first arrived at Indianapolis we were fortunate recently to find some notes made by Jim Endruweit at the time. These confirm that the prototype was, as to be expected, '29/1', the car initially designated Dan's was '29/2', and Jimmy's '29/3'. Although Dan was destined to hop in and out of '/1' and '/2', Jimmy was to drive '/3' from the start of practice, race it and continue to drive it at other venues that year.

It was never suggested that I should go to Indianapolis. We had so much going on both at the factory and in other races that it was logical for me to remain at home base on call for the usual 24 hours a day, seven days a week. The Indy project was classified as a one-off exercise at that time; Colin regarded every aspect and category of racing within Team Lotus as top priority, whether it was the supply of Lotus-Cortina engines or the new practice time charts expected from the printers. To be honest, it was quite a relief to know that he would be away for such a long period of time as he shuttled to and fro across the Atlantic!

In fact, it was quite rare for me to attend races, but it caused no disappointment as I always regarded the excitement and challenge of factory life as greater than any race, where it was merely a case of being dogsbody to the Guv'nor. Only telephone calls received in the middle of the night, prefaced by 'It's Colin here ...' would bring instant consciousness and a hand reaching for the papers piled beside the bed. Such calls might last two minutes or half an hour while I scribbled notes sufficiently detailed for me to act upon at first light. Even in those days there was an excellent telephone service available whereby all incoming calls were re-routed to wherever the recipient might be, and Team Lotus made good use of it. The only drawback was when one visited a friend for the evening and had to carry two briefcases full of the documents Colin might want to discuss in detail over the telephone.

Some idea of the amateurish arrangements prevailing at Indy can be gained from the way Jimmy's car arrived at the Speedway, as recalled by author, journalist and photographer David Phipps, a close associate and friend of Colin until the latter's death in 1982, and whom Colin had asked to accompany the Indy section to the 1963 '500'. In making our organisational plans for the month of May with Colin before he left, I assumed from what he inferred that David would be fulfilling all my working functions at Indy. It was not until 1993 that I discovered this was not the case! Moreover, several members of Team assumed that he was acting as European manager for Dan Gurney and that this was the reason for his trip, but again many years later David dispelled the impression.

'I was what might be termed "general co-ordinator" for Indy 1963,' explains David. 'I think my presumed managerial relationship with Dan came about because we were often seen together at race meetings; I was a struggling photographer at the time and with barely adequate finances I was using what could be described as a "box Brownie". But Dan had a Leica, and in exchange for whatever I might do for him he would (when he remembered to bring it!) let me borrow it at a race, after which I would give it back. Camera lenses at that time were very expensive indeed.

'Also, I lived next to Brands Hatch in those days, so it suited Dan to come and stay with me. He had a key to the house and could come and go as he pleased; in fact, Colin and Jimmy had a similar arrangement and one weekend when the trio were racing at Nurburgring on the Sunday and Brands on the Monday I came downstairs to find all three asleep. Dan was on a mattress on the floor of the sitting room and Colin and Jimmy were asleep on chairs in the kitchen.

'When I went to Indy I was expected to fulfil the job that Andrew Ferguson did. I was there for six weeks all told. I remember that Ford had promised us courtesy cars, but none appeared so I did a deal with General Motors! I had an Oldsmobile Starfire and one day Colin told me to get to the airport as quickly as possible as Jimmy's Type 29 had just arrived. Indianapolis's Weir Cook Airport was pretty relaxed at the best of times, and this was no exception – I had taken Jimmy with me and we were waved on to the airport apron and I drove right up to where the car was standing. There were no customs officials or documents to sign, and nobody in authority to be seen. We just hitched up the Indy car with a rope behind the Starfire, Jimmy jumped into the race car and we were off!

'At some stages during the journey I could see Jimmy waving to me and, thinking he was getting bored, speeded up each time – it turned out he was trying to get me to slow down! Not long

Lift-off – Jimmy trying out the Len Terry-designed whole-car jack platform, which arrived late at Indy '63, with the aircraft-attachment fuel feed hose also locked on to his ultimately second-placed Lotus-Ford '29/3'. Compare the cut-down Clark car windscreen with the tall moulding preferred on Gurney's. Firestone tyres here are mounted on Dunlop alloy wheels. Both the written and the photo records of which chassis did what are confusing, but it seems almost certain that this historic car was ultimately destroyed in Bobby Marshman's fatal testing accident at Phoenix in November '64, 18½ months hence. (Indianapolis Motor Speedway)

after we arrived at the track, about 8 miles from Weir Cook, the engine was started and Jimmy was out on the track.

'We rented a house from Rodger Ward that year. Of course, Colin being what he was, I was given several jobs, all of which he wanted done at the same time. As I looked strong and fit I was given the task of working the mechanical handle on the fuel bowsers, one for each car, but then Colin told me he wanted me out on the circuit to take photographs of other cars, to note certain items he wanted an answer to, plus close-up photographs of our own car, with the accent on the front suspension! I left it to him to decide his order of priority.'

Now that the cars, spares and personnel were safely at the track, it might be imagined that constructional work for the project would then tail off. In fact, Len Terry was still hard at work designing new or modified components needed urgently at the Speedway as running continued. The cars were now to run in asymmetric form, and revisions to front and rear suspension geometry came first, following which new components were fabricated and air-freighted out. The long hours of work spent building the cars had seen other items put to one side, and these were now receiving attention.

One such item was the pneumatic ramp, or jacking device, that would be placed on the pit apron in our designated area during the race and over which the driver would position his car when the time came for tyre changes. The design had been completed in the middle of April during the scramble to get the race cars completed; as a result it was not to be flown out until well into May, and this would ultimately play a detrimental part in our race procedure.

David Lazenby took to life at the Speedway like the proverbial duck to water. Facilities for the workers at Formula 1 events in those days were virtually non-existent, and when Laz had first arrived at the Speedway he could not believe his eyes. Just to have a roof over his head while he worked on our car was a novelty, and to have the same roof for over a month was an enormous benefit. The garages were allocated as soon as entry fees were received; for 1963 Lotus's were on the north-west corner of the block, Nos 85, 86 and 87, and we were to use them for the next six years. No 85 was a single-car garage where the third car and main spares were housed, the other a double in which all the work on the two race cars was carried out.

The daily temperatures and humidity levels during May were more often than not exhausting for those saddled with the standard Team Lotus working day. Whereas all the American teams enjoyed leased air-conditioning units (the Americans worked out of these garages throughout most of the USAC season), Colin would have none of this and he was not to relent throughout all the years we attended. Although much has been written of Jimmy's phobia for the place, I can personally remember hardly any derogatory statements from the Scot, whereas Colin's withering outbursts, made mostly in public, could – and invariably did – produce an embarrassed hush among those standing in the vicinity.

With interested onlookers tending to gather at the open doors of the garages, some anxious to chat with the incumbents, Colin decreed that the doors must be shut at all times, although when he was away at another race the crew luxuriated in leaving them open. With temperatures sometimes approaching the 100 mark, and humidity percentages into the 80s, the stifling atmosphere within our vintage clap-boarded double garage (measuring around 26 feet square) can be imagined. Add to this scene the simmering-hot racing cars fresh from running, plus the smell of fuel and oils, a number of Ford executives, race scrutineers (seemingly ever present), our drivers, Colin and the mechanics, perhaps the tyre and fuel engineers, intruders hammering on the doors to be let in, and our telephone ringing constantly (and more often than not drowned out by the garage paging loudspeaker calls), and the picture is nearly complete.

To visit other garages was a revelation, and Colin, always critical of what he felt was the typical English mechanic's lack of regard for what he defined as the finer aspects of life ('the pigs-in-shit brigade' was his description) was openly envious of the American team owners' spotlessly clean garages. A contract from a carpet and rug hiring company at Indy had arrived at Cheshunt, and being unfamiliar with the American way of racing and taken aback at the thought that any garage could ever boast such a thing, I had mentioned the subject to Colin. It had produced an instant and vigorous response.

'Complete waste of time and money,' he said, 'so forget it! What do our lads do when they arrive anywhere? First they pour a gallon of oil all over the floor, then slap their toolboxes in the middle of it and slip and slide for the rest of their stay!'

Naturally our Guv'nor's opinion sometimes leaked out in the company of our crew and later (after Colin had gone!) they would quietly remind anyone listening that it was their cars way up at the front of the grid, and perhaps if the Americans threw their carpets away, a lot more of them might be challenging our lap times. It was a thorn in Colin's side (and an equally sharp one for our lads) that never went away; only moments after arriving at the Speedway the following year, Colin whistled me around the top garages for a look-see with the order that I must do something about our own. On frequent occasions, when we might be dashing off somewhere together, he would suddenly slam to a halt, grab my elbow and point out another garage that impressed him, everyone inside it priding themselves that the English 'foreigner' was admiring their racing car!

To spend the month of May at Indianapolis as a mechanic is a very long time indeed. In 1963, with 22 full days of tuning, plus two days for qualifying (if you encountered problems en route it could add up to four days!), the total time available for practice was 174 hours. Or, put another way, just one month at the Speedway was equal to over 27 Grands Prix, or 2.75 years of Formula 1 practice! These figures might at first sight seem to exaggerate the case, but they are perfectly factual and formed part of a paper I circulated to Formula 1 teams and the sport's governing body of that period by way of clarifying the extreme conditions of competing at the Speedway.

While preparation of the No 1 and spare car was in the hands of Jim Endruweit, David Lazenby and Colin Riley, Dan's was maintained by his own crew led by Bill Fowler.

The track opened for running at 9 am each morning, seven days a week, and closed at 6 pm. Allowing for the high temperatures encountered (that year saw several days at 94°F with over 80 per cent humidity), our schedule was to run in the cooler hours of the morning, then returning to the garage for a job list of work detailed by Colin, which had to be completed by the time the temperatures cooled in the afternoon and running resumed. Then it would be a hurried return to the garage to complete another ACBC job list before running re-opened next day. A working day for the 'lads' would be a 6.30–7 am breakfast, with a 7.30 am arrival at the garage. Colin would arrive around 8 to 8.30 am, having given another job list connected with Cheshunt factory business to someone back in the UK. After working until the track closed at 6 pm, the evening work usually carried on until midnight or the early hours of the morning.

Colin and Jimmy would stay in the garage until 7.30–8 pm before leaving for dinner, and would return around 10.30–11 pm to see how work was progressing. Invariably Jimmy would return with Colin, and if given a nudge and a wink by the Chief Mechanic, indicating that the lads could get on quicker without the Guv'nor around, he would remark that it was time they were both in bed, and Colin would almost immediately disappear with his No 1. On most occasions Colin would have another bundle of telexes and mail awaiting him in his motel cubby hole, to which he would attend before turning in.

From opening day on 1 May the Speedway's promotional department issued endless reams of material guaranteed to entertain the European visitors. One newspaper listed race drivers' former professions; bus-driver, undertaker's assistant, sportswriter, motorcycle policeman, taxi driver, Hollywood stuntman. A previous winner of the race was reported to be driving taxis in Chicago …

Colin and Jimmy arrived at the track fresh from another 'Man of the Race' performance by the Scot. In the Formula 1 Aintree '200' Clark's pole-position car had refused to start. A battery change saw him set off 1½ laps down. With problems persisting, Chapman had called him in to switch cars with his team-mate, Trevor Taylor, then 1 minute behind the leader. Jimmy smashed the lap record to take third place just 24 seconds in arrears.

At Indy the tyre decision went to Firestone, still slower than Dunlop but of a harder compound, so more durable, thus minimising pit-stops. There is also a family link between Ford and Firestone, as would be made clear to us a year later. Firestone made special 15-inch tyres for us that were smaller in diameter but 1.25 inches wider than the roadster size. When Dan began lapping at over 149 mph as early as 6 May, with Jimmy only fractionally slower, all hell broke loose from other teams, convinced that these tyres were playing a substantial role in the performance. Their ultimatum to Firestone was that the company must make the revised profile available to all or withdraw Lotus's supply of 'specials'.

Month of May at Indy '63 with Jimmy in his Firestone-shod, now offset-suspension race car – '29/3' – tended by Colin Chapman (left, white shirt), and mechanics Colin Riley and David Lazenby (at tail). The car is now in virtually its full warpaint with BRG panels striped and coach-lined in yellow, but final decals are yet to be applied. (Indianapolis Motor Speedway)

Although Firestone was not happy at the thought of the new moulding being used on the heavier roadsters, they were forced to relent and more tyres were made. This must have proved an enormous undertaking, considering that Firestone had provided over 3,700 tyres the previous year and had no doubt set themselves the task of providing even more of the larger tyres for the current event. However, this was not the end of the matter, for everyone now realised that there were few wheels available to suit the smaller tyres, and wheel manufacturer Ted Halibrand set to work, openly admitting that there just was not enough time left to qualifying to produce the stock required; however, he resorted to working around the clock to do the best he could. A significant spin-off from the affair was that A. J. Foyt, in his frustration, had telephoned Goodyear with a heartfelt plea for them to enter the fray and bring along their 15-inch stock car racing tyres. This was to lead to the giant tyre company's participation in international racing from that day forward.

Dan's entrant of the previous year, Mickey Thompson, brought no fewer than five radically new Chevrolet V8-engined cars, nicknamed 'pancakes' for their diminutive height and flattened shape. They had minute 12-inch tyres, but no one complained about them as the cars were slow. Graham Hill practised in one, but its handling was unpredictable and after two lurid incidents, one of which included hitting the wall, he realised that it was most unlikely he could qualify early and compete in the Monaco GP (which he was to win), so he returned home.

Changing times, changing styles – the Indianapolis Motor Speedway's photographic library has compiled a matchless record of its great race's history, its cameramen seldom missing a chance to record the new and unusual. Here in 1963 the diverse approaches to race car design of (left to right) Mickey Thompson, A. J. Watson and Colin Chapman are graphically compared; Dan Gurney is in the Type 29. (Indianapolis Motor Speedway)

Another loud grumble concerned the British Racing Green colour of both Jimmy's and the spare car. Green had been a superstitiously unlucky omen at the Brickyard for years; 'Our drivers don't feel good passing a green car,' someone had said to Colin, to which he replied, 'I'm hoping they won't do so ...'

Saturday 4 May dealt another body blow to the American fraternity. Frank Harrison, from Chattanooga, Tennessee, had entered a vintage Formula 1 Lotus Type 18 with a 2.7 Coventry Climax engine installed against the establishment Offys in the Trenton 100-Mile USAC race with veteran Texan driver Lloyd Ruby at the wheel. Despite giving away 1½ litres, Ruby had set a one lap record of 106 mph for the mile oval in practice, his speed through the turns more than making up for the roadsters' superior speeds on the straights. He had led the race from the start, but succumbed to transmission failure on lap 40.

Back at Indy, our special Dunlop magnesium knock-off wheels were soon giving trouble; cracks were discovered radiating from the holes in the wheels, and each time the cars came into the pits the cracks were carefully measured to check growth. Soon Chapman had designed a strengthening plate, which fitted behind the wheels to provide more resilience. As the rears gave most cause for alarm, Colin chose to try Halibrands there instead, which would also provide 9-inch rims, an inch wider than the Dunlops, but none were available; even if they had been there was still the problem of fitting them to the Lotus hubs.

Only a few days of running were now available for Jimmy before he and Colin had to return home for the International Trophy race at Silverstone. The furore they left behind at the Speedway again alarmed Ford as their 'partners' took off. Before a 100,000 crowd at Silverstone Jimmy completely dominated, leading 49 of the 52 laps to win. Immediately the race was over he and Colin were back over the Atlantic heading for the next weekend's all-important Indy qualifying.

Bird's-eye view of Dan's Lotus 29 almost ready to go at the track entrance in May 1963. The Lotus-Ford's slender profile and gasoline-burning push-rod Ford V8 engine on carburettors mounted astern of the driver was preaching revolution to the most conservative establishment in international motor racing. (Indianapolis Motor Speedway)

Differential tyre wear is clearly evident on the front Firestones of the ill-fated '29/2' during pre-race preparation, with cheerful Dan strapped firmly into its cockpit by the mandatory safety harness that would not appear even in Formula 1 road racing until 1967–68. (Indianapolis Motor Speedway)

On the Thursday before qualifying driver Curtis Turner demolished his Smokey Yunick-entered car. That team had two Halibrand rear wheels left in its garage, which were quickly acquired and modified for the Lotus hubs. But with only these two, it was decided that Jimmy and Dan would share them. Meanwhile Parnelli Jones was shattering the Ford computers' calculations. Running his Watson roadster on 15-inch tyres designed originally for our cars, he was nearly 1½ mph quicker than his previous all-time best, at over 152 mph; three days later he passed the 153 mph mark.

With qualifying fast approaching, Ford made it known that they wanted to run methanol with fuel injection to ensure higher speeds, switching back to gasoline and carburettors for the race. This plan was nullified when it was discovered that our bag tank material would not tolerate the 'hotter' fuel.

The modified Halibrands were ready for trials the day before qualifying, which rain then washed out. The major event of the day was the highly publicised 'draw' for which entrants of the cars still striving to get on to the 33-car grid queued to take out of a hat a plastic phial containing their running order number.

Fresh Autolite spark plugs for Gurney. On the original print of this shot the chassis serial '29/2' is legible on the tiny chassis plate riveted on to that rear bulkhead flange to the right of the harness straps. Dan has had his steering wheel rim thickened with taped-on padding to enhance grip. The seat features that prominent right-side torso support to resist lateral loads on the left-turn-only Speedway. Dan needed it as '/2' was about to meet the Turn One wall, right side on, at speed . . . (Indianapolis Motor Speedway)

● 1963: THE ROAD TO INDY

Dan's '29/2', badly damaged by his qualifying crash, is dragged back across the infield towards 'Gasoline Alley' and soon to the Cheshunt works in England for repair to its badly crushed stressed-skin 'tub'. Of more immediate significance than Team's loss of the car was that of the smashed wide-rim Halibrand wheels which had only just replaced Dunlop's finest, as explained in the text. (Indianapolis Motor Speedway)

Team Lotus drew 7 for Clark and 11 for Gurney.

Around 220,000 spectators watched the first day's time trials, unprecedented traffic jams clogging the surrounding neighbourhood. In the 2-hour warm-up (there were 66 cars trying for the

33-car grid) Jimmy tried the new Halibrands. Scrubbing in new tyres, he was up to speed by lap 5 and immediately bettered his and Dan's previous times by more than 1 mph, lapping the 2.5-mile oval in just 58.3 seconds – 153 mph. Back in the pits the precious rear wheels were fitted to Dan's car, but the suspension geometry preferred by its driver remained unaltered. Whether this was a contributory factor to what followed makes no difference. Working up to the speeds set by Jimmy, Dan had his 29 get away from him in Turn One and he slammed into the wall. He was unhurt, but the car would not run again that month, and its all-important rear wheels were written off ...

'On that Saturday morning of qualifying,' Dan remembers, 'Colin told me that due to the wheel shortage they'd let me run Jimmy's wheels and tyres on my car. That phrase "the month of May" sounds like an awful long time, but in fact it all revolves around a small number of very specific slots that you have to meet, and approaching each of these critical moments you are always running short of time ...

'Wound up tighter 'n a nine-day clock' – a tense Dan Gurney ready to make his second qualifying attempt in 'The Mule', Team's original green-liveried prototype car '29/1'. With Dan are (left to right) his own veteran mechanic Bill Fowler, young Lamar Lippencott and a concerned Colin Chapman – dapper in shirt and tie on this very public day with a huge crowd present. Standing extreme right is drag-racer and Ford performance specialist Art Chrisman. (Indianapolis Motor Speedway)

'I had four laps to run to prepare for qualifying and of course I was wound up tighter 'n a nine-day clock. I wanted pole position, and I knew with our equipment it was within reach. I went out and did two exploratory laps without any way of knowing really how fast I was going. I was on Jimmy's tyres, which had been scrubbed in on Jimmy's car – ha, as much as you could scrub in those Firestone track tyres in those days. Story was they were so hard that if you got broadside they'd spark. But Jimmy preferred slightly different camber setting from mine, and now these tyres, which had bedded into his settings, were being presented to the pavement differently by mine. This meant that with me trying to run harder and with the tyres resisting less load on my car, I suddenly found myself going through Turn One backwards.

'I clearly remember that wall was a long time arriving – so long that I genuinely had time to think, "If I was Rob Slotemaker [who ran the famous Schlip School of Car Control at Zandvoort, home of the Dutch Grand Prix] I would know what to do right now. But I'm not – and I don't." And BANG, we got into the wall quite hard, right-rear first, then right-front.'

The 8-inch-rim, strengthened Dunlop rears were then re-fitted to Jimmy's car, the mechanics now hard at work not only preparing the Scotsman's car, but also salvaging retrievable components from Dan's ('29/2') and preparing 'The Mule' ('29/1') for his qualifying run later that day.

A troublesome wind had been blowing from early morning, and by the time the nail-biting runs began it was gusting to 35 mph and virtually all the times were slower. The whole atmosphere of an Indy Speedway filled to capacity, the constant shrieks from the crowd, interrupted only by the never-ending commentary booming in one's ears is an experience hard to forget. The commentator reeled off the lap time and speed immediately each car crossed the finish line, usually followed by applause, cheers, whoops and screams from the immense crowd. By midday three drivers, McElreath, Marshman, and Branson, had qualified, the last-named fastest at 150.188 mph. Then came Parnelli Jones in J. C. Agajanian's Offy-powered roadster, nicknamed *Ol' Calhoun*. Wind or no wind, Parnelli's adrenalin was flowing fast – his four-lap average was 151.153, his best single lap 151.847. It was to be his

The official IMS standard photo of Jimmy Clark's Lotus-powered-by-Ford posed before qualifying in the Indy pit lane, backed by Colin, Jim Endruweit, 'Laz' and Colin Riley. The car is rigged with Dunlop wheels carrying Firestone tyres front and rear, but will tackle qualifying on Halibrands. It has an aluminium blanking plate where the spring-loaded fuel-filler should be, no mirrors and racer-tape blanking the scuttle-top filler. Jimmy is also wearing a new white-peaked silver helmet just supplied by Bell, not his normal Scots-blue hat. (Indianapolis Motor Speedway)

second successive pole. As for Agajanian, as a young man he initially harboured aspirations of being a race driver himself, but his father, who had made a fortune from garbage collection ('second-hand food dealer' as Aggie described it) told him, 'You can own 'em but don't drive 'em', and Aggie followed his advice. Since those days he had entered cars in 22 consecutive Indy 500s from 1948, or nearly half the total run, only missing the race three times when his cars failed to qualify. His first entry had carried the number 98, and he had kept it thereafter. Involved in various aspects of the sport for over 30 years, he had been a car owner, race promoter, run charters from Los Angeles to the race and brought the '500' to cable TV in Los Angeles. By 1969 he was on the board of the multi-million-dollar Ontario Motor Speedway, then being constructed in California.

Seventh to run was Jimmy, on the narrower rims and on new un-scrubbed tyres with only three laps allowed to get up to speed. He gave a superb four-lap performance, averaging 149.750 mph.

Now Team's attention was focused on getting Dan's car to the line-up, and while running was suspended drivers waited for the wind to abate. After a superb effort by both the Ford and Lotus crews 'The Mule's' engine was started and Dan made ready with only 3 minutes to go. His first timed lap was over 149 mph, his second and third the same. It looked as if the tension was finally over, then on the last lap Dan made for the pit lane. A driver could make three attempts all told, providing he aborted each try before the four laps were up. As he rolled to a stop the gun signalling the end of the day's session went off, with only seven cars having qualified. Dan would now have to succeed the following day or forego the following weekend's Monaco GP. That night saw work continuing on 'The Mule', bringing it to full race standard; Dan's shunted car was too badly damaged to rebuild before qualifying (a driver had to drive the same car in both qualifying and the race), and was to be returned to Cheshunt for repair after the '500'.

'The accident had been my own fault,' concedes Gurney. 'It couldn't have come at a poorer time. They rolled out the back-up car and I remember getting out in it that Saturday evening only just before the gun went off to signal the end of running for the day. I ran three laps, then as I went to hit the brakes I got my foot caught up in the darned throttle toe-strap. It was required by the regulations so the driver could pull the throttle shut should it stick open, but I had it taken off my own car to prevent this very thing happening. I guess that wasn't strictly legal, but I wasn't aware of any scrutineers riding with me. Anyway, the strap was still in place on that old car and it wrecked my final qualifying attempt that evening. So I just had to stew overnight . . . It had all been entirely my own fault. And I was really disturbed about it.'

However, Sunday saw order restored. With the strong wind continuing, Dan completed his four-lap qualifying run at an average of 149.019 mph, but as it was the second day of the trials he went back on to the 'grid behind the grid'. Of the 18 cars so far qualified, Jimmy was in fifth place (second row), and Dan 12th (fourth row). When qualifying ended, the 33 fastest cars had averaged 148.895 mph, more than 1½ mph up on the previous year.

As soon as Dan had finished his run, he, Jimmy and Colin left for Monaco. They might as well have stayed at the Speedway. From pole, which he had taken 0.7 seconds faster than Graham Hill, Jimmy was outgunned by the two BRMs of Hill and Richie Ginther and was not to lead until lap 18 after a frantic duel. Jimmy told *Life* magazine, 'For the first ten laps I had seven cylinders. I dropped back 20 seconds on the leaders, then after ten laps everything fired up, but two laps later the clutch went. From then on I had no clutch – finally the poor old 'box seized and I was out.'

Dan was out early, his Brabham's crown-wheel-and-pinion failing on lap 24. His boss, Jack Brabham, had given Dan his team's only engine for the race. But Colin had come to Jack's aid, loaning him Team's spare Type 25 to drive! Such a gesture seems light years in the past; sadly, Jack also encountered gearbox problems, but soldiered on to be classified ninth and last.

There was no further all-day running scheduled before the '500', so our trio were able to leave Nice airport the day after Monaco for a more relaxed return to Indy. Joining them on their BEA Comet to London was RAC senior timekeeper Cyril Audrey, who had accepted Colin's invitation to 'give a hand with the watches' at Indy. Colin, busy designing changes to the Type 25's transmission, called into Cheshunt to leave the inevitable job list, then followed the rest of the party to Chicago and thence to Indy. Also on his way to the Speedway, as a reward for all his hard work, was designer Len Terry, laden with a large number of spares and components.

With Colin, Jimmy and Dan having been in Europe for the week leading up to the second weekend of qualifying, only a very short period of running time remained before the big event took place on the Thursday after Monaco. This period was confined to a single 'Carburation Day', when crews could make last minute checks on fuel and tyre consumption.

'I have a reasonable ear for an engine,' says Dan, 'and on Carburation Day I found my engine running rough and woolly. It sounded fine when we ran it up stationary, but under load out on the Speedway I was convinced that it was fluttering on to seven cylinders. When I came in and reported the problem, Bill Gay of Ford just didn't believe me. He told the crew "Fire it up", so they did and he took hold of the throttle linkage and slammed it wide open, revving the heads off the engine and floating all the valves.' Dan winces at the memory. 'Then he shut it down, they switched off and he declared, "It's OK, *nothing* to worry about . . .".'

The rear wheel saga was now resolved; more than sufficient Halibrands for the race, including tyre changes, were available for both cars; Ford's plant near the Speedway machined the wheels to suit. But there was another problem to resolve. The overwhelming work schedules foisted on the mechanics refurbishing 'The Mule' and race preparation of both cars had precluded both pit-stop practice and familiarity with related equipment.

Lotus design 'advantages' had not been so obvious in qualifying speeds through Turn One, showing the roadsters of Parnelli Jones quickest (143 mph) and Bobby Marshman second (142 mph), with Jimmy and Dan third and fourth quickest (141 and 139 mph respectively), and Rodger Ward fifth (138 mph). Admittedly our two cars had run on the narrowed and slower rear tyres, but those leading roadsters had proved ominously fast.

According to Ford records, Bill Gay initiated the move to get a more experienced crew to handle the stops, and Bill Stroppe's stock car crew was immediately flown up from Atlanta; according to Levine they only had the night before the race to familiarise themselves with the car, but there are photographs of this taking place in daylight with Len Terry and Cyril Audrey. Jim Endruweit was also part of this crew, and he would cater for Jimmy's needs at the planned single stop and any others that might occur.

In those days timekeeping by the teams was an individual hand-held-watch affair; with 33 cars flashing past the pits every 50–60 seconds Colin obviously required reliable assistance, and Cyril Audrey was an excellent man for the job. Extremely skilled and possessing a highly retentive memory coupled with a good sense of humour, he was an invaluable part of the set-up. Even so, the best that Colin and Cyril, aided by a 'watcher', could ever manage was keeping times and maintaining a lap chart for barely half the field, and this was to cause problems. Indy's well-known electrically operated scoreboard pylon, or 'totem pole', displaying the official positions of all 33 cars, was in full view of everyone, but Colin – unable to vouch for its accuracy – was not about to rely on it.

Almost 250,000 spectators flooded into the Speedway when an exploding 'maroon' on the infield announced the opening of the gates at 5 am on race day. Many had been waiting for several days, one having taken on almost cult status, parking his motor home at the main entrance on West 16th Street on the first of May and remaining there until the gates opened.

The opening ceremonies followed military precision; race cars had to be positioned on the track apron before their respective 'out' by 8.30 am. At 9.30 came the 'Spectacle of Bands', with musicians representing every American state. At 10 am the cars were moved to their starting positions to the strains of a local band playing 'On the Banks of the Wabash', and this was followed by featured events and the presentation of numerous national and international celebrities from astronaut Gordon Cooper and Stirling Moss to film, TV and radio stars. A 10-minute track inspection followed, then the local band played the 'Star-Spangled Banner' before a military band played 'Taps'.

By then only 10 minutes remained before the 11 am start, this being signalled by a sentimental rendition of 'Back Home Again in Indiana' and the release of an enormous cluster of balloons. At 3 minutes to go came Tony Hulman's instruction over the public address, 'Gentlemen, start your engines', and as the last engine burst into life the gaudily decorated pace car, destined to be one of the race-winner's prizes, moved off at the head of the grid. Its speed would then increase to 90 mph, and if all was in ship-shape order within the 33-car field, the rolling start would be released by the pace car diving into the pit lane and the start steward flailing his green flags.

Team Lotus's top brass for the Indianapolis programme discussing prospects in Gasoline Alley – left to right, Colin Chapman, Len Terry (who will on race day be sorely dismayed by a cruel decision of the Old Man) and team mechanic David Lazenby. This shot was taken by Swiss-born French journalist Gerard 'Jabby' Crombac, long-time Lotus supporter, friend of 'Chunky' and eventually flat-mate to Jim Clark. (G. Crombac)

The whole proceeding is guaranteed to set everyone's adrenalin building to a nervous tension that is unforgettable, particularly if you are one of the working participants! The weather that day was perfect, bright sunshine coupled with a light breeze keeping the temperature just above 70 degrees. Only one car proved momentarily troublesome in starting, then the 11 rows of three cars each accelerated away behind the pace car driven by 12-race veteran and past winner, Sam Hanks. As the field neared the start of its third pace lap, the pace car tore into the pit lane – and the race was on!

The brave Jim Hurtubise, second fastest in qualifying in the monstrous, screaming, supercharged 734 hp Novi of Andy Granatelli's STP team (STP's blurb said that it had been detuned for reliability), led over the line at the end of the first lap, but another Novi made straight for the pits with a clutch problem before continuing until its retirement on lap 18. The legendary 16-cylinder Novi, so popular with the spectators over two decades, was living up to its record of unreliability. Lap 2, and the race order was Parnelli Jones, Hurtubise and Bobby Marshman. Before lap 3 could begin the yellow lights were on; another Novi, driven by Bobby Unser, had hit the wall. It took eight laps to clear the track, and when the green light flashed on, the leader, Jones, increased speed dramatically, lapping at over 150 mph.

By lap 20 Jones was 14 seconds ahead of the two Lotuses, Dan ninth, Jimmy tenth and holding station. At the 100-mile mark, Dan slowed letting Jimmy past. Parnelli raised the average to 151 mph in an endeavour to build himself a cushion for the extra pit stops he knew he would need over the single stops planned for the Anglo-American Lotuses, but they matched his increased pace. More yellows, and on lap 62 Jones made his first stop for fuel and tyres. More roadsters followed him in, until on lap 67, Jimmy took the lead. Setting new records, the Scot now had Dan right behind him. Lotus-Fords ran 1–2!

On lap 92 Dan made his first stop. His aim for the platform jack was poor; the compressed air system eventually lifted his car but he had lost time. Three tyres (the left front was deemed safe to leave) were changed, fuel taken on, then Dan roared back into the race. His stop lasted a fraction over 42 seconds. Three laps later and Jimmy was in. Again three tyres were changed and fuel added. The Scotsman had stopped with his front wheels on the back wheel marker and his crew had to push his car on to the jack platform. His stop lasted 32 seconds.

Jimmy was now third, 40 seconds behind leader Jones, the howling Hurtubise Novi holding second place. Lap 102 and this last of the three Novis was out, black-flagged for losing oil. Jimmy lay second, Dan eighth. Clark was now encountering back-markers travelling visibly slower, and he was finding it difficult to pass them. The gap to Jones grew to 47 seconds. Another accident brought the yellows on again and Jones dived in for his second stop, rejoining without losing his lead. The green flashed on momentarily, quickly followed by the yellows again as another car smacked the wall. At 130 laps (325 miles) Jones was lapping at 149–150 mph with Jimmy maintaining station and Dan now fifth.

As the laps went by, the gap remained constant. Jones's third and last pit stop was imminent; then at 160 laps there was another accident. On came the yellows as Parnelli dived for his pit. A race official pointed to oil dripping in some quantity from the rear of his car. He was moving again just 21 seconds later, and two laps after that Jimmy was shown a pit-board reading 'PARN-11'. Dan was now third, and the Scot started to haul Jones in. By lap 177 the gap was down to 5 seconds. Lap 178 and Eddie Sachs spun, but continued.

Then Parnelli's car began to trail smoke as he backed off for the turns. Yet the gap between *Ol' Calhoun* and Jimmy increased. From 5 seconds it went to 7, then 9, then 10 as the oil leakage

Mid-race Lotus pit stops in the '63 '500'. The first shot shows Jimmy's car perched on the Len Terry-designed jacking platform. 'Big Jim' Gardner enthusiastically signals that a fresh right-rear wheel is secure on Jimmy's 29 as Jim Endruweit passes clean goggles to the Scot and opens the scuttle cap so the filling tanks can vent their air during refuelling. Brandishing the filler hose (right) is transmission designer Pete Weismann. Jimmy later described 'Big Jim' as a master of wheel-changing technique. Dan's second stop sees him signalling frantically for the right-rear to be re-tightened, Jim Endruweit executing the pas de deux (left). (Both Indianapolis Motor Speedway)

52

TEAM LOTUS: THE INDIANAPOLIS YEARS •

continued. Gurney's car, running a different set-up from Jimmy's, needed fresh tyres. His stop was a quick one, but two laps later he was back in – the right-front wheel nut had not been tightened sufficiently. This time it was jammed and the stop was a long one.

Parnelli's chief mechanic, Johnny Poulsen, went to the start line to talk to Chief Steward Harlan Fengler. Their conversation was animated. Meanwhile Jimmy did his best to keep his car on a track now awash with oil, waiting for the leading car to be black-flagged. Fengler had made it quite clear at the driver briefing that any oil seen discharged from a car would bring instant disqualification. But nothing happened. The car's owner, millionaire pig farmer, race-track-owner and USAC Director J. C. Agajanian conferred with Fengler. Now Chapman, his adrenalin running high, joined in. Fengler called for binoculars. He asked Colin to move away, as it was not his car they were discussing.

All this time Jimmy had been encountering more difficulty passing two slower cars. He had survived one heart-stopping slide towards the wall and was taking extra care at this late stage in the race, especially when Sachs lost a wheel and hit the wall in front of him. Still Parnelli continued; two officials reported it was water they could see leaking. Aggie claimed that nothing was being dropped. An official held the black flag, but no one used it.

The yellows came on again. Jimmy passed the two slower cars ahead of him, a manoeuvre he thought might bring disqualification. But he'd misinterpreted the rules. Nothing happened. When the green flashed on, Jimmy was a further 6 seconds down, the gap now 22 seconds. With three laps to go, Jimmy had to settle for second place, Dan for seventh.

For the record, the result was as follows (all seven completed 200 laps):

1st	Parnelli Jones	Agajanian Special	142.137 mph (record), 3 hrs 29 mins 35 secs
2nd	Jim Clark	Lotus-Ford	142.752 mph
3rd	A. J. Foyt	Sheraton-Thompson	142.210 mph
4th	Rodger Ward	Kaiser Aluminium	141.090 mph
5th	Don Branson	Leader Card	140.866 mph
6th	Jim McElreath	Bill Forbes Special	140.862 mph
7th	Dan Gurney	Lotus-Ford	140.071 mph

Jimmy kept his immense disappointment to himself; when asked

J. C. Agajanian is clearly delighted with Parnelli Jones's win in the '63 '500'. The crew-cuts had prevailed. (Indianapolis Motor Speedway)

what he thought of Parnelli's win, he replied, 'He did a damn fine job.' That was typically Jimmy.

Ford also expressed a mature resignation in keeping with the sporting interest. Benson Ford told Harlan Fengler, 'We're delighted with the outcome of the race, and I think you made the finest decision possible.'

Other drivers were nothing like as conciliatory. Eddie Sachs was convinced that his first slide and his final accident when running in the front group of cars had been initiated by Jones's oil loss. Before members of the press and public the next day, Sachs and Jones got into an argument over the affair, which terminated when Jones thumped his accuser. McCluskey, running third, had hit the wall on his last lap and also blamed Jones: 'I braked at the same time he did, but slid 100 feet past him ...'

Dan Gurney on his race: 'I was hustling the car pretty hard from the start, just trying to make it perform. Jimmy appreciated that 500 miles was a long way to go. He was holding back behind me while I confirmed to myself that my engine was pulling on no more than seven and a half cylinders, and I realised then that this just wasn't going to be my day ...After a few laps I waved him by and he came past on the straight like I was in reverse. After the race, when they unzipped my engine, they told me that one of the lobes had been worn off the camshaft.

'That was a disappointment ... but a 1990s audience ought to put that in context. In those days we went through so much mechanical disaster and disappointment it was virtually routine. Experience simply trained us all to be philosophical. In effect, most times you went out in a race car you knew it was likely you'd be walking back. To have sufficient reliability to finish could be a bonus.

'But the thought that the engine could have been changed if they'd believed me on Carburation Day is still ... disappointing.'

An event unseen by anyone, but deeply upsetting to Len Terry, had occurred towards the end of the race when Jimmy appeared to have a chance of winning. Colin had matter-of-factly told our Chief Designer that he was wanted back at the factory quickly. There were problems with the Type 25s and Lotus-Cortinas needing immediate attention. 'Here's your air ticket – the plane leaves shortly. There's a helicopter waiting for you over there.'

'I was flabbergasted,' Len said. 'After all those months of hard work I was dumbstruck.'

Dan Gurney looks back on that first Lotus year at Indy with very great affection. 'I think inevitably that Colin and the Lotus crew would really have preferred for Jimmy to win, and all I required was that I should be treated equally and given equal equipment, and as far as possible I'm happy that was so. In fact, you could almost say that if in any way I received *less* than equal treatment, it was by the American interests involved in the programme, not the British ...

'And you should also appreciate that Jimmy and I were on remarkably good terms for team-mates ... By the nature of racing, team-mates generally hate each other. They have to. It's an almost inevitable part of the job because each is trying to out-perform the other – to prove himself top dog. It's part of the inevitable psychology of the situation.

'But in Formula 1 at that time, Jimmy and I were racing against each other almost every other weekend – he for Lotus, me for Brabham. We had a clear idea of each other's capability. We shared an awful lot of mutual respect; I thought an awful lot of him as a driver and as a man, and I think he reckoned I was OK too. So when we came together on the Indy programme we worked together just fine.

'We both just enjoyed racing cars and everything about them. We both enjoyed trying out different kinds of cars – Jimmy tried driving an American stock car out of curiosity, and of course I drove them too. We both drove Lotus-Cortinas, which were a lot of fun, and we ran Indy cars on the road circuit at Riverside too ... We both got a real kick out of bringing together our two worlds of racing at Indy – the European-style road-racing design and USAC oval-track racing.

'Going into Indy racing with something so entirely new was one hell of a challenge – there was no place for in-fighting, neither of us was political, and above all it was fun tweaking the Establishment's tail ... Obviously we both came in for some comments from the traditionalists about how favoured we were, being allowed to run these kiddy cars in amongst the big roadsters. But the interesting feature there was that when more established US drivers began to run rear-engined cars they quickly discovered that these things were not viceless either – they really were *not* on the sweet spot all the time ... When they appreciated that we had to work at it too, we were regarded perhaps with a little more respect.

'To some degree, if you're a pro and times have been good, you've been drawing a good share of the prize money, and then some outsider comes along with a different angle and takes that from you – then he's going to be your enemy, because he's making times bad for you. A great many established Indy guys didn't want to see change, but truth is that most of those Indy guys who screamed loudest weren't current racers at all – the majority were retired veterans or some of the Indy-series journalists and writers. They saw that form of racing more as a tradition and way of life than as a living, developing branch of current auto racing, so really they made more fuss than the active drivers.

'The Indy establishment was also very insulated from the real world outside. The first time we drove up to the Speedway, we arrived at the entrance on the corner of 16th Street and Georgetown and there was a sign reading 'Indianapolis Motor Speedway – World Capitol of Auto Racing'. Colin instantly took exception and began grumbling!'

CHAPTER THREE

1963: Milwaukee, Trenton and the Quad-Cam Indy Ford

Jimmy's second place won world-wide acclaim and a flood of cables, telexes and correspondence. The oil controversy brought sympathy and understanding, particularly from Americans; nine times the yellows had slowed the race (totalling 50 minutes) and Parnelli's greater experience of how to turn these periods to advantage had settled the result. Experts judged that Jimmy's overall time loss from yellows had amounted to 59 seconds and he had trailed Jones home by just under 34 . . . Jimmy felt that if all things had been equal he would have lapped Parnelli; whatever, the man more experienced at the Brickyard had won. And Jones had not been short on skill. For others to blame him for their accidents on oil missed the point that he had driven over it safely . . .

The race had been run on a Thursday. By the Saturday Jimmy had already spent nearly two days in Canada, where he was to drive a sports Lotus Type 23 in the 'Players 200' at Mosport. This example of 'from the sublime to the ridiculous' was emphasised by the 23's sponsor, 'Honest Ed' of Toronto bargain basement fame. Parnelli Jones had also been due to run a Lotus 23, but withdrew after his Indy win. It would have been an interesting contest. Jimmy finished 8th overall against the larger-engined cars, one of which, Dan Gurney's Cooper Monaco, took third.

Immediately the race was over Jimmy was back in the air again en route to the Whit Monday Crystal Palace BARC meeting two days later, again in a Type 23, this one entered by the British Normand team. He won, his team-mate Mike Beckwith second. This was the Scot's fourth race on two continents in nine days!

Len Terry's memories of Indy were to remain sour. On his return to Cheshunt he had found the situation normal, with no job list of work needing immediate attention. Meanwhile, reports from America indicated that the Ford engineers directly involved in the project were utterly dejected by the 'failure' while their hierarchy viewed the result as the best they could reasonably have expected. The 'establishment' had been given a serious lesson, and the public's response to such a moral victory had probably been greater than if Lotus-Ford had actually won. Bill Gay, in his presentation to the Society of Automotive Engineers (US), detailed the achievement in some detail:

'While the race itself is history, the production push-rod engine turned in a distinguished performance. Jimmy Clark drove his car to a number of very interesting statistics:

- Bettered all previous times for Indy 500 winners.
- Fastest time ever recorded for a V8 or any other eight-cylinder engine.
- Best time ever recorded by a rear-engined car.
- Established race records on the 70th, 80th and 90th laps.
- Fastest average speed ever turned in by a first-time entry in Indianapolis 500 history.
- Required only one pit stop in 500 miles versus an average of three or four for the "Offies".
- The Ford-powered Lotuses were the only entries running on gasoline.'

He summed up the Lotus Type 29: 'The basic Lotus design had given a good account of itself at Indianapolis. It had proved itself well adapted to racing requirements there . . .'

A further glimpse into the future came on the Milwaukee 1-mile oval in the 100-mile race held on Belgian Grand Prix weekend, just ten days after Indy. Frank Harrison dusted down his old Lotus 18 again for Lloyd Ruby, the Texan qualifying seventh fastest. This time there were no problems with the car and Lloyd finished 12th.

After the '500' Ford's V8 engines were removed from our cars and returned to Dearborn for detailed analysis. The two race car chassis – Jimmy's '/3' and Dan's 'Mule' – remained in our Speedway garage, while the wrecked '/2' returned to Cheshunt to be rebuilt.

Team Lotus's share of income from the race, including Ford's initial development grant, qualifying bonuses and Speedway race prize money totalled $100,000 (then nearly £42,000). From that had to be deducted the cost of building the three cars, all the testing and development expenditure, air travel and freighting costs, living expenses throughout the month of May, plus the salaries of the Lotus staff involved. Indy was not quite the cornucopia of money the media claimed.

Although some pundits have since intimated that our running on two American ovals later in the year came as a result of Jimmy pressurising Colin, this is doubtful. Team Lotus had an Indy section to support until the next trip to the Brickyard. In the course of post-race debriefing, both the Ford personnel and Colin agreed to enter cars for the Milwaukee '200' (18 August) and the Trenton '200' (22 September), with a test scheduled at Milwaukee some time in July. Gurney was agreed as one of the drivers, with a question mark against Jimmy, as he was at that time due to drive for us in the Formula 1 race at Enna in Sicily on 18 August. This problem was soon resolved for us, as our Italian lawyers advised against Jimmy appearing in Italy; both he and Team Lotus were still involved in protracted legal proceedings following the fatal collision with von Trips at Monza in 1961. However, when I cabled the race organisers with the news that Peter Arundell would replace Jimmy, all hell broke loose, and they began threatening legal action . . .

When Colin returned to Cheshunt he clarified the on-going American programme, for which I drew up budgets, dispatching them to Ford for approval. At the same time Colin himself prepared an overall proposal to Ford that, if accepted, would secure a working relationship between the two companies until 31 December 1965. The presentation centred around a financial formula whereby 'the scale of return [to Team Lotus] would be in direct proportion to the actual successes achieved'. If unsuccessful, Ford would 'not be involved in anything more than a bare margin over the direct expenses incurred'. Income derived from additional sponsorship would be used to reduce the net cost of the venture to Ford, race and prize monies going to Team Lotus and being split with the drivers in the usual fashion.

An item of particular interest in view of what was soon to occur concerned the future of the race cars after Team Lotus had finished using them. As he had previously emphasised to Ford when the subject was raised some time before the 1963 race, Colin again laid down that any race cars passing to Ford 'are to be used for exhibition purposes only, and will not be used by Ford for re-sale or reproduction or used in any other connection'. Ford was to bypass this request, exposing the Lotus name to severe criticism when cars run by other organisations suffered mechanical failures; in other words, when a car won it was a 'Ford', but when it broke it was (loudly) a 'Lotus' . . .

Although this proposition appeared to be a result of Colin's desire to establish a sound base for future race programmes in America, he had other reasons in mind. There was news on the motor racing grapevine that a more than casual relationship was growing between Ford and Eric Broadley's Lola Cars company. Eric had announced his Ford V8-engined Mark 6 GT car at that year's Racing Car Show in London. Its monocoque chassis and fibreglass bodywork incorporated a Ford V8 4.2-litre power unit producing 350 bhp, which had been supplied direct from Dearborn. Colin was also looking to produce a big-engined sports car, and his proposal to Ford would have tied up the two categories for Lotus without Lola interference . . .

In the early months of 1963 there had also been lengthy discussions between Ford and Enzo Ferrari concerning a possible buy-out of the Italian concern by Ford. However, towards the end of May, while Team Lotus was at Indy, the talks had foundered upon Enzo's sudden withdrawal.

On the rebound just a month later, Lee Iacocca decreed that Ford was to establish its own high-performance vehicle department, and a group of the company's executives set off for the Le Mans 24-Hour race to survey the international sports-racing car scene. After the race they made their way to England to visit the Cooper, Lotus and Lola establishments.

Ford was looking to produce its own sports car to beat Ferrari fair and square, and the Lola GT, with its 92-inch wheelbase and 42-inch-high roofline presented a neat package on which to base such a vehicle. Ford also closely studied the two men at the helms of Lola and Lotus. According to Leo Levine, Colin's natural ego and inability to take direction coupled with his already multiple commitments counted against him. Broadley, on the other hand, suited Ford's requirement perfectly; a quiet, retiring individual, uninterested in personal acclaim, his GT car already existed and Eric had made it known that he was keen to work with Ford and would not haggle over the change of vehicle name. As Levine wrote, 'The car would be a Ford-Ford, not a Lola-Ford.'

When the Ford executives visited Lotus, Levine maintains that Colin offered them the company, lock, stock and barrel, but this is hard to believe. Fred Bushell, Colin's right-hand man in such matters, told Jabby Crombac years later (*Colin Chapman: the Man and his Cars*) that Ford had enquired through a third party if Lotus might be for sale, and Colin had agreed to talk to them.

The upshot of the talks was that an agreement was signed between Ford and Lola, and Eric Broadley subsequently moved his company from Bromley to Slough, west of London. Although Eric's GT had not been an overwhelming success, Ford was willing to accept that this was basically due to lack of finance and backing. After extensive re-engineering the car would be relaunched the following May as the Ford GT40.

As this Ford/Lola relationship became known during 1963, it was obvious that however much Colin wanted an agreement with Ford, to him the Lola arrangement did not exist and he continued to draw up his plans for a big-engined sports car of his own, the Type 30. This was not to be a direct rival; it was not a Le Mans car, but rather an unlimited-capacity sports-racer.

In Dearborn, despite the push-rod engine having given a good account of itself at Indy, it was obvious that if and when the next stage in the programme was agreed, the double-overhead camshaft (quad-cam) engine would be the way to go. Ford knew that the Indy car gained its success not solely through the lightness or economy of its power unit, but also by a chassis concept entirely alien to the 'establishment'. Other teams would soon, if not already, have similar designs on their drawing boards. Of immediate concern was the impending test session, now scheduled for 12 July at Milwaukee, followed by the two races now only weeks away in which the proven push-rod V8s would reappear. When stripped after the '500', both race units had been found to be in exemplary order, and had even gained horsepower since their initial test-bed running when new.

Some of the USAC old guard were still trying to neutralise the foreigners' advantage, notably Andy Granatelli, newly elected President of the STP Corporation, who had campaigned the legendary Novis. Like Parnelli Jones's entrant, J. C. Agajanian, before the race, Granatelli was now looking to drum up support amongst fellow American entrants and team owners. His plan was to introduce a weight limitation that would bring the Lotuses up to roadster weight and thereby nullify their advantage. The press, as usual without a penny of their own money invested, decried the move, saying that it was about time the 'establishment' woke up to the advances brought in by the Europeans.

Granatelli, on the other hand, had spent enormous sums of money on research and development in preparing the Novis and he was not prepared to go down without a fight. However, his pleas went unheeded by the governing body, who instead issued a statement hoping that it would not be long before Indy-style race cars would soon be running on road courses.

In August, just a few weeks later, Andy arranged an Indy-style test for the Formula 1 Ferguson P99 four-wheel-drive car to evaluate its capabilities at Indy. Still powered by its original 2¹/₂-litre Coventry Climax engine and handicapped by the weight of instrumentation it carried, this front-engined car was driven by veteran British racing driver Jack Fairman, who put in an impressive performance. Later, American star Bobby Marshman tried it and, although unused to its handling characteristics, was soon lapping at 142 mph. The venture was reported worldwide through STP's highly efficient promotions department, and soon it was further announced that the 1964 Novis would be built at Ferguson's facility in Coventry, and would employ four-wheel drive.

Ford soon approved my budgets and the initial Milwaukee test day, scheduled principally to evaluate gear ratios and tyre compounds, was set for 12 July. Practice periods for oval races were quite short, with qualifying on the morning of the race, so it was vitally important to finalise the set-up of the cars beforehand. As these oval races were only 200-milers, the faster Dunlop tyres would be tried. Our two race cars, which had been garaged at Indy, were trucked up to Dearborn for preparation and engine installation.

The Milwaukee results were more than encouraging. Jimmy consistently broke the two-year-old lap record of 34.09 seconds with a best of 32.65, raising the average speed fully 4.7 mph from 105.62 mph to 110.3 mph. Dan was only fractionally slower. After the test the cars returned to Dearborn where the engines were quickly removed.

Our crew returned home, and it was planned that they would return to the US some ten days before the race in order to prepare the cars thoroughly at Dearborn, then truck them back to the Zecol-Lubaid garage just south of Milwaukee, where we had received a warm welcome and fine facilities during the test. Unlike the European equivalent, our cars were given a large spotlessly clean area, all of which was free of charge in exchange for the local publicity generated by our presence.

Jimmy and Trevor Taylor were in Sweden the weekend before Milwaukee, driving Formula 1 Type 25s in the *Kanonloppet*, or non-Championship Swedish Grand Prix. Jimmy won, leading Trevor home to a Team Lotus 1–2. With typically nonsensical planning, the governing body had programmed the following weekend's non-Championship Formula 1 race in the middle of Sicily, at Enna, some 2,300 miles to the south! As our infamous Ford Zodiac-engined transporter 903 PMT (towing a trailer, let it be said) was prone to frequent breakdowns, even Colin agreed with my plan that the two mechanics from Karlskoga, Dick Scammell and Ted Woodley, should be relieved in Geneva, where Derek Wild and Cedric Selzer would take over for the remaining 800-odd miles. 'PMT' was basically a 15 cwt Ford van chassis with a plywood flat top 'body' to carry a Formula 1 car, with plywood 'cupboards' on each side supposedly large enough to carry all the race car spares that might be required. As I was now in the middle of a continuing row with the Sicilian race organisers over Jimmy's non-appearance, it was obvious that I should go to Enna, while Colin, Jimmy and Dan travelled to Milwaukee that weekend. Then, as I left Cheshunt, came news that 'PMT' had broken its back while being unloaded by crane from the Naples–Palermo ferry, and was now stranded on the dockside, fortunately in Sicily. All we had to do now was get the cars and parts the last 90 miles to Enna!

In Milwaukee our two cars dominated proceedings from the outset. The presence of the two 'funny cars' at another bastion of the American auto scene was a heaven-sent opportunity for the US media and the crowd of over 35,000 packed into the State Fair grounds to watch the occasion, reputedly the largest crowd ever to watch a 1-mile oval event.

In qualifying, Don Branson's 1961 lap record of 34.09 seconds was bogey time and Jimmy's four laps of 33.71, 33.72, 32.95 and 32.93 secured him pole position. Dan took second slot with times of 33.28, 33.04, 33.32 and 33.09 seconds, the American forced to cope with poor carburation in the turns, which seriously hampered acceleration. He was having to make do with 58 mm Webers which mounted transversely, whereas Jimmy had Team's only 48 mm Webers, mounted longitudinally. Behind them on the grid were A. J. Foyt (third fastest with 33.90, 33.82, 33.88 and 33.73) and Parnelli Jones (34.15, 33.83, 34.14 and 33.89).

Straight from the rolling start Jimmy shattered the first-lap record with a speed of 104.806 mph, pulling away into what would become an ever-increasing lead. Parnelli Jones, who had won the last two stock car events at Milwaukee, made straight for his pit with brake problems, and although he restarted in last place he was out for good by lap 43. Jimmy continued to demolish the previous best times; at five laps his 106.743 mph average was a new record, and the average speed records at 10, 15, 25 and 50 laps also fell to him. So it went on, the Scot breaking records at 125, 150 and 175 miles, only the yellow caution lights slowing his pace and preventing him from breaking every Milwaukee record in the book.

It was a Lotus 1–2 for the first 80 miles until Dan's carburation problems worsened, causing fuel starvation through the turns and erratic acceleration out of them, so he slowly dropped back. After Foyt passed him, Rodger Ward also challenged, but was then forced to ease off as the switch operating his auxiliary fuel tank started to restrict his fuel supply. So the race ran out, Jimmy lapping everyone except Foyt to secure a conclusive first victory for the Indianapolis Lotus-Ford. In fact he was right behind A. J. in the closing laps, but eased off rather than cause offence by lapping him! A. J. finished second, Dan third, Rodger Ward fourth.

'I got thoroughly hosed down again at Milwaukee,' remembers Dan. 'You'd think that a company the size of Ford would have had more than one set of suitable carburettors for their track-car programme. Well, they hadn't. They had two alternative sizes of Weber carburettor available, but only one set of the bigger ones. But it wasn't the choke size that was critical, it was the way they mounted them.

'They had big 52 mm Webers that mounted east/west across the valley of the engine, or smaller 48s that mounted north/south along the valley. And the problem was that with the 52s mounted east/west, one choke would starve under centrifugal load as you ran hard through Milwaukee's tight turns. I got the east/west ones, so my car would hesitate and stammer in the middle of each turn. That was an uncomfortable situation for me – but no way was I going to stand up and demand the carburettors off Jimmy's car . . . This was a team shortage.'

'A Record Smashing Spree' read the American newspaper headlines, and interviews with the senior American racing fraternity, 'some grudgingly, some exuberantly', admitted that the Lotus design was the thing to have. Car owner Robert C. Wilke announced that he already had a rear-engined car at the design stage for the following year. Three-time Indy winner Lou Meyer, builder of the Meyer-Drake Offenhauser engines, while declaring that it was more a chassis-over-chassis than engine-over-engine victory, accepted that in future American engines and chassis would have to be lighter. Chapman told the media immediately after the race, 'We could go another 200 miles now, both the car and the tyres', and the journalists noted that both were British.

The race purse money totalled $44,225, of which $2,000 was race leader money, from which our winning car earned $12,413. As the American media noted, it was 'not a bad day's work for a fellow who spends his leisure time raising sheep and cattle'. Other British visitors also did well in Milwaukee that day; just down the road, Lord Cowdray had led his team to an 11–3 victory over Don Uihlein's Milwaukean polo team. The British team captain was Major Ronnie Ferguson, father of the future Duchess of York . . .

Meanwhile the Team's Sicilian Formula 1 venture became a real saga. Fortunately, race organiser Rino Mingrino proved to be a man of the world regardless of his stainless-steel teeth, and he ended our confrontation over Jimmy's non-appearance with a warm smile and a choice comment. 'Here we have the Mafia and in England you have Colin Chapman!'

Peter Arundell finished second, Trevor Taylor fortunately emerging unscathed from a 140 mph accident right under our noses, being ejected from his cockpit and flashing past us in the driving position but minus his car (and preceded by his favourite Rolex watch!). A marshal very kindly delivered it to the hospital later that evening; he had seen a small object whistling towards him where he stood at the exit to the pits, and it had come to rest at his feet at the time of the shunt.

It took most of the evening to get the required call through to Colin in Milwaukee to report on the race. After my reassurance that Trevor was OK, he enquired after the condition of the car. First came the chassis (25/R3) – written off. Engine? Very badly damaged and with its ancillary items stolen by spectators in the grandstand enclosure opposite the pits where it had come to rest. Gearbox?

'It's in the lake!'

'Well, you better get the lads to jump in and get it!'

Enna's stagnant lake was alive with water snakes; when I told Derek and Cedric of the Old Man's command, they responded in unison, 'You drive the truck back, we'll pay our own fares home!'

In fact, they quickly fashioned a 'trawl' from welding wire and after a lengthy delay every piece of the shattered gearbox was retrieved. All that remained was the 1,400-mile journey back to base.

Following the Milwaukee win, our Indy section made for the oval track at Trenton, New Jersey, for a test; it was more steeply banked and the only tyres available had not been tried on the car before. In between stops to match the suspension geometry to the track, Jimmy ran progressively faster, unofficially breaking the track record ten times.

David Lazenby: 'Then we discovered that a steering arm was bent, and when we examined it closely we found cracks in it, so set about reworking the spares.'

Colin's reaction was to institute an immediate steering system re-design for both Indy and Formula 1 cars, an action that greatly impressed Jimmy, who wrote later that the cars had run with the same design and layout for five years without a breakage.

Dan Gurney recalled the lighter side: 'There was one testing episode at Trenton when Dave Lazenby and Colin Riley had made friends with two airline stewardesses who were coming down to see them after we'd finished testing. Trenton was a mile-and-a-half oval and we got into a deal of mutual leg-pulling about lap times. I finally bet them $20 each that they couldn't even run around the oval in less than 10 minutes, and they accepted my challenge.

'They both went off like Carl Lewis, but after the first hundred yards they began blowing hard. Finally Colin came round very close to 10 minutes, but not inside it, while Dave – the bigger man – was maybe a couple of minutes outside. They'd both been absolutely determined to take my $20. They'd both given their all, and they were both just about *totally* wasted. They were no good for anything after that, but eventually dragged themselves off to keep their dates. Next day I received a real "grateful" thank-you note – from the girls!'

The Italian Grand Prix at Monza saw Jimmy clinch his first World Championship title and Team Lotus its first Constructor's World Championship victory. It was typical of Jimmy that he was as thrilled by Team's award as his own, especially after so narrowly losing the title in the final race of the previous year, but his immediate enjoyment was short-lived. Completing his victory lap, he returned to his jubilant crew in the circuit garage area only to discover an official waiting to escort him to a nearby office. There, an Italian lawyer, attended by police, opened yet another chapter in the aftermath of the tragic accident that had killed Ferrari driver 'Taffy' von Trips and 14 spectators in the same race two years earlier. Although involved in the accident, Jimmy was in no way to blame, as the Italian courts were to confirm some four years later, but the lawyer, Signor Canpinelli, declared that as Jimmy had interfered with the German driver's entry into a corner, he had caused 'homicide by imprudence'.

The immediate aftermath had devastated our No 1, and the long-running legal proceedings, in which court action by the immediate next-of-kin were duplicated later by their next-of-kin, placed a considerable strain on both Jimmy and Team. On this occasion it was agreed that both were free to leave Italy, pending further action by the courts, but Jimmy's harassment by the press would continue unabated.

In Cheshunt, Team Lotus's Lotus-Cortina section was busily preparing for its long-awaited debut following the car's successful homologation. Its first race was at Oulton Park (21 September) where Jimmy and Trevor Taylor were entered in the Gold Cup Formula 1 event. Immediately afterwards Colin, Jimmy and Dan Gurney (who was driving a Brabham) were scheduled for a hurried departure for America, where both drivers were entered in the following day's USAC Trenton '200'.

Trenton was 'category one' in the team's plans, while so far as the Lotus-Cortinas were concerned, Ford of Britain's support extended to the Willment team and Ford was anxious that a Willment driver should sample the new car in anger as soon as possible. As a result, Jimmy was to forgo his saloon seat in favour of Willment's 'Gentleman' Jack Sears, Trevor Taylor driving the second car. Only the huge 7-litre Ford Galaxies of Dan Gurney and Graham Hill headed our two 1,558 cc Lotus twin-cam-engined cars, Sears and Taylor finishing first and second respectively in their class and third and fourth overall. The main race of the day, for the Gold Cup, saw Jimmy start from pole to lead virtually all the way, setting the first 100 mph fastest lap at Oulton Park along the way. Soon after the race, Colin gently coaxed our overloaded company Piper Commanche into the air en route for London Airport where he, Jimmy and Dan would transfer to a transatlantic flight.

For me, intercontinental travel arrangements, particularly including Colin's company aircraft and/or chartered aircraft, guaranteed floods of adrenalin. When I first joined Colin, he habitually made his own flight plans, leaving me to tidy up both ends of each journey in arranging rendezvous points and times for him to be met by his own or hire cars. As it was obviously essential for me to know his flight arrangements in advance, and he was loath to waste time discussing plans that he knew were odds-on for substantial changes as the run-up to events unfolded, it was not long before he asked me to produce his flight plans. This proved an unenviable task, as apart from the necessary alterations that constantly had to be made, Colin could be guaranteed to make changes, sometimes even en route, asking air traffic control at his new destination to telephone me.

John Blake of the Royal Aero Club was a true ally, keeping me constantly in touch with airfield and regulation changes, and for this trip to Trenton he provided the telephone numbers of contacts en route able to report that all was well. My original scheme had been for Colin and the drivers to take the Commanche to London Airport and there to transfer to a flight for New York, whence a chartered light plane would whisk them the short 70-mile hop to an early night in their Trenton motel. The essential point to keep in mind was that the two drivers had had a very tiring 18-hour day, with two or three races thrown in for good measure, to be followed by practice and a 200-mile USAC race after breakfast the following day.

The finalised Oulton Park race-day timetable put paid to my plans. Arrival at London Airport was too late to catch the New York flight; the next was bound for Canada, and here Ford America came to my rescue, positioning one of their executive aircraft to take care of the final stage, although the longer journey meant that the drivers would not be in their beds until the small hours.

After the post-Milwaukee August test at Trenton, the Type 29s had returned to Dearborn for a thorough strip and rebuild. From there the cars (now both sporting 48 mm Weber carburettors mounted longitudinally) and spares were trucked the 766 miles to the New Jersey track. Our usual crew of Jim Endruweit, David Lazenby and Colin Riley followed a spares package weighing 350 lbs freighted out from Cheshunt.

Jimmy and Dan, revitalised after the barest few hours' sleep, dominated practice and qualifying, leaving the other 45 entries in their wake as they took first and second places on the 26-car starting grid. Both 29s were over 3 mph quicker than the old record, first Dan and then Jimmy settling pole, the Scot averaging 109.356 mph (32.92 seconds) round the 1-mile oval.

But the race was a disaster for us. Although the cars took a commanding 1-2 lead from the start, the gap to third man A. J. Foyt increasing every lap, on lap 49 a plume of blue smoke began to trail from Jimmy's car. An engine/chassis scavenge hose had failed, a problem later attributed to damage sustained in transit, although Ford's initial press bulletin blithely attributed blame to our crew's preparation. As the smoke billowed from the car, Jimmy's mind took him back to the Indy 500 earlier in the year and the controversial Parnelli Jones oil spillage. Later he wrote: 'Now what was going to happen? Would I be black flagged for losing oil or would someone overlook the fact since I was leading and since the Indianapolis shambles? No black flag appeared and I retired gracefully to the pits, but you can well understand why I was smiling quietly to myself.'

Dan donned the leader's mantle in comfortable fashion, further extending the gap between himself and second place over the following 100 miles until an internal engine failure took him out. Dan's car, like Jimmy's, also trailed blue smoke, but for a different reason – oil was being lost through the engine breather, and when the unit was later dismantled, a piston was found to have broken, a piece being lodged in an engine oil line.

This race marked a disappointing end to what was in retrospect a most successful venture overall. It also marked the end of the Indy-Ford push-rod V8 programme, a Lotus-Ford collaboration that had turned the USAC world on its head.

Immediately after the 1963 Indy race the spotlight had been turned on Ford's double-overhead camshaft, or 'quad-cam', engine, which had been researched at the same time as the push-rod unit preferred by Chapman for his Indy debut. In motor racing's natural progression it was clear that more power was essential for the continuing programme, and work was well progressed on the 'quad-cam' as its predecessor swept the board at Milwaukee and nearly repeated the story at Trenton. However, considerable development work remained to be done as the year went by.

The Offenhauser engine that Ford purchased for comparative studies, provided an interesting comparison with the two engines Ford subsequently built. An in-line four-cylinder unit running on methanol, its twin overhead camshafts operating 16 valves, it produced slightly over 400 bhp at 6,000 rpm. Ford's 1963 push-rod V8 engine produced 375 bhp at 7,200 rpm on gasoline; it was 100 lbs lighter and its fuel consumption significantly better. Ford had run the engine on a mixture of 30 per cent nitro-methane in methanol, but its 20 per cent increase in power had been obtained only at a vastly increased fuel consumption, some $2^{1}/_{3}$–3 times more than that of gasoline, a fact that had swayed Ford to follow Chapman's thinking. Its successor, the quad-cam, initially produced 400 bhp at 7,000 rpm on gasoline. It scaled 60 lbs less than the Offy and promised much, although when more details became known our chief designer, Len Terry, felt that a more exciting package had been missed.

'Although I was a car designer I knew enough about engines to realise that this one was not achieving its potential,' he reflected later. 'The Ford engineers had obviously sat down and said to each other, "Let's have a look at the most successful Indy engine to date". So they acquired an Offy, but overlooked the fact that it was simply a four-cylinder. They made a Dutch copy of its cylinder head as far as valve and port sizes and so on, then put one on each bank of their own V8. Now the valves and ports were far too big, not generating the gas velocity that was so essential, so they got nowhere near the power and torque out of the V8 that they should have. It was immediately apparent to me that the engine people involved knew little of what should have been achieved by the engine – they had got gas flow but not the velocity required. With an engine of that capacity and with four valves per cylinder they should have been getting around 550 bhp on methanol; in other words, 75 to 100 bhp more than they actually got.'

As thousands of test and race miles had revealed no inherent weakness, the sand-cast aluminium block (with cast dry liners made from, as Ford literature described, 'exceptionally high-quality cast iron') and bottom end remained virtually unchanged, but the new heads were to be subject to extensive research as the programme continued.

In its early running the quad-cam had used four twin-choke Weber carburettors (and one engine would run in this form in October testing at Indy), but for various reasons these were discarded in favour of a Ford-modified Hilborn fuel injection system. The prototype incorporated outside exhaust ports by reason of the carburettors being sited within the vee, and it was clear that the exhaust layout required for improved engine efficiency would be almost impossible to fit into a rear-engined scheme. Then, when the head porting was improved, the re-design brought a more versatile arrangement. For the rear-engined cars the unit had its exhaust ports on the inside of the vee, and to adapt the unit for a potential front-engined Indy roadster (or sports car) the heads were simply interchanged, turning them 180 degrees at the same time.

Fuel injection also corrected the supply of over-rich mixture and inconsistent delivery on high-speed corners that had afflicted Gurney at Milwaukee. It was also felt that fuel loss through the carburettor air intakes eradicated by injection would help offset the increase in fuel consumption expected (but in practice this proved minimal). An overriding factor was the supply of sufficient numbers of Weber carburettors now that Ford was proposing to build 25 engines, not only for us but for the other teams they were contemplating.

Exhaust pipe design was a matter of protracted research. The final layout incorporating two slightly flared megaphones was found to improve response during throttle opening.

As the engine would be producing more power and running faster, improvements to the lubrication system were deemed necessary. In testing, Ford had also fitted larger pumps and nozzles to run on methanol, releasing an additional 50 bhp; as this was obviously the ideal mode for qualifying, but would increase overall loadings, various detail refinements were incorporated for longevity.

The use of carburettors had already plagued the project by reason of the over-complicated throttle linkage required, and 30 years later chief mechanic David Lazenby recalled the problems involved as well as the fact these would continue with fuel injection.

'Finding an efficient and consistently reliable throttle linkage was a headache that never went away, be it for carburettors or fuel injection. We tried all sorts of layouts when the engines were first installed, but no satisfactory solution was found, and in the end we just came to accept it. I clearly recall being with Jim Endruweit at the enormous Ford engine research and development facility, tickling and fiddling with numerous designs and redesigns of linkages, and a multitude of angled levers and bell cranks – a very time-consuming exercise.'

Mike Underwood, a former aircraft technician who joined our Indy section just as preparations for the 1964 race began (later he became Chief Mechanic for the 1967 '500'), also clearly recalled the frustrations involved with the various schemes tried.

'Throttle linkages were always a problem. There was a hideous bar attached to the front of the engines on which a section of the throttle linkage was mounted. As the bar was bolted to the cam covers in the vee, it "grew" as the engine heated up, which threw all the settings out. If you take a close look at the accidents that befell both our cars and those of the other teams, many had a throttle linkage deficiency of one sort or another as a contributory factor.'

David Lazenby: 'We thought of alternative schemes for a number of items connected with the engines, but the Ford people were not at all happy with our suggestions. For instance, I sometimes used the cam cover studs as attachment points, but Ford engineers vetoed every one; I don't think it was the idea that was vetoed, but the fact that we were touching or suggesting changes to the engines when we were Lotus people, and Ford had decreed these were not to be "tampered" with in any way, shape or form by those they always regarded as outsiders.'

Although a test was scheduled at the Speedway for a quad-cam installed in a modified Type 29 to follow the US Grand Prix at Watkins Glen, it was postponed until after the Mexican GP on 27 October, where Jimmy took pole, led from start to finish and set a record fastest lap. After the race our Formula 1 crew returned home, while Colin, Jimmy, Dan, Jim Endruweit and Dunlop tyre technician Vic Barlow set off for Indy, where 'Laz' and Colin Riley, together with the Ford engineers, were preparing the new combination.

Chassis number '29/1', 'The Mule' that Dan had driven in the '500', had the new engine installed in Detroit by 'Laz' and Jim Endruweit. Meanwhile the shunted chassis, '29/2', was back in the factory at Cheshunt being slowly rebuilt but awaiting modifications to accept the new quad-cam engine.

Tuesday 29 October finally saw the white Type 29's new engine fired up for the first time at the Brickyard. Attached to an additional frame above the gearbox was an oblong shoe-box-sized aluminium container housing electronics to record temperatures, pressures and lap-by-lap progress data.

'It churned out reams and reams of paper that was earnestly studied by everyone,' remembered David Lazenby. 'What drew most plaudits was the record of Jimmy's spells in the car – no one could believe just how smooth he was.'

Dan drove on the car's first run, but the following three days of testing were far from conclusive, as Jim Endruweit's notes reveal. Running on Dunlop 5.50 front and 7.00 rear tyres, the fuel injection system was initially slow to pick up after the driver had lifted off. Over-rich mixture was suspected. With the rev-counter tell-tale left at 7,700 rpm, the session was halted for the injection to be thoroughly examined. Soon after running resumed, the cooling system lost water; no fewer than 7 pints were required to top it up. The engine now ran to 7,950 rpm, but water loss continued, raising oil and water temperatures to a worrying level. When Dan stopped for replenishment he reported that even prior to overheating the engine 'felt strange' near maximum revs.

That evening saw a routine Team Lotus late night as the chassis was stripped for inspection and the Ford engineers played with their new baby. For the second day, Dunlop 'Green Spot' tyres were changed for D9s and the fuel injection leaned off. A 17 lb radiator cap replaced the previous 13 lb one in an attempt to cure the water loss, and a different grade of spark plug was fitted.

The engine now ran only fractionally quicker, but running was halted when the car's handling deteriorated due to failure of the right-rear damper. The chronic overheating and associated water loss continued throughout the day; a trial run holding the engine to a consistent 7,700 rpm was tried, but again the system boiled. Gear ratios had been continually juggled over the two days, and after the fourth session of the second day the Dunlop tyres were changed for Goodyear Blue Streaks. Later, tyre pressures were lowered from 40/45 (front/rear) to 30/35 for the final period, but overall the car's performance remained disappointing.

That evening our crew together with the Ford engineers closely scrutinised every detail of the chassis and engine, but no explanation could be found. Eventually it was decided to change the engine for the last day and a carburetted version was fitted with 58 mm Webers and side-stack exhausts.

It was now Jimmy's turn to drive, but first he could not select fourth gear then oil began to blow out from the breather. After these setbacks had been attended to, he reported that he could get the car up to the 7,950 rpm limit, but in so doing the carburettors were acting up in the 7,000 to 7,550 rpm range before uninterrupted power resumed; and now oil was pouring from the breather. This malady had already been encountered previously; eventually it was found to be due to severe agitation of oil by the increased number of gears, and the solution came with the addition of a second scavenge pump. The carburettor jets were changed, improving performance throughout the range, but again at the 7,950 rpm barrier both fuel-injected and carburetted engines went flat.

An experimental set of Dunlops had been used for the third day, but for the final session Goodyears, pressured to 30/35, were fitted. Now Jimmy broke the barrier, but only by 50 rpm, the car coming off the turns at 7,200 rpm. Then a peculiar noise was heard and he was signalled into the pits, where it was found that a rear tyre was beginning to shred and the other three had heated up substantially.

Later Jimmy wrote, 'Now one of the most dangerous things for a driver is test driving a new car, or some new development which has never been tried before. It is here, where you are proving whether design ideas work and groping virtually into the unknown, that danger lies. On this occasion we were testing tyres at Indy, and I had been running with different tyres all day. Towards the end of testing, the engineers said, "Now try these". After they had fitted them I asked if they were going to put the pressures up, explaining that the previous week I had raced a sports car using the same tyres. On that occasion I had used higher pressures than they had put in the Indy car, and without getting into top in the sports car I found I couldn't even put my hands on the tyres, they were so hot. To my mind going out on Indy on these tyres I wanted more pressure.

'But no, I was told that the concern had been running this type of tyre on Indy cars before and they were all right. I didn't argue any further and took the car out. I was lapping at about 150 mph and getting quicker and quicker every lap. I never felt a thing wrong with the car but down in the pits the mechanics suddenly heard this extraordinary noise, and thought I had blown the engine up. They signalled me into the pits, and here was one tyre with chunks of rubber out of it and just about to blow. Now, I had been doing 175 mph or 180 mph on the straight, and this sort of thing happening is not so funny. You don't have much of a chance if anything should go wrong.'

This final setback closed the three-day session, but before the participants went their various ways the chassis and engine were subjected to another close scrutiny before 'Laz' and Colin Riley cleaned the car, reloaded it on to the Ford transporter and rode back to Dearborn for further evaluation. It had been a disappointing test; the fastest lap achieved had been only fractionally above Jimmy's 150 mph qualifying earlier in the year with a push-rod V8, while unresolved problems had provided continual interruptions.

That same month Ford publicly announced its plans for 1964, confirming it would be running the quad-cam at Indianapolis again on gasoline. Contrary to rumours that Meyer-Drake would be involved in provision of racing engines, Ford also confirmed that it would be building the engines itself and providing them both to Team Lotus and to those entrants of cars driven by Foyt, Bobby Marshman, Rodger Ward and to entrant Mickey Thompson. However, unlike us the other entrants would run independently of Ford support.

In Cheshunt a dummy version of the quad-cam engine had been delivered from London Airport, enabling chief designer Len Terry to start installation drawings centred initially around the shunted chassis '29/2', but which would continue as preparation for the 1964 car, the Type 34. At this stage '29/2' was earmarked as the reserve, or third, car for our next assault on the Brickyard, and while work on the project continued at Lotus, the Ford engineers were striving to find more power and reliability, plus cures for the recent ailments.

As our Formula 1 crew completed their preparations for the South African 'tour', quad-cam test-bed running continued. 'Laz' and Colin stripped down chassis '29/1', 'The Mule', then rebuilt it to test readiness. Around this time Ford's competition executive group was reorganised, the most senior member, Bill Gay, moving up the ladder. In taking over his vacated post, A. J. (Gus) Scussel from the stock car engine research and development department took overall charge of all Ford of America's racing engines.

As test-bed running began to pay off, so Ford's winter plans of 1963/64 evolved. With the company's desire to get as many test miles as possible under its corporate belt, and with Jimmy's and Dan's busy calendars likely to prevent them being available at the drop of a hat, Ford turned to US organisation on home soil. Jimmy's race calendar took him through to the end of December (South Africa), followed by a series of test periods leading up to his first home race in March, and it was clear to Ford that we would not provide the continuity required.

The company therefore turned instead to Lindsey Hopkins, a senior and respected member of the established team who had been entering Indy cars since 1950, and his undoubtedly talented driver, 27-year-old Bobby Marshman. Bobby's father George had sown the seed for what would become his son's all-consuming passion for a career in auto racing, and had become an established name in East Coast midget and sprint events of the 1930s and early '40s. Bobby had taken up the challenge with sprint cars at the age of 19 in 1955. He was soon angling for a 'big car' drive, and destined to be a high flyer – he finally landed himself a drive in the top flight of USAC in 1961. In only his second season he had won a race and ranked fifth in the Championship table that year. In his Indy debut he had literally clawed his way on to the last row of the grid (in fact, last place at 33rd), but had finished seventh. The following year he finished fifth.

'Laz' found him a quiet and reserved character; as he put it, 'in the Jimmy Clark mould, and very likeable. I clearly remember how, like the rest of the Indy community, he harboured a clear dislike of what they all regarded as the unlucky colour of green for a race car, and how he mumbled under his breath when on arrival to test for us, he discovered the car he was to drive was Jimmy's, resplendent in its British Racing Green.'

Colour preferences aside, Bobby was not slow to recognise the Lotus as the car with which to succeed, and he was fortunate in having the wealthy and enthusiastic Lindsey Hopkins as his mentor and team owner. Lindsey had been a USAC entrant over many years and was a USAC director. A confidant of Henry Ford, the company had already approached him for advice when it had first sought a chassis builder. Lindsey's continuing enthusiasm and faith in 'funny cars' like ours was to play a large part in what was to become his close involvement with the Ford effort, and his team, under chief mechanic Jack Beckley, now prepared for an extensive winter test programme with a quad-cam-engined Type 29.

It has often been stated that the car used for this period of testing by Marshman was Dan's damaged '29/2', presupposing that it had been rebuilt and returned to America, but this is not so.

From correspondence and cables between Ford and Team Lotus it is evident that '29/2' was nearing the end of its rebuild in Cheshunt that November/December, while '29/1' and '29/3' were at Dearborn, since Ford had completed their purchase.

In fact, '29/2' remained at Cheshunt without a quad-cam engine because there was still no contract between Ford and Lotus for the 1964 '500', and Len Terry was immersed in a wide-ranging design programme. Added to this, Team faced practical problems caused by the sheer number of cars to be built, particularly since the new 1-litre Formula 2 created an extra racing category to contest. Certainly chassis '29/2' was still in push-rod form at the time of the London Racing Car Show in January 1964, where it was displayed on the *Daily Express* stand. And it was still in the factory in March, as evidenced by my notes and scribbled drafts of cables answering Ford's anxious enquiries over its availability.

A red herring that has contributed to this confusion about which chassis was where during this period is the Type 29 subsequently displayed in the Indianapolis Speedway Museum. Its chassis plate, taped on rather than riveted as it would have left us (which would have made Customs officials both in America and the UK blanch), reads '29/1' and the information board alongside it claims that it is Jimmy's 1963 second-place car. This is incorrect, and is possibly a misunderstanding dating back to when Ford handed over the car, some considerable time after its running life ended. In fact, Jimmy drove this prototype in its early life prior to arriving at Indy for the month of May, and from Jim Endruweit's notes we can see that Jimmy then drove only '29/3' throughout Indy practice, qualifying and the race, and also at Milwaukee and Trenton later that year.

Also its windscreen is of the deeper variety preferred by Dan. Obviously Ford's enormous volume of spares might have allowed them to utilise whatever was available for the display car regardless of authenticity. In addition, its nose cowling is wrongly painted, both nose badge and 'Lotus powered by Ford' inscription are missing, and it is on Goodyear tyres, whereas we ran Dunlop and Firestone on the 29s.

Perhaps, like many of the cars we raced in other categories, the chassis plates *were* swopped over. The cost and time-consuming paraphernalia involved in obtaining either the RAC or the London Chamber of Commerce carnets to permit Customs passage were prohibitive. If we had four or five chassis but only required three cars at each race, it was more economical to have only three carnets and to swop the chassis plates around to suit. There was nothing illegal in this practice, as all the cars involved returned to the UK. In the case of the USAC cars, when they were sold to Ford we paid import duty in the proper way, then charged it to the new owner.

Certainly the Type 29s had a most active life, accumulating many thousands of test miles in addition to their practice and race running. Their air freight mileage was also impressive, as chassis were returned to Cheshunt for the quad-cam engines to be installed and for rebuilding after their numerous accidents. Lindsey Hopkins had at least two of the cars for his 1963/64 winter programme, and as they were now the property of Ford America we at Lotus were not concerned with keeping detailed

movement records of individuals coupled to chassis numbers. We were more concerned with simply planning the next season's build and test programmes than keeping track of what were, after all, cars that we at Lotus would not race again.

Perhaps a more reliable clue as to the destination of Type 29 chassis can be found in Jabby Crombac's report in the magazine *Sport-Auto* of December 1965, after he had interviewed me for an in-depth study of Team Lotus. He listed the three 29 chassis, but without their all-important suffixes – the cars driven by Jimmy and Dan in the race are shown as 'destroyed (or shunted) by Marshman', and Dan's shunted practice car '29/2' as 'sold to the Jerry Alderman stable for Al Miller'.

In February 1964 work finally began on installing a quad-cam V8 in '29/2'; Denis Jenkinson, making a tour of Cheshunt, wrote: '. . . interest in Ford V8 engines naturally led one to the racing shop where the Indianapolis Type 29 that was on show at the Racing Car Show was being fitted with one of the new 4 ohc Ford V8 engines . . . this particular car was the one Gurney should have raced last year, but he bent it in practice, and it has now been rebuilt and sold to an American private owner . . . nearing completion were the two new Indianapolis chassis frames, full monocoques as last year, but known as Type 34 models . . .'

It is interesting to note that Jenks, like his journalistic colleagues, described the 'tub' as a 'monocoque', whereas Team Lotus press releases, approved in detail by Colin personally as always, still described them as 'twin-tube, ladder frame, stressed-skin riveted structures' – not quite so catchy, but more precise.

Len Terry: 'Yes, Colin was correct in not calling them monocoques . . . we initially described them as a "bath-tub" concept, which they were to look at . . . It wasn't until the Type 38 came along that we built a true monocoque.'

In December Jimmy went mud-plugging with a twin-engined Mini-Moke representing the London Motor Club against the British Army – he learned quickly after becoming bogged down in deep mud, and went on to win two heats. It was an excellent example of his enjoyment when driving any type of vehicle.

Meanwhile, the 1963 motor racing season had ended with the South African Grand Prix on 28 December. Jimmy took pole and his seventh World Championship victory in the 10-round series. As well as securing both Formula 1 World Championships, Team Lotus had scored points in every World Championship round, a feat not to be repeated until Benetton's similar achievement in 1992, 30 years later.

Our South African tour also included the Rand Grand Prix on the old Kyalami circuit near Johannesburg two weeks before the Championship finale in East London, and as the deal with the race organisers stipulated appearances in both events, Jimmy had to forego an Indy car test arranged by Ford at Kingman, for which Bobby Marshman took his place. As it turned out our programme would have been better served if Jimmy had gone to America, as at Kyalami both his and Trevor Taylor's Type 25s succumbed to fuel pump problems.

CHAPTER FOUR

1964:
Team Lotus Developments

As one journalist wrote, '1964 was the year the whole world beat a path to Cheshunt.' Lotus Elan production was well under way and that of the Lotus-Cortina was accelerating, while our hard-worked Team Lotus personnel felt that their World Championship success reflected well upon the Group in general. From the three unpaid employees of 1948, Lotus now employed over 350 people, and total car production per week was running at 60–70.

As the New Year began, the Team Lotus build programme lagged behind in some areas, the Indy schedule possibly suffering most. As the Indy mechanics were later to reflect ruefully, 1964 was the year in which they had to struggle against almost insurmountable odds in order to get anywhere near acceptable battle readiness, and although the Type 34 was to show enormous potential, sadly this was not to be proven until the cars had passed into the hands of American private owners . . .

Adverse factors seriously affected Team's Indy effort, and sad to relate they emanated from Colin. Len Terry: 'I was quite simply devastated by his premeditated action in having me removed from the Speedway at the previous year's Indy 500 just as Jimmy's car seemed to have a chance of winning first time out. It was his utterly cruel instruction that I was to leave on the helicopter then whirring away nearby; I just couldn't believe it. I might have forgiven him if his explanation at the time that I was needed back at base to attend to important Formula 1 matters had proved true, but when I got back to Cheshunt it was clear there were no problems worth talking about. All I could think was, "You sod!".

'The 1963 season went by and there were so many racing categories needing attention that we were all too busy to harbour grudges, but as the winter began and Colin piled the work on to all of us I thought, "This is enough". I really had no heart for the long hours and continuing very hard work; I had spent the previous winter working all the hours God sent; it seemed that I was never at home, and with the memory of my ejection from the 1963 race still fresh in my mind, no way could I work flat out for him . . . I had already made up my mind to leave him again, but I would honour my three-year contract, so I was just biding my

time to find a suitable team to go to; as a result the Indy programme slipped back so much that Dunlop couldn't fit in their scheduled tyre tests, and we all know now what happened as a result . . .'

Coupled with these problems concerning the Chief Designer, and forgetting the other projects connected with Formulae 1 and 2 and saloons and small sports cars, came the new big sports car programme and its disastrous Type 30. That concept in effect combined the backbone chassis of the Elan and a 'big banger' Ford America V8 engine, so administratively the 30s built and raced by Team Lotus became the Indy section's responsibility.

Colin still seemed not to acknowledge the rival Ford/Lola GT relationship. We continued to integrate our big sports car budget into the Indy financial structure with Ford time and time again, only for Ford to distance itself at every turn. But Colin indomitably persevered, and perhaps if the Type 30 had proved a success Ford might have merely accepted involvement as part of a two-pronged effort. As it was, our Indy section's efforts, with the mechanics constantly toiling for long hours building, testing and running two categories of cars, were seriously diluted, and only their superhuman dedication kept the section afloat at all! Someone once told me that this was the only way Colin could operate; racing personnel keeping comfortably to schedule meant a relaxed team, and a relaxed team was one most likely to miss the obvious and thereby bring disaster upon itself. It was a wicked two-edged sword. However, looking back Colin could very easily have been right . . .

The Type 30 and its replacement, the Type 40 ('. . . a 30 with ten more mistakes,' as the late Richie Ginther put it), both became celebrated engineering disasters. Len Terry: 'Colin brought in some sketches of his new sports car [the Type 30] for me to look at, and my first thought was that he had had another of his engineering brain fades. Admittedly he didn't have them often, but when he did he really went overboard. Mike Costin summed it up when he said that Colin sometimes lacked a real understanding of engineering principles, and that sometimes he couldn't (or wouldn't) accept clear explanations however hard you tried.

'He planned the 30's backbone chassis in 20-gauge steel, and I said that was nowhere near strong enough. The serious weakness was the rear engine bay, or "tuning fork" like the Elan, which he designed in channel section. The kink where the chassis opened up was also a major weakness. I gave Colin my thoughts and he boxed in the channel-section legs, but left the kink as it was – it was never, ever going to be stiff enough for the V8's power, but Colin simply would not budge. They put the prototype chassis through a torsion test and before they had really begun to apply serious load it kinked permanently! They threw that chassis away and went up to 16-gauge with the next one . . .

'That car was never going to be right. The trouble was that while the majority of people could see this, Colin couldn't. The Type 23 sports car had hinged bodywork sections to make it easier to work on, but the 30 body was all one piece, like a saddle, so you had to take this unwieldy shell off just to make minor adjustments. To work on the front or rear suspension meant working inside the wheel arches . . .

'Mind you, that body was a magnificent shape. Jim Clark, our New Zealand stylist (no relation to the driver), did it, but unfortunately he lived in an airy-fairy world. He had an aptitude for line and shape but forgot that wheels go up and down, and the fronts also turn in and out, so he didn't provide wheel clearance. That was the only change I had to make, though. Colin, for his part, continued his disastrous path by putting 1½-litre Formula 1 wheels *and* brakes on a car weighing twice as much with an all-enveloping body to prevent the brakes cooling!

'Colin always had a bee in his bonnet over Eric Broadley and Lola. It started when Eric began making his name in the '50s; Colin was determined to prove he was a better designer, so when Eric's Lola Mark I sports blew off the Lotus Elevens he produced the Type 17, which had all sorts of problems. Then came Eric's Ford deal, which seemed to affect Colin's mind, as he brought out the Type 30 in reaction. He must have gone quietly berserk at Indy when he thought Jimmy had won in 1966 only to find his lap chart was wrong and Graham had won, *in a Lola*! Colin was always a brilliant concept man, but he needed nailing to the ground on detail; Mike Costin and, before him, the Allen brothers have never received the credit they deserve for doing just that.'

January 1964 had also seen an additional workload for me. I was secretary of the Formula Junior, later Formula 2, Association, which I had founded in 1961. Formula 1 teams had been watching its fairly rapid progress in obtaining safeguards and additional income for entrants, and Brabham, BRM, Cooper and Colin for Lotus asked me to do the same for them. Initially we had kept the arrangement a matter amongst ourselves, but by the end of 1963 it was decided to 'go public', and an announcement was made in January, creating the Formula One Constructors' Association. Under the impression that I could hardly wear two hats (the two groups were sometimes in conflict), I only agreed to a post in the new body as a temporary measure. I was given £15 by each team to get the thing off the ground, with the explicit request that it must cover the first year's expenses! In fact, I found myself in a post that was to endure for ten long years.

Team's proposed racing programme for 1964 had, as previously, been initiated early in the previous year. My card index file contained regular updates on circuit information, comments from other teams, drivers and mechanics, as well as circuit owners and race organisers together with the problems and deficiencies I had noted from the previous year and which had to be put right before our next appearance. I kept a similar file on airfields, landing strips and favourite farms that Colin liked to use on his constant trips around the UK and Europe. For instance, when Colin flew to Silverstone we had a friendly farmer who owned land adjoining the circuit and who would very kindly move his cows if I phoned to give him an arrival time.

This was in the early days of company aviation, when Lotus's sole aircraft was an elderly Miles Messenger. On the last occasion we used this particular field, Colin landed safely and hurried off to the paddock with his passengers. Unknown to anyone, the farmer then let his cows back into the field where they immediately ate the Messenger's doped fabric wings, which meant that Colin was forced to journey home by car, 'surrounded by plebs' as he described other road users. As a result I found myself with two disgruntled people: Colin, who lost the use of his plane until repairs could be completed, and the farmer, who had in future to keep his cows out of his field until our tasty aircraft could depart.

With a race programme as complex as ours, coupled with a governing body with a lackadaisical attitude towards finalising race dates in good time, we were forced to keep our ears to the ground to keep one step ahead of the opposition. My own advanced calendar for 1964, based on supposition, rumour and plain common sense, initially listed 72 meetings, and by year's end we had actually totalled 70. These comprised 18 Formula 1, three USAC, 25 saloon (Lotus-Cortina) events – 13 in the UK and 12 in the States – five sports car races, 16 Formula 2 and three for Elans.

The American saloon, or sedan, season was funded by the English Ford Line Organisation – EFLO – located in Ford America's Dearborn site, but operating independently, marketing British Ford products in the US. The first I knew of it was one evening when EFLO's Peter Quenet, trying to get a call through to Colin, was switched through to my office. The Lotus-Cortina had been rapturously received by the press world-wide and Peter thought an excellent promotional campaign could be built around a race team competing, even though out of category in American events. When I discussed Peter's thoughts with Colin later that evening he showed little interest.

'I'm really too busy to think about it,' he said, 'but if you feel we can do a good job and you want to take it on then go ahead. But it has to be done well and I want to see your budget proposal before you send it off . . .'

Colin's ice-cold manner was not new to me. It was as if he had immediately classed the conversation as surplus to requirements, and did I know I was making God late for dinner? I had scored no points; the proposed revenue appeared to hold little interest for him, so what was I doing proposing that he go all the way to America just to watch saloons race for neither trophies nor prize money? To be fair to him, the logistics did seem unnecessarily complicated – it was all strictly promotional and there was nothing tangible to win.

However, to me it presented an ideal challenge, provided useful income and would ensure that we had additional mechanic strength on hand, which we could fly cheaply and quickly into Indianapolis in the event of a dire emergency. I produced a budget to suit Colin, fired it off and received immediate approval from EFLO. Years later Colin was to hark back to the two-year EFLO programme in unusually appreciative terms; to his way of thinking it had been a clean and neat package that had pleased Ford and earned a useful revenue.

'Pro rata, it proved to be the most profitable category of racing we took part in,' he commented.

Following EFLO's approval I set about restructuring Team Lotus. It was now to comprise six sections, each with its own budget and operational staff, complete right down to its own notepaper. There was 'Team Lotus Formula One'; 'Team Lotus Racing with Ford America' (Indy and big sports cars); 'Team Lotus Racing with Ford of Britain' (Lotus-Cortinas UK); 'Team Lotus Racing with EFLO'; and a racing Elan development team. We were also closely involved with 'Ron Harris-Team Lotus', running the Formula 2 section, and Ian Walker-Team Lotus, running another Type 30 and Elan.

Our fabrication section had to be enlarged to cope with the additional work. John Lambert, initially the section's one and only employee, had been joined the previous year by Roy Franks (still with Team Lotus in 1993), and more sheet metal workers were to be added during the coming year.

My budget proposal for 1964 catered for the building or refurbishing, preparation and racing of 22 cars; five Formula 1, four Type 30s, four Type 34 Indy cars, eight Lotus-Cortinas (four UK, four USA) and, last but not least, a racing Elan. Sixteen of these were new cars. Colin insisted that I continued my 'pencilled accounts' system, which ran parallel to but not linked with the Lotus accounts department. He regularly called for my version, which I liked to think was never more than a week in arrears and listed 21 areas of expenditure within each racing section. New additions were the EFLO, Elan and Type 30 sections.

A pragmatic attitude was essential if I was to cope with Colin's allocation to me of 'financial responsibilities'. With absolutely no control over his spending, it was intensely annoying to be called to his office for a dressing down on overspending in an engineering or R&D department that he controlled entirely. It was taboo to suggest any restriction within engineering schemes (the life blood of Lotus, as it was often described) unless Colin was obviously trying to score points off another engineer who might be present. Then you had to be careful not to tread on the Guv'nor's toes, otherwise you suffered the wrath of both participants! It was deemed sacrilegious even to whisper a hint of engineering extravagance, especially if Colin was involved. Eventually such

arguments would rise in temperature until Colin would demand an answer instead of a grimace. My response in most cases was the retort, 'It's a bog-rolls and *Motoring News* job, Colin,' reminding him of an argument we had had some time previously when I had first been accused of overspending.

'You've *got* to do something about it,' Colin had shouted.

'Come off it, Colin,' I had replied. 'You know very well the only items I have direct control over are toilet roll purchases and whether we should pay the subscription to *Motoring News* each year.'

This wasn't quite the case of course, but for me to establish restrictions in Colin's favoured areas would be an open invitation to him to break them immediately and, what would be worse, in full view of the staff. He frequently displayed such spiteful habits, and I had long before determined that he would not back me into such a corner; I had seen it happen too many times with other managers. In many ways his leadership was laudable, but it seemed to me a complete waste of effort for him to enforce such a loss of face on his managers; the senior members of Team Lotus had discussed this failing a number of times, and somehow an unwritten code had been established whereby no one took personal advantage of his often cynical comments in order to score points off one another. The matter was finally put to rest, amongst Team personnel at least, after some of us had seen a TV programme on the psychological pitfalls of rearing children, and we agreed that Colin hadn't been pottied properly. From then on we felt we held the upper hand!

Securing drivers for the EFLO operation soon became the head-scratcher that Colin had predicted, and I continually had to chop and shuffle names so as not to be left short. The over-riding problem was to find drivers of sufficient calibre who were not already signed for other drives on the weekends I needed them; by the end of the season we had 23 on our books. One was Jim Spencer, the Lotus Cars distributor in Chicago whom Colin had asked me to sign as reserve for the Marlboro 12-Hours race (Lotus-Cortinas); Jim had agreed to supply Elans for our road use at Indianapolis in 1964, and his sales efforts deserved reward. Although Colin had made it clear to me that Jim would not have a drive (Colin felt that it was sufficient for him just to have his name in the programme listing), Jim had other ideas, but more of him later.

By February our plans were sufficiently well advanced to enable me to dispatch 'priority calendar' letters to our three primary drivers, Jim Clark, Peter Arundell and Mike Spence. These gave them early notification of working weekends and detailed those dates on which they could, with our approval, drive for other teams. As there were 35 'Team' weekends in a span of 43 (with Jimmy down to drive in a minimum of 44 races) we felt satisfied that they would have few idle moments. Test programmes still had to be arranged as the season progressed, and Jimmy would also spend most of May in Indianapolis.

By now the original plan that the Type 29 displayed at the London Racing Car Show would act as back-up at Indy '64 had changed, and Ford indicated that it would like the car to be shipped to them as soon as possible. This caused Colin considerable concern, as he had already made his thoughts clear to the Americans that the 29s should not be raced again. First, he was unhappy at the thought of anyone outside Team being responsible for preparing the cars, and second having to set up a separate spares supply arrangement would place a strain on Team. His worry about Lotus's name being jeopardised by outsiders' unfamiliarity with our techniques and standards of preparation was to be proved correct time and time again, underscoring our proven adage that 'if it wins it's a Ford, if it breaks it's a Lotus'. The media focus on incidents that befell privately owned Indy Lotuses always placed responsibility at our door, even when we had not set eyes on the vehicle for a year or more!

Colin's opinion was that such cars, outdated as they undoubtedly were and fitted with engines producing more power than had been contemplated when the chassis were designed, should be relegated to promotional or museum displays. Unfortunately, each contract with Ford stipulated that they could purchase the cars after their Team Lotus participation, so their eventual use was a matter entirely beyond our control.

Although described as merely a developed version of the Type 29, the Type 34 was hardly a repeat of its predecessor, and this is clearly emphasised by the vast amount of entirely new drawings involved of virtually every aspect and detail.

Len Terry: '. . . the main changes came about in the "tub" to accommodate the quad-cam unit. The suspension geometry changed, so new designs of front and rear uprights and new wishbones were required, but there were no radical changes of thought. Richard Parker in our design office produced the suspension geometry for the rear end, and uppermost in his mind was elimination of any tendency for it to "steer". Richard's major task was the design of the racing Elan (Type 26R), and he was to take a year completing that. I regarded him as a mathematical genius; he had an MA in engineering and, whereas I would have laid it all out on my drawing board working from first principles, he was able to lock himself away and work it out mathematically.

'Richard was extremely bright and had previously designed the Rochdale Olympic, a monocoque fibreglass car very similar in concept to the first Lotus Elite. Like many bright people, however, he was prone to forgetting the practicalities; he progressed the 26R right up to being built, then rushed off to Snetterton to test his year's work, only to discover that he had to come home again because he'd forgotten to book the circuit! But he was extremely pleasant and easy to work with, and his rear geometry on the 1964 Type 34 carried over on to the 1965 Type 38.'

Len also designed new knock-on four-spoke magnesium wheels for the car to replace the Dunlop pressings that had cracked the previous year. The Type 29's Colotti gearbox was now to be replaced by the German Zahnradfabrik Friedrichshafen (ZF) 2DS20 two-speed unit, and Len was responsible for the design and production of the gearbox casing; this gearbox, in five-speed form, was also to be used in the Type 30.

The new quad-cam engine, of which two 'live' versions had now followed the dummy to Cheshunt, was some 40 lbs heavier than its predecessor, and overall the Type 34 weighed some 70 lbs more than the Type 29. Again, a Lotus bell-housing mated the gearbox and engine. The latter now employed a Ford-developed Hilborn fuel-injection system, its mechanical pump driven from an inlet camshaft, eradicating the three electrical Bendix fuel pumps of the Type 29 sited under the driver's legs. The five fuel compartments within the 'tub' again housed FPT rubber bladders produced by Fireproof Tanks of Portsmouth, a manufacturer whose products and British base were later submerged in the flood of promotional material issued by the Speedway when Firestone USA introduced similar products. A sixth fuel tank (of aluminum encased in GRP) was positioned over the driver's legs ahead of the instrument panel.

Again the chassis was offset to the left (by 2^3/$_8$ inches). Len Terry: 'We definitely had to restrain our enthusiasm for having a more pronounced offset because if you went too far it made the car really unbalanced if the driver had a "moment" and it became more difficult for him to straighten it up again. It would steer

Ford's experimental quad-cam ran at the Speedway early in 1964 with this simple uncoupled exhaust system and Colotti gearbox on a Firestone-tyred Lotus 29 chassis, identifiable by the hub-height attachment of the upper rear radius rods, whereas the definitive Type 34s for the new season would have upper radius rods picking up at the top of the rear hub carriers. It is extremely difficult to identify with any certainty which of the 1963 Type 29 chassis this particular car may have been, but it was probably '29/1'. (Indianapolis Motor Speedway)

better one way than the other. I don't think the offset gave a huge advantage; it prevented weight transfer through corners and therefore helped to reduce tyre wear, but I don't think it increased cornering speeds. Nowadays, of course, they jack car weights and choose tyres of specific rolling diameters – it's all much more technical, but in some ways more of a compromise as the cars now race on both ovals and road circuits. I found the same situation when I joined Dan Gurney's All-American Racers team after leaving Team Lotus in 1965 – Dan wanted a design that could be used for both Indy and Formula 1, so I had to incorporate symmetrical suspension.'

Unlike the Type 29 and the 38 and 42 that were to follow, the Type 34 had no provision for fitting symmetrical suspension. One obvious change was the two-piece slotted (or air-deflector) windscreen on Jimmy's car; Dan preferred the previous style, possibly due to his extra height when seated in the car. He also experimented with various screen changes during practice, but kept to

Later testing, still with a Type 29 chassis, Ford's latest iteration of its quad-cam V8 engine now features cross-coupled in-vee exhaust manifolding and a German-made ZF transaxle in place of the former Colotti. The car is also shod here with prototype Dunlop racing tyres on Halibrand cast-alloy wheel rims. (Indianapolis Motor Speedway)

one that was considerably deeper and which can now be seen on the Type 29 in the Indy Museum. Jimmy's two-piece air-deflector version had first appeared on his Formula 1 car in practice for the previous season's Belgian Grand Prix, but he had gone back to the usual one-piece for the race.

Len Terry: 'When Colin explained what he wanted he said he had taken the idea from the windscreen design on the bridge of a destroyer. It gave improved vision in rain by the passage of deflected air through the opening, but there were doubts about whether large bugs and stones would be so deterred. However, Jimmy soon grew to like it, so it was adopted.'

In mid-January 'Laz' and Colin Riley were at Kingman for a test at which Bobby Marshman drove, while at Cheshunt Ford's Frank Zimmerman was outlining to Colin and myself his company's plans for 1964, seeking details of our financial proposals for the next stage of our relationship and clarifying the supply of quad-cam engines for our new Type 34s. Two of the new engines would arrive within a few days, one to go into chassis '29/2', the other into '29/1', which was to be returned to Cheshunt from Dearborn for the quad-cam installation before returning to America for a test programme.

After Frank returned home, a mass of cables flashed back and forth between Cheshunt and Dearborn, with additional confusion caused by Lotus Components' order for engines for its production Type 30 cars, which some people assumed were engines allocated to Team Lotus. At the same time I was chasing Ford's Dave Evans for the return of chassis '29/1'; I had also received a request from Ford of Britain for the loan of '29/2' for display on its stand at the Geneva Motor Show in the first two weeks of March, and as all three cars were now the property of Ford I asked their permission. The request was turned down on the basis that Ford had already sold '29/2' to Lindsey Hopkins and it was wanted for an Indy test in the first week of March. Dave's confirmation of this came on 13 February, while Colin Chapman and Steve Sanville, the Lotus engine and transmission engineer, were in Dearborn for meetings to discuss the quad-cam and its transmission; Colin was also scheduled to sign the on-going contract. It was obviously too late by that time to have '29/2' converted and delivered to Indy in time for the test at the beginning of March, and Colin reported the situation to Ford. He was obviously still keen to prevent the car being used, as he asked Ford to give him a rebuild specification, another time-delaying tactic. On 17 February, the day after Colin and Steve left Dearborn, came confirmation from Ford that Colin was carrying the refurbishment spec for '29/2', by that time referred to as 'the Hopkins car'.

March came and the still unconverted '29/2' remained in Cheshunt as our mechanics concentrated on building the new Type 34s. Some idea of how late the programme was running can be established by the dates of Len Terry's drawings. That for the new Lotus four-spoke magnesium-zirconium rear wheels was not finished until 24 February, that for the fronts, 4 March. These still had to go to the outside pattern-makers, then for casting and finally to be machined. Three weeks after the rear-wheel drawing had been approved came a design change altering the rim of the wheel, and three weeks after that, on 9 April, came another rim design change negating all previous progress; remember that we were due at the Speedway just three weeks after final design approval, complete with 12 front wheels.

As in 1963, the new quick-lift scissor jacks were among the last items to be made, and early running in the first week of May saw major changes to front and rear suspension geometry drawn at Cheshunt and air-freighted out. Regardless of the test scheduled for the first week in March, on the 12th I sent Evans a specification of the changes being made to '29/2', and this crossed with an almost irate and lengthy cable from Ford. In this they stated that 'due to confusion on your [Lotus's] part and the car not getting here until the end of March, we shall use the car we still have here, complete with latest engine for a 10/14 day test at Indy commencing March 16; we would like a Team Lotus mechanic to attend.' Later the same day, when someone obviously tumbled to the fact that Ford was now short of engines and had already sent a suitable engine to us in mid-January, came another cable requesting that we send it back for updating without delay!

From all this it can be accepted that Lindsey Hopkins/Bobby Marshman *were* initially scheduled to have '29/2', the car Dan had shunted at Indy, but that in view of our delayed rebuild they were forced to make do with '29/1'. It is also obvious that in the months to come the Ford test vehicle, whether run by Ford or by Hopkins, could have been any one of the three existing Type 29 chassis.

The 1964 contract that Colin signed followed the same lines as before and called for three new cars to be built, one to be the spare. Both the Milwaukee '200' (23 August) and Trenton (20 September) were included. Team Lotus was to continue as an 'independent contractor', Ford 'making available a sufficient number of Fairlane engines and parts built to a design and specifications agreed upon by the parties.' There would be a contribution to Team Lotus by Ford of $46,000 towards the design, development and manufacture of the three cars, together with those costs incurred in transportation, accommodation expenses and entry fees for the month of May at Indy. Any other costs, such as those incurred for entries at the two oval races, were to be approved after acceptance of detailed budgets. In addition, there would be a retainer of $20,000 payable on 1 May when the Brickyard opened, together with qualifying and success bonuses. Ownership title of each car would be in Lotus's name, that of the engines in Ford's, except that when a Ford engine was installed in a Lotus chassis, the title to the engine would pass to Lotus, such title reverting to Ford when the engine was removed. Team Lotus also agreed that it would not enter the oval races if Ford 'so request in writing before June 3rd 1964', a condition that was destined to play a large part in the story of that year . . .

Any publicity or statement issued by Lotus involving the name 'Ford' required 'prior written consent', and the words 'Powered by Ford' appearing on the cars were to be in a 'different size, color or script from the word "Lotus"'. Any additional sponsor-ship monies secured by Lotus would pass to Ford in their entirety (to help offset Ford's expenditure on the project), and additional testing agreed by both parties would be to Ford's account. Lotus would also extend to Ford, for a period of 30 days after the last oval race, the option to purchase any one, or all three, of the cars.

In converting a Type 29 from a push-rod to a quad-cam engine, the main differences, apart from the obvious changes of engine mounting (the unit was moved 7/16 inch towards the driver), concerned the fuel system, breathing arrangements, gear shift and body alterations, the roll-over bar moving from its previous mounting on the engine to one on the chassis. The gear shift for the Colotti's replacement ZF two-speed gearbox now incorporated a flexible drive to clear the changed engine and gearbox contours, and the three Bendix fuel pumps installed under the driver's legs in the Type 29 were replaced by a Hilborn-Ford pump mounted on the engine. The alterations to the chassis moved the top radius arms outboard of the pick-ups, while the lower arms were lengthened by 1/2 inch by fitting a longer-stemmed rose joint.

Mid-March also saw Fred Bushell chasing Ford's accountants to pay our Milwaukee and Trenton races and tests dues from 1963; apart from the usual aggravation and wastage of time involved, this also brought us into conflict with Jimmy's lawyers. Colin and I called them 'those Scottish bullocks', a particularly apt description for two most tiresome fellows, who, like most lawyers, appeared to keep a constant stream of letters flowing about nit-picking items in order to ingratiate themselves with their client while also earning as much as possible from him in fees. Jimmy's first year of driving for Team Lotus (1960) had been accomplished without a contract, and it was natural for Colin, running a business, to make a more secure arrangement for the second year, especially as organisations such as the fuel company supporting us financially required their own peace of mind.

For Jimmy's second season, he and Colin agreed terms personally, but the third year (1962) saw Jimmy leave such discussions and arrangements to lawyers; he was either not at ease negotiating with the highly skilled Chapman, or perhaps he felt that they would get a better deal for him. The bullocks' approach did nothing to soothe Colin, or anyone else at Team Lotus. They appeared unable, or possibly unwilling, to accept the standard financial structures of motor racing, causing us much exasperation and frustration. For instance, if we mentioned a retainer for Jimmy, payable upon qualification, they were soon in print insisting that it be paid up front. On one occasion they learned of the money refunded to us by Ford for the payment we had sent with our entries for Indianapolis, and claimed this as Jimmy's 'start money'. If such aggravations could have been settled by a quick telephone call, then all would have been well, but they could only convey acceptance or otherwise by means of copious correspondence. In desperation I tried another tack, talking to Jimmy about any item in dispute, saying that I could arrange payment as soon as he had quietened his beagles; this did little to enhance my relationship with Jimmy, but as I made clear on numerous occasions, I was employed by Colin, not by our drivers.

Chassis '29/2' was finally ready to return to the States in mid-March 1964. Its completion coincided with that of the first two EFLO Lotus-Cortinas, which were entered for two races at Sebring, a 350 km stock car race on 20 March followed by the International 12-Hours event the next day, and these left London Airport the preceding Sunday. Our crew for Sebring consisted of Colin, Jimmy, Dan and Ray Parsons – manager, two drivers for two cars, and one mechanic! The first race brought great amusement when Dan was sidelined out on the circuit, having shed a wheel, but he rejoined after a fine piece of mechanicking. In deciding to catch Jimmy by fair means or foul, he dodged through the straw bales lining the circuit, cutting out a part of each lap, a manoeuvre he repeated without being noticed other than by Jimmy, who couldn't understand where Dan had found the extra speed to catch him! Later they both enjoyed the joke immensely ...

After the race, in which Jimmy finished first in class and third overall behind a 7-litre Galaxie and a 5-litre Falcon, his Lotus-Cortina (registration 168 RUR) was prepared for the international 12-Hours race starting at 10 am the next day. Although Colin was keen to be his co-driver, eventually discretion won the day and Ray Parsons, no mean driver himself, got the seat. Incredibly the car survived the 12-Hours amongst the Ferraris, Porsches, Cobras, Corvettes and Alfa Romeos; of the 66 starters it finished second in class and 21st overall amongst the 35 finishers.

The Indy car followed the two saloons across the Atlantic three days later, complete with 12 Dunlop tyres to test, the continuing saga of its late appearance evident to the last. The BOAC air-freighter carrying it was caught in an airline strike in New York, and only a superb effort by our brokers saw it off-loaded on to a truck, its driver managing to evade the pickets on his journey to Newark Airport where a hastily arranged Slick Airlines reservation saw it safely on its way to Weir Cook at Indy. The Sunday of Sebring saw its final preparation, Colin, Jimmy and Dan arriving at the Speedway direct from Florida.

No Lotus records of this test survive, but from Jim Endruweit's cable to Ford a few days after running it can be seen there had been problems with the throttle linkage triggering a re-design programme at Dearborn. The engine had also run with an exhaust system by Derrington, our usual supplier, and Ford had taken this, along with our new-style Type 34 radiator, for further tests and examination.

David Lazenby and new recruit Mike Underwood serviced this session, and when they left Indy it effectively marked the end of our association with the Type 29s other than the rebuilding of one or two cars for Hopkins. All three cars were now the property of Ford of America, as I reminded them during talks regarding insurance for the forthcoming race; it was our responsibility to provide third party insurance cover for $1 million as well as insuring the cars themselves. The insurance cover premiums for our other racing cars while 'self-propelled' was prohibitive, yet I could find extremely good terms for our Indy cars; the scheme lasted three years until a British TV programme depicted Indy racing complete with the usual thrills and spills, and the next morning I received a call from one of our underwriters announcing an enormous premium increase. None of them had previously had any idea of the dangers involved!

With the programme of work within our Indy section (which now of course included sports cars) increasing in 1964, it was necessary for us to take on more staff. Mike Underwood had joined David Lazenby and Colin Riley at the beginning of the season, and now we recruited Graham Clode, John Duxberry and an Australian former ship's engineer, Jim Smith. Mike had joined Lotus Components the previous year, having served an aircraft fitter's apprenticeship with Armstrong Whitworth in Coventry before spending three years in the RAF. His initial salary was £11 a week: 'It was terrible money, but the work interested me – my first task was working on the Formula Junior Type 27 and for accommodation I moved in with David Lazenby.'

Mike began the 1964 season as a member of our Indy section, working first on the buck for the new Type 30 sports car; it was not until mid-February that the Type 34 build commenced, in parallel with quad-cam installation in the rebuilt Type 29.

Mike recalled a typical Lotus incident that took place shortly after he joined: 'A Lotus sports car needed delivering to a customer in Portugal and as Jim Smith, a mechanic with Team, had some free time it was suggested that we go together. Driving a small Ford van and trailer, we did the round trip to Lisbon without encountering any problems, but there was some surprise when we returned to Cheshunt. Firmly convinced that they would not see the van or trailer again, management had purchased a cheap old rig specially for the trip!'

CHAPTER FIVE

1964: 'It's Only a Sport'

Our first Indy Type 34 was air freighted to America on 27 April 1964, the second and third on the 29th. David Lazenby set off the same day, Jim Endruweit and the rest of the crew two days later, a great deal of car building destined to continue in our Speedway garage.

As Indy running opened, Colin, Jimmy and Dan were at Silverstone for the Formula 1 race. That was a busy Saturday for Jimmy, driving Formula 1, a Lotus Elan, a Lotus-Cortina and a Type 30. He won his class in the Elan and Cortina, but fuel-injection problems sidelined the Lotus 30 on the start line. He joined the race eight laps down and, although excluded from the results, promptly set fastest lap! In the Formula 1 race his engine seized solid after he had led for the first five laps.

That same weekend Ray Parsons had run the two Sebring Lotus-Cortinas at Laguna Seca in California with drivers Sir John Whitmore and Mike Spence. Running out of class, they

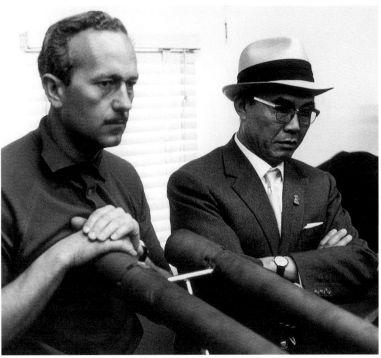

Grim-faced, Colin Chapman and Soichiro Honda ponder the quad-cam Ford V8-engined Lotus 34s in Gasoline Alley in 1964. The Japanese industrialist's motor-cycle company had only recently entered the four-wheeled world, and at this time its original transverse-V12 Formula 1 car was under test prior to its racing debut in the German Grand Prix at Nürburgring in August. (G. Crombac)

Team's garage in Gasoline Alley was often a shambles until the Guv'nor would appear on the scene and the hard-pressed, dog-tired mechanics would have a tidying blitz. Here's Dan's 34 stripped out, revealing the 'bath-tub' stressed-skin chassis structure, right-hand gearchange and linkage and suspension detail. That dartboard is a nice reminder of the pubs back home . . . (Indianapolis Motor Speedway)

Maintaining a low-profile – the author's loaned Lotus Elan courtesy car with friend – Ella English – waiting in the queue to enter the Speedway, 1964 . . .

had finished fifth and seventh respectively.

Colin decreed that I should go to Indy this year, and I arrived there on 2 May. As he and Jimmy had had problems with laundry and meal arrangements during their stay in the house Rodger Ward had arranged the previous year, this time all Team personnel stayed at the Speedway Holiday Inn.

An interesting facet of Team Lotus life throughout the association of Colin and Jimmy was their preference for sharing a twin-bedded room if they were at a circuit on their own. Bearing in mind how professional each of them was, this provided an ideally relaxed debriefing period for each to talk to the other. Compared to the extravagant motor-homes evident at race meetings today, it was also highly cost-effective!

When I arrived at the Holiday Inn's front desk I was handed a wad of messages from people around America, most unknown to me, wanting me to contact them. After speaking to the third or fourth caller it occurred to me that such a thing was likely to become a fact of life in Indianapolis. Some were American Lotus road car owners who simply wanted to make contact with someone from the factory, while some had detailed lists of spares required, and hoped that I could have them shipped out with ours. Others were rather more difficult to pacify; some were girls anxious to meet Jimmy or Dan, some, of both sexes, were simply race fans keen to obtain a pit pass, and others – already hooked

by the Beatles – merely wanted to hear an English voice to ask, inevitably, did I know or live near them?

Others again were mothers or fathers keen for me to meet their son and daughter. This was middle America – they were not seeking employment or any favours, but simply wanted their offspring to meet an Englishman. My apology and explanation that I had only minimal time to myself was not always accepted in good grace, and more calls would follow. To ask the front desk not to pass through such calls did not work; there were many different switchboard operators and it was ridiculous to expect them to judge which were genuine calls and which were not.

On occasion the callers would present themselves at the motel's front desk saying that they had an appointment. One was an English-born mother who had, she assured me, married into a Red Indian family, and was accompanied by a daughter in her 20s. That was one of a million stories I was to hear, which to an Englishman seemed barely plausible, added to which the mother suddenly got to her feet and left, saying that she knew her daughter had lots of things to talk to me about! Perhaps, strange to relate, both turned out to be thoroughly straightforward people with whom I was to enjoy home cooking and family parties over the following two years . . .

In 1963 Ford had hinted at, but failed to provide, courtesy cars for the Team, and when Lotus Cars' American mid-West dealer,

Span Inc, run by Jim Spencer, offered to help in 1964, Colin gladly accepted the loan of three red, suitably decalled Elans for our use, while the crew had the standard and enormous American rent-a-cars. It was not long before I wished I had drawn one of those, as the minute Elan was way below other drivers' mirror vision and seemed highly vulnerable. With my month's mileage totalling 2–3,000 miles, I was quite pleased when the time came to hand the Elan back.

To explain this high mileage when the focus of our attention lay within walking distance of our motel rooms, I should clarify my role as 'competitions manager' at Indy. Everyday tasks entailed everything associated with the title, and Colin generally gave me free rein in providing organisational structures, budgets, detailing forthcoming Team movements, arranging contracts and all the minutiae of motor racing detail that I found completely fascinating. 'On-track' management, or responsibility for running the cars, was solely Colin's – no written rule was required to establish that. The fact that I had no technical background (and no pretensions in that direction) suited both of us admirably, and he would sometimes remark as much. My brief period as a trainee mechanic at Allards in 1949–50 had left me in no doubt that such work was not for me. In those now far-off days I assumed that my lack of interest in the mechanical side spelled the end of any ideas I might have about securing a job in motor racing. Management seemed to be the domain of either former racing drivers, skilled engineers or those with an 'in' through personal or family contacts. Additionally, such jobs in those days were extremely few and far between.

When John Cooper had allowed me to become involved with the administrative side of his Cooper Formula 1 team, I could not believe my good fortune; I was actually being *paid* merely for some imagination and a fascination for motor racing. With Esso backing, I produced a booklet *The Cooper Golden Years*, of which 20,000 were sold; I sent a copy to Colin Chapman, and later, when I was about to join the Camoradi team, we met at a party and he invited me to join Lotus to write a similar book. I am doing it now, 33 years later!

One event that I assumed was an Indy tradition was explained to me one evening as I sat in the bar at the Holiday Inn. I had noticed a gathering of girls and women – always the same – of a wide range of ages, who regularly occupied one corner of the room, laughing and joking, obviously thoroughly enjoying themselves. I commented on them to an Indy regular one evening.

'Yes, it's a sad little group,' he replied. 'They're the widows of racing drivers killed in racing around the States over the years, and they always meet up here in the month of May . . .'

That rather steadied me.

Although I enjoyed my free-ranging tasks within Team Lotus, I have to admit that a large percentage of them were focused on nursemaiding Colin. Although anyone with a macho inclination would have turned up his nose at some of the jobs, I have to say that I thoroughly enjoyed it. I treated the whole thing as a highly competitive game, always striving to stay one step ahead of the Guv'nor, and trying to imagine what might come into his mind next so as to be well prepared. To win was mighty satisfying, especially when Colin suddenly realised that I had read his mind well in advance and had all details catered for! His knowing smile and accompanying comment was ample reward. Mind you, there were also explosive blasts when I expounded my theory only to discover that I had picked wrong, but his comments were more often than not entirely fair. As to my views on racing drivers in general, Colin always considered that I was too lenient in my judgement of their merits, and he soon dubbed me 'President of the Down-and-Out Brigade'!

As 'nursemaid', thoroughly bored with endless hours of track running, I became Team's 'gofer', hence my Elan's high mileage. Collecting components made by outside workshops, visiting the heat-treatment facility, arranging meetings away from the track to explore financial deals or business relationships, returning to the motel to make confidential telephone calls, visiting local airfields to investigate the latest 'mod cons' for the company aircraft – these were just a few of my missions around Indiana. To my mind, keeping the lid on our administrative pot was far more exciting than any motor race!

Bobby Marshman had completed an enormous test mileage in one, or perhaps both, of Ford's Type 29s over the winter and this showed as soon as he began running. It remains uncertain whether he was now driving Gurney's shunted car from 1963, but it became obvious that he was fully acclimatised to a 'funny car'. Considering that Ford had produced around 25 quad-cam engines for Indy, it seemed strange that front-runners such as Parnelli Jones and A. J. Foyt were not on the company's list; one can only guess at what politicking had gone on behind the scenes, but the fact remained that both Jones and Foyt were again in Offy-engined roadsters; Ford had approached Colin to allow a drive in our third car, but the importance of our retaining it in case of an unforeseen problem was too great.

It was Jimmy who first introduced me to A. J. Foyt. He had suggested that we go around the track watching others at work, and we had first walked down to Turn One where a smiling A. J. hurried across to Jimmy with some cheery cracks delivered in his Texan drawl. Later, when we collected one of our cars that we had driven around to other parts of the track, Jimmy gave me a word of warning.

'If you take my advice,' he said 'don't shake hands with the bigger lads here – give a wave or keep your hands in your pockets. When I first came here I shook hands with one who had the most enormous hands. He sort of rolled my hand over and gave it a great squeeze and I couldn't use it properly for a hell of a time!'

Watching practice was an entertainment shared with other race drivers standing in ones and twos and comparing notes on their current situations while watching those running. They were, without exception, extremely pleasant and anxious to chat and compare notes on European-style racing, but what struck me immediately was the tremendous age of some of them. On my first visit to the pit lane I had seen one car hurtle down the main straight on only three wheels, the fourth bouncing against the retaining wall but fortunately not running into anyone's path. An American standing next to me offered the news that it would be a little while before the driver re-appeared back in the pit lane; it transpired that he was well into his 50s, a rotund grandfather who could only vacate the cockpit with the help of his crew!

Walking across the competitors' car park one morning, who should come roaring towards me on a large motor-cycle smoking a pipe, complete with a very attractive girl on the pillion, but my old friend from Cooper and Camoradi days, Masten Gregory. Masten was godfather to my elder son, and while we did not meet up very often, we enjoyed numerous telephone chats.

'Good Lord, Masten, where have you appeared from?' I asked.

'New York,' he drawled in his deep voice, grinning through his heavy-lensed spectacles. (He used specially made goggles fitted with similar lenses, and on one occasion found that his latest batch had had the lenses reversed; he maintained that his new braking distances had been frightening, but worth at least

Dan Gurney's white and blue US-liveried works Lotus-Ford Type 34 ready to be fuelled at the Humble depot in Gasoline Alley, jacked up at the front to ensure full filling and thus a true tank capacity measure. The moulded glassfibre-clad scuttle fuel tank above the driver's legs is clearly visible in this shot. (Indianapolis Motor Speedway)

Masten Gregory, works Cooper Formula 1 driver during the time that the author managed that team's affairs – an Indy hopeful.

another second a lap!) He had indeed come from New York – nothing special in that, except that he had come on his motor-cycle complete with the lovely popsy now smiling so coyly at me.

In 1963 he had been bumped from the '500' grid, and now he had a drive with Mickey Thompson. His delight at the thought of the forthcoming race was, as usual, infectious, and I enjoyed his quips about life in general. Later, when Colin noticed his name among the list of runners, he said, 'Cor, your old mate's here – shall we sign him up?'

All I could think of on the spur of the moment was, 'Well at least we'd have more laughs around the place.'

Colin's response was a heavenward roll of the eyes!

Almost the first person to offer genuine help on my arrival was Nancy, wife of racing driver Eddie Sachs, the much acclaimed 'Clown Prince' of American auto racing. Possessor of the great sense of humour of a music hall comedian, Eddie had competed at the Speedway for the past seven years, his sense of fun coupled with an expertise that had seen him rewarded with a second and a third place, and frequent front-running. He had a soft spot for the foreign invaders and asked Nancy to see that everyone in our crew was well looked after. For all his sense of fun he was a strict disciplinarian, and unlike some of his fellow drivers he did not drink and was always in bed by 10 pm; no doubt his suggestion that Nancy should look after us was two-edged, and would guarantee that he could sleep in peace!

Nancy's female friends were, to an Englishman's eyes, a wild

Dan ready for an early run in the spare new Type 34, showing off its high top-rear radius rod suspension geometry, roll-over bar mounted upon the chassis – rather than the engine – and hastily taped-on taller windscreen section to protect the lanky American's head from undue aerodynamic buffeting. The car has Dunlop tyres on Halibrand wheels, by modern standards tiny disc brakes, blue stripe, numbers and lettering on overall white livery. (Indianapolis Motor Speedway)

bunch, keen to have fun at the drop of a hat. On Monaco Sunday some of our crew decided to have a few hours' relaxation and, led by Nancy and her group of friends, we soon found ourselves seated at lunch in a smart restaurant. After some drinks and an excellent meal, one of Nancy's friends suggested that we all go on to her home. I asked where she lived, and when she told me, it didn't mean a thing. I asked which direction, as we all had our own cars.

'It's down in little ol' Tennessee,' she beamed.

It sounded a long way to me, and with only a short break planned away from the track I felt uneasy.

'I think it might make too long a drive,' I said.

'Oh, we're not driving,' she said. 'It's around 350 miles away, but my plane's at the airport and we can all go in that.'

We all made our polite excuses, and returned to the Speedway.

Coming from Silverstone right at the start of May meant that Jimmy and Dan did not start running until Monday the 4th, and with Monaco the following weekend they and Colin would be leaving again the following Thursday. On Tuesday the celebratory flags were out for A. J. and his fastest laps to date at just over

154 mph. That held for three days until Parnelli got up to speed, turning in a 156.223 mph lap.

Meanwhile Jimmy was securing pole position in Monaco; he led away but an uncharacteristic error, giving some straw bales a heavy thump, eventually led to his car's rear anti-roll bar coming adrift. Dropping to third place in a pit stop, he was forced to stop near the end with zero oil pressure. Dan, driving a Brabham, had

Dan at high speed in his Type 34, chassis '34/1', sans engine cover but with his requisite tall windscreen transparency fitted. He never really managed to get it together throughout the month of May for the 1964 '500'. (Dave Friedman Photo Collection)

also led the race, but retired with a defunct gearbox; he had also suffered petrol burns on his legs, which with the rush to return to Indianapolis could not be treated properly until he arrived.

I met them at Weir Cook airport on the Monday, and with Dan still obviously in some considerable discomfort, attempted to find a doctor willing to give some attention 'after hours'. Used to 24-hour service in Europe, I was amazed to come up against a brick wall, and eventually Dan had to settle for some jars of ointment from a local hospital, also devoid of doctors.

While they had been winging their way from Monaco, Bobby Marshman had really got into his stride, lapping at 156 mph. On Tuesday he went over 157, with Rodger Ward in a rear-engined Watson (also Ford quad-cam-powered) next at 155 mph. Then, as Jimmy re-familiarised himself with the Brickyard, Marshman was lapping at over 158, but the Scot worked up quickly and lapped faster each time he appeared on the track. Soon he began to nudge Marshman's times …

This was a media man's dream, and the press besieged our garage. Local TV coverage meant that every member of our team became instantly recognisable, which made life outside the track somewhat hazardous. The crush of people swarming all over our motel made it virtually impossible to walk anywhere without being accosted, either by fans, hangers-on or the press. Lotus owners also flocked in, seemingly from all over the country, anxious to show us their cars and seeking local accommodation as the build-up to the coming qualifying weekend approached fever pitch, quite unlike anything we had previously experienced. Our Elan road cars, instantly recognisable even without their large decals, provided no cover, and trips around the surrounding area triggered a carnival atmosphere as other enthusiastic drivers tagged on behind; the moment we parked they would leap out and instantly engage us in conversation.

An example of the natural promotional attitude of America came in the form of a free gift for anyone purchasing more than a certain amount of gasoline; Autolite, the sparking plug arm of Ford, produced a 7-inch-long plastic model of our Type 29. Remarkably well detailed for a give-away, it was complete with offset suspension and 'chromed' components, and surprisingly – considering our American team driver – depicted Jimmy's car in its green and yellow livery, not Dan's in good old American white and blue.

I always preferred breakfast in my room, if only to prevent Colin attacking it. He refused the kind of dish ordered by Jimmy and myself, convinced in his own mind that by ordering instead a simple plate of toast he was sticking rigidly to his latest diet, and was thus able to complain loudly about the uncivilised quality and quantity of American food. However, he would then 'peck away' at both our two breakfasts, virtually devouring them if we should be called away to the telephone.

Colin's attitude to all this razzmatazz was inconsistent. He always made it plain that he wanted me to join him and Jimmy in the restaurant for breakfast to discuss the forthcoming day. We

British Racing Green beauty – Jimmy's Lotus-Ford 34, believed to have been chassis '34/3', all dolled up and ready to run at Indy '64. Spoked Lotus wheels have replaced the Halibrands among myriad other design changes from the 1963 Type 29. (Indianapolis Motor Speedway)

also had to contend with being stared at by people on adjoining tables, who after a short time could contain themselves no longer and would come to our table for autographs or a chat. Colin and I were always being called away to the telephone, and when we returned poor Jimmy would be surrounded by 'fans' all earnestly talking away at him, and we would have to ask them to leave; then another call would come and the whole process would be repeated.

Colin's request for people to desist could take various forms, the majority of them relatively rude to an American way of thinking. However, when I suggested that we all have breakfast in one of our rooms to accomplish a lot more in considerably less time (and be able to enjoy warm food!), he brushed the idea aside. Yet within the confines of the track he would harbour no nonsense from people he did not know starting conversations, cutting them dead in their tracks almost as soon as they opened their mouths. 'Where we come from we don't speak until invited to,' he might say, or 'Do you mind?', continuing on his way without pausing.

During practice we had run with both Firestone and Dunlop tyres, the latter proving faster than the American products, but with a reduced life. As qualifying approached so talk turned to which tyres to use. One day I was talking to someone through the wire fence surrounding the garage area when Colin walked over looking forlorn.

'Looks like I'm the one who has to decide which tyres we're going with,' he said.

I asked him what the drivers' opinions were. 'Oh, you know them,' he replied. 'When it comes down to actually making a decision they just shuffle their feet.'

I asked him what Ford's thoughts were.

'They're much the same, but I decided this morning to get a positive answer from them and they're either at meetings or just plain uncontactable. I've been on the phone to Dearborn several times today but can't get hold of anyone.'

He stood looking into space, his mind miles away, then said, 'Get onto Firestone and arrange a meeting for tonight. Don't broadcast it to anyone. Let's make it in your room and I'll meet them there – it's quiet. See how you get on and let me know the arrangements – I'll be in my room later.'

My motel room was ideal for a confidential meeting. It was a large single at the rear of the building and people could park beside an outside staircase which went straight up to it.

Although we had a phone in the garage, the calls I had to make were classified, so I drove back to the motel. When I called the Firestone office at the track there were only tyre fitters there; management had gone. I tried the Speedway Motel where they stayed, which was the mecca for the gin rummy and poker tournaments that seemed to be the highlight of off-duty hours for the motor racing executives that month of May. Again no luck. Next I tried the Cove, a favourite watering hole for just about everyone connected with auto racing while at the track. Still no luck.

In desperation, as it was well past office hours, I telephoned

Tail-on, the ZF transaxle uncowled at the rear of Jimmy's assigned '34/3', aiming into Turn One at the Speedway. (Indianapolis Motor Speedway)

Firestone headquarters in Akron. Security put me through to the office of Bill McCrary, Firestone's Director of Racing, and his secretary answered. Mr McCrary was at that moment in New York attending an important meeting; he was with his boss, Mr McCrory (a similarity of names that sometimes created confusion). As head of Firestone racing, Bill was the man I was after, and perhaps the fact that he was with his boss would prove useful. I explained that Mr Chapman would like to meet Mr McCrary as soon as possible, and the secretary said that she would get back to me.

Half an hour later the phone rang. The secretary explained that she had managed to get through to the corporate aircraft they were using; it was about to leave New York, and had been re-routed direct to Weir Cook. They would be with us in around 2½ hours. It was obvious both had recognised the importance of the call. I then rang Colin, who said that he would be in his room waiting for me to let him know when they arrived.

I had calculated when that would be, and when the time came and passed I phoned Colin to make sure he had not gone to bed. His response took me aback.

'I've changed my mind,' he said in a matter of fact tone. 'I won't need to talk to them now – you deal with it.'

Waiting for the now dreaded knock on my door I rehearsed my explanation and words of apology. I had been stunned by Colin's action, particularly as he did not consider that it would be good manners to clarify the situation personally to our two guests who had travelled so far.

Eventually, after what seemed like years, there came that dreaded knock on the door. Bill McCrary, whom I had met before, opened the conversation with a brisk, 'Hi, Andrew, are we meeting Colin here?'

Jimmy and the 34 back on Team's pit lane marks after his new qualifying record of 158.828 mph and a new one-lap qualifying record of 159.377 – (left) 'Tell us what it was like out there . . .' The Lotus-Ford's Dunlop tyres might have been sticky and quick over four laps, but they would not endure come race day. (Both Indianapolis Motor Speedway)

I fumbled my selected speech, and went straight in.

'I'm very sorry, but I'm afraid the meeting is off . . .'

Before I could get any further, both turned and walked away without saying a word. The sheer discomfort of that occasion has remained with me ever since . . .

As David Lazenby was to remark later, '. . . in 1963 we ran Firestone tyres and should have had Dunlops. In 1964 we ran Dunlop when we should have had Firestone . . .'

On the Friday night before first qualifying we attended a Ford press conference at the Speedway Motel. There Benson Ford and Lee Iacocca talked of their company's involvement in the forthcoming race, and detailed the progress of the nine Ford-engined cars to date. Ford's saturation of the Speedway was immense; they had taken over the ground floor of the Tower building at the track, inviting the press to use it as their headquarters for the duration. Everywhere you went there were Ford Mustangs, the new model announced only the previous month, and numerous examples had been loaned to the press corps and race committee so that their special car parks would be awash with sparkling Mustangs; the City of Indianapolis also succumbed to the excitement of Ford's increasingly revitalised sporting image, and put on a parade of suitably decalled Mustangs around the streets.

The area immediately outside the Speedway had been congested with parked vehicles waiting to get in for qualifying some days prior to the trials, and the members of our crew, led by Colin, agreed tactics for speedy entry and exit manoeuvres; in case of dire emergency, such as a requirement to get quickly to a machine shop in the town, a car was left in the motel car park, which was readily accessible on foot.

According to the Speedway's publicity machine, over 250,000 people and 48,000 cars attended the first day of qualifying. Even at 6.30 that morning the atmosphere within the track was electric and quite unlike anything I had experienced before. Jimmy's composure throughout the day never changed; calm and methodical throughout, he could just as easily have been waiting to drive his Lotus Elite around Brands Hatch. His qualifying run was quite extraordinary; when his speeds were announced after each lap there came a thunderous roar of approval from the enormous crowd. One lap was over 160 mph, his average for the four laps 158.828 mph, over 7 mph quicker than the old record.

I had received assurances from many throughout my stay that American fans in general had felt very badly about Jimmy's treatment the previous year; whether it was this or just the crowd's approval of his completed run, their noisy appreciation as he returned to the pit lane was unforgettable. Like us, A. J. and Parnelli were running on alcohol, and both had run into engine problems during the morning's warm-up, requiring engine changes before their timed runs.

That day belonged to Lotus-Ford; the front row were all rear-engined cars. Jimmy took pole, Dan was sixth (154.487 mph) and Marshman in his Lindsey Hopkins-entered Type 29, or *Pure Firebird Special* was second with 157.867. We had run with a Pure Oil contract the previous year, but later our principal sponsor in other spheres, Esso Petroleum, had introduced us to their American counterparts at Humble Oil in Houston, and now we carried their Enco decals. Strangely, I had initially contacted Clark Petroleum, but they failed to connect the two names as worthwhile.

To Ford's American supporters it had been their day, with the new quad-cam engine installed in all three cars on the front of the starting grid (Rodger Ward's new rear-engined car was third fastest), and with a fourth, Dan's, on the second row alongside the roadsters of Foyt and Jones, Parnelli faster but nearly 4 mph adrift of Jimmy's best. The advantages of the 'funny car' concept had been confirmed . . .

As soon as Jimmy had finished his run, he changed quickly and left for the airport. It was the three-day Whitsun holiday in England and he was entered for a small race meeting at Mallory Park the very next day, followed by another minor meeting at

Formidable combination – respected Indy car entrant Lindsey Hopkins with his star driver Bobby Marshman in the Lotus 29 Pure Firebird Special. Note the outrigged oil tank modification since the '63 '500'. Livery was red on white. (Indianapolis Motor Speedway)

Crystal Palace the day after that! After an overnight flight into London Airport he enjoyed a police escort up to Leicestershire, where he won both the Formula 2 and sports car races, the latter in a Type 30, as well as establishing new record laps in both events. Then it was on to Crystal Palace where he won the saloon car race, but a plug lead came adrift in his Formula 2 car and the pit stop dropped him from contention. Winner of that race was an unknown Austrian driver named Jochen Rindt . . .

Meanwhile Colin and Dan stayed on at the Brickyard, using the time to try full-tank running. However, the beginning of the week brought disquieting events. First, Dan's car began throwing chunks of rubber from its Dunlop rear tyres, the failure bringing hordes of Ford personnel and pressmen, not to mention alarmed members of the USAC safety team, or scrutineers as we would call them, to our garages. Interminable discussions then followed, Colin spending ages on the telephone to Dick Jeffrey, racing manager of Dunlop Tyres, back in Birmingham, England. Soon a plan was agreed: there must have been a rare production mishap when the tyres were made, and Dunlop would now produce more and fly them to us as soon as possible. Unfortunately, as we all ruefully guessed later, with the Whitsun holiday scheduled the following weekend a makeshift workforce was enlisted to whom the name Indianapolis meant as much as Constantinople. We did not know it yet, but ours was a lost cause.

Not long after our tyre discussions had quietened down, our

garage was visited by the police. Our senior local helper, Forrest Hughes, had been reported missing and they questioned us over what we knew of him. Forrest had been enlisted the previous year for his local knowledge, and our crew had taken to him immediately; when he had presented himself at our garage just two weeks previously we were delighted to re-engage him. He was 68 years old, had a 35-year-old mistress and a gun in the glove pocket of his car. To us he was the archetypal movie American.

We had last seen him the previous evening, when we had given him $400 cash to pay local bills. We all rejected any suggestion that he might have taken the money and run, and a quick phone round confirmed that he had indeed made all his calls. Two days later his body was found floating in a gravel pit; he was still wearing his glasses and baseball cap and the coroner recorded death by drowning. This whole sombre episode has remained a mystery ever since.

When Colin, Jimmy and Dan left for Europe again for the Dutch Grand Prix, the sense of relief was almost tangible. The lads, our workers, were exhausted, and Nancy Sachs came to the rescue with an invitation to Team Lotus to accompany her to The Embers niterie in downtown Indianapolis. It was an hilarious evening suitably enhanced by copious amounts of firewater, although the main act was deemed as below standard by Nancy. Her shouts of 'Get off!' resulted in her being invited to take over, which she did to roars of enthusiasm from the audience. Whether Nancy's tap dance and singing act was an improvement is not for me to say, but the experience was certainly enlivening!

The crew was soon back at work, weighed down with Colin's inevitably long job list, and some members asked what I could do to provide some female company, regardless of how brief a time. They had worked solidly from the beginning of the month apart from two fleeting excursions lasting mere hours, and now they were approaching the end of their third week of round-the-clock labour. I sought advice from an American acquaintance, and the next day he said he could provide an excellent solution. So that others could sleep, we agreed to use my room for the tryst, and I would move elsewhere for the night. I sorted out the finances and, spot on 2 am, a young lady arrived at my room. The lads had drawn straws to establish who the lucky fellow would be; I duly knocked on his door and we swopped rooms.

Some of the crew were gathered in my 'new' room and we sat around chatting idly, surmising how well the liaison might be progressing. About half an hour later our colleague returned to derisive comments regarding his staying power, but he was white faced.

'The Old Man's on the phone for you in your room,' he said.

Cursing my failed plan, I hurried back. The call was a long one and I soon became engrossed in making notes, sitting on my bed in which lay a complete stranger, no doubt wondering what all the commotion was about.

When I put the phone down I apologised to her for the interruption and went back to the other room, but two had gone to

bed and the remainder were sitting fast asleep in their clothes where they had been chatting only half an hour before. I could only rouse one, and he summed it up: 'Forget sex, we've got to be up at six. G'night.'

I paid the young lady, telling her that it was an advance for our next attempt. There never was one.

One evening towards the end of the month we met my acquaintance who had helped us, and he was with the young lady. He introduced her to us. She was his wife.

The Dutch Grand Prix was being held on the same weekend as final Indy qualifying. Dan took pole, but retired; Jimmy won. Then it was back to the Speedway for 'Carburation Day', the one period of practice allowed prior to the race. The newly moulded Dunlops had by now arrived, but there was insufficient time left to accumulate the running required to prove that they were safe …

The extensive and excitable media coverage of our front row success no doubt helped to swell spectator numbers on race day, over 350,000 cramming themselves into the Speedway on an early morning that was far from warm and noticeably windy. The size of the invasion had already been brought home to me; we had been inundated with requests from close associates of Team Lotus for rooms over race weekend, and I had finally had to hand my room over and seek another elsewhere. The best I could do was at a motel 40 miles away!

After the programmed pre-race fanfares and displays, the cars lined up on the grid. David Lazenby, scrutinising the various cars, remarked on the new oil-pipe arrangement on Bobby Marshman's Type 29; instead of it being hidden away in the safety of the inverted 'V', which was part of the underside of the 'tub', the Hopkins car now carried it outside the 'tub's left-hand curvature, vulnerably close to the track.

'I wonder if they know what they're doing?' mused David.

As the Ford Mustang pace car pulled off to release a clean rolling grid formation, Jimmy, using his low first gear, leapt into an almost instant and appreciable lead. His first lap was a new record, at 149.775 over 6 mph quicker than Parnelli's 1963 143.335. His second lap set another record at 154.615. Behind him was Marshman, Lotus thus running first and second.

RAC timekeeper Cyril Audrey was supporting us once more, and he, Colin and myself were seated at a lone table on a platform resting on the low wall that separated the pit lane from the rear walkway. Holding a thick sheaf of paper strips, it was my job to write down the race numbers of as many cars as I could as all 33 flashed past us every minute. To do this I never moved my head and wrote blindly, as to look down could mean missing four or five cars. A lap over, I would pass a strip to Colin, to enable him to compile his lap chart, a formidable task with so many cars covering such ultra-quick laps.

As Jimmy went past us for the second time I saw a great mushroom of thick black smoke abruptly billowing skywards above Turn Four, like a mini atom bomb. Colin, his mind full of numbers, yelled 'Where's Jimmy?' When I bawled that he had gone by, Colin's next thought was for Dan. Almost as Colin shouted his

Pace lap – the 33-strong starting field for the '64 '500' streams in formation out of Turn One behind the Mustang pace car. Clark, Marshman and Ward are in row one from Jones, ultimate winner Foyt and Gurney in row two. Dave MacDonald and Eddie Sachs are respectively in the centres of rows five and six. (Indianapolis Motor Speedway)

name, I saw his car go past and told Colin so. By this time all hell had broken loose – fire wagon and ambulance sirens blasted our eardrums as they appeared as if from nowhere. Even in those far-off days, the Speedway's safety services were second to none, making Europeans deeply embarrassed with thoughts of what passed for 'safety' at other circuits. Here at Indy the 'wrecker trucks' were often on the move before the car even hit the wall.

The yellow lights immediately flashed on, quickly followed by red, stopping the race. The fire-fighters on Turn Four were still struggling to extinguish the flames when Jimmy slowly led the

Pace lap – Bobby Marshman signals that Rodger Ward is breaking rank as the front row grumbles round behind the pace car. Jimmy's 34 is on pole, the Firebird Special *29 centre, Ward's* Kaiser Aluminum Special *Watson-Offy – following the Cooper and Lotus lead into rear-engined configuration – on the outside. Qualifying speeds were, respectively, 158.828, 157.857 and 156.406 mph. (Indianapolis Motor Speedway)*

Team's lap scoring set-up on the pit wall, wholly unprotected from the weather. Colin sits on the left, RAC timekeeper Cyril Audrey to the right, with the author in natty suit and suede shoes taking the Guv'nor's latest instructions . . . (G. Crombac)

surviving field through the smoke after a brief halt caused by a total lack of visibility. He told us that there were cars lying and burning all over the place, but could give no specific details.

Finally, a dreadful tragedy was officially confirmed. Eddie Sachs had been killed, Dave MacDonald critically burned, Ronnie Duman badly burned, and Johnny Rutherford slightly burned. Of the others caught up in the accident, Norm Hall, Bobby Unser and Chuck Stevenson were badly shaken but unhurt. Perhaps the most fortunate was Duman who, dazed by his car's impact with the wall, had sat in the cockpit as it began to burn, then clambered out slowly to roll on the grass as the safety crew reached him. Not long afterwards the flames reached his car's fuel tank, which then exploded. Fortunately flying debris had not gone into the packed spectator enclosure, although a great many people had been forced to move away quickly due to the intense heat.

Jimmy released his seat belts and slowly climbed out to sit on the track, using his car's left front wheel as a back rest, quietly chatting to members of our crew kneeling around him. After a while he beckoned me over.

'Don't look so worried,' he said. 'It's only a sport.'

It was to take nearly two hours to clear the track and resume the day's programme, and I walked back to our garage to enjoy a comforting cigarette. As I got to Gasoline Alley I had to push through a crowd of people gathered around a large vehicle

resembling an estate car, into the clear glass windows of which the spectators were peering. Brightly painted, it had been halted by the crush of race crews going about their business as they prepared for the re-start. Impossible to distinguish what it was because of the throng, I pushed my way through and peered in to see something completely unrecognisable lying under crisp white sheets. I asked a bystander what it was.

'It's Dave MacDonald,' he replied.

He was quite obviously very badly hurt, but unknown to me the Shelby Cobra star had only a very short time to live. I couldn't believe what I had seen, nor could I understand the unforgivable thoughtlessness of the ambulance curtains not having been drawn. The onlookers' curiosity was completely beyond me. Deeply shocked, and not a little sickened, I moved on.

Dan Gurney: 'Dave MacDonald was a team-mate of mine with the Shelby Cobras – a friendly guy, not much experienced, very much a car-control kind of driver. But at Indy he was a Babe in the Wood. His Mickey Thompson car, with the small Sears tyres, all independent suspension and that exceptionally low build, was also equipped with a 100-gallon tank to minimise pit stops. One

'Don't look so worried . . . it's only a sport.' After the horrendous opening lap multiple collision in which Sachs and MacDonald were fatally injured, Jimmy sits against the front wheel of his 34, parked on the front straightaway, awaiting the restart. He had taped his face as protection against flying grit. Note the tiny pressure-air slot provided in the Lotus's ingenious air-deflector clear-vision windscreen. (Indianapolis Motor Speedway)

hundred gallons of gasoline is enormously heavy, and I guess that opening lap at Indy was the first time that Dave had handled the car fully loaded at racing speeds, and its wheel cambers would have been exaggerated under such a load. I've always suspected that this factor over-loaded the inner edge of his tyres, which would have just about gone liquid, so he spun.

'The big collision happened behind us, and by the time we came round to it on our second lap we just picked our way through as directed, then came the long wait while the mess was cleared up. I'd had a long chat with Dave just the previous evening. It's so often the good guys ...'

At 12.46 pm the pace car moved off again, the field now following in line-ahead formation, in the order in which they had finished lap 1 behind Jimmy. Rear-engined cars held the first four places, Jimmy leading Marshman by a narrow margin, then Ward and Dan Gurney. On lap 5 (the first two laps prior to the accident were included in the total) Dan went ahead of Ward to make it Lotuses first, second and third. Marshman's winter running was obviously paying off, as by lap 10 he had passed Jimmy and now had a 4-second lead, lapping at 153.917, up 8 mph on the previous record. Lap 20 and Marshman's lead was an impressive 14 seconds, and increasing with every lap. Dan had by this time made a pit stop, convinced that his car had a problem, but he had merely forgotten a tank switching procedure, dropped him right back.

Lap 39 and Marshman was out; balked by a slower car, he had swooped down below the marker line through one of the turns and, bottoming out as the other car had moved down with him, had gone on to the uneven surface, removing that vulnerably re-positioned oil pipe as well as the oil drain plug from his engine's sump.

Literally minutes later came a great roar from the spectators in the enormous grandstand opposite us; they had a full view of the main straight, whereas my vision, hampered by other team crews, took in only half. Then Jimmy appeared, so close to the low wall bordering the track that only the top half of his car was visible. He was still travelling very fast, but on only three wheels, the left rear perched on top of its suspension at a drunken 45-degree angle. When he disappeared from sight, Colin was all for some of our crew going out to find him, but when he was reminded of the prompt rescue services he changed his mind.

Just minutes later, Parnelli Jones, the new race leader, made his first stop for fuel. His pit was next to ours and I vaguely took in the scene as I continued spotting and timing gaps. Soon I was aware of a heat haze over Parnelli's car, but it did not alarm me. Then, as he was about to depart, members of his own and other crews, along with Bear Safety officials, started dancing all over the place trying to attract his attention. As the fuel nozzle had been withdrawn, alcohol had gushed copiously over the car's tail and hot exhaust pipes, instantly igniting; but alcohol burns invisibly without the smoke and flames of gasoline. At that very moment Parnelli began to roll and with an enormous 'boomph' the fire really erupted. Suddenly aware of what was going on

Embarrassing failure – Jabby Crombac in the grandstand caught the moment when Jimmy's left-rear Dunlop threw its tread, collapsed the suspension corner and sent the Lotus 34 skittering into retirement, pit wall officials and signallers reacting suitably. The World Champion showed masterly skill in keeping the car away from the wall, eventually abandoning it on the grassy infield entering Turn One. (G. Crombac)

around his fully laden fuel tank, Parnelli unlocked his harness and baled out quicker than it takes to write. Unfortunately the car was still rolling, albeit slowly, and with around 65 gallons of alcohol enveloped in fire, it posed a frightening prospect. However, true to form the safety officials swarmed around the thing with their foam fire extinguishers and soon had it quenched. Parnelli sustained burns to his arm and leg and was immediately taken to hospital.

It was not long before Jimmy was back in the pits with us explaining what had happened. He had felt a sudden and violent vibration from the rear going through Turn Four, but without a rear-view mirror on that side had been uncertain what had occurred – the car had settled into a lop-sided attitude, leaving him with his hands full keeping it out of trouble and running in a straight line, avoiding the end of the pit wall as he did so. As soon as he had got out of the car at Turn One, he had discovered that large chunks of tread were missing from the tyre, the resulting heavy vibration having broken the suspension.

This whole episode must have been extremely frightening for him, but he remained outwardly calm, and after a short while he said to me, 'Oh well, I'd best be off now; can I borrow your car?'

As he did not know where it was parked, I said that I would go with him to find it, and the two of us walked back together, slowed by fans wanting his autograph. A very attractive girl stood in the crowd smiling at Jimmy, and when he noticed her he quickly edged in her direction.

'Would you like a coffee?' he asked her, and when she nodded they walked along behind me chatting. I pondered where I had seen her before; from their conversation, Jimmy obviously knew

Post mortem – Jim Endruweit (foreground), Dave Lazenby and Jim Smith examine their No 1 car's shattered suspension. In the second shot the overheated and separated tread on the car's left-rear Dunlop bears silent testimony to a fine British cock-up, one which triggered a major humour failure at Detroit. (Ozzie Lyons/Dave Friedman Photo Collection)

her well. Still in his overalls, and having put his crash helmet in the boot of the Elan, he drove off, accompanied by his friend . . .

Back in the pits, Colin and Cyril were still hard at work on the lap chart, plotting Dan's progress as everyone on the crew, with Jimmy's tyre failure in mind, kept as close an eye as possible on the tall American's Dunlops. He had fought back well from the unheralded pit stop made shortly after the restart; from initially running below our lap chart 'barrier' of 15th place, he was eighth by lap 60, sixth on lap 80 and had moved into fifth ten laps later. On lap 96 he was in for three new tyres and fuel, and Colin anxiously examined the treads as the worn tyres were discarded. As Dan went back into the race, Colin detected the self-same signs of impending failure. He quickly gave the order that Dan be brought in without delay, and withdrew the car.

Dan Gurney: 'That second season was really clouded by the tyre problems at Indy, but throughout I just never got my car working for me . . .

'After the first-lap accident and the re-start, I just ran as best I could until the second pit stop, but we were obviously in trouble with tyre chunking, and I wasn't that disappointed to be pulled out . . .'

It was a bitter pill for the Team to swallow, and even worse for Colin, who had been left to make the decision in the first place. As for Ford, our garage soon filled with the company's executives appearing to accept the affair as one of the twists of fate not uncommon in the sport. Most of them appeared to commiserate with us.

Unknown to us at the time, the scenario was still being played out on the track and the full force of Ford's displeasure with Team Lotus was yet to develop. A. J. Foyt, Offenhauser-powered, had taken over the race lead on lap 54, and as the talking continued in our garage, he was building up a sizeable time cushion over Ford-powered second man Rodger Ward. As we learned later, Ford had been trying to get A. J. into its camp since late 1963; subsequently Colin was asked to hand over our third Type 34 to the Texan, but such a suggestion had been a non-starter. First, we needed to keep a spare in reserve in case of an accident, as in 1963; second, if it had gone to A. J. it would have meant further depleting our workforce at the track by providing assistance for its preparation and running; third, it would have called for additional spare parts and components, while we had consistently run behind schedule in preparing just the two Team cars; fourth, Colin would have been doing his two drivers a severe injustice by handing over the latest factory car to a major competitor.

To an outsider, the simplistic answer would surely have been to provide A. J. with engines in the same way as Ford had supplied them to other teams. Mickey Thompson's creations, while attract-

ing a great deal of media attention for reasons other than their reliability and speed, had been allocated five engines; why hadn't these gone to Foyt for some chassis of his own choice?

To make matters tragically worse, race day had seen the deaths of two drivers in Ford-engined cars in an inferno that the press was already attributing to the use of gasoline rather than alcohol, and it was Ford who had favoured gasoline. When the race ended, only one Ford-engined car had finished, albeit in second place; but it was a second place that could so easily have led to Victory Lane. Against Ford's wishes Rodger Ward's engine had been run on methanol for extra power, but its higher fuel consumption had brought the penalty of five pit stops and a race-losing loss of time. Then, to cap it all, race-winner Foyt, delighted to have brought what he called his 'antique' into the winners' circle, made disparaging comments about both Ford and the 'funny cars' that he had beaten. Ford's very public loss of face was complete, and scapegoats would be needed . . .

Dinner that evening was a subdued affair, as Colin and Jimmy went over the day's events as well as discussing the forthcoming race programme back in Europe. The early evening's TV coverage of the race, together with the evening paper reports, centred on the fiery accidents together with the pros and cons of gasoline versus alcohol.

On a lighter note, at one point I mentioned to Jimmy that I had never met his girl from Gasoline Alley.

'Nor had I,' he replied.

Next day came the awards banquet at the Murat Temple in downtown Indianapolis. The previous Tuesday the same venue had hosted the Mechanics' Dinner, when our crew had enjoyed celebrity status as well as sharing the financial fruits of Jimmy's pole position. Now we were present more from good manners than anything else. One part of the proceedings was the confirmation of the 33 finishing positions and the presentation of race awards. Winner A. J. Foyt's share of the total purse of $506,575 (which included $19,300 of qualification prizes) totalled $153,650. Dan was credited with 17th place ($6,450), Jimmy with 24th (his $12,400 including pole position money); the third Lotus, Marshman's, was 25th, for which he earned $12,000. It was all a far cry from our 1963 pay-out.

Later Colin told me that next day we would both be guests of Ford in Dearborn, and he would let me know when the corporate aircraft would be departing Weir Cook. He went on to describe warmly the lavishness of Ford hospitality; it was something I would not forget, he assured me. I should have heard warning bells ringing when he later altered the travel arrangements by suggesting I should buy two air tickets on a local airline . . . Then when our elderly turbo-prop landed, its door was jammed shut and it took nearly half an hour to secure our release. Bad omens were multiplying.

From what we learned later, the executive block at Dearborn had been fairly humming prior to our arrival. Lee Iacocca, furious at the lack of results from a much larger field of operation compared to the previous year, was out for blood, threatening his

executives that he would have theirs if they did not get the show properly back on the corporate rails.

Hush Puppy shoes were very popular at that time, and while they were delightful to wear in Europe, they proved deadly in America, their man-made soles acting like generator brushes on the corporate deep-pile plasticised carpets; whenever a metal door knob was touched, the wearer sustained a sizeable static shock! Colin had it down to a fine art, hanging back for others to open doors, and if it was down to him to close them, he did so with his foot. I remember that on arrival at Dearborn we visited one or two offices with our hosts, and the higher we rose in the building, the greater the static produced by the ever-deeper pile.

In my naivety I still had no inkling of what was to come. Any suggestion that we were about to be held to blame for sheer incompetence I would have laughed out of court; we had done our best throughout that month of May and Colin would hardly have chosen Dunlop tyres without first carefully weighing the pros and cons. As to whether Colin suspected a grilling I cannot say; certainly he had given no prior hint of a clash of some proportion, and on the flight up we had engrossed ourselves in my budget proposals for the remainder of the year, in which Colin's

Compensation – retaining a sense of proportion, Jimmy accepts his lap-leader money cheque beside the still-stricken 34. (Indianapolis Motor Speedway)

dreaded sports car programme was again clandestinely enmeshed.

Eventually we were ushered into an empty conference room, in the centre of which were two chairs surrounded by perhaps 20 or more in a circle. These were quickly filled as we sat down, then without delay a full-blooded inquisition burst around our heads.

All the Ford top brass concerned with racing were there, including a top man new to Ford's racing world, Leo Beebe. Probing his background after the announcement of his new post, I was told that he was a well-known former newspaperman and his appearance fitted the bill perfectly – tall, dark, thin and hawkish, and usually to be found chewing a medium cigar down to a stub. He exuded a serious business-like approach, which emphasised that he was not a man to mince words, nor one in whom any sense of frivolity might surface. In truth, newspapers had played no part in his career; he had first joined Ford 20 years before, and had filled a variety of increasingly important posts before having been promoted to Manager, Special Vehicles, earlier that year.

Now, flanked by people we knew such as Don Frey, Jacque Passino, Frank Zimmerman, Dave Evans, and a host of others, the inquisitors piled straight in with outright condemnation of Colin's actions during the month of May. I was taken aback at the stream of insinuations that followed, as if addressed to an embarrassed stable-boy who was explaining why he had shut the door after the horse had bolted. It was as if Ford had given us their multi-million-dollar ball to play with for a month and we had merely spent the 30 days of May kicking it about with senseless abandon.

Why had we gone to a British tyre company? Did we know that a member of Harvey Firestone's family was married to someone in the Ford dynasty? (I couldn't see the point of this last question.) What was at the back of it all? What were our plans now? Then came the bombshell. Ford had come to the opinion that we were incapable of running an efficient ship, and Colin must now hand over the complete Team of cars and spares to Ford for them to run.

Colin's reaction was remarkably calm, and he quietly clarified the events of the past month. But it was obvious that our Indy section was in dire straits, and it surprised me that Colin appeared not to have realised the full impact of Ford's demand. Then the focus of attention momentarily shifted from us as the Ford executives discussed among themselves the practicalities of the 'take-over', and I quietly suggested to Colin that it was perhaps time for a coffee break. The meeting had gone on for over an hour and we had had an early start to the day.

'Why not give Fred [Bushell] a call?' I suggested. It would give Colin a breather and it was odds-on that Fred's measured thoughts, delivered from a clear environment back in England, would do much to remove Colin's glazed expression and help revitalise his thinking.

We emerged from the room to find Carroll Shelby already enjoying a coffee. After exchanging greetings, we discovered that he was also there, as he put it, 'to get a bollocking'. The Nürburgring 1,000 Kms sports car race had been held the previous day, and Carroll had been summoned to explain the 'failures' of the sole Ford GT40 – making its debut there – and three out of the four Shelby-AC Cobras, the sole survivor winning its class. Meeting another member of the racing fraternity provided welcome relief, as well as some laughs. As Carroll put it, Ford could have taken four out of the first five places in Germany, and he would still have got a dressing-down over the failure of the fifth car.

Colin had had his chat with Fred when we returned to the conference room. Most of the Ford executives had now departed, leaving a small contingent to draft a contract covering the Indy Team's hand-over. But Colin was now absolutely back on song, and he waded in with all guns blazing; it was as if the first part of the meeting had never taken place at all.

The Ford men were aghast, but Colin was adamant that Team Lotus must be allowed to redeem itself at the Milwaukee and Trenton races later that year. Some of the executives who had left the meeting were called back, and although one re-read aloud the minutes of the initial discussion, it made no difference to Colin's new position.

Under the terms of a new agreement, which was then thrashed out, Colin agreed to sell the spare Type 34 to Ford immediately; selection of drivers, pit personnel, tyres and maintenance procedures would from now on be Ford's responsibility, and Team Lotus agreed to take part in a minimum of one week's practice at each of the two ovals of Milwaukee and Trenton prior to the 200-mile events of 23 August and 20 September respectively. Both parties were given eight days in which they could change their minds.

Immediately we were back in England, Colin returned to his old theme of incorporating a sports car programme in the Ford-Indy structure. As laid down in the new contract, he was required to signify his acceptance in writing, and this he did, pointing out that now Ford wished to race our third and spare car we would require more financial assistance to provide the additional spares, as well as covering our expenses for the two additional weeks of testing. Colin's letter, dispatched three days after his return from Dearborn, also contained a reminder that Team Lotus was still awaiting the contract for a sports car programme, which Ford had indicated would be with him nearly eight months earlier. In addition to his request that we should have four engines made available to us before Indy car testing began, Colin also asked that an additional quad-cam be sent to us for our sports car programme.

Considering the strength of Ford's feeling over what they regarded as Team Lotus's debacle at Indy, Colin's renewed effort to resurrect the sports car deal, when most would have been more concerned with healing the recent breach, was audacious to say the least. A sting in the tail of his letter was his request 'to get these points cleared without delay, so we can proceed with a one hundred per cent effort not prejudiced by indecision right up to the last minute.'

This was followed by an ominous silence from Dearborn, and after two weeks we sent Beebe a cable suggesting that as we had not heard from him, could we assume that the contract was to proceed as written? The contract referred to was the one we liked to think would include sports cars. Leo's reaction came by return cable. The delay in consummating the new contract, he said, was due to our insistence that sports cars be included; they must be regarded as an entirely separate matter and Leo would visit us immediately after the Le Mans 24-Hours race to settle arrangements for Milwaukee and Trenton.

Almost simultaneously came news that Bobby Marshman had shunted one of the Type 29s at Milwaukee, and damage was sufficiently serious for Ford to airfreight it back to Cheshunt for rebuilding. Again no record remains of which chassis number this was. Jimmy's damaged Type 34 from the race was also at Cheshunt, and with no settlement of the on-going arrangements with Ford America it had been put to one side for rebuilding, our Indy section now being engaged instead in building Type 30 sports cars.

On the Wednesday following Le Mans, Leo Beebe arrived at Cheshunt, accompanied by Jacque Passino and Bob Hefty. The primary subject for discussion, in Ford's mind, was to settle the arrangements for the forthcoming races at Milwaukee and Trenton, but again Colin raised his pet subject of the sports car programme. The Ford men continued to distance themselves, saying that our budgets for the five races we had scheduled in North America were financially prohibitive, and that any returns that could be envisaged would not warrant the investment by Ford that Team Lotus called for. However, Beebe agreed to make five engines available, as well as limited finance to cover development costs, and suggested that it was now up to Team Lotus to secure financial support elsewhere if it wished to race its Type 30s.

Shortly after the meeting ended and the Ford executives had departed, Colin gave his approval for work to begin on rebuilding Jimmy's green and yellow Type 34, and for the three engines we still retained to be returned to Ford for preparation for the ovals. But Ford's alteration of the agreement for running the Indy cars, together with what Colin saw as their withdrawal of support for the Type 30 programme, still rankled with him, and when Beebe's minutes of our meeting in Colin's office were received, he fired off a final salvo at Dearborn in his desire to place matters in their proper context.

He pointed out that Ford had gone back on both programmes detailed the previous September, and that he was seriously worried as well as disappointed that a small company such as Lotus could not rely upon the integrity of agreements made with a company the size of Ford. He again stressed that Ford had also gone back on its assurance about the future of the race cars passing into Ford ownership, and was worried about rumours that Jimmy's 1963 Indy car – '29/3' – was now being prepared for racing.

A short time later I found myself having problems with drivers for the first race at Milwaukee, the date of which coincided with the Formula 1 Austrian Grand Prix. Dan Gurney was making noises about his shortage of World Championship points, a cry that was soon taken up by Jimmy, both of them asking to be allowed to miss Milwaukee in favour of Austria. Colin's reaction was to leave any decision regarding their replacements with Ford, although our own inclination was to plump for the two stars, Parnelli Jones and A. J. Foyt. Bobby Marshman had had another accident with a Type 29, which meant that he might also be free, but his record of 'incidents' was not in his favour. We were not to find out until later of Ford's continuing displeasure with A. J., which meant that he was out of the running, and a phone call from Jacque Passino quickly passed the responsibility for signing Parnelli over to us.

Then someone slipped Walt Hansgen's name into the equation, Colin signified his acceptance and a deal was done with him instead. A distinguished sports car driver of Jaguars, Listers, Corvettes, Ferraris and Maseratis, Walt was a popular figure in the sport; despite being 44 years of age, he was still a driver to be reckoned with and had run as high as third at that year's Indy '500' before being delayed by mechanical problems. Having raced since 1951, he had become associated with Briggs Cunningham's team, and had taken three SCCA National Championships in the millionaire's sports cars.

The deal to secure Parnelli was another story altogether. Firstly it meant dealing with his car owner, J. C. Agajanian, whose extrovert personality hid as bright a business mind as one could find anywhere. As well as taking some little time to strike an agreement, and obtaining Ford's approval to Aggie's stipulation that we change the name of the car to the *Bowes Seal Fast Special*, Parnelli also had a bullet-proof fuel contract with Mobil Oil, which meant that we had to unravel our exclusive Humble contract for that race.

Following Ford's initial requirement that we should have a week's testing at both ovals, we had left it to Dearborn to make the necessary arrangements with the track owners, but subsequent events went against us. The to and fro of paperwork, which was a prerequisite of work starting on the preparation of both cars and engines, was only completed in July, and by that time the Milwaukee race organiser had resisted Ford's approach for an extended test, offering instead only 2 hours of track time on the Thursday (20 August) before the race. The offer from Trenton was a three-day session, 17–19 August, so it was agreed to combine both these much-reduced test sessions into the same week.

Some race mechanics from our Indy section were required in Cheshunt, to rebuild Jimmy's damaged car from the '500', Marshman's shunted Type 29 and Type 30s, while others were required to go to our Indy garage (where Dan's Type 34 and the spare car remained) to remove the engines that Ford still had to rebuild, and to re-prepare the cars. Fortunately our EFLO (English Ford Line Organisation) programme of running Lotus-Cortinas in the States had just entered a lull between races, so I moved our sedan chief mechanic, Ray Parsons, and some of his crew to Indianapolis to work there with David Lazenby.

Ford's research into the changes of car specification required by running on the tighter 1-mile ovals was soon complete, and the company confirmed that as the engine oil system needed modification, it would provide the systems required as well as an extra oil tank that would be hung on the outside of each car, although in the end these were made in England by our own suppliers, Williams & Pritchard. Ford engineers had approved the new Lotus lightweight copper-core radiators that we had been testing at Cheshunt, and also wanted to revert to the clutches we had used in 1963, as they had found the current versions unsuitable.

In the meantime both Ford and ourselves were badgering the Milwaukee track promoter for more test time, but all our efforts came to naught. Ford admitted that tests on its 289 cu in engine, which Colin wanted for his sports car programme, had proved unsatisfactory, and the company's suggestion was that we wait

instead for delivery of its 325-inch version, due some time in August.

Eventually the two groups of our Indy section, complete with three Type 34s and an enormous stock of spares flown out from Cheshunt, rendezvoused at Trenton the weekend before the Milwaukee race, Colin forsaking his role at the Austrian Grand Prix to oversee events in America. Anticipating a heavy week's work ahead, I wanted more EFLO personnel at Trenton; these included Bob Dance and Bob Sparshott, who on the Sunday of that weekend had helped run three Lotus-Cortinas in the Marlboro 12-Hours race where, with drivers Jackie Stewart, David Hobbs, Sir John Whitmore, Mike Beckwith, Tony Hegbourne and Dave Clark, they had finished first, second and ninth in their class, as well as taking the Team Prize and Index of Performance. Colin had also attended the race, and first thing on Monday morning offered a genial invitation to those scheduled to return to England to 'drop off for some Indy-style racing'.

Sent out from England was our gearbox man, John 'the gear'

The green-and-yellow liveried Clark 34 – now fitted with Firestone tyres – is rolled on to the top deck of a Ford transporter at the Indianapolis Speedway en route to Milwaukee.

Davies, whose life style created even more attention than the other characters within our Team. For reasons he kept to himself, John's address was the boiler room of his local swimming pool, and his personal travelling gear consisted solely of a couple of changes of underwear, which he carried, even on intercontinental flights, in a plastic shopping bag. His entry through American immigration channels was a source of both concern and delay; he had spent time in East Germany (again for reasons he kept to himself), and the relevant visa in his passport was guaranteed to alert officialdom on his arrival anywhere in the USA.

Bob Dance's work diary, which he has kept since his earliest days in motor racing, bears testimony to the pressures of that week of Indy racing, which saw him and the other members of the crew work a total of 141 hours out of a possible 168!

Shortly after running started at Trenton, Parnelli had a steering arm break; this took him into a wild spin, which he managed partially to control so that the car only 'kissed' the retaining wall. A new nose, together with a radiator, its plumbing and other components, were needed to repair the damage, but the main work centred on making new steering arms. The uprights into which the arms fitted had been incorrectly machined, and lack of time forced the production of new arms locally.

Late on the second day of running Hansgen also hit the wall, and the decision was taken to move on to Milwaukee so that repairs on both cars could be completed safe in the knowledge that they were at least 'on site.' The 900-mile journey took 36 hours out of the working schedule, and it was a very tired crew that arrived at their new garage in Milwaukee ready to plunge into preparing the two cars in the small hours of Thursday morning.

After Hansgen's car had been refurbished and its shakedown runs completed, Walt began working up to speed, but he hit the wall again, this time inflicting more serious damage to the car and to himself. Apart from severe shock, he had also injured a leg badly, the initial diagnosis suggesting that it was broken; fortunately, however, it was found to be severely bruised with only possibly minor fractures. He was back in a sports car a month later, winning the Bridgehampton Double 500 in John Mecom's Zerex.

Unknown to us at the time, Ford was still in the process of formulating a deal with A. J. Foyt, and with the Texan now present at Milwaukee the pressure was on to reach a suitable agreement without delay. This done, attention turned to the car. Although the majority of our crew who were present maintain that they rebuilt Hansgen's damaged car for Foyt to drive in the race, our factory records show that it was still in its damaged form in Cheshunt as late as November, so the all-night session that followed must have been spent transferring the useable parts from the damaged car to the spare. As mechanic Mike Underwood recalled, 'Components were not easily interchangeable between tubs, and "fudging" could be a lengthy process.'

Race day saw Parnelli, in Jimmy's Indy '500' race car still in its green and yellow colours, dominate both practice and the race, breaking Jimmy's qualifying and race times from the previous

Jimmy's 34 as set up with an external oil tank for the short-oval 200-mile post-Indy races at Trenton and Milwaukee. (Bud Jones)

year. Both Rodger Ward (in his American-built rear-engined car with Ford power unit) and Foyt broke the 1963 qualifying record, a feat that promised a 1–2 Lotus finish, but it was not to be. A. J. encountered a problem with his gear-change mechanism at the start; it merely required a quick adjustment, but strangely he drove round to the back of the pits for attention, an error that disqualified him from the race. This was enormously disappointing for our hard-working crew, who by this time were virtually out on their feet from fatigue. But Parnelli's achievement brought consolation, as he won by two laps from second man Rodger Ward, his winning prize money totalling $13,840.

Ford was delighted with this result, and congratulatory cables became the order of the day, together with the early arrival of qualifying and victory bonus cheques to put a distinct gloss on the whole affair. Indeed, at a motel meeting between Beebe and Chapman, Leo broached the subject of the 1965 Indy race, sketching out his company's thoughts as well as its budgetary considerations, but these showed a severe reduction over each of the two previous years. Gone were driver retainers, qualifying and race bonus monies; proposed was a lump sum payment of $50,000 to cover all expenses plus a $25,000 management fee. Ford would provide five engines, spares and servicing, and would be satisfied with two new cars, a Type 34 being allocated as the spare. The company required 'immediate and close liaison in respect of product development testing as well as the selection of drivers', and would require Team's participation in the Trenton race scheduled before running opened at the Speedway.

Colin made no bones about his severe disappointment at the limitations imposed, and put his thoughts in writing immediately upon his return to Cheshunt, adding that the suggested programme was considerably less attractive than an alternative he had been actively considering. A week later he repeated his views in a cable, suggesting an early meeting to discuss the matter further.

For our regular Indy crew, the Monday and Tuesday after Milwaukee were spent taking the cars apart in preparation for the Trenton race before they hurried back to Cheshunt for departure to Goodwood for the Tourist Trophy the following Saturday, where Jimmy would drive a Type 30. There they went straight into another all-nighter after Friday's pre-race practice, the car suffering serious problems with its suspension and cooling system.

For the members of our EFLO crew who returned to England with Colin after the Milwaukee race, memories of the journey still remain clear. Bob Sparshott: 'We had won some very nice silver trays and trophies in the Marlboro 12-Hour race. The Old Man was always addicted to trophies and carried these around himself to make sure they didn't get lost. Unfortunately for everyone, they went astray somewhere between his hire car and the check-in desk when we left Milwaukee, a disaster he blamed directly on the airline. The journey home then became a series of encounters with airline staff, Colin verbally abusing every official that crossed his path until we were safely outside London Airport.'

Ford was keen to have Jones and Foyt drive our cars again at Trenton on 27 September, but without a clashing Grand Prix date Jimmy was keen to return to oval racing. Ford held firm on its decision until, exasperated that his No 1 was being cold-shouldered, Colin cabled Beebe laying it on the line that if Jimmy did not drive at Trenton, he would not drive at Indy in 1965, and without Jimmy Colin would personally forget the '500' altogether. Because Ford's primary objectives for 1965 were to spend less money and to secure Jimmy as its No 1 driver, he was quickly reinstated in the green car that Parnelli had driven at Trenton, Jones switching to the white car in which Foyt had been disqualified there.

On 15 September Leo Beebe arrived at Cheshunt to finalise arrangements for Indy '65. As usual, Colin was well versed on every aspect of what he considered essential, and although Leo's gesture of throwing his wallet on to Colin's conference table with the immortal words 'You can have all that to race for us and no more' has been well reported since, the facts are rather different, and Colin did a far better job than he has been credited with. The original offer of $75,000 overall was obviously unacceptable; forgetting the income derived from selling the cars, the 1963

Indy programme had cost Team Lotus nearly $143,000, and 1964 $147,000. Colin therefore pressed for double the amount suggested by Ford, detailing summaries of previous expenditure in one of his highly persuasive presentations.

The cross-table discussions lasted 2 hours, the end result being one of which Colin could have been proud, but which to him was only barely acceptable. Of his target of $150,000, Ford agreed to pay Team Lotus $147,000 to cover our management fee and expenses, plus a $25,000 contingency fund set to one side to underwrite unanticipated expenses. Ford also agreed with Colin that three new cars were the minimum requirement; the third car, which would become Ford property upon completion, would be loaned to us as our spare during the month of May. In the event of our winning the race, Ford would pay $30,000 for the winning car. The icing on the cake was that the five engines provided by Ford and maintained by them free of charge during the month of May would become the property of Team Lotus. Team Lotus was to settle the drivers' retainers.

Jimmy was invited to attend the final part of the meeting to give his own views on the forthcoming Indy programme, and here we ran into an unexpected hiccup. When he learned that the Ford-Lotus deal was as good as finalised, and was asked if he was looking forward to his third attempt at the Speedway, he made no reply. Those sitting around the table gave an informal account of what was planned, but the reasonably relaxed atmosphere in the room became increasingly tense as our No 1 listened but still did not comment. It soon became obvious that something was seriously worrying him, and the group went back over the latest engine developments, the possibility that we would forsake running at Monaco due to clashing dates, and the various back-up plans that were in the pipeline. Still there was no response.

Then someone asked Jimmy outright if there was something worrying him. He agreed that there was, and eventually explained what.

'It's my mother,' he said.

For the businessmen and engineers who had been thrashing out their plans for the high point of their year, Jimmy's reply came as a complete shock, and there was a lengthy silence. Eventually Jimmy elucidated.

'This year's accident really upset her, and she has heard all kinds of stories about the place – I have to say I'm not keen to do it again.'

Eventually it was left for Jimmy to think it over; the meeting continued, with Jimmy taking part in the discussions, but I did not hear of the subject being raised again. Presumably Jimmy made his decision when he learned that the programme would be null and void without his participation.

Two weeks before September's Trenton race, our crew arrived in our Indy garage to work on the cars. With memories of the Milwaukee workload, and with our spare car still awaiting its rebuild, any damage to our remaining pair of 34s would require on-the-spot repairs, so our advance party consisted of four mechanics, with three members of our EFLO team flying in as support for the second week, when testing was scheduled for the Wednesday and Thursday.

Fortunately there were no accidents to hinder our progress on this occasion, and a record crowd of nearly 40,000 spectators packed into the New Jersey State Fairground on race day. In his white Type 34, Parnelli again set the USAC world alight, breaking the lap record with a phenomenally quick time of 31.54 seconds around the 1-mile oval; a speed of 114.140 mph ensured the Californian's pole position.

The opening stages of the race heralded a Lotus 1–2–3 finish as Parnelli, Bobby Marshman (Type 29) and Jimmy led the rest of the field, even the fourth place car of Jim McElreath being another foreign 'funny car' in the shape of the Brabham-built *Zink Trackburner*.

Although the media and even the Ford PR reports suggested that Jimmy was having an off-day, he was actually trying his hardest to make up for a down-on-power engine; David Lazenby and the Ford engineers had spent practice trying to trace the problem without success, and when rubbish from the track was sucked into his car's nose cowling, Jimmy soon suffered serious overheating and went out just before half-distance. Only 12 miles later, Marshman was also out. The Scot earned a mere $459 race purse money for his effort, Marshman $643. Parnelli finished one lap clear of Don Branson in second place, taking home a race purse of $9,686, which with accessory money added totalled over $13,000.

The results from the two oval races went a long way to healing our breach with Ford, and Leo Beebe set the date for a meeting just two days after Trenton to discuss detail matters in preparation for the 1965 programme. The USAC had just announced that two stops would be mandatory in the '500', and Ford wanted to settle the question of pit crew procedure; also the question of whether to go with alcohol fuel needed investigation. Colin's day ended when he and Lee Iacocca jointly signed the 1965 agreement between the two companies.

Towards the end of October I visited Dearborn to discuss budgetary details both historical and future, clarifying outstanding billings and other matters that had so quickly built up as more practical events took precedence. I had kept in touch with Nancy Sachs since the tragic month of May, and she met me at the airport on arrival.

'I'm taking you to dinner tonight,' she said, 'and no ifs or buts. You're going to see some people that'll soon be known the world over ...'

At the local Playboy Club we were shown to a table almost on the stage, and were about to tuck into our main course when to loud applause the evening's main attraction was introduced. A local group who had become the centre of attention for miles around, they were Diana Ross and the Supremes ...

One item for discussion with Ford was the Type 34 that had been written off in the Hansgen shunt at Milwaukee, the remains of which were by that time in Cheshunt awaiting a decision.

● 1964: 'IT'S ONLY A SPORT'

During late-autumn tyre and engine tests at the Speedway, Bobby Marshman ran ever faster in the Lindsey Hopkins Pure Firebird *29, wearing Goodyear tyres. Here, after lapping at a record-shattering 162.3 mph, leadfoot Bobby demonstrates how. Crew chief Jack Beckley is bare-chested below during a summer session. (Both Indianapolis Motor Speedway)*

November 1964 – the Phoenix '200' with Parnelli Jones at speed in the Ford/Agajanian Lotus-Ford 34. The outrigged left-side oil tank pannier is well disguised by the car's dark livery in this shot, but its filler cap is visible just above the race number, the pannier's rear extremity curving round just short of the side fuel filler neck.

The Hopkins team stayed on at Phoenix post-race to conduct engine tests for Ford. Running what was almost certainly the ex-Clark second-place '29/3' from 1963, Bobby Marshman suffered an appalling accident caused reputedly by an engine intake instrumentation probe falling into an induction trumpet and jamming the throttle wide open. The car exploded upon impact with the Phoenix wall, inflicting fatal burns upon this quietly talented and very popular driver. One Lotus team member recalled him as 'An American Jimmy Clark . . .' There is no higher praise. (Bob Tronolone)

Under the terms of our agreement, Ford was to purchase all three cars, so it was now faced either with a bill for the purchase of a wreck or a substantial charge, estimated at $22,000, for rebuilding it. One suggestion was that as Ford had gone back on its decision to have a 1964 Type 34 as a spare for the 1965 race, the salvageable parts from Hansgen's wreck could go some way towards the construction of the third Type 38 for 1965, but this was sensibly deemed unacceptable from a practical point of view.

Eventually it was agreed that the wreck would not be rebuilt. Ford paid the original contracted cost of the car, and all the Type 34 spares that still remained with us were handed to Ford for use in running the two surviving cars.

Although by that time we at Team Lotus had accepted, unwillingly, that our former cars would be raced by other organisations, a point I raised at the meeting (and here I quote from a letter I sent to Ford on my return to England) concerned the components that I anticipated Team Lotus would have to supply 'for the 1964 cars which will be run in all probability by A. J. Foyt and Parnelli Jones as well as that of the Marshman car next year'. In the absence of any other records from the period, this infers that the two Type 34s were already allocated, and that Marshman would continue with his Type 29. Early in November came reports that he was circulating Indianapolis very rapidly indeed during Goodyear tests and was approaching lap speeds of 162 mph. These and other reports indicated that he was piloting the Type 34 Parnelli had driven to win Trenton; if this was so, his change of car must have been at the behest of Ford (which still owned the 34) because his Type 29 was not available, rather than of the tyre companies, as Parnelli was a front-line Firestone driver.

On 27 November came tragedy. While testing at Phoenix Marshman went into the wall and was badly burned when the car caught fire. At Cheshunt in those days I had useful contacts at Reuters, and they confirmed that his injuries were critical and that he had been flown to a military hospital in Texas where he died a week later.

The scant inferences that still remain point to the car he crashed and destroyed as being a Type 29, whereas various scribes have since pinpointed it as a Type 34. There were just two 34s in existence, both owned by Ford, and two 34s continued to run through 1965. No communique came from Dearborn as to which car had crashed, yet if it had been a Type 34 the company would surely have required some components from us in order to rebuild it for 1965.

On 5 December I received a cable from Ford's Danny Jones reporting that the 'Parnelli Jones Agajanian 1964 Lotus steering rack and pinion gear did not pass a Magnaflux test – we presently have two sets on order and big help if you can supply as soon as possible.' Much later came American newspaper reports that Bobby's widow was taking legal action over her husband's accident in a 'dangerous 1964 Indianapolis car'. The case was not directed at Lotus, but suffice to say that the description of the car suited either a Type 29 or 34.

Jim Hurtubise, a driver and personality much liked by Jimmy and our crew, had been badly burned at Milwaukee earlier that season, and three drivers of Ford-engined racing cars had died in fires during the year. Two of them, Eddie Sachs and Bobby Marshman, had been good friends of ours. It was a gruesome thought on which to end the year.

CHAPTER SIX

1965:
First Fruits

The year got off to an irritating start. En route to the South African Grand Prix in the last week of December, Jimmy, Colin and myself had met at London Airport to sign Jimmy's contract for the coming year. It was obvious that Colin was not in the mood to concentrate; various editions of the document were flooding the table and floor, and after some discussion Colin had hurried the whole thing along by saying that a copy should be signed or they would miss the plane. I had been left to collate the various altered pages, only to find the wrong version had been signed. Colin was accompanying Jimmy to the Tasman series that followed, which meant that I would not see either of them again until mid-March, so Jimmy would be racing without a strictly valid agreement. The Tasman was a resounding success for him, his Type 32B Formula 2-based car winning a total of nine races.

USAC regulations for the coming season had been radically changed very late in 1964, catching both Ford and ourselves on the hop. Following the fiery accidents, both gasoline and pressure refuelling had been outlawed, triggering substantial design changes. Yet construction of the Type 38 'tubs' had already begun, incorporating five individual and interconnected fuel cells à la Type 34 (the GRP-encased aluminium fuel tank over the driver's legs having already been banned through a 'no fuel forward of the driver' ruling). However, the scheme depended upon pressure refuelling, and a redesign thus became necessary, adopting just two large fuel cells, one in each sponson plus a third behind the driver. Fortunately, in answer to our pleas that the cost of such work had not been allowed for in our budget, Ford agreed that it would accept the additional costs involved.

Another USAC ruling called for all cars to be fitted with bag tanks similar to the FPT British style that we had introduced two years earlier. For 1965 Firestone and Goodyear were producing rupture-proof fuel cell bladders, filled with polyurethane foam cellular material. The foam prevented serious leakage if a bag was punctured and also minimised the volume of air available in the event of an explosion. These American bag tanks were slightly heavier than the British units, but also incorporated various designs of baffle. By first running at Indy three drivers were

reported to have been saved serious fire injury as a result.

The fuel bowsers sited in the pits were also subject to new regulations; there was to be just one 3-inch outlet combining two 3-inch hose off-takes. The bowser's maximum capacity was to be 400 US gallons (333 Imperial), with no addition of fuel allowed during the race. Buckeye-type connections were mandatory.

Ford's detail engine improvements spoke well for their V8s' basic design. Its induction and lubrication system had required revision to cope with increased power, previous gallery and passage restrictions being eradicated, while an aircraft-style oil filter was incorporated to remove all but the most minute particles. The con-rod bottom ends and caps had been strengthened to cope with the inertial forces of higher rpm, and camshaft diameters were increased to reduce deflection. Valve springs were also now assembled by selective fit to avoid repetition of the previous season's failures. Pistons and piston rings had been modified, the fuel system now employing new boost venturi injectors for improved fuel mixing before the charge entered the cylinders, giving a significant increase in fuel economy. The system could be calibrated to run methanol, gasoline, or 80 per cent blends of methanol with toluene, benzol, naphtha and gasoline.

Oil-flow rate was increased from the 10.5 US gallons per minute (8.7 Imperial) of the 1964 unit to 16 US gallons (13.3 Imperial). As a result, Ford's flow tests of the Cheshunt-designed oil cooler demanded less restriction and they suggested that we should fit a pressure-operated bypass and adopt a redesigned oil tank with increased expansion area.

Ford's transmission research approved of the 1964-type Borg & Beck clutch, and we were able to confirm that new gear ratios already received from ZF would amply accommodate the new unit's 8,800–9,000 rpm, our own test runs with it seeing 9,300 rpm.

Following the 1964 race Ford had been deluged with calls from teams anxious to confirm engine orders for the following year. Accepting that they would be unable either to build the numbers required or to handle servicing, Ford had sought a suitable outside contractor, while still overseeing quality control of the parts supplied.

Three-time Indy winner Lou Meyer (of the famed Meyer-Drake Offenhauser engine partnership) had signalled interest and ultimately he opened a 'Ford' engine shop at 4709 1/2 West 30th, right next to the Speedway. We would become regular visitors there in future years. While the engines sold for $15,000 each, Ford's initial subsidy amounted to $16,500 per unit. This figure would later be greatly reduced.

Meanwhile, Dan Gurney was going his own way: 'Looking forward to '65, I just concluded it would be better if I had nobody else but myself to blame for any shortcomings, or shortages, affecting my Indy programme. I came to a very amicable deal with both Ford and Colin for a new Lotus 38 – strictly speaking, I think Ford owned both the car and the engines. Bill Fowler and Ken Derringer had both been employed by me to work on my '64 car, and they formed the nucleus of what would become All-American Racers, the major trigger for which had been Firestone pulling strings to block Goodyear out of Indy at their first attempt in '64.

'Indianapolis had been a Firestone preserve since the Constitution. But for 1964 Goodyear had set up a depot there in Gasoline Alley offering rival track tyres. You had Goodyear's place painted all blue and gold, facing Firestone's red and white, and it was clear that the knives were out. Then, just before the race, Firestone went around – with a bunch of dollars – and painstakingly convinced every qualifier to race on their tyres, and to ditch Goodyear.

'Well, that piece of politics worked fine short term, but long term it was a terrible mistake, because Goodyear is the world's largest tyre company, and what Firestone had done was just to wake up a sleeping giant. That '64 Indy incident was a huge slap in the face to Goodyear, and the directors decided that wasn't ever going to happen again. And the way to stop that happening would be to have a car builder contracted exclusively to run on their tyres. Carroll Shelby of Cobra was close to Tony Webner, race tyre director of Goodyear, and he asked me, "Do you think you could build and run your own cars like Brabham does in Formula 1?", and I said, "Yep, I think I can . . .", and that was it.

'Vic Holt was Chief Executive Officer of Goodyear then, and when we got together he asked me what I was proposing to call my new team. I hadn't really thought about it, although I knew that I didn't want to use my own name since so many important people were involved in setting it up that I just felt it would be "politically correct" not to use my name.

'Holt was a great, tall ex-basketball player from Indiana, an Abe Lincoln-type commanding presence, and he said, "Why not call it All-American Racers?", so we did. And I added the "Eagle" bit later . . .'

Mid-January's dyno readings saw the methanol-fuelled prototype already exceeding 500 bhp, with improvements in fuel and oil economy as well as easier starting and response. On the 'customer' front, both Parnelli and A. J. were encountering problems with their Type 34 ZF gearboxes, including their crown wheels and pinions (no doubt due to component age), and Ford requested that we press ZF to supply spares by return so testing

could continue in the run-up to the first '65-season race at Phoenix in March. In addition, Ford was also anxious that we ship them all the Type 34 components we still possessed. Yet when Colin called from 'down under' to check the current situation, his primary concern was the date that his new Galaxie was due to arrive from Canada!

His extended absence on the Tasman series was a bonus for Len Terry, who was able to enjoy carte-blanche on the design of the Type 38, which he has always regarded since as *his* car. With work commencing earlier than previous years, construction remained on schedule regardless of the redesign and the fact that a third car was to be built for Dan Gurney's new All-American Racers. Ford requested, however, that if the third was needed following damage to the other two, Gurney would forfeit his ride. These plans not only required a third car to be ready to run from the outset, but also another driver to partner Jimmy.

In mid-January I was chasing Ford for engines, with specially designed 'Lotus throttle linkages' to suit our chassis. We had a tyre test at Phoenix scheduled from 5 April and a visit to Kingman, so time was of the essence.

For 1965 Ford was producing around 50 engines to meet much increased demand from other teams, and I was keen to ensure supply at the earliest possible time before production problems arose. Ford's reply was that its prototype was still undergoing tests; anticipating that we would then request mock-up units to fit in our cars, the company confirmed that all its stock had already been supplied to its new customers, so we should resort to using a 1964 engine we still held at Cheshunt. Even Ford's special Autolite racing batteries were yet to be produced, and we were told that these would not be available until the beginning of February at the earliest.

Jim Endruweit and 'Laz' were also experimenting, as usual, with throttle linkages. Ford later asked for drawings and a prototype from Cheshunt for further evaluation in Dearborn, adding that further design changes and production, once approved by Ford, would be the responsibility of Team Lotus, which would fuel controversy at the first running in America. The same conditions applied to the smaller radiator designed at Cheshunt, which was permitted by the cooler running on alcohol fuel. With so many customers, Ford had organised a nine-day engine school for mechanics from the various teams and for this they would provide the special tooling required.

At the beginning of February Ford suggested that we fit their wiring harness ourselves, but with one of their electricians ready to fly over in case we encountered problems. They had just completed prototype engine running with an A. J. Watson chassis on the 1-mile Phoenix track and supplied us with detailed instructions on the changes made to throttle linkages as well as design changes needed to be made to our radiator. There would also need to be another style of radiator required for running on mile-oval tracks.

Our first 'live' Indy engine finally arrived at the beginning of March, the second a week later. Time was running short. Ford also supplied us with relevant test data on its engine, on which it had accumulated over 5,000 miles of running.

One interesting item concerned Ford's provision of Type 34 components to another constructor for comment. We had heard the story on the grapevine, and I had immediately jumped at Ford, but the company's response was that if this had happened it could only have been actioned by a current owner, completely outside its area of jurisdiction.

The Type 38 was the first true monocoque constructed by Lotus and torsional stiffness was estimated to have increased 50 per cent over previous 'bathtub' designs, the completed car weighing a fraction over the 1,250 lbs minimum weight. Employing outer skins produced by Williams & Pritchard (who also again built the aluminium prototype body shell), the remainder of the sheet metal work was in the hands of John Lambert heading Team's own fabrication shop, which had come into being the previous year, building the Type 33 Formula 1 cars.

In the space behind the instrument panel vacated by the previous fuel tank, Len Terry introduced his 'birdbath' oil reservoir to take care of the increased oil requirement for which there was insufficient space in the usual place in the front of the car. Shown in Len's drawing, an hermetically sealed tank sited above the driver's knees fed the vented tank, which, as usual, was situated for cooling directly behind the radiator in the nose of the car. This was fed through two pipes that joined the lower tank just below its required level. Immediately the oil level in the main tank dropped, the two pipe ends became exposed; one allowed air into the top tank and the other allowed oil to flow down until the required level was restored.

Len enjoyed the opposition's confusion: 'With the quite large

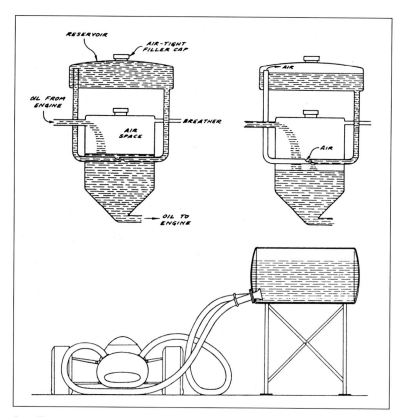

Len Terry's automatic oil tank replenishing device, and the double-sided refuelling arrangement that gained an enormous advantage for Lotus.

reserve hidden away in the monocoque, all they could see was the relatively small tank behind the radiator. Since oil consumption for the race was considerably more than the amount that could be held in the front tank, and the regs forbade adding oil, they became convinced that we had made a big error. I found it all very amusing.'

Although Ford and Lotus both claimed credit for the design of the bowser outlet, which was to increase the flow of fuel into the car during pit stops and which would play such a large part in the outcome of the race, it was Len Terry who had produced the drawings. As we were the only team to get round the problem (it obviously could not have been a Ford idea as then all its top runners would have benefited).

Len: 'When the gravity feed regulations became known, it was obviously a matter of vital importance to increase the replenishment flow during pit stops to gain an advantage, and it became clear later that no one else within the other teams had considered a solution too deeply. I based my design on a venturi shape for the 3-inch-diameter outlet that fed into a "Y" from which two 3-inch lines individually fed fuel to each side of the car. My calculations promised a delivery of around 50 US (41 Imperial) gallons in under 20 seconds, and if no one else thought of a similar scheme we would gain an enormous advantage. Fortunately, no one else did . . .'

Len Terry's ultimately race-winning Lotus 38 'full' monocoque chassis taking shape on the trestles at Cheshunt.

March brought another problem to overcome. In applying for his Trenton race date of 25 April, track manager and promoter Sam Nunis (known as 'Slippery Sam' by the racing fraternity) had omitted to schedule it for international status, thereby excluding Jimmy, with his British licence. Jimmy had already been entered for Pau automatically under the Formula 2 Association contract some time earlier, and the French organisers refused to allow his withdrawal, even if we could iron out the Trenton problem. While Nunis applied to the sport's governing body for his event's required upgrading, I cabled Jimmy for his thoughts on revoking his British licence in favour of an American version, to which he quickly agreed. Nunis's plea had to be agreed by race organisers of conflicting international events on that date, and those of the Pau Grand Prix quickly opposed it. I explained the reasons for the switch in Jimmy's licence to the British representative on the Commission Sportive Internationale (CSI), Dean Delamont of the RAC, who, as a staunch ally in times of need, vouched his support, together with his doubts that such a move would be trouble-free.

But events quickly took the matter out of our hands; Pau's opposition increased in volume, the CSI agreed they had a case and ACCUS (the US licensing authority) was ordered to oppose Jimmy's application. While all this was going on, I approached Parnelli Jones to drive Jimmy's car at Trenton. By now Colin had returned to Cheshunt and his view was that the affair presented the perfect reason for reducing our Trenton entry to just one car; he was seriously worried about the possibility of damaging both immediately before running began at Indy, so we sought Ford's approval for Parnelli to drive a single entry.

When it was announced that Parnelli (a Mobil contracted driver) would drive Jimmy's car, our own fuel company, Humble, threatened to annul our Indy contract, but Esso in London quickly calmed the storm.

Leo Beebe's response was that we should contract another American driver for the second car. Colin's plan from the outset had been to sign a capable, up-and-coming driver rather than another star in case Jimmy's car should develop a problem in the race, requiring us to call in the second car for Jimmy to take over. The first name on my list was NASCAR driver Paul Goldsmith, but he already had an Indy seat; the matter was still not resolved by the time of the Trenton test, and Colin arranged with Gurney to 'borrow' his driver, Roger McCluskey, for both the test and the 100-mile race that followed it.

Compared with earlier years our build schedule for all three cars was well advanced, and in the second week in March Jimmy was able to have a cockpit fitting when he returned from the Tasman series. The first engine to arrive was then being fitted, and a shakedown test took place at Snetterton on 3 April. Both Jimmy and a rather cramped Dan drove the car anti-clockwise around the circuit to compensate for the car's asymmetric suspension and 'left-hand' turning fuel system. We had personnel 'guarding' the entry on to the track to warn arrivals of the car's approach from the wrong direction. Running on alcohol, the

Friendly rivals – 1963 '500' winner Parnelli Jones (left) listens in as very-English-looking Colin discusses matters with very-American-looking J. C. 'Aggie' Agajanian, Parnelli's car entrant. (G. Crombac)

maximum revs attainable in top gear were 7,500 (slightly over 160 mph) compared with the 9,000 rpm Indy norm, but only minor adjustments were called for and the test was declared a success. Two days later the car was announced at a press gathering in the factory car park at Cheshunt.

We had still not signed a tyre contract, and by this time the Phoenix tyre and Kingman test programme had both been cancelled in favour of the Firestone and Goodyear session at Trenton at the end of the month, so more running could take place nearer home before leaving for the States.

A week after the Type 38's announcement, Dan's car (chassis '38/3') was winging its way to the US. This car, which he paid for, was entered by his All-American Racers team and sponsored by Yamaha, a surprising achievement in view of Dan's regular Spanish Montesa motorcycle dealership. The two Team cars were also now complete and being prepared for a test at Silverstone where Jimmy drove them both, along with a Formula 1 car, in less than ideal weather. One Type 38 had Indy ratios fitted, but running was curtailed by a fuel filter problem. The other car was set up for the Trenton 1-mile oval and performed faultlessly. It was fitted with asymmetric suspension (chassis offset to the left), but running the usual (clockwise) direction around the track, Jimmy found that its handling demanded extra concentration on the right-hand corners, especially Woodcote. But power was available in plenty, and he was having to back off halfway down the straight. Jack Brabham had set the outright lap record the previous year at 1 min 33.6 secs (112.58 mph), and Jimmy circulated

The prototype Lotus-Ford 38 upon its unveiling to the press at Cheshunt, April 1965. The 'suits' are, from the right, the author, the Guv'nor, Len Terry, Jim Endruweit and David Lazenby. (David Phipps)

The new 38's three-quarter rear view simply breathes power – here '38/1' demonstrates its Firestone-shod, knock-off hub, cast-spoked wheels, rear nerf-cum-push-start bar, massive driveshafts and the Ford quad-cam V8's hungry injection trumpets and snake-pit, centre-vee exhaust system. The heat-sink fins of the electronic ignition transistor box project through the cockpit coaming skin just above the right-rear tyre.

The head-on aspect of '38/1' demonstrates its offset suspension set-up, cockpit rear panel detail sans seat upholstery, fuel filler and tank-vent fixtures. The suspension offset certainly played eccentric tricks with rear radius-rod angularity.

consistently in 1 min 38 secs without real effort, neither using the brakes nor changing out of top gear!

A few days later our Indy section was in Trenton preparing the two new cars for Jimmy and Roger McCluskey to test. I had kept Sam Nunis informed of progress over the problem with Jimmy's entry, but as the Trenton race programmes went to press, Sam went off at a tangent and announced to the world that Jimmy would run.

Ford's PR department was out in force as Trenton testing opened, accompanied by a large media contingent, which severely displeased Colin. On a similar occasion he had resorted to arranging for everyone to eat in a nearby restaurant to get them out of his hair, and later ruefully reported that he had had to pay for 98 hot dogs . . .

An initial brake problem soon found Colin cabling Girling for a specification change, then Jimmy suffered a jammed throttle, which he managed to control without hitting anything, but a more serious setback was about to occur. The day was cold with a blustery wind affecting times, and when Colin learned that the track officials were about to go home, he rushed around to them all, successfully negotiating cash payments to extend running. Then 10 minutes after resuming, McCluskey smashed into the wall, seriously damaging chassis '38/2'.

Mike Underwood: 'The familiar bogey of a jammed throttle had struck again, and immediately we found ourselves getting the

blame for it from the Ford people, which we felt distinctly unfair, especially as the press referred to it as "the usual Ford malady" and the same thing would happen to another Ford in race practice. When the wreck was brought in, there was a meeting to decide the best plan of action. There were nine days to go before the Speedway opened, but when it became obvious the damage meant that virtually a new tub would have to be built, we realised we were in for a lot of work. We immediately set to, removing all the salvageable bits and taking the engine out; then we airfreighted the car back to Cheshunt with me following while the rest of the crew packed up and moved on to the Speedway, rather than risk anything happening to Jimmy's car.'

Graham Clode: 'I can still remember very clearly arriving at Indy with Jim Smith and the crowd that gathered round when we unloaded Jimmy's 38. Quite soon the scrutineers called for the car to be weighed. I remember the occasion so well because it was so far below the weight of the lightest roadster that they made us take the car off the weighbridge while they checked their scales! Then we had to loosen every water and oil pipe to prove the car was dry. Finally they asked us to remain in our garage for an hour or so while they went over all their figures again . . .'

For Jimmy, the end of testing meant an early return to Europe and a superb Formula 2 win at Pau.

Colin telephoned me shortly after McCluskey's accident to ask

Dan Gurney's Yamaha-sponsored private Type 38 – chassis '38/3' – all set up and ready to run during Indy '65 pre-qualifying. Dan's personal crew chief, Bill Fowler, is to his right. (Indianapolis Motor Speedway)

how long a new 'tub' would take to build in this emergency situation. John Lambert was in charge of our fabricators, Colin Knight, Roy Franks, Ron Chappell, Mick Barry and the 'boy', Colin Hawker, and his estimate of completion of 6 May, just 13 days away, was cabled back to Trenton.

Roy Franks: 'We had a few components completed for the fourth tub that had been scheduled, but nothing to speak of. There may have been some Williams & Pritchard skins – I can't remember – but we set to work immediately, our people doing shifts and the shop operational 24 hours a day. Then, when the Old Man got back, he rushed round to see how we were progressing, promising us a cash bonus, which delighted us all!'

It was an immense task facing both the fabricators and the crew at Indy, who would have to race-prepare the car; around six weeks (865 hours in total) was the norm from starting a car build to actually rolling it out of the door. Construction of a Type 38 front box alone was scheduled to take 85 man-hours, and now a complete car was required within a matter of days.

As this new 38 took shape, Ford asked us to supply the Jones and Foyt cars with 1965-style ZF gearboxes, but with the one damaged at Trenton as our only spare, this was out of the question.

I arrived at the Speedway at the end of April. New stands had been erected over the winter, and seating capacity was now increased to 160,000. In addition to the three British marques – ourselves, Lola and British Racing Partnership (BRP) – there were four American monocoque designs entered. Sixty-eight entries had been confirmed; 45 were rear-engined, of which power units 24 were Ford products. Of the field, 21 would be Firestone-shod and 12 on Goodyear. The Cooper-inspired revolution of the Speedway was almost complete!

Although the new tub being built in Cheshunt was the fourth Type 38 to be built, Team fabricator Ron Chappell recalled why the chassis plate he riveted on the car designated it '38/2' and not '38/4': 'You were already at the Speedway and when I asked what number should be put on the plate I was told "38/2" as all the Customs & Excise paperwork for the shunted car was still relevant.' Expensive bonds were in force and as the procedure to obtain new paperwork was very time-consuming and expensive it was more sensible to leave everything as it was and ship out the 'new' car under the old chassis number.

The fabrication shop excelled in producing the new 'tub' on time, but a great many tasks demanded completion upon its arrival at the Speedway before it could run. An engine and its ancillaries had to be fitted, together with running gear, and this was not a task to be accomplished quickly.

Mike Underwood: 'In those days the cars did not have readily interchangeable components; each had its own set of bits, and when you were forced to change between tubs, such as we now found ourselves doing, there was a lot of fudging to be done, which all took time.'

Fortunately we could again draw upon our EFLO section mechanics to help with the reassembly work, while Jimmy's run-

ning continued unhindered. The Bobs – Dance and Sparshott – had run the Lotus-Cortinas at Riverside on the first weekend in May, and the following week they were at Laguna Seca, also in California, again running cars for Jackie Stewart and Tony Hegbourne. Immediately before the second race they were on their way to Indy. As the work continued, our second Indy driver arrived on the scene – a note from Colin left in my motel pigeon hole announced, 'Our driver Bobby Johns will be at the garage today – sign him up!'

As soon as I set eyes on our new recruit I realised that Colin had followed his original thoughts to the letter. Johns was ideal. He was the same height and weight as Jimmy (making changeovers in the race trouble-free) and displayed just the same pleasantly quiet, reflective attitude and sense of humour. Then 31, he was a NASCAR veteran who had started driving roadsters in 1950. Four of his years driving stock cars had seen him as Florida's NASCAR Champion, and he had won an Atlanta '500', finished second in a Daytona '500' and third in a Charlotte '600'. At Indy he had passed his driver's test in 1964 driving Smokey Yunick's extraordinary rear-engined sidecar device, only to write it off just before qualifying. His first visit to our garage could hardly have assured him of a relaxed spell with our team; it was now well into the month of May and the rebuilt car had still not turned a wheel in anger.

Back home Jimmy opened his May schedule by driving a Type 30 in the Tourist Trophy at Oulton Park. It was going to be strange programme for Team Lotus – Jimmy would miss the Silverstone race (15 May) in favour of qualifying (Mike Spence and Pedro Rodriguez would drive the Formula 1 cars there), and the Monaco Grand Prix (30 May) would be missed altogether, since new rulings stipulated that 24 hours had to elapse between international race appearances.

Both David Lazenby and Mike Underwood reflected on their personal satisfaction during May 1965. 'Laz': 'It was a superb feeling – with the Type 38s we were in bloody good shape all month. The cars had been built in good time, the design was right, the engines were good. Everything on Jimmy's programme went according to plan. Apart from the problems with the second car, we felt confident right from the start that this could very easily be our year.'

Jimmy was equally pleased. After what was for him a leisurely transatlantic schedule, he was running at the Speedway just two days after the track's opening, lapping a little over 152 mph and delighted with the car's handling, which he attributed to both increased power and weight. Ford, however, still harboured doubts about our race crew after the McCluskey stuck-throttle accident at Trenton, and made it known that it would not tolerate any interference with its engines at Indy.

Mike Underwood: 'We had Ford "engineers" or mechanics allotted to us, and one of their responsibilities was to drain and refill the engine oil every day. Almost immediately we found they were suspect – on two occasions we found that they had forgotten to wire-lock the drain plugs. So we said to them, "Look, if that's all you have to do and you can't do that properly, you can piss off!" Which they did and we never heard another word ...'

Much heralded arrivals were the new Lola-Fords for Parnelli and A. J., both being described as replacements for their Lotuses. Perhaps now we would be able to sit back while another British constructor enjoyed the attentions of the press!

Initially our team focused on fuel settings for the alcohol-burning engine, a task demanding much concentrated tweaking to persuade it to function efficiently throughout the whole rev range. Then once this had been accomplished came fuel consumption calculations, and when this looked a trifle marginal, a 2-gallon reserve tank was installed to ensure that a fuel-starved car could make it back to the pits. Trials with the gravity refuelling system were accomplished only in parts, to ensure that our advantage was not broadcast to the world; then by the end of the first week the calculations and tweaking had been finalised.

The total time required to fill the fuel cells was clocked at 16 seconds, so a quick stop would rely upon the refuelling crew's ability to get the hoses out, attach them to the car, refuel, cut off, then get the gear back behind the pit wall. The task was allotted to a crew well renowned for their skills in stock car racing, where they held the record for a four-wheel change and refuel in 21.20 seconds. Bobby Johns had initiated their recruitment; known as the Wood Brothers, the group had been formed in 1956 and was composed of five brothers and two cousins from Stuart, Virginia. They now held top place in the world of pit crewmen, and were to perform outstandingly well in the race, going through the 'out and back' part of their allotted task in just under 4 seconds. They flew in a couple of days before the race and

Refuelling practice before the cameras but deserted grandstands – the 38 is standing normally in the pit lane, but during a race stop it would be raised upon its platform jack enabling fresh wheels and tyres to be fitted simultaneously with the tanks being filled. (Indianapolis Motor Speedway)

Bobby Johns in the back-up Lotus 38 – chassis '38/2' (2) – with Mike Underwood on the John Deere mini-tractor pushing him towards the pit lane.

quickly impressed Colin with their professional appearance and efficiency, but their presence was not viewed too favourably by our own mechanics, who still felt under the shadow of the unfair criticism they had incurred in a previous race.

If progress with Jimmy's car seemed almost leisurely, events with the second car more than made up for it! When it was finally completed, Colin left instructions that it was not to be run until he came out on to the pit lane. So '38/2' (B) was pushed there, the mechanics making last-minute adjustments. They then started the engine to warm it up while Bobby operated the clutch as he sampled the gear change. Suddenly the car leapt forward under power. Bobby, shocked, attempted to steer round the car in front, but the Lotus's left-front wheel struck the other's right-rear and the Type 38 'tub' instantly 'banana'd', its right-front wheel cocked clear of the ground!

In utter dismay, accompanied by a very embarrassed driver, our stunned crew began pushing the car back to the garage. On the way we met Colin, hurrying out to the pit lane.

'Where are you going?' he demanded. 'We've got to start running.'

'Er, we've got a problem and we're going back to the garage,' I explained.

'How can you have a problem?' said Colin. 'It hasn't run yet.'

'We've had a shunt,' I said.

'*Shunt*! How could you have had a *shunt?*'

I explained, briefly.

'I don't believe it,' he snorted.

At that moment the car appeared alongside, its damage all too evident.

'Oh no!' Colin gasped, and together we returned to the privacy of our over-heated garage.

Repairs took two days and two full nights. Once again the car had to be reduced to a bare 'tub', then taken to the Bear Safety Service centre near our garage where Mike Underwood and an American sheet metal man, Lujie Lesovsky, using chains and hydraulics, immediately set to work stripping panels for re-shaping before reconstruction could begin. After this relentless 48-hour effort the car was ready to run again.

Mike Underwood: 'We never did get it back to proper shape during May – when we checked the wheelbase on completion it was half an inch out on the left-hand side, and that's how it ran for the rest of the month, including the race.'

It was Wednesday 12 May, with just two days to go to the first qualifying weekend, before Bobby Johns could drive around the oval, and he quietly set himself the task of working up to commendable speeds without fireworks. Rookie driver speeds had been increased to 145 mph, and Bobby – and even such veterans as Masten Gregory – had to take their tests again.

Meanwhile, despite our May schedule for Jimmy running almost to plan, late-night working remained the norm, as his car enjoyed meticulous and unhurried preparation and the No 2 car's mechanics struggled to complete their tasks.

Very late one night, anxious to have Jimmy's car running at

'crack o' sparrow's', Colin bemoaned the absence of the official signwriter, George Gruber, to paint the number '82' on its nose. He then asked if I had hidden painting talents; I said that it was not my forte, but agreed to have a go. I did my best, but it hardly satisfied me; nor Colin, who, when he surveyed my handicraft, remarked, 'Good Lord, you're no good at all!', confirming my own opinion.

Colin's concern about Ford allowing private American owners to run our earlier cars with considerably more powerful engines was justified soon after the Speedway opened. On 5 May A. J. Foyt's Type 34 hit the retaining wall twice after a rear hub broke, and following examination the scrutineers announced that six cars – our two and the Lola and Lotus entries of both Parnelli Jones and A. J., who had one of each – would be 'temporarily grounded' until the components were strengthened. Although we had experienced no problems with our own uprights, stronger ones were hastily sent out from Cheshunt, Jimmy continuing to run on the previous components as they were passed as perfectly safe in the compulsory USAC tests. However, the officials restricted Jimmy to 30 laps, after which the uprights were removed for another crack test, which again they passed.

Then on 9 May it was Parnelli's turn to experience a breakage when one of his Type 34's hubs sheared; this time there was no contact with the wall; Parnelli reported that he had slowed down after feeling something was wrong prior to the wheel coming off.

Again both Lotus and Lola entries were officially grounded, but not for long in Team's case as further detailed inspection of our rear uprights revealed no inherent flaws, not surprising since they had been designed for the current car! Then Foyt, who had been fighting a close duel with Jimmy on lap speeds since the track had opened, clocked a record lap of just under the magic 160 mph in his Type 34, but returning to his pit he declared that he would from now on drive his Lola, as the Lotus felt 'unsanitary'.

This comment provided another cherry for the media, who had been mounting an increasingly hostile campaign against rear-engined cars, and the fragility of Team Lotus vehicles in particular, reciting 'facts' that were completely false. They also reported a 'resentment towards foreign teams that goes beyond normal competitive instincts'!

Colin might have followed his usual stance in not responding to press criticism, but when the reports went on to suggest that McCluskey's Trenton accident might have been caused by the loss of a wheel, and that Jimmy had only finished in five of his last 29 races, our Guv'nor's touch paper was lit and he asked me to issue a Team press statement.

In this it was pointed out that in his last 29 races, Jimmy had in fact scored 19 wins, been placed in four more, and had only retired from four for reasons not attributable to Team. It also made the point that currently the cars being run by American teams were year-old designs that had been extensively altered (not by us) and which were now employing engines producing considerably more power, subjecting them to stresses in excess of their original design. In contrast, our new cars had already recorded a considerable mileage and 'had not suffered, nor shown any sign of suffering, any weakness whatsoever in their mechanical components'.

The statement perhaps slowed but did not stem the rot, but we all felt better for delivering a broadside; Parnelli's entrant, J. C. Agajanian, responded with a press interview stating that he had bought his Lotus from Ford but its running components from us. 'They knew we were preparing for 1965 – the '64 race was over'. Just two days later A. J. was back in his Lotus and notching up even faster times.

'Laz': 'I don't know who made them (I heard it was Ford), but when Parnelli's car appeared again it had the most horrendous hubs fitted – they looked as if someone had used almost plate steel.'

None the less, Jimmy in particular as well as Colin remained in a good mood for most of the month of May, reflecting their confidence in the Type 38's efficiency, but there were exceptions. Colin was a stickler for following the procedure for accurately measuring the amount of fuel pumped from a car when calculating its fuel consumption. In fact, the solemnity of these occasions was so awe-inspiring that I always carried copies of a step-by-step instruction sheet I had drawn up in case a mechanic forgot the rules, or, heaven forbid, I was the fellow in charge.

Colin noticed that the device for extracting fuel at our Humble Oil (Enco) fuel depot at Indy incorporated a dial to record the amount of fuel pumped out. He immediately suspected its accuracy and instructed 'Laz' and the crew that it was on no account to be relied upon when calculating fuel consumption. It could be used, but only to pump fuel into churns, in which the amount could be more accurately measured by us, first-hand.

After the track had closed one evening, the usual large crowd was tight-packed around our garage doors and a group of crew members were standing outside in the cool with Colin and 'Laz' as they discussed fuel consumption for the day; Colin recorded the details in his neat pencilled handwriting on a notepad fastened to his clipboard with its three stop-watches. Finally 'Laz' was asked to repeat how many churns and fractions of churns had been filled, and with an unusual attack of brain fade he stated that the Enco fuel man had used the dial for the calculations.

There was a momentary pause before the so far reasonably relaxed conversation was punctuated by a loud bellow of 'f—-!', as Colin executed a perfect overarm delivery that saw his clipboard hit the ground with such power that watches flew in all directions, the board itself landing on the edge of the garage roof 8 feet from the ground. This was all good stuff for the spectators; even as Colin, like a prison warder, quickly herded us all into the garage and slammed the doors behind us, more came running to swell the crowd, convinced that an event of major significance had occurred. For us, indeed, it had . . .

When I eventually emerged to seek the remains of the watches (only one was intact, but distinctly unwell), the crowd was still looking on in stunned amazement.

• 1965: FIRST FRUITS

With our tyre contract as yet unsigned, the cars ran both Goodyear and Firestone in practice; the former were faster by 2–3 mph and, surprisingly, initially more durable as well, but when signs of chunking similar to our Dunlop experience the previous year threatened, we settled for the slightly slower but trouble-free Firestones.

Certainly the 1965 Indianapolis '500' provided a good example of how to win a race. Most of our data collation – full-fuel running, shock absorber data, fuel-injection tweaking, fuel consumption calculations – had been completed by the beginning of the second week, when several cars, including our No 2, had not

Time for adjustment – a dubious-looking Foyt with his modified Type 34 as the crew adjust the right-rear suspension set-up during the month of May. (Bruce Craig Photos)

even ventured on to the track. Although early morning and late afternoon running was best thanks to cooler temperatures, it was also essential to experience the midday heat, when the race would be run, and even this spell of testing was accomplished satisfactorily.

One afternoon Ford's Dave Evans invited Colin, Jimmy and myself to go for a flight from Weir Cook in his single-engined aircraft. By no means an enthusiastic flyer, I soon got the message that perhaps Dave was not as skilled as Colin or Jimmy. Colin sat alongside Dave and they chatted about radio equipment and weather, but both Jimmy and I were alerted by Colin's observation to the pilot that some knobs were missing from the instrument panel.

'Yes, I know, Colin. There's a pair of pliers somewhere about – perhaps they're under your seat. Can you have a look-see?'

A nudge from Jimmy alongside me, accompanied by a rolling of his eyes, appraised me of the situation, and from then on both of us paid rapt attention to everything going on up front. After something like 45 minutes we were back on terra firma, and as the three of us drove back to the track Jimmy said to me, 'I get the feeling you worry about me going around the Speedway – I just want to say that you have possibly just survived something a lot more dangerous …'

We were delighted to see Jim Hurtubise back on the scene after his terrible crash and horrifying burns sustained at Milwaukee 11 months earlier. Jimmy was visibly shocked to see the brave extrovert driver's injuries, his hands reduced to claws, but he went on to qualify a front-engined Kurtis Novi at close on 157 mph after another huge crash in practice. He went out on lap 1 of the race, but his prize money of $6,000 was considerably more than Graham Hill's Monaco GP win brought him … Known as 'Hercules', in 1968 Hurtubise was to drive a roadster called a 'Mallard', and he kept ducks of the same variety in his Speedway garage. Mechanic Doug Garner: 'As well as the ducks he kept two large fibreglass balls hanging in a fisherman's net outside his garage door. When you asked him what they were for he'd tell you he strapped them on for qualifying!'

It was not long before one of our engines had run over 1,000 miles, and as the second week neared its end another unit was installed, tuned to run for qualifying with 20 per cent nitro fuel additive. This called for a fine setting of the fuel injection system, since from now until the end of qualifying the car would be running on minimum fuel loads. Just prior to first qualifying, Jimmy's car was officially timed at 195.5 mph on the straight and 148.9 through Turn Two.

As first qualifying approached, the ding-dong battle for top speed honours still swung between Jimmy and A. J. as they both broke Marshman's 1964 Lotus record of 160.081. Soon the Texan was over the 161 mph mark, Jimmy close behind in the mid-160 mph zone. Parnelli was still attempting to get to grips with the top men, running like Dan in his '38/3' above 159 mph, while rookie Mario Andretti kept a watching brief on both with his *Dean Van Lines Special*, a replica Brabham that even Black Jack

would not have recognised, also powered by Ford. Brave Bobby Unser in the 760 bhp STP Novi Ferguson 4WD also achieved speeds above 160 mph before the car was wrecked when another spun into it.

With 'Beatlemania' still the rage, particularly in America (where we were asked by total strangers if we lived near them!), some of our mechanics sported 'Beatle' hair-cuts, a style in sharp contrast to the Americans' crew-cuts. One early evening there was a commotion in the garage area, with the sound of running feet and slamming doors. Foyt and Parnelli had got together to teach our crew a lesson; both drivers and their crew members were attempting to ambush our lads on their frequent trips around the area, Foyt armed with a large pair of scissors.

'Laz': 'I can still see Bob Sparshott in my mind's eye flying through the toilet block with A. J. and a pair of scissors in hot pursuit. Eventually all our lads returned safely to our garage, locking the doors behind them and not venturing out again until the early hours of the morning.' Round one to Team Lotus!

For the first time qualifying order at Indy was determined by a draw, after previous years had witnessed a mad dash as cars were pushed into line, their crews anxious not to miss first-day attempts for the leading grid positions. The new scheme would be much more civilised.

The settling of the draw was another event for media attention, as well as some bluffing and humour. The queues started early the day before in the garage area's central roadway. Anxious to be in at the start, I arrived to find J. C. Agajanian, as usual resplendent in cowboy hat, standing on the north side talking to a group of fellow entrants. He called me over with his customary bonhomie.

'You're in second place behind me,' he said, then, to prevent any bad feeling among the others, 'I've kept it open for you like we agreed …'

The queue grew and the sun blazed down making the long wait for the USAC officials a decided bore. Then Andy Granatelli arrived, taking station on the south side.

'The queue starts here,' he bellowed over to us. 'You guys are in the wrong place …'

J. C. made a sarcastic response, but amazingly some of the others broke rank and lined up behind Andy. Very soon the two growing lines were almost the same length. Still the sun beat down; the last thing we should be doing was to have a hassle …

Finally the officials' table arrived, to be plonked down in front of Andy! Chaos erupted as we all fought for a place near the front. I eventually landed seventh or eighth place amidst 50 or 60. Small plastic capsules containing the running order numbers were drawn from a hat.

There were over 200,000 spectators on hand to witness an incredibly exciting battle. Eleventh to run was rookie Mario Andretti, and he set the initial pace, averaging 158.849 mph over his four laps and breaking the previous 10-lap speed record. Next to run was Jimmy. It had already been accepted that his faster Goodyears gave A. J. the edge on us, but Jimmy put in a typically superlative effort, his second lap a sniff under 161 mph, his four-lap average of 160.729 mph easily breaking Mario's record, which had stood for all of 4 minutes. Later Jimmy was to apologise for 'making a mess of it'. He had been affected by a blustery wind that had made the car feel nervous, and remained convinced that he could have done better.

As the hullabaloo erupted around him upon his return to the pit lane it was A. J.'s turn to go out in his *Sheraton Thompson Special* Lotus Type 34. No doubt the initial difficulty in getting his car to start helped his adrenalin to flow, and his first flying lap was stupendous, at just under 162 mph; his four-lap average was 161.233 mph. However, it is interesting to note that regardless of his faster tyres, A.J.'s total time over his four laps was only seven-hundredths of a second quicker than Jimmy's.

Dan Gurney was 2 seconds slower, but his 158.898 mph was good enough for third spot, his drive clinching an all-Lotus front row for the 33-car grid. Parnelli's year-old Lotus was fifth fastest, on the second row with Dan and wonder-boy Mario Andretti, with Al Miller's two-year-old Lotus Type 29 seventh (third row). The huge crowd had been royally entertained.

While Jimmy enjoyed a break back in Scotland the following week, Bobby Johns consistently improved his times; with his first run in the rebuilt car so near to first qualifying, it was decided to let him gain more experience, and he qualified comfortably the following Saturday with third fastest of the day, taking 22nd slot with a four-lap average of 155.481 mph. During this period the Goodyear runners suffered the Dunlop malaise of the previous year, their tyres chunking, and although there was considerable agitation, Goodyear soon put the matter to bed.

Under the regulations, the engine installed for qualifying had to be used in the race, and Ford stripped and carefully inspected it as well as converting it back to run on methanol without the hot additive in time for carburation trials on the Thursday before the race. Meanwhile Colin's lengthy job lists as usual kept our crew working long hours, but come the night before the race they were finished at 10.30 pm.

Mechanic Graham Clode: 'I couldn't believe it! Although Jimmy's car just ran and ran and ran throughout May I was convinced that the night before the race would be a real saga, so at such an early hour it seemed impossible that we had really finished – we checked and double-checked but it was true and we could actually look forward to a relaxed meal and early bed. There was to be no partying *that* night! As was the unwritten rule, we went off to clear our departure with Colin ...'

Mike Underwood: 'We drove round to Colin's room in the Speedway Holiday Inn where we all stayed, and Hazel Chapman answered the door. Colin was in the shower and Hazel said, "Hang on, I'll give him your news." When she came back she said, "Colin says are you really sure you're finished?" We said yeah, yeah, and Hazel looked at us as if to say, "Well, you should know best", and off we went ...'

For the hour or so before the start of the race Jimmy sought the peace and quiet of our garage; he later reckoned that 20,000

In the queue for qualifying – 'Laz' and Mike Underwood with Jimmy's Lotus 38. (Indianapolis Motor Speedway)

Deep discussion – focus of the ever-present film camera and microphone (left), Jimmy reports on Type 38 behaviour to 'Laz' (right), Jim Smith (left) and Colin (dark glasses) as dusk gathers at the Speedway. (Indianapolis Motor Speedway)

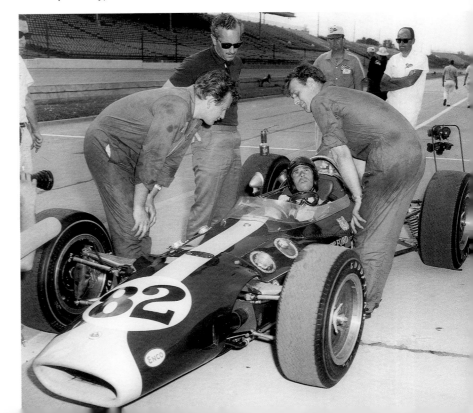

The front-row line-up after qualifying for the 1965 '500' – A. J.'s Eddie Kuzma-modified '64 Lotus 34 (right) is on pole, Bobby Johns deputising for Jimmy in the Lotus 38 (centre), and Dan Gurney (far left) in his privately-entered Yamaha 38. George Bignotti, 'Laz' and Bill Fowler are the three crew chiefs honoured in the line-up beyond. (Indianapolis Motor Speedway)

members of the media were waiting on the track where the cars had been lined up on the dummy grid, every one intent on conducting a pre-race interview. For the 350,000 spectators the

Graham Clode on the doormat working on the 38's gearbox. The car is shod here, unusually, on Goodyear tyres. (Indianapolis Motor Speedway)

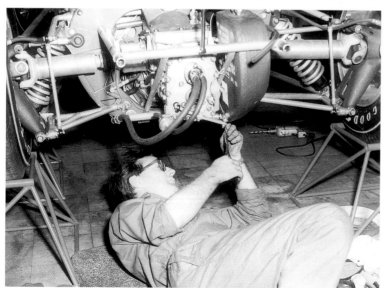

weather was superb, the sky cloudless, the temperature into the high 70s, with a slight breeze.

When the pre-start running and pace lap got under way, Jimmy was taken by surprise as the pace car turned into the pit lane after only two laps. Anxious to trail pole-sitter Foyt into Turn One, he changed into top gear early, taking the Texan unawares and passing him to lead into it. The manoeuvre provided a picture to thrill every Lotus enthusiast, Jimmy leading the race and heading four Lotuses in line-ahead formation. The time for that first flying $2^{1}/_{2}$-mile lap, 59.45 seconds (151.380 mph), was a new record, over $1^{1}/_{2}$ mph faster than Jimmy's first lap average of the previous year.

A. J. moved ahead on lap 2, Jimmy tucking in behind him, Gurney third, Parnelli and Al Miller fourth and fifth – five Lotuses in the first five places, although to be fair A. J. had already made it clear that there was hardly anything Lotus remaining in his car – until something would break on it!

But lap 3 saw Jimmy back in front, and he was destined to lead all but ten of the race's 200 laps. Later he was to report that he had dropped back in order to weigh up Foyt's pace, but had found himself being delayed so had retaken the lead. In addition, Foyt was running on an alcohol/nitro methane mixture, which meant that he would require more fuel and possibly more stops, and there was also the possibility that the Texan would encounter the tyre problems with his Goodyears that had

Jimmy at speed in his Type 38, 1965 Indy '500'. (Dave Friedman Photo Collection)

Dave Friedman's superb study of Jimmy's Lotus 38 during the Indy-winning drive plainly demonstrates its sleek lines, subtly fuel-bloated midships section, offset suspension and neat engine installation with only fuel injection velocity stacks and up-raked exhaust megaphones protruding beyond the monocoque/roll-over bar section. Leaving one of the shallow-banked 90-degree turns, Jimmy is back on the loud pedal, the 38's rear suspension is squatting down and the car is nose high, front top rocker arms virtually horizontal, lower wishbones drooped . . . The Type 38's replacement as a Lotus Indycar would attempt to correct such unseemly pitch change. (Dave Friedman Photo Collection)

Out of luck yet again – Dan Gurney stands on it at Indy '65. (Dave Friedman Photo Collection)

Pit stop flurry – Bobby Johns hustles in with Team's back-up 38, which he drove at Indy '65 with impressive, quiet competence. (Indianapolis Motor Speedway)

emerged during qualifying. Jimmy was also surprised to find his encounters with back-marker traffic resolved quicker than A. J.'s, a man he had always rated as quickest of all in such situations.

By lap 33 Jimmy was 10 seconds ahead of Foyt and Parnelli, with Dan dropping back with engine problems that would take him out of the race on lap 42. By 100 miles Jimmy and A. J. had lapped the field up to 6th place.

Parnelli pitted for fuel on lap 63, taking 45 seconds. When Jimmy stopped three laps later, he was away again in just 19.8 seconds and tongues began to wag – no doubt the Scotsman would soon be back for more fuel. In fact, our leading car had taken on fully 50 US gallons (41 Imperial), which with the fuel still remaining in his car would be more than enough for him to cover the 175 miles to his next scheduled stop on lap 136. After all, both cars had a 2-gallon reserve fuel tank fitted during practice, which would enable them to return to the pits should consumption unexpectedly increase.

Foyt briefly took the lead while Jimmy made his stop, but his 34-second cushion was cut to a deficit when his own fuel stop on lap 74 took over 43 seconds, returning the lead to the Scot. As the race progressed, so this battle between Jimmy and the Texan continued, first one then the other clocking record speeds, the race average sometimes running more than 5 mph faster than in 1964.

Working his way competently and consistently through the midfield, Bobby Johns meanwhile was more than holding his own. His first fuel stop took 40 seconds, setting tongues wagging again as the press, armed only with their fact sheets, compared his stop time to Jimmy's. What they did not know was that he had been allowed to carry on until he was taking fuel from his reserve tank, thereby giving a stable fuel consumption figure that could be used when estimating Jimmy's second-stop requirement. Consequently Bobby had taken on more fuel in more time, but had also fumbled his getaway, adding more grist to the media's mill.

At 100 laps Jimmy led Foyt (the only man he had not lapped) by just over a minute, but 15 laps later the Texan toured into his pit, transmission broken, his race over. Now Clark was something over 2 minutes ahead of Parnelli, himself some 10 seconds clear of Mario Andretti.

The fuel consumption check after Johns's stop showed it to be slightly higher than expected in the first part of the race, so to play safe it was decided to increase the amount to be loaded at Jimmy's second stop on lap 136, 58 US gallons (48 Imperial) going in for the remaining 160 miles in a longer 24.7-second stop.

At 400 miles Bobby Johns was up to ninth place, while his No 1 set new records at virtually every distance and averaging over 4 mph faster than Foyt the previous year. Jimmy was never keen to slow his pace as he felt that his concentration eased off pro rata; the middle stage of the race had also been a lot easier than he had expected, and he had been forced to pay extra attention to avoid even the slightest mistake. It was something that was to

1963: New shapes and sounds at the Indianapolis Motor Speedway as early in the month of May the push-rod-engined Lotus-Ford Type 29 V8s of Dan Gurney (white) and Jim Clark (green) rasp along the pit lane preparatory to some pulverising practice laps . . .

Above Pit-stop practice during what to Team Lotus's crewmen seemed to be the interminable month of May. USAC veterans George Bignotti (left) and A. J. Watson (background) look on – was the writing on the wall for their kind of racing? In fact, the former would flourish in the coming rear-engined era, but the latter would find his technology outpaced.

Left Race-day morning 1963 – Jimmy's '29/3' is drawn out of its garage and towed towards the pit area. It is on the brink of confirming the revolution engulfing the world's most conservative motor race. In contrast the yellow car, No 6, is Bobby Unser's Kurtis-chassised Novi V8 Hotel Tropicana Special, which will become the race's first retirement, tagging the south-west wall after only two laps.

Above right 1964: In dazzling spring sunshine Colin (right) and Jimmy (sitting beyond on the pit wall) ponder prospects for their latest Dunlop-shod Type 34.

Right The fastest man at the Speedway throughout much of the 1964 practice, test and race running was Bobby Marshman, here in the Lindsey Hopkins team's Jack Beckley-prepared, Firestone-shod and now Ford quad-cam-engined ex-works Type 29 Pure Firebird Special.

1965: Heading for the big one – Jim Clark in his Lotus-Ford 38, averaging 150.686 mph, en route to his record-shattering victory in the 1965 Indianapolis 500-Miles classic.

A good job done well – Bobby Johns, Lotus-Ford 38, heading towards his respectable – and unexpected – seventh place. The intention had been merely to provide team leader Clark with a healthy back-up throughout May. Team invited Johns back in both 1966 and 1967, but he could not accept.

Dan Gurney's All-American Racers-entered Yamaha Special *Lotus-Ford 38* gave him an unhappy ride at Indy '65, the engine stripping its timing gears after 42 laps to leave him classified 26th.

A. J. Foyt's Lesovsky-rebuilt Sheraton-Thompson Special *Lotus-Ford 34* stripped its final-drive gears after 115 laps, leaving the Texan to be classified 15th.

Parnelli Jones's Agajanian Hurst Special *Lotus-Ford 34, as reworked by Eddie Kuzma, had the legs of everything in the 1965 Indy field apart from Clark's Type 38. It finished second behind the factory car, having averaged 149.200 mph for the 200 laps.*

Al Miller's Jerry Alderman Ford Sales Special *Lotus-Ford 29 – Carroll Horton-modified chassis '29/2' – provided perhaps the revelation of the '65 '500', running reliably home as a two-year-old car to a superb fourth place finish, at 146.581 mph.*

1966: What Colin Chapman would describe as 'Granatelli Green' became the works Lotus-Ford 38s' team livery for 1966 as STP sponsorship backed the twin cars of Al Unser (18) and Jimmy Clark (19). Al's '38/7' sadly clouted the north-west wall after 161 laps, while Jimmy's '38/4' finished second – at 143.843 mph – and he thought he had won . . .

Above *A. J. Foyt's impeccably presented Type 38 was severely damaged in the start-line pile-up that eliminated 11 cars – including this latest* Sheraton-Thompson Special *– even before the 1966 '500' had really begun.*

Left *1967: A cheerful Jimmy before STP-Lotus's appalling 1967 Indy '500'. His demeanour in the face of depressing strife and failure buoyed team morale even when the crew was at its most grossly overworked and utterly exhausted. He would be placed 31st after holing a piston at 35 laps.*

Above right *Team Lotus Formula 1 Chief Mechanic Jim Endruweit giving Graham Hill a thumbs-up ready to leave the pit lane in his practice symmetrical Type 38 – '38/8/S' – which he was unable to qualify, finally running the hybrid 42F instead. Like his fellow Formula 1 World Champion team-mate Clark he would go out of the '500' with a burned piston – after 23 laps – and be classified 32nd.*

Right *Larry Dickson's* Vita Fresh Orange Juice Special *shows off its heavily reworked Lotus-Ford 38 lines during the 1967 '500'. It is the ex-Gurney '38/3'. After spinning out on the main straightaway at 180 laps he was classified 15th.*

Left *1968: Celebrating pole position at a four-lap average of 171.599 mph, Andy Granatelli poses proudly with former motor-cycle star Joe Leonard in the gas turbine-powered '56/1', its chisel nose already thoroughly sand-blasted by record-breaking passage around the historic Speedway.*

Below *Graham Hill's Lotus Type 56 turbine car, chassis '56/3', was the only one of the three contesting the 1968 '500' that could conceivably have survived the fuel pump drive failures which robbed STP team-mates Joe Leonard and Art Pollard of victory within the last 12 laps. But the Londoner had long since retired, hitting the south-east wall after 110 laps.*

Right *Day-glo identification paint on the left-front wheel and tyre of Joe Leonard's '56/1' in addition to the nose cone as the Californian runs hard into Turn One on race day '68.*

Below right *Dick Scammell conferring with Art Pollard at the wheel of '56/4' pre-race, the turbine car's vulnerable nose-edge racer-taped as protection against hurtling grit and debris. Four years later this faultlessly friendly veteran driver would break a leg here in a practice crash, returning in 1973 only to crash fatally during first qualifying.*

TEAM LOTUS: THE INDIANAPOLIS YEARS •

1969: A racing rarity – Jochen Rindt queasily finding his way around the Speedway in the unloved turbocharged, four-wheel-drive STP-Lotus-Ford 64 during practice for the 1969 '500'. The peculiar high-rise mirror frame ahead of him was necessary to provide a clear rear view over that enormous upturned rear wing.

For 1969 Andy Granatelli hedged his bets by entering this Lotus 56 look-alike with a conventional turbocharged four-cylinder Offenhauser engine, and water radiator within that opened-up wedge nose. This was a new STP-built car. The experiment was not notably successful – after qualifying very respectably 12th fastest at 167.123 mph, Art went out after only seven race laps when the car's drive line let go. He was classified 31st. (All colour photos Bob Tronolone)

happen to him on one occasion with almost dire results, and now he continued to build a time cushion over Parnelli. As the race neared its end Jimmy did ease from his 154-157 mph rhythm to 148-152, worried that a noise from the rear of his car heralded a transmission problem, but when the car was examined later, no such fault could be found.

Jimmy's glorious win, over 2 minutes (5 miles) clear of second-man Parnelli Jones, was the first by a foreigner at Indy for 49 years, and found him more mentally than physically exhausted (he only reported a sore right wrist later). From his first pit stop he had maintained an overwhelming superiority virtually in seclusion, and the lack of a good battle had drained him.

Bobby Johns had also done a magnificent job, working his way up to eighth in the final stages and nipping past Don Branson, literally on the last lap, to take seventh place by 32-hundredths of a second! With Al Miller's fourth place in the Type 29, Lotus had taken first, second, fourth and seventh places. The new refuelling system had worked, and the Wood Brothers had played an important part; Jimmy had made two stops totalling 44.5 seconds, while Andretti's two had taken 77 seconds and Parnelli's three had totalled 98.5. An hour after the race ended, Jimmy was on the phone to his mother in Scotland.

I had returned to Cheshunt after the second qualifying weekend, and a number of Team personnel had retired to Jim Endruweit's home to listen to a crackly broadcast commentary on American Forces Network in Germany. When we eventually got our congratulatory telephone call through to Colin, there came a most unpleasant surprise.

In reply to my opening 'Heartiest congratulations!' came Colin's coldly strained comment, 'We've been locked up!'

Apparently the cars had indeed been locked in our garage by the local sheriff, and the doors sealed; instead of enjoying a pleasant conversation with Colin, it boiled down simply to me giving him our lawyers' home telephone numbers in Indianapolis.

The matter stemmed from Parnelli Jones's drives in our Type 34s at Milwaukee and Trenton the previous year. In financial arrangements with trade support and sponsoring companies there were 'posted' and 'non-posted' bonuses; 'posted' bonuses were those that were made public and appeared on all the bonus sheets available to anyone who cared to obtain them, while 'non-posted' ones were those amounts paid on top of the 'posted' bonuses, which were not shared with the driver but went straight to the entrant, or car owner.

Payment of most success bonuses was usually a lengthy process, not helped by the fact that there was a time delay before the sport's governing body ratified a win or a placing; it was only after the rubber stamp in the top office had been inked that application for payment could be made. In the case of the two American races, receipt of such payments had not been finalised until March 1965, and in sending Parnelli his statement and cheque our accounts department had, in error, included details of both types of bonus. It may have been the first time Parnelli had encountered such an arrangement, but when he spotted that

Team Lotus with their victorious 38 in Gasoline Alley. 'Charlie Chins' (Mike Underwood) is looking up at the camera bottom right, with 'Laz' (hat), the Guv'nor and Jim Smith beyond. (Indianapolis Motor Speedway)

Superstars '65 – Dan Gurney, Jimmy Clark and A. J. Foyt with the Borg-Warner Trophy. (G. Crombac)

How do they do that? Jim Clark displays the pre-prepared but allegedly 'hot off the press' edition of the Indianapolis Star *reporting his record-breaking victory. 'Laz' (left) shares the moment, Colin reflects on a job brilliantly completed, and the sculpted figure topping the Borg-Warner Trophy is framed as the victor's crown. Look at the filthy state of the 38's windscreen – yet again there had been a lot of oil and rubber sprayed around the Speedway. (Indianapolis Motor Speedway)*

what he regarded as monies owing to him had not been received, he resorted to the legal action in which Colin was now involved. The matter was resolved in court the next day, and Colin never mentioned the matter again.

As to be expected, Ford America was delighted with the victory. Of its 17 engines in the race, only three had failed, including that of the unfortunate Gurney, and of the 11 cars running at the end, eight were Ford-powered. The American press was over the moon with so many 'firsts' in which to glory. It was the first win by a rear-engined car, the first for a Ford power unit, the first

for 49 years by a foreigner, and the first for a Briton with a British-built car. Jimmy had broken 19 of 20 record distances and speeds for the race. It was also the first non-Offy victory since 1946.

The winning car, as detailed in our agreement with Ford, was transferred to that company's ownership, and shortly after the race it was made ready for its first engagement, display in the Ford pavilion at the New York World's Fair; Colin and Jimmy flew there for the unveiling and press interviews. Ford Vice-President Donald Frey, talking to the media under a mass of dazzlingly

Job done – Team Lotus's Indianapolis section at Indy '65. Jimmy is in the car, with Colin and Mike Underwood squatting beside him. Chief Mechanic Dave Lazenby sits on the right-front wheel, then Graham Clode, Peter Jackson of Specialised Mouldings, who attended for the fun of it and was press-ganged into helping, Bob Sparshott, and Australians Alan Moffat and Jim Smith. Bob Sparshott went on to found his own one-time BS Fabrications Formula 1 team, Alan Moffat drove Team Lotus-Cortinas on occasion and became a leading light in Australian racing, while Jim Smith was a former ship's engineer converted here to lighter-weight technology. When 'Laz' later became General Manager of Lotus Components Ltd, Mike Underwood took over as Lotus's Indy Chief Mechanic. (Indianapolis Motor Speedway)

bright spotlights in front of numerous TV cameras, described the Indianapolis-winning Lotus-Ford as 'the greatest engine and the greatest chassis in the world', the 'result of a marriage between one of the world's largest and one of the smallest of car manufacturers.'

Ford's pavilion proved an immense attraction, a tunnel ride displaying the many ages of man to visitors seated in nearly 50 Ford vehicles attached to an endless belt, which transported over 45,000 people a day. Jimmy's Type 38, together with the Indy '500' winner's famous Borg-Warner trophy, was positioned on a turntable, which gently rose and fell as it revolved, set against a backdrop of an enormous photograph nearly 80 feet long depicting the car in action at the Speedway.

In Dearborn, EFLO's General Manager, Ron Platt, also joined in, stating that their sales of Lotus-Cortinas to dealers had increased by 54 per cent over the previous year, with retail sales increasing every month. As the publicity proudly proclaimed, the Lotus-Cortina victories had 'astonished the racing world'.

Ford issued historical pamphlets listing the 11 Ford-powered Lotus products to date, from the Mark II trials-cum-racing Lotus through Lotus 7s and Lotus-Cortinas to the Indy winner.

Sadly, like so many much-fanfared associations, the marriage Frey had referred to was already coming to a close. Quite soon the close-knit working programme that had existed between the two companies for over three years would wither and die, Ford's interest refocusing upon Dan Gurney's All-American Racers team. To be fair, Ford was to confirm its new relationship by helping us when our replacement BRM plan turned sour. As for the 'world-wide fame' that the press claimed now shone on Lotus, a Cheshunt sales department survey estimated that the Indianapolis win had brought them one more sale than the previous year – a Lotus 7, no less!

Of the total race prize money of $628,399 (then £224,400), which included lap and accessory prizes from 26 organisations, on paper the win brought us $166,621 (£59,150), of which £28,500 was leader cup money for Jimmy's 190 laps in front, figures that were bandied about in the press without mention of both the Federal Withholding Tax (around 32%) and a further Indiana Gross Tax, both of which were deducted at source. Of the $102,681 Speedway prize money, the Federal Tax accounted for nearly $33,000, the Indiana Tax just over $2,000.

There were also, however, goodies in kind, ranging from the Plymouth Sports Fury convertible pace car to sets of spanners, a wardrobe full of clothes, a diamond-studded pin, an engraved watch from Premier for Jimmy, together with replicas that he shared with us, a 'merchandise certificate' and many more, including a 'race winner's blanket'. Of these, after I had obtained cash equivalents for some (of which 45% went to Jimmy, 10% to the mechanics and the remaining 45% to Team in the usual way), Ford diplomatically exchanged the Plymouth pace car for a 1966 Galaxie 500. Bobby Johns's excellent seventh place had totalled $16,886 (£6,030) before deduction of tax, the split of which followed usual Team practice.

It is interesting to compare Jimmy's Indy income with that earned in his other categories of racing. For the Tasman series of ten races (of which he won nine) his total of start, prize and bonus monies was £4,000; for his Formula 1 season of 13 events, which included his World Championship, it was £13,340. For his one race at Indy it was over £46,000 . . .

Shortly after his Indy win Jimmy was contracted by an English national newspaper to write his account of the race. Reading it in the office one day I came to the part where he touched on the finances of the thing, saying that although it might have seemed a lot of money, he still had his expenses such as motel bills and laundry to pay. As I smiled to myself, the red light and buzzer on my phone indicated that Colin wanted me in his office without delay. He had the same article spread out on his desk.

'Have you seen this?' he asked, jabbing the newspaper with his as usual faultlessly manicured finger. I nodded.

'Oh dear, poor Jimmy!', wailed Colin. 'We spend a fortune and endless hours of work providing a winning car, and he has to spend good money paying for his underwear and socks to be laundered . . . my heart bleeds for him!'

One of the bonuses of Indy was to find that 1-cent coins were exactly equivalent in weight and size to the UK sixpence, which was worth six times as much and common currency in British parking meters! As a result the crew would collect 1-cent coins for shipment back to England in the spares crates, and when we let Jimmy in on the news he asked for some too. Several months later he told me that he had given up using them; he had come out of his London flat one morning to find 1-cent coins in little piles on the roof of his Elan, and a parking meter attendant waiting to talk to him . . .

As the five engines supplied to us for the month of May were now our property, the two units used in the race were removed the evening after the race, and Jimmy's engineless car was then cleaned and prepared for Ford America to take away.

Mike Underwood: 'As we relaxed after the race I remember looking forward to some time off, but "Laz" told us that the engines had to come out and we started work again almost immediately.'

One aspect extensively discussed since the race has been the fabricated rear uprights used on Jimmy's car. Some American parties have even suggested that since these uprights were not on the World's Fair and later Ford Museum car (which remains in the Museum today) it cannot have been Jimmy's car at all, but Bobby's.

However, as already mentioned, during USAC's initial grounding of both Lotus and Lola entries due to its suspicion that the uprights might be prone to failure, our 1965 Type 38 components had been found to be perfectly satisfactory and running had continued. At the last moment, to ensure that no future crack-test findings could immobilise Jimmy's car, fabricated uprights had been produced in Cheshunt and flown to Indy. Since time was fast running out, and they seemed unlikely to be needed, only one set was made.

But in the immediate pre-race period our latest magnesium/zirconium uprights failed crack-testing, so the newly arrived fabricated set was fitted to Jimmy's car. A repeated search for components to fit to Bobby's car was at last rewarded with success, and they passed crack-testing so both cars started. In the immediate post-race strip-down, since Jimmy's car was destined to live out its life on display, its fabricated uprights were replaced by two that had failed the test. This change was of no consequence as the fabricated uprights' appearance would be acceptable on a show car, as Colin would have made very clear.

David Lazenby: 'When I was first asked to recount what I remembered of the fabricated set, I had to work backwards. The next events in which a Type 38 took part were two Swiss hill-climbs that I attended with Graham Clode [described later]. That car used the fabricated uprights, and at the second event Graham recalled that we found cracks in them, which I then remember

Committed direct from Indianapolis into the care of Ford, Jimmy's 1965 Indy-winning car was allowed to fall into this disgusting condition in the Ford Museum through lack of understanding and respect. Its outer screen moulding has gone, suspension links are battered and bent, and the glassfibre moulded nose cone, engine cover and gearbox cowl are delaminating, split and crazed . . .

re-welding before the next run. The point of all this is that they would never have cracked after just short runs up a hill, which means that they must have run extensively prior to that, which could only have been the 500 Miles, since only one set was in existence . . .'

Ford also exercised its right to purchase the Bobby Johns Type 38 (the fourth Type 38 chassis, it will be remembered, but numbered '38/2'). However, here memories are vague as to what hap-

pened to it immediately after the race. Mike Underwood recalled working on both cars after the 1965 race, and that A. J. had a green Type 38 at this period. Since Jimmy's had gone to Ford, this can only have been the Johns car, but Ford confirmed that it had both cars well into July 1965, and in August I requested that Ford should loan us the Johns car for the September Trenton race (without success). Mike Underwood recalled that it had run throughout practice and the race with its wheelbase half an inch out, a condition that must surely have been put right before the car was disposed of.

David Lazenby well remembered taking a Type 38 to Ford, and seeing enormous machines there. Mike Underwood recalled being with him, '. . . and we saw a bloody great surface plate. We asked what it was used for and the Ford bloke proudly told us they used it for their GT40s. When we said, "Why bother? They're not quick enough to need it!", he wasn't too impressed.'

At this range it is not possible to say if this visit to Ford *was* with the Johns car, but no other visit to Ford with a Type 38 for repair is recorded in our files. A fly in the ointment, however, is Mike's recollection of A. J. Foyt collecting a green Type 38 from us after the 1965 race, an event that cannot be explained satisfactorily other than perhaps the Texan was delivering Jimmy's car to Ford. Both 'Laz' and Mike felt sure (27 years after the event) that the Johns car never returned to Cheshunt.

Back in Europe Colin and Jimmy were universally feted at a multitude of celebratory functions. Requests came from all over the world, including as far away as Australia, for the winning car to be displayed, but it remained in America.

In amongst the party dates, Jimmy went to Brands to take part in an extended test of a Ford 'D300' series truck; against Jackie Stewart and Sir John Whitmore he put up the day's fastest time of 1 min 29.8 secs, before two bald front tyres brought testing to an end.

After clearing up our garages following the Indy win, our mechanics were off to Mosport to run a Type 30 Series 2 for Jimmy. David Lazenby: 'I shall always remember Mosport for personal reasons. In all the bustle of preparing the car it suddenly occurred to me that I should telephone my mother, a quite unusual event. She had been reading all the newspaper reports of our win and we had a long chat. The next day she died suddenly from a coronary . . .'

Jimmy retired from the race with a driveshaft failure, then flew back for Crystal Palace, where his Formula 2 win earned £150. We were back to earth again! He also drove a Lotus-Cortina there, and the mechanics still remember it as one of the rare examples of him losing his cool.

Bob Dance: 'With only a day between races Jimmy was late arriving at Crystal Palace, so could only practice on race morning. Before the cars went out he asked a Galaxie driver who was in another class if he would let him go in front so he could really see what the car was like. The fellow agreed but forgot his promise when they were out on the track, which was hard to understand as Jimmy was simply climbing all over him trying to get past in the 20-minute period. The Galaxie was like a mobile chicane, and when Jimmy returned to the pits he had a mammoth wobbly with the chap, going at him as if the World Championship depended on it – he was just fuming! Amazingly Jimmy then outdragged him at the start and the fellow spun at the first corner . . .'

In America that same weekend Parnelli Jones won the Milwaukee 100-miler with his Lotus 34, Roger McCluskey, in Gurney's white and blue Type 38, finishing sixth. A. J.'s heavily disguised Type 34 had started from pole, but retired early when its transmission again failed.

That week drawings were approved to convert a Type 38 to symmetric suspension. The components that could be salvaged from McCluskey's Trenton shunt car (the original '38/2'), together with the spares left from Indy, now went into the building of a fifth Type 38 ('38/4' proper), the 'tub' of which was now nearing completion.

Although there were no more USAC races on our programme, there were good reasons for constructing this extra car. Many requests came from show organisers for such a vehicle, and the indications were that Ford America already had a busy schedule for the two Team cars it had acquired. Colin suspected that Ford would not be staying with us for 1966, and securing a sponsor was very much on his mind, an exercise that would benefit from the existence of an available car. He was also anxious to keep the Indy section mechanics intact. Enquiries for the purchase of Type 38s, some requesting symmetric suspension layout, were flooding in and there was a possibility that we would set up a production unit.

Also our Formula 1 plans, like those of some other teams, were in flux. Coventry Climax was withdrawing at the end of the year as the new 3-litre Formula was beginning, and without an engine in sight it would be a waste of money to start designing a car before such power unit details were available. In the meantime, for test and development purposes the layout of a Type 38 would prove ideal. Additionally, a Monsieur Pettavel of the Swiss Automobile Club in Lausanne had invited us to demonstrate the car at two of their events counting towards the European Mountain (hill-climb) Championship, offering over £2,000 plus all expenses. These events would provide ideal time-fillers . . .

Initially the club's proposal had been for only one event, but the resulting publicity and interest from the Swiss public, starved of motor racing since the ban of 1955, was such that a second event was quickly added, both organisers taking on the chore of providing methanol fuel; however, as Colin was concerned that this would emanate from an aviation supplier and would not be the required mix, our crew took their own drum as a safety measure.

Of the five Ford engines we had acquired following Indy, Ford sold four for us, and the fifth, still tuned to run on methanol, went into '38/4' for a shakedown and test at Snetterton that proved satisfactory but not shatteringly quick. The car was fitted with a five-speed ZF gearbox, larger brakes than those used at Indy, and a modified fuel system to cater for both left- and right-handed corners. Jimmy's fastest lap of 1 min 37 secs (compared to Graham Hill's 1½-litre BRM test time of 1 min 37.2 secs in the same month) used only two of the five speeds.

Colin's concern about our former race cars being supplied to American owners continued, requiring me to write again to Leo Beebe. By return came his assurance that the winning car would definitely remain a show vehicle, the ex-Johns car being used for development purposes only, and that neither would be raced again.

The first hill-climb took place at Ste Ursanne-Les-Rangiers, a 2.85-mile course near Delemont, south-west of Basle, and attracted 350 entries. David Lazenby and Graham Clode took the new 38 there on a trailer behind our hard-worked 15 cwt Ford van, Jimmy flying down with Colin in the company aircraft direct to Delemont's small airfield.

Practice opened at 6 am on Saturday 21 August, and we were allowed six practice runs, our 'start money' dependent upon completing two of them. The first two-thirds of the course comprised slightly ascending high-speed curves followed by three hairpin bends on the steep rise towards the finish, 1,000 feet above the start.

Only a few straw bales were scattered against the numerous pine trees, and although everyone recognised that Jimmy's main task would be simply to keep the 500 bhp car on the course rather than attempt to break the record, he kept the crowd enthralled, plumping to do all six runs, each more lurid than its predecessor as he fought immense wheelspin from start to finish. Although the majority of other drivers were hill-climb specialists, a few faster than Jimmy in his unwieldy car, he still succeeded in breaking the previous outright record of 2 mins 15.9 secs with 2 mins 13.1 secs, a performance warmly appreciated by the enormous crowd and 0.9 secs quicker than his friend, hill-climb exponent Peter Westbury, in his Ferguson 4WD 2-litre BRM. Jo Siffert's Rob Walker team Formula 1 Brabham-BRM was quickest of all at 2 mins 9.5 secs (81.4 mph).

After sunny practice it rained for Sunday's event, making Jimmy's task a fearsome prospect. Two runs were allowed, of which one qualified for the agreed start money, but in typical fashion the Scot opted for both to entertain the crowd. The rain had ceased by the time he fought the car every inch of the way to a first run of 2 mins 43.9 secs, compared with Siffert's best of 2 mins 27.5 secs. Rain then began to teem down again, and in places where other cars had left the road coated in mud, Jimmy's second climb was even more memorable than his first, the large crowd braving the appalling weather to witness what was the last, but possibly the most exciting, run of the day. Jimmy seemed to cope better with the decidedly worse conditions, knocking a whole 7 *seconds* off his previous best, a superb performance in a most inappropriate car. His enthusiasm was all the more creditable when it is remembered that in this National Open event he was ineligible for any award. Siffert was fastest man of the day (2 mins 25.1 secs), and Jimmy's Type 38 classified eighth overall amongst cars much more suited to the task.

The Ollon–Villars hill-climb, south-east of Montreux, was run the following weekend. With Jimmy scheduled to drive at Brands Hatch on the Bank Holiday Monday, his tight itinerary was a one-day trip to Switzerland slotted between Brands practice and the race. As a result he missed official practice at Ollon and was given three trial runs on the morning of the event. Jimmy had driven the Filipinetti-owned Lotus Type 21 there in 1962, so had

some idea of what to expect – on that occasion he later laughingly told me that the car had no brakes or shock absorbers to speak of, and he had overshot a corner and entered a farmyard at high speed, scattering a multitude of chickens as he screeched to a halt.

Set amongst fashionable ski resorts, the tricky 8 km course had no proper straights and eight hairpins. It started in Ollon, located in a valley of the Rhone, then climbed steeply (sometimes at 1 in 9) negotiating the narrow streets of a village to terminate in Villars, 2,000 feet above the start.

Jimmy's first run of 4 mins 49 secs (the record of 4 mins 23 secs being held by Jo Bonnier), was made before the crack was found in one of the celebrated ex-Indy fabricated uprights, and 'Laz' resorted to nickel-bronze welding before Jimmy's second run. He completed that climb in 4 mins 34.5 secs, his third, hampered by an off-song engine, being over 35 seconds slower. The problem proved impossible to cure, so his single run in the event that followed was a disappointing 4 min 45.3 secs, against Scarfiotti's new outright record of 4 mins 9.8 secs.

The first flight available on which Jimmy could return to Brands was not until the following morning; Colin waited for him at Heathrow with our company plane and whisked him off to the circuit. Both mechanics also flew back to England, while Bob Dance drove the van and trailer to take the Type 38 to the Festival of Speed at Monza in Italy.

Anticipating Ford's withdrawal of support, Colin was constantly on the look-out for a sponsor, and when STP's Andy Granatelli enquired about the possible purchase of a Type 38, a door was opened. At the end of August came Andy's confirmation that he was very interested in taking the matter further. Colin had earlier met with a member of the Granatelli family when brother 'Big Vince' had visited Lotus at Andy's instigation for advice on the suspension of the ill-handling 4WD Ferguson Novi.

Ever since the Indy win, numerous enquiries had been received concerning the possible production of Type 38s; several owners had approached Colin immediately after the race, and now there came letters and cables. As some of these also asked for cars with symmetric suspension, and we now had a car running in this configuration (Colin was still contemplating the possibility of Team's Indy section building customer cars), we were able to produce a retail price list for both configurations.

On our hill-climb car the conversion from asymmetric to symmetric had proved an expensive and time-consuming exercise. Pivot point alterations demanded 60 hours, chassis stripping and rebuilding an additional 90 hours, the total cost (without profit margin) amounting to £662.00. The scheme required fuel line rerouting, a different fuel catch tank, new suspension and dampers, brake discs and callipers (rear), radius arms, and steering complete with a different rack and pinion.

Enquiries came from A. J. Foyt, Mario Andretti's entrant Al Dean of the Dean Van Lines trucking and removals business, Masten Gregory (on behalf of entrant George Bryant), Weinberger Homes, Dayton Steel Foundry, Vita Fresh, Alderman Ford, Gig

Stephens, Rolla Vollstedt, Lindsey Hopkins, Bob Wilke and others. Eventually the price was agreed at £12,000 for a chassis without engine or gearbox.

Colin had been mightily impressed with what he had seen of Mario Andretti, and in July we cabled him with an invitation to drive the second Type 30 sports-racing car alongside Jimmy's in three North American races starting at Mosport in September. His acceptance was not long in coming, but sadly the big sports car programme fell behind and the drive never materialised.

On its return from the display at Monza, our symmetric 38 was prepared for a test at Silverstone, in company with a Type 40 sports, Team wanting to compare Dunlop and Firestone tyres. With our principal drivers away at Albi for a Formula 2 race, Jack Sears was recruited.

Graham Clode: 'Mike Underwood and I took the two cars to Silverstone. First we warmed up the Indy car, still in its symmetric form and with its five-speed ZF gearbox. Jack did his runs and when he came in he was ecstatic and just kept saying, "What a beautiful car, what a beautiful car". Then he tried the Type 40 on Dunlop R7s. He was very quick, and when his run came to an end we all went off for lunch.

'Immediately afterwards, running on Firestones, he went off at Abbey curve on his first lap – a marshal said he had seen the back of the car come out, and it then went backwards off the track. Everything seemed OK, but then it went into a ditch, turning over. Poor Jack suffered severe arm fractures and a broken collar-bone, and they whipped him off to hospital. He was a popular chap, and it's very sad that the accident spelled the end of his career. He just thought it best that he should call it a day . . .'

Another person to call it a day was Len Terry. After his organised early departure from the 1963 Indy '500', he had made up his mind to leave Team Lotus, but not before honouring his three-year contract. Colin had asked him to find someone to replace himself, adding that if he was successful he could leave early. Len left the company on 31 May, and in September our new chief designer, Maurice Phillippe, arrived.

Len: 'I had come across Maurice through the 750 Motor Club in 1959-60; he and I were both designing Formula Junior cars, completely separately, but they were very similar in concept. We were never what you could call friends, as we only crossed each other's paths infrequently, and I was introduced to him by Brian Hart. His car, the Delta, was not as successful as mine, principally because Maurice drove his himself and I had Brian, who was very quick, driving my Terrier. Later Maurice bought Keith Duckworth's Lotus 7 Series II and started winning many races. But I certainly went along with his thinking, so when I needed to recommend someone I immediately thought of Maurice. There was just no one else to fit the bill, and I was able to join Dan Gurney's team in California that much earlier. As it turned out Maurice was very much in the Chapman mould . . .'

Maurice was another product of the de Havilland aircraft company. Born in 1932, he had joined the company in 1949 for his technical education and apprenticeship as a design draughtsman,

Maurice Phillippe, the former de Havilland structures engineer who took over from Len Terry as Colin Chapman's Chief Designer. Maurice was no stranger to automotive monocoque structures, having designed and built his own MPS monocoque sports-racing special as early as 1955. (Jutta Fausel)

and after ten years had moved to Ford of Britain to work on its Cortina and Corsair models while continuing to build his own racing cars. With a name like his, most of us at Team were preparing to welcome Lotus's first Frenchman, so we were a little disappointed to find he was from east London.

His first jobs were to convert a stillborn Formula 1 design into a Tasman car, then to design both a Formula 1 and an Indy car for 1966, but the question of a suitable power unit – should Ford bow out – still hung over us.

For Formula 1 it was becoming increasingly obvious that we would have to rely on BRM for the 3-litre H16-cylinder engine it was then in the final stages of building, so we were told. In discussion the suggestion was made that BRM could also supply 4.2-litre versions for Indy, and once their estimated power output was mentioned, Colin was hooked. With the two versions boasting virtually identical external dimensions, it was obvious that the two new cars could be matching images of each other, which would simplify production as well as maintenance schedules and costs. As a result Maurice designed the Type 43 for Formula 1 and the matching Type 42 for Indy.

By November 1965 the idea that Team mechanics could build the production Type 38s was fast fading. With six listed for customers and with new cars wanted for our anticipated entries at Indy '66, it was plain that there would not be enough time to pursue both programmes. A Type 38 'tub' alone demanded 815 hours labour, making it a 'runner' then taking two mechanics three further weeks. Colin was still intent on continuing his big sports car programme, so by the end of that month the task of building customer Type 38s was handed over to the Lotus Components side of Group Lotus.

Maurice had technical discussions with BRM, as a result of which that company revised the profile of its three-speed Indy gearbox to fit Maurice's concept. BRM was providing information to the motoring press on its H16 Formula 1 engine, and by December the new car was reportedly nearing completion, although it would not be unveiled until the end of April. For such a complicated box of tricks, the engine's size compared well with its 1-litre predecessor, being 22 inches long and less than 19 inches high if certain ancillaries were moved elsewhere. Externally both Formula 1 and Indy versions would match, internal differences involving crankshafts, con-rods, liners, piston assembly, valve gear and cam drive.

Significantly, weight was not disclosed. Maurice had been told that the 4.2-litre Indy H16 would weigh around 425 lbs (without its BRM gearbox), so he quickly looked into weight reduction elsewhere. His surprise can be imagined when the first unit exceeded the estimated weight by 140 lbs.

As 1965 ended, Colin surveyed the car build programme for '66, studying our stock-take of car parts remaining. After a meeting with Jim Endruweit (who was continuing in his role as engineering manager and co-ordinator), Maurice issued his 1966 guidelines to section-leaders Colin Knight (car build), Steve Sanville (engine and transmission engineer) and chief mechanics Dick Scammell (Formula 1) and David Lazenby (Indy). Maurice's project paper highlighted essentials. With Keith Duckworth's DFV Formula 1 engine coming to life for the 1967 season, the 1966 Type 42 Indy and 43 Formula 1 cars were to be regarded strictly as interim models, and for economic reasons only one

vehicle would be designed to fulfil both functions. Innovation would also be limited, and in view of the parts common with our Types 30, 38 and 40, 'maximum possible use is to be made of existing components'. Skins would be 16-gauge for the Indy and 18-gauge for the Formula 1 monocoques, the latter being similar to the Type 38 in construction but 'cleaner aerodynamically if possible'. The engines were to be secured to the bulkhead behind the driver as a fully stressed chassis member, attached by only four bolts.

A smoother undertray was desired, the oil and water pipes previously sited within inverted underside 'Vs' now reduced from concentric to single pipes of minimum cross-section 'built in' flush with the exterior of the 'tub'. Brake discs were planned to be lightened Ford Galaxie, the system otherwise being Type 40 sports car. However, a development project was to investigate the use of the standard and lighter Formula 1 braking system, since Indy braking requirements were modest. Both front and rear suspension would 'make maximum use of Type 30 and 38 components', with a redesign of rear uprights 'to eliminate completely the casting and Zyglo test problems of 1965'.

Wheels were to be of 'best quality at minimum price, so that very expensive alloys need not be used, with rim sections redesigned to utilise new Firestone weights and clips'. The fuel system would be redesigned to ensure extraction of all but the last half-gallon, with 'massive fuel lines to eliminate the possibility of fuel starvation'. The 16-pipe BRM Formula 1 exhaust would be used initially, but would probably be altered to suit the Indy engine's different power band.

In summing up, using his initial engine weight figures, Maurice prophesied that it would be difficult to meet the minimum weight figures in Formula 1, but that 'no difficulty should be found in achieving the Indy requirement'. December saw design work under way, chassis jigs were completed as the New Year was celebrated, and the build of '42/1' began.

As it turned out, events outside our control were to play a decisive part in our fourth assault on the Brickyard. But for the meantime the Team Lotus Christmas party was a wild affair, as well it should have been considering the successes achieved. Apart from Jimmy's Indianapolis win, he had taken the World Driver's crown in Formula 1 and had brought us the Constructors' Championship too. We had won the British Saloon Car Championship and the British and French Formula 2 Championships, as well as the Tasman series at the beginning of the year. As the cherry on the cake, Colin had been awarded the Ferodo Gold Trophy for the second time in honour of his Team's dominance of motor racing worldwide.

CHAPTER SEVEN

1966:
'Spinning Takes Practice'

Jimmy's successes made him the uncomfortable focus of media attention. In contrast to today's Formula 1 stars, who contest only the 16 Grands Prix each year, Jimmy's name, and to only a slightly lesser degree that of Team Lotus, provided a worthwhile story virtually every *weekend*. His giant-killing drives in the humble Lotus-Cortina saloon provided a constant attraction, as did his enthusiastic races in sports cars big and small as well as Formula 2 events.

The few media scribes fortunate enough to secure an interview were prone to study him in depth, some alluding to his Latin and quite non-Scots looks, and 'monkeyish' expression, more Mediterranean than Berwickshire, with his dark brown, lively eyes, wide laughing mouth, flinging his palms outwards as he walked bouncily, his head jerking left and right, dapper and dark suited with a Lotus badge in his button-hole. 'Like a kettle lid on boiling water – explosive energy restrained only by effort.'

Even so, Jimmy was delighted to report that he did not have a memorable face. 'I sat next to a bloke on a long-distance flight talking about motor racing and he didn't know who I was!' Another Scotsman once asked him where he came from, and when told asked, 'Good heavens, do you know Jimmy Clark?'

Such observations were accurate, although no doubt Jimmy took umbrage at 'monkeyish', as he did when he discovered the photograph someone had pinned up behind my office door depicting him in a peakless crash helmet and with the ballooned comment: 'I was alright until my third orbit when my banana stuck in my throat.' Even Jimmy's listed recreations in the contemporary *Who's Who* brought media attention: 'Water-skiing, shooting and parking in London.'

In New Zealand for the 1966 Tasman series, Jimmy made a tape recording of his opinions of the latest products of Firestone, our new tyre suppliers, and when Colin sent Jimmy his customary up-date letter, he expressed his concern: 'I hope you weren't too bloody rude!'

Colin reported that the first Type 42 hull had been completed, on 4 February; the 4.2-litre BRM engine had not yet run, but the 3-litre version had, and he mentioned his concern at the torsional vibrations between the two crankshafts affecting the coupling gears. However, he was confident that the first Type 42 would be ready for Jimmy to sample immediately he returned from Australia in March, the engine initially tuned to run on gasoline. BRM's Peter Spear had promised Colin that the engine would soon be available and its output would be 650 bhp, a statement contradicted by BRM owner Sir Alfred Owen's comment a whole two months later that he had just given the units the go ahead! This was way after STP press releases announced that we were on our way!

Colin and engine specialist Steve Sanville had recently met Alejandro De Tomaso in Italy in the quest for an improved and light-alloy version of the Ford 351 cubic inch engine, which would employ better con-rods and pistons and with six cylinder-head studs around each bore instead of four. If the project was unsuccessful Colin was contemplating an end to our big sports car programme (Team's Type 40s were about to be sold) since 'the other constructors had monopolised the four best power units'. However, he had already started design of a multi-tubular space-frame chassis (using the design principles of the Type 41) to accept this Lotus-De Tomaso V8 engine, Frank Costin drawing 'a negative lift body from the word go', as Colin put it. He hoped the car would be ready by the end of May, when 'Laz' and his Indy crew would begin 'sorting it out'. The Type 30/40 programme was, at last, dead.

Finally, Colin told Jimmy that he had acquired a new 'plane: 'I have my magnificent, immaculate, fantastic, superb, well-equipped, perfect condition Twin Commanche available forthwith. If you wish to secure this outstanding bargain please cable me at once! Love, Colin.'

As the Type 42s neared completion, sans engines, contract wording between Team Lotus and STP was finally agreed and arrangements were made for Colin to meet Jimmy on his return from the Tasman series for a press conference at STP's HQ near Chicago.

From the day we first met and throughout the next seven years of our association, I found STP's head man, Anthony ('Andy') Granatelli, one of life's rich characters. Along with his brothers, 'Big Vince' and Joe, and Andy's son, 'Little Vince', they presented the very essence of American-Italian immigrants who had 'made it' in the New World. Their father, another 'Big Vince', had left Campofelice (a small town on Sicily's Targa Florio circuit) for America when he was 18 years old. His three sons, all born near Dallas, Texas, had in the late 1930s and early '40s taken numerous jobs from filling station attendants and mechanics to garage operators and used car salesmen. Born in 1923, Andy himself later acknowledged that their schemes employed the 'low-budget, high-confidence approach', but he himself was to prove to be a business executive-cum-salesman extraordinaire.

Their first motor sporting involvement was in the dirt track world – hot rods and later stock cars, even a rocket-car – but since first listening to the 1934 '500' on radio, they had set their sights on Indy. Their first appearance there in 1946 reads like a Hollywood script. Without anything like sufficient finance but consumed by ambition, they purchased one of the pre-war front-wheel-drive Miller-Fords. Without the cash to buy a trailer, they drove the thing from Chicago to Indy on public roads. Their arrival made them the talk of Gasoline Alley; their driver, midget racer Danny Kladis, then qualified what they called the *Grancor V8*, 33rd at just under 119 mph. In the race itself Kladis was classified 21st but disqualified for, in official jargon, 'a tow'! He had stopped on Turn Two, and Andy had driven the car back through the infield to the entry to the pit lane, accompanied by his driver, intent upon rejoining the race.

The following year the Granatelli's driver, Russian-American Pete Romcevich, qualified 17th and finished 12th. Their third '500' in 1948 saw Andy himself driving, until a substantial practice crash put paid to that, and he retired from active participation. However, by 1957 his automotive equipment business had made him a millionaire, so he sold it and 'retired' aged just 34.

Unable to settle, he used his retirement fund to purchase the financially troubled supercharger manufacturer Paxton Engineering in Los Angeles, whose products were not noted for their reliability. Andy's management soon solved the manufacturing problem, and brought Paxton back to profitability. The redesigned supercharger's success persuaded Chrysler to give the Granatelli brothers an engineering contract, and in 1962 Studebaker – seeking to rejuvenate its dated designs – took over Paxton, and with it the brothers. Money was tight, but Andy focused on their Avanti model, fitting a Paxton blower.

Publicity-conscious as ever, Andy and his brothers turned to Bonneville Salt Flats, breaking scores of records with various Studebaker products, sometimes with Barbara Nieland and Paula Murphy co-driving, to rewrite nearly 350 American marks.

In 1961 the Granatellis were back at Indy, having acquired the enormously powerful Novi V8s, first seen at the Speedway in 1941. Under their management and with Andy's matchless promotional skills, these legendary cars enhanced their aura without unfortunately achieving any success, but remained enormous favourites with the crowd. In 1962 Andy became President of Studebaker's STP Division, which then had 13 per cent of the world's oil and gasoline treatment market. Within four years Andy

The Money – Andy Granatelli's STP Corporation replaced the mighty Ford Motor Company as Lotus's prime Indianapolis project sponsor for 1966–69. Here's 'Big G' (left), whom the author came to like and admire very much indeed, with his brother 'Big Vince', to whom Andy persistently gave public credit for Lotus innovations in a manner that utterly incensed Colin, and estranged Lotus's own Indy crew.

had quadrupled sales and secured 60 per cent of the market, a bigger share than all the opposition combined and worth many millions.

His brothers and son moved with him to the company's base near Chicago, and it was thus there that Colin and Jimmy met them in March 1966 for the much-publicised contract signing. When the news was announced my first problem came from our mechanics. Remembering the STP crew's official garb of white jump-suits, polka-dotted with hundreds of STP logos, they stipulated that there was no way they would follow suit! We settled instead for a plain red variety.

'STP-Team Lotus' plans at that time were to enter five cars of three different types. STP would run a single front-engined Ferguson 4WD Novi, its V8 Paxton-blown engine producing a massive 837 bhp at 9,000 rpm from its 2,738 cc (167 cu in). Team Lotus would enter two Type 42 BRM H16-engined cars, along with two Type 38s, updated from the previous year and given the 'B' suffix to prove it.

Andy was not over-impressed by the thought of using the H16. He felt sure that such a device (he called it a 'mechanical sandwich') could never be reliable, and he made his feelings known to Colin, prophesying that harmonic resonance between the two crankshafts would produce torsional vibrations sufficient to destroy the coupling gears. But when Colin convinced Andy that BRM had the problems solved, he confirmed his support.

Our oil company, Humble, like all oil companies, had muttered long and hard about this additive tie-up, and on a business visit to New York the previous month Colin and I had visited Mobil, but without success. Fortunately the London branch of Humble (Geoff Murdoch of Esso) calmed the waters once again, and 'Enco' went back on our cars.

From New York I went to Dearborn for a meeting with Leo Beebe and Jacque Passino. Budgetary details from as far back as 1964 still required finalisation, together with the rebuild (for sale) costs of the Ford engines that had passed to us after the 1965 race. One had gone to Foyt and there were rebuild details to agree with Lou Meyer, whom I was about to visit in Indy.

Leo made it clear that he had not supported Ford's decision to break with us for 1966; but he felt that after spending large sums of money on our joint three-year project and achieving excellent results, if we were now to be successful with another power unit it was all water under the bridge. At that time, he reported, Ford was experiencing serious problems with its Le Mans project, and he much regretted Colin's lack of interest in the French endurance classic (Ford was to finish 1–2–3 in that year's race).

Before departing for Indianapolis, I met Ron Platt of EFLO, his office literally 'just across the road'. Our 1966 programme and budget had been agreed, and we discussed various aspects of the coming season, one small point requiring verification about which I would need to phone him the next day. When I did, it

The H16-cylinder BRM engine mock-up slung on the rear of a Type 42/43 monocoque with the mocked-up 'Indy-winning' show Type 38 bearing Jimmy's race numbers beyond. The actual winning Type 38 was presented to Ford immediately after the '500' victory – as required by contract – and to the time of writing has never returned home.

was to hear the disturbing news that we had been 'released' from the programme, and that they had signed an alternative deal with Alan Mann! Such are the ways of big business ...

From Ford I visited Firestone's Bill McCrary in Akron, Ohio. Here the main topic was the possibility of Parnelli Jones driving our second car in the '500' alongside Jimmy. Colin and Bill had already discussed this, and now we settled the finer details, principal amongst which was how to reconcile our own fuel contracts with those of Parnelli.

Later the matter of a recent press report was raised; Firestone was most upset to read journalist Charles Fox's assertion that we had been paid $150,000 plus free tyres for 1966, a matter that both Firestone and ourselves regarded as being of the utmost confidentiality. Firestone was conducting an enquiry into the matter and requested that we do likewise. Charles later told me that A. J. Foyt had given him the information, although the Texan subsequently denied it.

Before leaving Firestone I had a meeting with Del Cline of the company's Coated Fabrics Division to discuss their fuel cell test findings following several simulated race car accidents. They were presenting data to USAC, who had announced stricter requirements in 1967. One survey had centred on the delightfully titled 'slosh mitigation', all of which I noted at full length for Colin, but Firestone expressed their regrets that we were staying with our usual British supplier, FPT of Portsmouth.

From Akron I flew to Indianapolis to meet Lou Meyer. His share of the Ford race engine work had increased substantially for the coming season, and he had 35 customer engine orders at that time. Now called the 'C' series, minor updates included a more efficient oil pump together with a change of oil gland design and the choice of running oil lines fore or aft as desired. The unit price had increased from $15,000 to $22,000, and the charge to update 1965 engines to current spec was $1,200.

My next stop was Los Angeles and a meeting with a promotional company responsible for a four-month programme of filming the Team Lotus/Firestone relationship at European races. From Los Angeles it was a short drive to Riverside and the 500 Mile NASCAR Grand National stock car event (won by Dan Gurney). There I had meetings arranged with Parnelli Jones and his patron, J. C. Agajanian, not only to discuss the relatively minor matters of settling our joint accounts ('Aggie' and Team had mutually exchanged or supplied numerous components during the past season) but also to predict Aggie's component requirements for his Type 34, or his proposed Type 38 purchase in the coming year. Most important of all were the details to be agreed for Parnelli to drive for us in May, but as expected I left for Europe merely with an agenda for further discussion. Sadly the matter was to end there. Parnelli had already driven a supercharged Offy-powered Shrike from the stable of his friend Ted Halibrand and, after completing a considerable mileage, reckoned 'it was a winner'; he still had a lot of time for the Offy engine.

However, what finished it for Colin was Parnelli's insistence on the traditional monetary arrangement existing between himself

and J. C. Agajanian, who would run the car, whereby 50 per sent went to the driver, 10 per cent to the mechanics and 40 per cent split down the middle for Aggie and Halibrand (or in this case Team Lotus). This met with Colin's usual response of, 'Oh no, we can't agree to that.' Neither was he happy with STP's attempt to get Mario Andretti's signature on a contract. Later I cabled Bobby Johns, but he was already signed to drive for George Bryant. Before returning home I paid a courtesy visit to Dan Gurney's base at nearby Costa Mesa, settling minor points connected with his Type 38, and meeting his new Chief Designer, Len Terry, and his wife Iris, both now enjoying life there in the sun.

Meanwhile, back in Cheshunt the prototype BRM H16 engines were still eagerly awaited, for both our Formula 1 and Indy cars. Lotus Components had farmed out production of the monocoques for the customer Type 38s, now reduced to just three positive orders. The contract had gone to Abbey Panels of Coventry, an event of some controversy much written about since.

The hard-pressed Lotus build crew proudly show off the two Type 38 'soft alloy special' customer cars freshly completed for 1966. (Artricia Industrial Pictures Ltd)

Later dubbed the 'soft alloy specials', these Abbey Panels monocoques were constructed from the specified L72 aircraft-specification aluminium alloy, but the material suffered a deterioration possibly during the annealing process.

David Lazenby: 'If you tried to bend the sort of aluminium that was specified it would be quite difficult, but if the annealing process went wrong and the applied heat process lasted either too long or was too hot, the material would become as soft as a flannel. In this case you only had to poke it with your finger and it left a dent.'

Len Terry: 'The monocoques built by Abbey would, regardless of the media description, have been just as stiff as the other cars, but would not have been so strong. There are lots of people, including engineers who really should know better, who do not know the difference between strength and stiffness. People have suggested that the Abbey-built structures would fatigue quicker, but that is rubbish. Remember that the stiffer L72 could be brittle; also the "softer" cars would be easier to repair and were also weldable, which the stiffer material wasn't.'

Eventually, shortage of time coupled with inexperience in building the Type 38 saw Lotus Components falling back on our Indy mechanics to assist them, while all the time our crew was listening aghast to disturbing rumours emanating from their counterparts at BRM in Bourne.

As the delay increased, Colin turned for help to Leo Beebe at Ford, requesting the loan of two Ford-built V8s rather than customer versions. The deal he was still trying to agree with BRM was to secure three engines on loan in exchange for 50 per cent of prize money earned, his argument being that once seen to be successful there would be a ready market for the engines amongst American teams. Meanwhile Sir Alfred Owen himself entered the arena to express his personal wish that we switch our Indy fuel deal to his BRM team's contracted backer, Shell.

With our much reduced support or sponsor money compared to previous years, that from STP amounting to $75,000, Colin obviously needed to resort to loan deals rather than outright purchase, and in an attempt to secure additional income we had already set in motion approaches to large corporations in both America and Japan, while also seeking additional payments from our trade supporters.

With no instant response from Ford to his engine suggestion, Colin now called in Ford of Britain's Walter Hayes, and it was not long before a deal was struck, which emphasises the generosity of the giant American concern. We were to receive one new engine on loan, while Ford would be responsible for updating the engine we still had left over from 1965. However, as Ford America made clear, we would need more than two engines for the month of May, and it would be up to us to acquire these as customers through Meyer's facility. However, coming as it did so late in the day and with Meyer's increasing customer list, as well as a distinct shortage of con-rods and injector parts, the best delivery he could confirm was early May, so we had to go back to Ford, cap in hand, asking it to exert influence on our behalf and

also to chivvy up its spares programme. Again the company obliged, but it would be some time into April before the engines appeared.

As March neared its end even Colin accepted, with much chagrin, that if a BRM engine did appear – and there was still no hint from them even of a delivery date – it would be too late for sufficient testing to take place before shipment to the Speedway. BRM was still trying to solve problems with the Formula 1 version of its new engine, so it was obvious that the Indy derivative would be ever further behind. With only one Team Type 38 available (chassis '38/4', the car built after Indy 1965 and used in the Swiss hill-climbs), we were obviously in dire straits; then, quite suddenly, one of the Abbey Panels cars became ours! Whether this was due to a customer withdrawal, voluntary or otherwise, I never discovered. The happy fact remained that suddenly we now had two cars.

It is interesting to note that USAC's latest rule revisions, this time concerning inspection procedures for wheels and safety systems affecting drivers (attachment points for seat belts, etc) arrived as late as April '66 following ratification in mid-March. But not all our problems were mechanical, as we found when the first batch of STP epoxy 'day-glo' rocket-red paint arrived from the States.

Arthur Birchall: 'I had joined the Indy section in January 1965, my first experience of working for Team Lotus being memorable in as much as I started at 8 am on Monday and didn't leave again until 11 pm Wednesday night! And for 1966 painting the cars fell to me. The base colour supplied was white, and anyone who knows what it's like to paint a red or an orange will know it takes a lot of work and a lot of paint. Considering the constant battle to reduce weight, I used to wonder if the weight of all the coats of paint were ever considered. The other problem was that it was photo-sensitive; the Old Man used to go crazy if you even put tools on the bodywork, and when the word went out he was on his way we would shift them in a flash. The trouble was that if you left tools in the sun on the STP livery, their outline would remain for some time after!'

Maurice Phillippe's assistant, Geoff Ferris, had drawn a multi-tubular De Dion structure for both the Type 38 and 42, and this was duly tested on the symmetrical 38 at Goodwood in mid-March during an official Firestone test. The layout called for a revision of the suspension, which included upper radius arms 2 inches longer (the lower only unequally longer) and revised spring/shock absorber units. Possibly due to the cold weather, the engine ran badly at first, but this was cured by enriching the mixture. Both the tyres planned for the forthcoming race and those used in the 1965 '500' were tried.

Initially Jimmy found the revised rear end 'very twitchy' on the new tyres, but reported that it became steadier when tyre pressures were raised. Then, when the 1965 tyres were fitted, he reported that the car was 'much more precise', but 'could not be thrown about'. From his 'slow' laps of 1 min 22.7 secs Jimmy got up to a fastest of 1 min 20.8 secs, which compared with Jackie

Stewart's Formula 1 pole position at Goodwood the previous year of 1 min 19.8 secs, and his and Jimmy's record fastest lap in the race of 1 min 20.4 secs. The handling problems he had commented on would be revived at Indy.

Meanwhile Firestone investigated on our behalf the possibility of the Wood Brothers forming our race pit crew again; this they agreed to do provided that the cars were Ford-engined rather than BRM, due to their Dearborn links.

On the sponsor front, the situation was positively bleak; provision of detailed proposals to companies such as Alcoa, Johnson Wax, Hitachi, NGK, Bosch and others had drawn a blank, although some would join our cause in years to come. Now that the possibility of running BRM-engined cars had faded, the two otherwise completed Type 42s were set aside and we concentrated all our energies instead upon the Type 38s. Even though BRM itself announced in mid-April that no Indy versions of the H16 would appear at the Speedway, Andy, ever keen to keep the publicity kettle boiling, issued an STP press release confirming that it was hoped one car would still run, but that the earliest

delivery date at the Speedway would be around 18 May, only two days prior to the final qualifying weekend!

As running got under way the American press reported the theft from BRM of major parts for both the 3-litre and 4.2-litre engines together with specialist tools, and the media kindly took it upon themselves to use the story as the reason for the engines' non-appearance at Indy.

The three Abbey Panels cars, continuing the Type 38 chassis number sequence, saw '38/5' go to Dean Van Lines for Mario Andretti and '38/6' to A. J. Foyt, the third car, '38/7', being retained by Team to be driven by Al Unser. The 26-year-old American had passed his Indy rookie test only the previous year, although he had been racing for eight years. From Albuquerque, New Mexico, he had an impeccable racing pedigree; his father, two uncles and three brothers were all racing drivers. Of his brothers, the late Jerry Unser had first driven at the Speedway in 1953, and Bobby in 1963. The family had made the 12.4-mile Pikes Peak dirt-track hill-climb in Colorado, with its summit at over 14,000 feet, virtually their own over the years, with outright fastest time taken by

Mario Andretti trying Al Dean's brand new 'soft alloy special' Type 38 – chassis '38/5' – for size in Gasoline Alley, Indy '66. He did not race the car, preferring instead the Dean Van Lines team's Brabham-derived tube-framed Brawner. (Indianapolis Motor Speedway)

'It's not going well, is it . . ?' – a reflective moment from '66 for Colin and Jimmy in the Gasoline Alley garage, captured by the sympathetic camera of Jabby Crombac. (G. Crombac)

father, uncles and then sons and nephews, Al's reign as King of the Mountain coming in 1964 and '65.

In 1965 Al had passed his Indianapolis driver test in the Arciero-owned Maserati-powered entry, then got a seat in the Sheraton-Thompson Lola for qualifying, with which he scraped on to the last row, finishing ninth in the race.

Jimmy's car would be '38/4', its suspension now asymmetric, its fuel tank system similarly returned to 'left-hand running', and its five-speed gearbox replaced by a two-speed.

In April Jimmy was in Japan as a guest at the newly opened Mount Fuji circuit. To his acute embarrassment, he was accorded Royal Family status, being driven to and around the circuit in a splendid Rolls-Royce. To add to his discomfort, his hosts then rolled out a brand new Cosworth-engined Lotus Type 35 Formula 2 car, which they invited him to drive, although he was warned that its brakes needed attention, the engine wasn't running properly and its wheels had not been balanced . . . Borrowing a crash helmet, he set off to do his best, and within a few laps set a new record! On taking his leave he told his hosts that he would be delighted to return, not knowing that his next visit would be only months away and would prove to be even more uncomfortable than the first.

Mario Andretti, the talk of the Speedway the previous year, had gone on to win the 1965 USAC title, and Ford engines had taken 11 pole positions and eight wins in 13 Championship events. At the opening USAC race of '66, a Ford engine had won again, although Offy-powered cars had proved more reliable. At the rain-shortened second race of the year at Trenton, a blown Offy had beaten the Fords. Mario had tangled with Foyt in the first race, and had been delayed by a puncture in the second, but now, as running opened at the Speedway, Mario dominated from the start, again driving his Clint Brawner-built 'replica' Brabham.

For our Lotus Indy '66 programme, David Lazenby was again Chief Mechanic, supported by Mike Underwood, Graham ('Tick') Clode, Liverpudlian Arthur ('Butty') Birchall, and New Zealander Alan McCall from our Lotus-Cortina section.

Jimmy experienced handling problems with '38/4' right from the start of running; it suffering excessive understeer, possibly because it was now 100 lbs over its 1965 weight (regulation changes) and on a new low-profile, new compound Firestone tyre, which, due to lack of time, we had been unable to test.

But there were lighter moments – Jimmy in his STP-sponsored jacket being presented with his 1965 winner's award replica of the legendary (and hefty) Borg-Warner Trophy during the month of May '66. In the back row of the stand above the trophy, Graham Hill shares a quip with Jackie Stewart in the row below, while A. J. Foyt (dark glasses) effects complete disinterest in the Scotsman's presentation. (Indianapolis Motor Speedway)

Maurice Phillippe and Colin set about investigating the 38's suspension geometry, their mathematical calculations and daily findings having to be put into practice by our crew making the required alterations . . .

David Lazenby: 'I think we shipped every spare we had out to Indy in 1966. There were Type 38 bits, components for the Type 42, possibly even Type 40 spares. We had the feeling that we were going to be in trouble . . . Colin and Maurice carefully examined the Type 42 spares and in the end we ran with Type 42 front uprights on the 38s complete with their dinky-doo steering arms.' 'Laz' has continued his habit of making his own carefully defined descriptions of spares together with consistent noises to illustrate a point, in which 'schuuk' and 'cluunk' combined with expressive gestures of the hands play an important part.

Mike Underwood: 'We were really hard pressed in '66. We had persevered with the Type 42s until almost the last moment, then had to dust down the hill-climb car and prepare the new one. They handled badly, Jimmy complaining that it felt like he was continually driving on oil. Then Colin and Maurice started trying to solve the problem and each day, after they had buried themselves in their calculations, we found the garage doors shut behind us so we could cut and fudge the suspension without anyone seeing us. We cut the rocker arms and re-welded them to different angles, the final solution being very steep angles, then refitted them to the car and went through the whole setting-up process again ready for the next day. We also tried alterations to numerous shock absorbers. Then Jimmy would go out and have a run and the whole thing would start all over again.

'We had brought all the suspension and other ancillary parts from the proposed BRM Type 42 with us in our crates of spares and Colin and Maurice soon started playing with them as well to see if they held the secret. It was a period when the Old Man and Maurice would go off for dinner and very quickly come back and stay with us until quite late – for Colin at any rate.'

'We still had the "birdbath"-principle oil-tank up front hidden away in the monocoque, and these were a real pain for the "workers" to get at.'

Arthur 'Butty' Birchall: 'A lot of the time you were working blind with your arms inserted through relatively small holes in the monocoque; the steering column and everything else around it had to come out for you to get at it, then the whole lot had to be re-fitted later. There was a cork liner around the tank to stop it overheating the driver; it had attachment brackets, and if you got one in, the others fell out. I remember having to refit one in the middle of the night and it took for ever . . .'

Mike Underwood: 'I had to weld more fittings on to an oil tank in the small hours of the morning – "Laz" had just renewed the fluid in our cleaning tank and unknown to us until then it was initially as potent as gasoline. I used it to clean out the oil tank and had started welding when there was a great "whoosh" and the tank distorted like a rugby ball, the explosion blowing my welding glasses off my face. The Old Man was still there – his face went white and he asked me if I was OK. Then he looked at his watch and said, "It's getting late – I think it's time I went home," and he was gone.'

As primary sponsor of Team's effort, Andy Granatelli maintained a commendably low profile during these days of drama, although no doubt he had enough troubles of his own overseeing preparation of his thundering Novi. A distinctive whirring noise would herald his approach on his STP-logo'd golf cart, and his 24-year old son 'Beau' Vince would usually dash into our garage to confront the selected person with 'My dad would like to have words'.

If the weather was hot, Andy would mop his brow during our meetings with an enormous handkerchief the size of a bath towel. If the meeting was in Andy's usual ground floor room at the Speedway Motel – which he used as an office – he would be sitting in the large black rocking chair always brought specially from Chicago with his legs crossed and invisible beneath him, looking like an enormous Buddha.

It was obvious that during the meetings Colin's lightning-quick clarifications and sometimes almost hostile responses to his questions initially left Andy slightly bemused, particularly as he was footing all the bills. As Colin's imminent departure from these meetings was signalled by a rapid shutting of his briefcase and an 'I've got to go', I was inevitably the second to leave. Andy's face would then break into a huge smile accompanied by a 'Jesus!' or a 'Can you explain what he meant, Andrew?'. Later on in our association he said to me, 'When you decide to leave him, or he fires you, just let me know. There's always a place with me for you any time . . .'

Sadly, the Novi, the love of Andy's life after his lovely wife Dolly ('I know Andy likes my cooking because he's gained 80 lbs since we married'), was to be irreparably wrecked while warming up for qualifying. Now it was down to the 'old' Type 38s of Clark and Unser to succeed for STP.

To an Englishman, one of the discomforting aspects of the Speedway's garage area was the men's toilets, the quaintly named 'rest rooms'. While a European would take for granted that there would be separate cubicles, there were instead merely long planked structures with holes over which numerous bottoms rested, the sort of structure normally associated with jail life, or under canvas in military service.

Fortunately, my natural cycle was well-timed for the early morning, so I was never forced to use the facility during busier times, but I always found it disconcerting when paying even a short visit to be confronted by men reading and chatting like Boy Scouts at a jamboree. Colin could not handle the situation at all, and with his bodily functions not as disciplined as mine, he would hot-foot it in his car back to the Motel whenever the need arose.

We had to wait until Graham Hill returned to the Speedway for a civilised move to be made. His presence at Indy attracted great attention, and one day the track's owner, Tony Hulman, arrived to welcome him as Britain's ambassador. Asking Graham what he thought of the Speedway, Graham recited the usual platitudes then dived in with a comment about the uncivilised 'planks'. That night the carpenters and workers were brought in to rectify the matter, and from then on we could all relax within the newly built cubicles ...

Other problems also beset our crew. As a follow-up to his failure to enforce American-style haircuts on our mechanics the previous year, A. J. Foyt had another plan up his sleeve for 1966. With his 'Coyote' cars, it was perhaps inevitable that the Texan would evolve a plan around that name, and one evening a pick-up truck loaded with a large crate slipped quietly past the guards at the vehicle entrance to the garage area. Soon after, a breathless mechanic arrived at our garage gasping that a real-live coyote was prowling around outside. Caught in the wilds of Texas by a member of A. J.'s crew (who was reputed to be, and who bore a striking resemblance to, a Red Indian), our lads were told that the animal was irritable and quite hungry after his long trip, and it would be as well to shut the garage doors and sit tight, advice that was followed ... (Another year the Vita Fresh team arrived at the track to find the word 'Don't' painted in front of 'Drink Vita Fresh' on their fuel bowsers.)

With our search for sponsors continuing, Chuck Barnes of Sports Headlines, his promotional company in Indianapolis, had indicated in March that the Gulf Oil Corporation, which had backed Indy cars in the 1930s, might be interested in a deal for 1967, and that their representatives would visit us at Indy at the beginning of May. Then came the news that Gulf might like to involve themselves in a worldwide deal covering all our racing activities, and Colin was invited to visit the company's Pittsburgh headquarters in the run-up to qualifying.

Quite suddenly, the night before his departure, Colin requested that I make a complete re-appraisal of our anticipated 1967 worldwide programmes and produce several brochures to outline our proposal in detail. It had to set out the income likely to be derived from each race for the eight sections in which we took part, together with our expenditure in car building and research and development. The report was also to include individual race success bonus sources for ourselves and our drivers. With Colin set to depart at 6.30 am, it was obviously going to be an all-nighter. Still hard at work around 4 am, Colin phoned me to say that he had decided not to go himself; the plane was scheduled to leave at 8 am and he would like me to be on it ...

I forgot breakfast in the Motel, deciding to have one on the plane, but this plan was scuppered when the stewardess announced that due to bad weather they would be unable to serve it. It was a desperately unpleasant flight, the plane's yumping and yawing showering dislodged ceiling panels on the unfortunate passengers. As someone not blessed with a love of flying, it was an unforgettable experience for me.

A limo met me at the airport and I was quickly swept to the office of Grady Davis, Executive Vice President, where his original prospecting boots were displayed. It was not a good meeting. Although my reception could not have been warmer, as events turned out Gulf did a sports car racing deal with John Wyer the

following year. However, continuing their generous hospitality the company put me back on its four-engined executive jet aircraft for the trip back to Indy, and as sole passenger I tucked into a meal fit for a king. At Weir Cook I disembarked with the engines still running and returned to a late-evening meeting with Colin.

Although the saga of our cars' bad handling might well have seen us way down the lap time sheets, Jimmy was more than holding his own, and at first qualifying he dominated all except the flying Andretti, although not without problems. Mario had already shaken the Speedway to its foundations with an unofficial lap at 168.5 mph, and now he clinched his anticipated pole position with a four-lap average of 165.899 mph.

Jimmy's morning practice in qualifying was severely hampered by his car jumping out of gear, and it was not until late in the day that he was ready to make what would have to be his one and only attempt if he was to gain a place at the front of the grid.

Later, Andy Granatelli disclosed the drama of the occasion. He had the habit of checking 'his' driver's seat belts before seeing them off, but when he attempted to check Jimmy's, the Scot grabbed his hand in a vice-like grip, shaking his head impercepti-

Jimmy about to sample Unser's 'soft alloy special' for size during practice in '66. An 'Enco' fuel decal is being hastily smoothed into place on the new car's shapely nose. (Indianapolis Motor Speedway)

Jimmy at speed in practice in his STP-Lotus-Ford 38 – chassis '38/4' – running four-spoke cast Lotus front wheels and Halibrand rears, but as yet no white walls on the tyres, which would be so adorned come race day. (Indianapolis Motor Speedway)

bly as he looked at Harlan Fengler, USAC Chief Steward in charge of the qualifying procedure. It was then that Andy discovered the problem that Jimmy was trying to hide; his left leg strap had broken and he had tucked it under his leg to hide it. If Harlan had noticed, his run would have had to be postponed until the fault had been rectified, and at this time of day that would have meant waiting overnight and losing the chance to gain a place on the front of the grid.

Jimmy was to make no public comment on his achievement in driving the car without the essential security given him by his harness, a feat that added considerably to Andy's unbounded admiration for him. The Scot's courageous four-lap average of 164.144 mph gave him second place on the grid. Third best time went to George Snider of A. J. Foyt's Sheraton-Thompson team, just under a whole 2 mph slower than Jimmy.

The first day of trials was marred by Chuck Rodee's fatal accident in his Offy-engined Watson when he hit the wall. However, on that first weekend of qualifying, of the 79 cars entered 23 ensured their place on the starting grid, which meant a hard time ahead over the second weekend as the remaining cars entered for the race fought for the last ten spots.

Immediately after Jimmy's run he and Colin left for Europe in preparation for the Monaco Grand Prix the following weekend. The problems concerning Jimmy's car in practice, and cockpit alterations to suit Unser's larger frame, meant that Al's part in the proceedings had been given low priority, but he had been remarkably consistent and fast, quietly acclimatising himself to the car while lapping quicker and quicker. As it turned out, it was not considered prudent for Al to qualify during the first weekend, and with Colin's departure it was left to the Indy crew to see him through the following weekend's trials. But then came a mysterious and serious problem.

David Lazenby: 'The track officials wanted some form of safety arrangement in the areas under the car where bits might drop on to the track, and we settled for a chicken-wire concoction. Then as standard practice got going again after first qualifying, Al's engine suffered an enormous explosion – I can tell you it was a big one as it flew into a million pieces, and not unexpectedly took the chicken wire out with it. We rushed the remains down to Lou Meyer's place and got another engine. It wasn't long before this one went as well, but I recall that Al was prepared this time and shut if off before serious damage occurred.

An uncharacteristically grim-faced Al Unser picks up a tow back to Gasoline Alley after the engine of '38/7' has let go. Back in the garage the car on its beam-ends reveals detail of the under-tub pipe runs and a ruptured sump-pan on its Ford quad-cam engine. Note the detail of the asymmetrical rear suspension with its differently designed lower wishbones. (Both Indianapolis Motor Speedway)

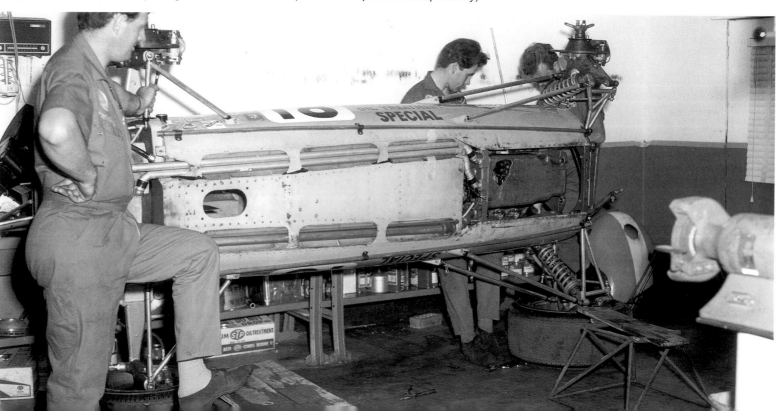

'We took it all to Lou's again and started installing a third V8, and when we came to bolt the gearbox to the bell housing we noticed a distinct gap between the two. As a stop-gap we used lots of washers, and when we had more time we made up a proper spacer. We soon discovered that the ZF quill shafts were a sniff too long, and these had put an end loading on the crankshaft thrust bearing. In the first blow-up this had then taken a main bearing out, but luckily Al had caught the second before too much damage occurred.'

Unlike the Cosworth DFV unit of more recent times, which could be removed from a chassis and replaced in something like 75 minutes, the Ford V8 demanded much longer.

Graham Clode: 'All the engine changes we were forced to make took a great deal of time; if you were waiting for particular components you could reckon on it taking anything up to 6 or 7 hours, while a quick change was in the 2–2½ hours range. There were also a number of "modifications" we had to make to the engine each time, which didn't impress the Ford guys. I don't know whether the engine got larger or the space for installation in the chassis smaller, but I can't remember any occasion when an engine slotted neatly into one of our chassis. There were six or seven areas on each engine that we had to attack with files before installation could start, and later there came a modification to the chassis that also made the job harder. One year there was a change to the regulations that called for a dural plate to be fastened on the "tub" beside the engine for protection supposing an engine really exploded to prevent pieces penetrating the fuel tanks.

'I remember that final week of practice saw a number of engine changes, so much so that we were in desperate problems, lasting literally right up to the time Al had to make his run. The engines had a four-bolt fixing low down with others up top, and time was so tight that Al's car went out for qualifying with only the four lower bolts fitted!'

Al was fastest of all the qualifiers on the second weekend of trials, averaging a very quick 162.272 mph for his four laps, a time that if recorded on the first day of qualifying would have placed him sixth on the grid.

One event that brought distraction concerned an apparent death threat to one of our mechanics. Well-respected as an acquaintance and judge of attractive women, he was engaged in an affair with a married American lady. Upon discovering the liaison, her husband adopted the movie-script ploy of sending the mechanic a letter composed of words cut from newspapers and glued to a sheet of paper. It stated that he had a rifle with telescopic sights and would be present in the stands opposite the pits during practice and the race. Plainly our worthy crew member was as good as done for . . .

We all took this as a huge joke. Then Colin demanded to know what the lads kept laughing about and I recounted the saga. Unfortunately I forgot Colin's apparent abhorrence for anything to do with death – he would never call identical lap times 'dead heats', but 'evens', and anything even remotely connected with

Unser, cheerful again, in his 'soft alloy special' Lotus '38/7' rigged with asymmetrical suspension in the pit lane line-up prior to qualifying. Car 55 is Joe Barnett's veteran Offy roadster for Ron Lux, which failed to complete a qualifying run. (Indianapolis Motor Speedway)

poison he would order out of his near vicinity, or better still 'Let's chuck it'. He was therefore not at all amused by our levity.

'You realise that 90 per cent of the population here are nutters, don't you? You've got to make him understand never to be near us when we're out of the garage. These things can ricochet so put him a few yards away from the rest of the crew if he goes out to the pit wall, and get some small blackboards and chalk so we can relay messages to him easily.'

We kept up the blackboard routine for a day, then as practice hotted up it was forgotten and we carried on an usual. Fortunately, the marksman must also have forgotten his shooter, but I feel sure that for the next week or two we all made certain that our lady friends were single.

On one occasion at breakfast Jimmy drew our attention to an item in the Indianapolis newspaper relating how a father had shot dead his daughter as she returned home through an open window at 2 in the morning, having forgotten her door key. Colin was simply horrified by the story, and kept referring to it for the rest of the day.

'Jesus, what a place this is,' he kept repeating. 'Dreadful, dreadful . . .' It really affected him.

On another occasion our motel car park attendant, a man of retirement age with whom we all had a nodding acquaintance, was shot dead in the middle of the night, apparently for no reason. Colin was dumbstruck. 'I can't believe it,' he kept saying, to no one in particular. Such senseless violence was an aspect of America he abhorred.

Our third, single, garage (two were knocked into one) was my office, somewhat cramped with a car in it but boasting a table and folding aluminium and canvas chairs, all under a bare light-bulb and complete with a fridge, all our crates stacked neatly along the walls and with spare wheels piled up. This year of course there was no spare car, so I had plenty of room. With the doors closed to keep out onlookers and press, the cool semi-dark-ness in the humid heat of the day was appreciated. Sitting in the 'office' talking with Colin one day, I noticed him looking around, as if sizing up the place.

'This really isn't good enough,' he said finally, his mind momen-tarily oblivious to the subject we had been discussing. 'Just look at it – crates piled up, you crammed in a corner, a bare table, uncomfortable chairs, no lamp shade – you really have no idea about these things.' Then without a moment's hesitation he returned to our original subject.

When he departed for Monaco I visited a nearby furniture hire company, selecting two comfortable chairs, a typist's chair, a more sanitary desk, and a table lamp. I also bought a lamp shade for our single bulb and some table mats. We were in business!

Jimmy and the revised team pose with his STP-liveried Type 38 for the official Indy photograph, a praiseworthy tradition which the Speedway authorities had far-sightedly instituted in 1911 and have maintained ever since. Behind the car are (left to right) Graham Clode, Andy Granatelli, Colin Chapman, Dave Lazenby, Arthur ('Butty') Birchall, Mike ('Charlie Chins') Underwood, Maurice Phillippe and New Zealand newcomer Alan McCall. (Indianapolis Motor Speedway)

When Colin returned, once more seated in the 'office' but now in a more comfortable chair, he said nothing. It was as if nothing had changed. The next day as we sat talking he suddenly glanced around him at all the various additions.

'What's happened here?' he said. 'What's all this new stuff doing in here?'

'I've hired it.'

'What for?'

'To make it more comfortable and not so grotty.'

'What? You've got the chairs, the table lamp and the lamp-shade?'

'Yes.'

'I don't know – there's something effeminate about you . . .'

Over 300,000 spectators were in place on a comfortably sunny day for the 50th running of what would be an extraordinary 500-Mile classic watched live in England courtesy of John Player and selected Gaumont cinemas around the country via the Early Bird satellite.

Once again, Cyril Audrey, the chief RAC timekeeper, flew over to assist us and he was in place at our timekeeping table as the opening ceremonies got under way. Of the 33 cars on the grid, 24 were Ford-powered, the remaining nine being Offy-engined. However, the latter came in various guises: three were unblown, three were turbo-charged and three supercharged. Only one car on the grid was front-engined, and 16 were British designed. Apart from Jimmy, rookies Graham Hill and Jackie Stewart also represented the Grand Prix world, both driving Lola-Ford T90s.

As the pace car pulled off into the pit lane, the field was already out of formation as it accelerated away. When the leading cars entered Turn One all hell broke loose behind them: one car either got out of shape or accelerated too quickly and hit the car in front. Whatever the cause, the effect was disastrous, with cars hitting and bouncing off each other and a debris of wheels and suspension parts spiralling above the dust.

Graham Clode remembers seeing Unser 'treading his way through the wreckage'. Mike Underwood doesn't: 'I was flat on the ground to avoid the flying debris.' Considering his starting position back down the grid in 23rd slot, Al did a remarkable job to stay clear of the carnage; one car alongside him and five imme-diately in front of him were involved, with another two up front!

Although 11 cars were wrecked (ten Ford and just one Offy-powered car), amazingly only one driver was hurt, A. J. Foyt cut-ting a finger as, with the speed of a jack-rabbit, he climbed up the wire fencing protecting the spectators.

The race was restarted nearly 1½ hours later following removal of the wreckage, and was run under the yellow for five laps to help clear the dust left around the crash area. Then as the field got under way another car went into the wall and the yellow caution lights stayed on for another 23 minutes.

The enforced cruising speeds did not help race leader Mario Andretti at all, and after the green light flashed on and with Jimmy immediately behind him, his Brawner-Brabham's engine poured smoke, Mario out of the race by lap 35 with a dropped valve.

Indy's official front-row line-up photograph for the 1966 '500' shows Mario Andretti on pole in his tube-frame Brawner-Ford (average 165.899 mph), Jimmy's '38/4' occupied here by Mike Underwood alongside at 164.114 mph and George Snider's 38-based Coyote-Ford – based on Bobby Johns' '65 car, '38/2' (2) – third on the outside at 162.521 mph. (Indianapolis Motor Speedway)

Now Jimmy led on his white-walled Firestones, followed by Lloyd Ruby (in the Len Terry-designed Eagle-Ford) and Parnelli Jones. Graham Hill (John Mecom-owned Lola) was eighth, Jackie Stewart (Lola) tenth. Then on lap 65 Jimmy lost control on Turn Four, his gyrations bringing the huge crowd to its feet as he managed to avoid contact with the wall, finishing his pirouettes on the grass from where he drove straight to our pit for a check. Rejoining the race he found himself behind Ruby, but catching him at around a second a lap; then the Texan pitted for fuel and Jimmy was back in the lead.

By lap 83 Clark still led Ruby, Jimmy's fellow Scot, Jackie Stewart, now third, Graham Hill still eighth. Just two laps later Jimmy spun again, kissing the wall slightly and pitting again for a check, plus fuel. It was the quickest stop in Speedway history at that point, Andy's STP crew getting him away in 17 seconds.

But now Jimmy's Type 38 was not handling as it should, possibly as a result of touching the wall; later he was to report ruefully, 'I actually spun six times, but caught four of them.'

As the race progressed past the halfway mark, Jimmy was passed by Stewart for second place behind Ruby, and Jimmy stayed with him until lap 131, when the two leading cars stopped for fuel and our No 1 took the lead for 11 laps until he too stopped for fuel, another rapid stop lasting just 22 seconds. He rejoined the race still in the lead, but Stewart

Prelude to chaos – hurtling into Turn One immediately after taking the green flag for the start, Snider is closing down on Andretti with Jimmy third. Meanwhile, back at the timing line, Billy Foster's Vollstedt is bouncing off the outside wall minus its right-side wheels, a car is broadside in the pack and 11 starters are about to become zero-lap retirements. For the second time in three years the '500' will be red-flagged and restarted only after a lengthy delay to clear up the mess. (Indianapolis Motor Speedway)

was right behind and soon passed him.

Graham Clode: 'The night before the race the Old Man got the fuel information from Ford and decided to run 10 per cent nitro.

We had three jets, one lean, one normal and one rich, and we had a control in the cockpit for Jimmy to choose what he wanted – he could run lean to save fuel, or if he wanted to have a boost he could run rich. But after the first refuelling Jimmy said the thing went flat and just wouldn't pull, and we suspected that Enco hadn't put the nitro in. He said the lack of power was embarrassing . . .'

Now Al Unser was third, Graham Hill fourth. Four British-built cars and three British drivers in the first four places! However, a number of cars had now retired with engine problems, flooding the track with oil.

Lap 162 brought a severe setback for Al and Team Lotus. Mike Underwood: 'It was a huge disappointment for us all as Al had done so well. In the reports of the race, Al was supposed to have lost it and hit the wall, but in fact he was coming up on another car when it blew up and Al hit an oil pump that was blown off and went into the wall in a big way, losing a wheel and crumpling the "tub" badly.'

Now the race was being led by three Brits, two of them rookies, in three British cars, all running in close proximity in a field of only ten surviving cars, three of them in trouble. Approaching lap 180, according to the electronic scoreboard Graham passed Jimmy into second place, although it was later believed to have

Al Unser's lap 162 impact with the wall in the North-West Turn was a heavy one, amputating the right-front wheel of '38/7' and punching it back hard into the soft-alloy-skinned tub. Evidence of track conditions is smeared all over the windscreen. (Indianapolis Motor Speedway)

happened during Jimmy's first spin in Turn Four; Colin and Cyril Audrey's lap chart had Jimmy retaining second place behind Stewart, and this information continued to be displayed on Jimmy's signal board.

Then, with just 25 miles to run, Stewart's oil pressure zeroed and he was out. Now both Graham's and Jimmy's boards showed each to be in the lead, and when Graham took the chequered flag he drove straight into Winner's Circle. Jimmy, after stopping to commiserate with Stewart, also followed the winner's route, only to find Graham already there, earning the first of his many bonuses by drinking a glass of milk and enjoying the plaudits. Without a moment's hesitation Jimmy was out of his car, warmly congratulating his old friend . . .

How had such a dreadful error upset our lap chart? Apart from the possibility of a simple mistake, we had two other factors to consider. First, we accepted that Colin's excellent chart-keeping could only be relied on down to 15th place; he knew this, and whereas his Grand Prix charts could be guaranteed correct right down to last place, on a track such as Indianapolis where the field would pass the pit area at very high speed every 55 to 60 seconds, he was faced with an impossible task, even for him. Graham Hill had started in 15th spot, but there was the dust and debris of the start to cause confusion. However, the second start had been more sedate and Hill had started 12th.

Second, there had been the two chilling commentator announcements (some people later reported three) that Jimmy had spun wildly; such news might easily have seriously disturbed Colin. In addition, Andy Granatelli reported later that Al Unser's shunt on lap 162 had been announced over the loudspeakers as an accident to Clark, another possible distraction . . .

Colin was convinced that his chart was right, especially as his had agreed with the official scoreboard until it had, late in the race, stuttered and winked, then flickered back on to show a different leader. He went completely over the top, shouting and protesting the result and haranguing Chief Steward Harlan Fengler. As Andy said later, Colin was even more excited than the STP chief, 'if that can be believed!'.

Eventually the race officials agreed to allow Colin and Cyril to investigate the official lap scorers' records and when, after a thorough check, the two agreed that it was their own error, the matter was allowed to rest. What appeared to upset Colin more was the fact that at the time he went out, Al Unser had, from third place in the race, been catching the leaders hand over fist, and that if he had been able to continue, he would have won!

Andy Granatelli remained unconvinced – how was it, he reasoned, that the official scoreboard, the announcer, the press and even Graham's John Mecom crew had Jimmy ahead before the tower scoreboard changed? Andy was willing to bet that the scoring official in charge of Jimmy's car (there being one official to each car) had turned to light a cigarette, or perhaps pour himself a drink, when Unser's Lotus had crashed, followed by the commentator's shout that it was race leader Clark who had come to grief, thereby missing Jimmy passing the pits. As Andy was to pro-

'Spinning Takes Practice' – Jimmy's famous explanation of the initials 'STP' was triggered by his two brilliantly controlled but costly mid-race spins that denied him and Lotus-Ford back-to-back victories in the world's richest motor race. (Indianapolis Motor Speedway)

claim on many occasions when reminded of the 1966 race, 'How can we put men on the moon and yet be unable to track one little old race car?'

Bearing in mind the handling problems suffered throughout May, which had returned for the race itself, and a track awash with oil (Colin added a point to the next USAC meeting agenda recommending that a 2–3 gallon catch tank for discharged oil and other lubricants be mandatory), together with the fact only four cars were classified as running at the time the chequered flag had fallen, it could all have been much worse. Needless to say, it was Jimmy's inherent skills that had brought home the bacon, even if it was second place and not another win. Perhaps it is best to remember Jimmy's summing up of the race, that 'STP stands for "Spinning Takes Practice"'.

Graham's win earned a total of $156.297, and Jimmy's runner-up position, reported as 44 seconds in arrears, brought $76,992, both before tax. Al's 12th place grossed a little over $14,000.

Immediately after the race Jimmy's car, chassis '38/4' complete with engine, was sold to A. J. Foyt. However, in practice for the Milwaukee 100-Mile race the weekend after Indy, A. J. crashed badly and was quite badly burned about the face and arms. The car was quickly returned to Cheshunt, arriving with Al's badly damaged car (chassis '38/7') from the '500', covered by our Team insurance.

Both required extensive rebuilds. While work on A. J.'s 'tub' continued until the end of July, the insurance assessors took their time before approving repairs to our own car. Quite regardless of his value as a customer, A. J. was regarded with much affection by everyone at Team Lotus. Both he and his father Tony were perfect customers; if payment was not made up front prior to order con-

firmation – usually because we were unable to price items instantaneously – subsequent invoices were always paid by return. As a result everyone involved, from accountants to store-keeper, responded instantly to A. J.'s requirements, and in so doing

Jimmy receiving his second-place award from Tony Hulman at the 1966 '500' Victory Awards Banquet. (Indianapolis Motor Speedway)

● 1966: 'SPINNING TAKES PRACTICE'

we probably set up an all-time record for trans-Continental urgent parts delivery to a customer.

A. J. called us from California late one night with a list of items required. It was early morning UK time, and the package was made up and dispatched to London Airport to arrive in Los Angeles that night, completing the whole transaction within the day. Colin soon became aware of the excellent service A. J. was enjoying and made it clear that he would personally bring it all to a stop if A. J. didn't display the Lotus name on his Lotus cars. Early in August, only a month after his accident, A. J. told us that he was back in the pink and his repaired car left Heathrow on the 13th.

While the rebuilding of Al's race car awaited the insurance company's approval, work started on the tenth and last Type 38 'tub' to be built, chassis number '38/8', which as a symmetrical car took the suffix 'S' in subsequent test and development reports. While it was progressing, USAC contacted us about a race to be run at Mount Fuji in Japan on 9 October. All the qualifiers from Indy were invited by the Japanese, and Rodger Ward was responsible for organising the freight and passenger charters required for the American teams, quite a considerable task.

Again the organisers had not thought to apply for the necessary FIA international permit to allow the 'big-three' from Indy, Messrs Clark, Hill and Stewart, to compete, and the American sporting politicians now proceeded to pull out all the stops to obtain one. When political progress appeared to be slowing, the Japanese arranged for their ambassador to France to present himself at the FIA office in Paris.

Symmetrical chassis '38/8S' ran at Snetterton on 22 September for Jimmy to test, complete with a ZF 5DS25 gearbox; a Lotus-Cortina was also present. I am not sure if this was the test in which Jimmy showed his extraordinary skills, but people who were there remember it as Snetterton in 1966 and Jim Endruweit recorded that Jimmy 'spun off' twice on that date. The car was running with a modified version of the multi-tubular De Dion rear-end structure tested earlier in the year, and there were several different Firestone Indy compounds to try. Initially Jimmy found the car's braking inconsistent, and when light rain began to fall 'R107'-pattern tyres were fitted to cope. Jimmy was lapping faster after each stop, and after one particular run he reported that the car was 'prone to swop ends' as well as suffering 'front-end washout', as he had just demonstrated!

Colin suggested that he and Maurice Phillippe should watch progress from the bridge at the esses. From there they could hear the car all around the circuit, and as Jimmy approached he snicked from fourth to fifth gear. At the turn-in to the corner the car suddenly went into a lurid spin and disappeared under the bridge.

Maurice: 'Colin shouted, "This is going to be a big one", but when we ran down the ramp there was no sign of the car or Jimmy. Then we noticed skid marks that went through a 20-foot-wide gap in the earth bank. On the other side we found a sheepish and embarrassed Jimmy, who had already got out of the undamaged car. He admitted that he had simply lost it – frankly, I suspected he had spotted us up on the bridge and thought he would put on a masterly display. The point was that the spin marks plainly changed direction to aim through the gap in the bank. I was intrigued how Jimmy had got off the brakes at the crucial moment so that the car had changed direction and passed neatly through that gap; Jimmy calmly agreed that this was what he had done to save the car and himself. I was a little sceptical that any human being was capable of retrieving the situation in such a violent spin, but the evidence was clearly recorded there on the road surface.

'Later that day the engine sound suddenly stopped, again in the direction of the esses, and we all jumped in our cars and raced to the scene. Another set of tyre marks evidenced a similar set of circumstances, and again the car was neatly parked in an almost identical position, again with no damage. The gap in the bank required a precise aim to avoid contact, yet the man had the ability to do it twice in one day!'

With only a week left before departure to Japan, and the car still not right, Jim Endruweit and Mike Underwood were back at Snetterton with it five days later. The brakes had been the main problem, so this time Ferodo's man was present. The previous test's ventilated discs had been replaced by solid ones, with DS 11 pad material unchanged. Jimmy tried the car both light of fuel and with 45 gallons on board, and now pronounced it, if not perfect, at least better and with none of the brake-fade experienced before. After a trial 'race start', the car was returned to Cheshunt and readied for the long trip to Japan. To cope with the 200-mile race without a fuel stop, additional pannier-style fuel tanks were hung on each side.

As Mike Underwood and Arthur Birchall were winging their way to Japan, Jim Endruweit was once more immersed in the H16 Indy engine programme, which had been revived. With Jimmy having gained the H16's sole Grand Prix win (the 1966 United States Grand Prix at Watkins Glen) just a day or two earlier, we were talking to the people at Bourne from a more advantageous position!

The 2.7-mile variant of the Fuji course was selected, running anti-clockwise. Some records suggest we took two cars, but only '38/8S' was there for Jimmy, resplendent in its bright red STP livery. For some reason the race promoters, generous to an extreme in providing additional air tickets to all and sundry, restricted the weight of tools and spares to a mere 75 lbs. This was no doubt a limit imposed for the charter, but the fact remained that 11 cars were excluded from the race due merely to lack of parts. Another strange item, considering the limitation on freight, was the adoption of the Indy regulation that only the engines used in practice could be used in the race, a requirement that now caught us out.

The Fuji road circuit was not suited to the American entries as most used standard two-speed gearboxes, and it was soon obvious that it placed unnecessary strain upon engines and transmissions, further reducing the number of starters. Mario Andretti was reported to have blown his engine trying to match Jackie

146

Stewart's and Graham Hill's pace with the four-speed Lolas, and although there were reports that Jimmy had also blown his engine, this was not so.

Mike Underwood: 'I would say that by this time in the season the Old Man had got so used to the method of starting the H16 F1 engines that he quite forgot where he was! Due to the BRM's tremendous resonance in the 2–4,000 rpm range, as soon as we fired them up we took them over 4,000 rpm. With the Indy Ford we would disconnect the throttle linkages and rev them by hand. On the last practice day before the Fuji race "Butty" (Arthur Birchall) and I had just started the engine from cold when the Old Man suddenly appeared in the garage. He looked the car over, then started vigorously revving the engine with a great "vrooom, vrooom"! Jimmy was standing in the corner and he reacted immediately, leaping over to the car and knocking the Old Man's hand off the throttle. But it was too late – the engine was well and truly knackered.

'All of this would have been OK – it was the Old Man's car after all – but there was a smart arse from Ford there who told the Old Man that the engine's bearings were identical to the Mustang's, to which Colin replied, "Oh really?" The Ford bloke immediately took off for Tokyo, while "Butty" and I, without any proper tools, started taking the engine apart. The bloke was gone

hours and when he eventually returned there was no way the bearings he had would fit. The whole affair was a complete waste of time. Then to cap it all, when "Butty" and I arrived in New York I found that the airline had lost all my baggage; they tried the old story that it would undoubtably arrive on the next day's flight, but I had a stand-up row with them, saying I was on my way to an important meeting in New York, and they coughed up for a new suit, shirt, tie, everything. That's all I want to remember about that trip!'

For me, the Fuji race was to rumble on for some years like a distant earthquake. First, we received no money for the race (we had not started, although this was the last reason acceptable to Colin, who preferred to call it 'appearance money'), and I had to chase after just about everyone in the motor racing world for support in trying to recoup the £5,500 travel expenses and appearance money owed. Years later I was told that the promoter's money had come from a pornographic publishing house, and that the company set up for the race had gone into liquidation soon after.

When I left Team Lotus three years later, the missing money was still a thorn in Colin's side, and he would frequently ask if I was doing my best to secure it. Even when I returned to Team in 1976, ten years after the race, it was not long before Colin

Group Lotus moved lock, stock and barrel from Cheshunt to Hethel aerodrome, Norfolk, at the start of 1966. Here's the assembly plant (right), office block (left), company aircraft hangar and airfield control tower (foreground). The former US 8th Air Force base's perimeter track, passing between hangar and factory building, provided Lotus's on-site test circuit. (Focalpoint, Norwich)

The 1966 Type 42 Indy cars intended for BRM H16 power units sitting in store at Lotus's new Norfolk factory, No 10 having been the intended Clark car for '66 that would eventually be fitted with a Ford V8 engine for Graham Hill's use at the Speedway in '67.

brought up the subject again, saying that as a Japanese Formula 1 race was being held at Fuji I should now approach the CSI and seek their support – in other words, pay Team Lotus or cancel the race! If that did not work, I should seek out the 1966 race promoter when I went to Japan at the end of the 1977 season . . . Needless to say, I had no success. Even more aggravating was the affair of the Japanese doll.

As is usual with Japanese hosts, everyone at Fuji '66 was given a traditional Japanese present, in this case a doll. Colin promptly put his in his suitcase and brought it home, giving it to his wife Hazel as a memento. At some stage it was removed to the loft at the Chapman home in Barnet, North London, and was left behind when the family moved to Norfolk.

One day in 1977 I was summoned to Colin's office where he was entertaining his old friend Alan Richardson, a furniture dealer from Highgate, who had purchased Colin's house when they moved. Alan had found the doll in the loft and had subsequently put it into an auction.

'Do you know what it fetched?' Colin asked me. '*Nine hundred pounds*! So while you're chasing the money in Japan, tell them they still owe us a doll.'

Again, I was unsuccessful . . .

October finally brought the underwriters' approval of our claim for nearly £7,000 to cover the rebuilding of Al Unser's '38/7', as well as their confirmation that we could dispose of what remained of the car.

Plans for the 1967 Indy '500' were now being sketched, the H16 BRM programme was revived, and the two Type 42 monocoques were dusted down in preparation. Geoff Johnson, the BRM engineer who drew the engine, later joined Lotus Engineering and he

recalled that 'the original 4.2-litre Indy version of the H16 engine was identical in general layout to the 3-litre Formula 1 version, with single-plane crankshafts and thus firing as a double-eight-cylinder unit – cylinders firing in pairs simultaneously, not all 16 separately. Obviously the bore and stroke were increased and the crankshaft interconnecting gears made stronger than the 3-litre's.

'Initial running was plagued by the failure of the metering unit drive belts until heavier duty ones were incorporated. The driving pins in the metering units then failed, and a special pair of dog-drive metering units were made. The next component to suffer repeated failure was the distributor driveshaft, which was replaced by a new design. This allowed the engine to run for short periods until failure of the camshaft-drive-pack dowels occurred. These were increased in size and the engine ran sufficiently to pass it off at 585 bhp.'

This dyno run took place as the New Year began, but the unit was not to be delivered to Team Lotus until February.

Meanwhile, in October the Fuji Type 38 was airfreighted back to Indianapolis for an extended tyre test, while the move of Team Lotus to its new factory site at Hethel, Norfolk, was being orchestrated by Jim Endruweit. In the Indy section, Mike Underwood was promoted to Chief Mechanic as David Lazenby, who had held the role since 1963, moved on to become General Manager of Lotus Components Ltd, a move he was to describe later as a 'big mistake'; he would leave Lotus for good in 1968.

A major addition to our ranks for 1967 was former World Champion driver Graham Hill. With the Ford-promoted Cosworth DFV Formula 1 engine about to be unleashed, initially for the exclusive use of Team Lotus, it had been decided to employ two front-line stars. Thus Graham made his return to the Team he had left at the end of 1959 to join BRM, for whom he had driven for the intervening seven seasons.

In December he arrived for his cockpit and seat fitting, which because of his larger frame and height compared to Jimmy demanded major modifications, which Colin decreed should apply to all Team cars. Steering columns were to be raised 2 inches, windscreens were to be wider and legroom longer. When it became clear that the insulated water pipe in the cockpit also needed to be re-sited to provide more elbow room, it became clear that all the cars' cockpits needed redesigning. Colin stressed that they must all be completed before the first race. Graham, the arch-detail-man, also wanted a discussion on spring rates, but Colin decreed that be left until after Graham's first trial runs.

We were reminded of BRM's apparently bottomless budgets when Graham mentioned in passing that all his travel was to be first class. Colin quickly countered by saying that since he himself never enjoyed first class, he could not see why anyone else should. After considerable haggling, Graham agreed to pay the fare surcharge himself. Colin asked me to inform Jimmy about this arrangement, to avoid any misunderstanding over who was paying for what!

This marked the start of a new era for Team Lotus, and one that would be both highly invigorating and most enjoyable . . .

CHAPTER EIGHT

1967:
Recipe for Disaster

Our experiences with the Formula 1 BRM H16 F1 engine in 1966 must have raised very serious doubts in Colin's mind regarding the promised Indy version; if it did, he gave no hint until the very last moment. Although BRM had indicated that the Formula 1 unit would be shown to the press in September 1965, it had not made its bow until several months later, and a complete car had not been seen until April 1966. Described by *Motoring News* in June as 'undoubtedly one of the most controversial of all racing cars ever built, next to the ill-fated V16 BRM', the engine had been savaged by some areas of the media with horrifying tales of excessive vibration and other maladies, while others had suggested that BRM was about to scrap the whole idea.

Early in January 1967 Colin and I flew to the BRM works at Bourne to discuss the situation affecting both Indy and Lotus-Cortina engines – which BRM also built for Ford – with Director of Research, Peter Spear. I was immediately cagey about Spear, as I wondered if he really meant what he said. Even at this late stage in the programme there was still much umming and aahing, although Peter confirmed that BRM's board had agreed that there should be three engines, and he also assured us that the H16 Indy unit would give 600–650 bhp and first delivery would, at the very latest, be at the end of February, or two weeks earlier if eight-pin crankshafts became available.

Colin said he was not entirely happy with that proposed power output, as the Offys and Weslake-headed V8 Fords were already giving 600 bhp and would no doubt give more by May. Team Lotus had already agreed with Firestone to test the Type 42-BRM car during one of two periods at Indy between 1 and 18 March, and the damage caused by delays was emphasised to Peter. Neither would we contemplate testing at all unless two H16s were available. BRM would provide a mechanic for this test – only his wages would be our responsibility – while BRM would accept the cost of mechanical failures up to the start of the race itself. Although we argued that our primary intention had been to accept the engines only on loan (it was, after all, a BRM R&D project), Peter could not accept that, and it was eventually agreed that Team would pay $28,000 each for two units, with the third

to be loaned. It was left for BRM owner Sir Alfred Owen to confirm the final agreement.

His thoughts were made known to us the day Ford reported promising progress on its turbo-charged V8 R&D programme, and Lou Meyer, the man looking after our 'customer' order, reported that he was some two months behind schedule, so our first Ford engine would not become available until the end of March. Life was becoming complicated . . .

Sir Alfred wanted to charge us $33,000 per H16 engine. In addition, four major items in our 11-point draft were radically altered, and only after much haggling was the price finally settled at $32,000 (the price of a 255 CID Ford V8, less exhaust assembly and battery, was $22,500).

The H16 engine's considerable weight has already been mentioned. As Maurice ruefully noted when the first Formula 1 unit was delivered, it took five or six mechanics just to lift it off the truck; in fact it weighed 140 lbs over the original estimate! It was not until the Belgian Grand Prix in June 1966 that our H16-powered Formula 1 Type 43 had appeared at a race, but only briefly in practice before being reloaded on to the transporter.

From then on the tale of woe had continued, brightening slightly at Monza for the Italian Grand Prix. There, Colin later reported with glee, the H16 car had completed 64 laps in practice, suffering only minor problems with clutch drag, poor gear selection and a continuous oil leak from a rear clutch assembly bearing 'that obviously needs a re-design'. He had also discovered a gearbox fault caused by soft gears.

At the start of that race in the 43, Jimmy had been slowed by vaporisation in the H16's fuel injection lines, but got going quickly after that to regain more than a second a lap on the leaders. Then, a wheel had gone seriously out of balance due to the inner tube's bonding melting. When he had stopped for a new wheel, the hot engine had proved difficult to restart and the battery's depletion had caused poor ignition and low fuel pressure from then on. Another inner tube then gave trouble, and at that pit stop the battery was replaced. Again Jimmy rejoined, this time lapping within one-tenth of a second inside the fastest race lap, but just two laps from the end the H16 had let go in a big way.

Then had followed the extraordinary United States Grand Prix at Watkins Glen, where, against all odds, Jimmy had won.

It had fallen to me to report our experiences to Bourne (BRM had generously loaned us its spare engine for the race after our last H16 had blown up in practice), and I had pointed out that our exuberance must be tempered by the fact that there was no one left in the race to press Jimmy when he had taken the lead. The car's water had all but boiled away in the closing stages, its oil pressure had run dangerously high and the BRM gearbox had been virtually useless. I concluded by reminding them that the winning engine had subsequently blown itself apart only 50 miles after the race, during practice for the Mexican Grand Prix. Costwise, the engine had also not been cheap, rebuilds costing over £1,500 and standard overhaul around £60 – peanuts today, but horrific at that time.

At the end of December 1966 Colin had requested that I work on my own in establishing contact with our friends in Ford America to secure an engine allocation for our back-up Type 38s at Indy '67 – he wanted the affair to be kept completely confidential to avoid disinterest and inertia at BRM in the Type 42 BRM-engined project. On New Year's Eve I therefore telephoned Leo Beebe in Detroit . . .

I also contacted Bobby Johns again, hoping that he would drive a third car, but again he had already signed elsewhere.

As February neared its end we were still awaiting delivery of the first BRM Indy engine. The week of testing the car at Indy some time between 1 and 18 March was still on our programme, and when the engine finally appeared work recommenced, along with discussions on the proposed financial arrangement between BRM and ourselves. BRM's suggestion was that as it was almost certain that it would only be able to supply sufficient engines for one car – Jimmy's – the split of race income should be 45 per cent to the Scotsman, 10 per cent to the mechanics, and the remaining 45 per cent to be split equally between ourselves and Bourne. At first Colin was unhappy, but he eventually relented upon the acceptance that all bonuses should be split equally between ourselves and Jimmy. On this basis our four entries of two Type 38s, one Ford-engined Type 42 and one BRM-engined 42 were dispatched. February also saw an H16 on test at BRM, where it achieved 5 hours' full-throttle running, as already described by BRM's Geoff Johnson in the previous chapter.

In March the first complete Lotus-BRM Type 42 was ready for testing, Mike Underwood and his crew taking the car to Snetterton for Jimmy to sample. It would be one of the last tests in England that Jimmy attended, for in April the press got news of his tax exile at the same time as his favourite girlfriend Sally Stokes announced her engagement to Dutch racing driver Ed Swart.

Mike Underwood: 'I took the car out for three laps to warm it up, then Jimmy tried it. It only lasted another two laps before the engine let go in a big way. It was a case of what the Formula 1 lads had called "mumps" in the H16 the previous year. I don't think one ever blew apart; they just had immense internal disruptions, and you could see these little lumps distorting the outer

surface of the engine, hence the term "mumps". So that was all a waste of time and we took the engine out and sent it back to BRM.

'What amazed us all was that Colin still insisted we would be going to Indy with BRM engines, and in all the months and months of talking we had only done five laps with the thing. Remembering what had happened the previous year, we spent our time waiting for Bourne to send us another unit by preparing our two 38s . . .'

Geoff Johnson: 'We found that bearing and centre gear failure in the power-pack gears had caused extensive damage and the engine was not run again with that crankshaft configuration. During this initial development, the engine was dynamically and torsionally rough, its torsional vibrations being responsible for all the failures encountered. However, it was impossible to increase the mass of the counterweights owing to the crankcase limitations, so a new design of two-plane crankshaft was drawn to allow the engine to fire as a full 16. It was not possible to make the crankshafts to the eight-pin form of the 3-litre with individual big-end journals. The change in firing order also necessitated new camshafts with different cam-lobe dispositions. This engine was run initially on eight primary exhaust pipes on the bottom banks and a cross-over coupled exhaust on the top banks. Also the centre gear and bearing in the power-pack were strengthened. The engine appeared slightly smoother than the Mark 1, but was still rough. And we saw only 525 bhp from it.

'When it was returned for inspection, it was found that the cage on the power-pack centre bearing had failed, and also the studs retaining the power-pack had fractures adjacent to the centre bearing. Larger studs were fitted and a larger-capacity bearing fitted. Further running with a variety of exhaust systems, fuel mixtures and various settings failed to produce any more power, but continued failure of the centre bearing cage occurred. This was due to misalignment of the centre gear, mainly due to distortion under load, so a further re-design of the power-pack was evolved to stiffen up its bearing housings. The temporary stiffening plate was run successfully, but the full improved system had not been run when the project was temporarily shelved. At no time during the running of the Mark 2 engine in any condition did it produce more than 530 bhp, even though it had its correct high-lift inlet camshafts, whereas the Mark 1 engine had given 585 bhp with low-lift 3-litre inlet camshafts.

'The engine was run as a double-eight as well as a full 16, but to no advantage. The usual fuel that it ran on was 40 per cent methanol/petrol mixture, but other mixes were tried, also to no advantage . . .'

At the end of March BRM's Chief Engineer, Tony Rudd, reported that the Indy H16 run on their test-bed with our design of exhaust system was 'down on power' to a reading of 625 bhp, but having changed to the BRM cross-coupled exhausts on top and bottom banks, its power output had returned to the 640–655 bhp they had predicted. Our exhaust design, enforced by our car's rear suspension layout, produced different power outputs

BRM design engineer Geoffrey Johnson with the Bourne company's Tony Rudd-masterminded H16-cylinder Formula 1 engine. Johnson had doubts about the unit's double-deck coupled twin-crankshaft design from the outset. Sadly they proved to be well founded . . .

from top and bottom banks, which overloaded the engine's centre output gear, causing the bearing failure.

Tony discussed the problem with both Jim Endruweit and Mike Underwood (neither of whom were great advocates of the H16 concept) and the point was raised concerning the car's ability to reach the pits supposing that something simple, like a loose ignition wire, put one 'deck' of the engine out of action, causing failure of the output gear bearings. Tony accepted the point and put in hand modification to fit bearings of an appropriate load-carrying capacity, a task he reckoned to complete in seven days. Bearing in mind that it would now be some time into April before such a modified engine was available, Mike Underwood reckoned that it was too late to set about such work, and Tony now sought Colin's approval to dispose of the engines elsewhere. The rumour at that time was that Texan team-owner John Mecom was a possible customer.

Meanwhile our crew was having to contend with a multitude of pieces to fit into their jigsaw, quite apart from the H16; there was also the updated Ford V8, as well as the possible turbocharged version. On the gearbox front alone there were, apart from the BRM, no fewer than four types of ZF gearbox to cater for, and a multitude of different chassis and suspension components required for asymmetric and symmetric layouts on both the Type 42s and Type 38s, and now another permutation was necessary. If the 42-BRM would not work, we would have to convert a 42 to accept Ford power.

In America, Autolite's Chickie Hirashima, testing our Ford V8 used at the Indy test, found it down on power; it had used a modified injection system, but Chickie later reinstalled a standard layout and it regained power, although a valve spring problem now arose and the unit went back to Meyer, who was already overloaded with work.

It was as late as March before the decision was finally made to go ahead with the conversion of a Type 42 to a Ford V8 installation and, with only a few weeks to go before departure to Indy, everyone who could be spared from the other Team Lotus sections set about the horrendous effort required. During the month we went to Indy for a test with '38/7', then came back to rebuild the test car and to all this feverish activity with the 42.

Mike Underwood: 'It was simply mind-blowing; with the Ford V8 considerably longer than the BRM unit, the car really grew – its wheelbase was a whole *10 inches* longer. This necessitated revised suspension parts with new pick-up points for the radius arms (moved from the "tub" to a new rear engine-frame), eight types of shock absorbers that might be interchanged on each of the three cars – the work seemed endless. We all worked 24-hour shifts in order to meet the deadline; I was living 30 minutes from Hethel and it was obviously a waste of time doing that twice a day, so for two weeks I slept in a bed in our Formula 1 transporter parked just outside the workshop.'

We also retained a sizeable Indy customer list to whom we were supplying suspension and gearbox components, all these orders being looked after by our hard-pressed Indy section. One of our most helpful customers was Jerry Alderman Ford, who not only supplied us with components but also transport and trucks during testing.

Towards the end of April the 42 (asymmetric chassis '42F/1') and the two 38s (symmetric chassis '38/8S' from Fuji and Unser's rebuilt asymmetric chassis '38/7' from the '66 race) were air-freighted to Indy still unfinished, and the exhausted crew followed them to continue working around the clock before running could begin.

It was lucky that during my first week at Indy I happened to overhear a conversation between Ford executives indicating that Harley Copp was about to leave for Monaco in order to take part in the Ford presence to celebrate the first race of the Cosworth DFV. Knowing that we had abandoned any intention of running there some months previously, but not wishing to get involved in the political game, I swiftly asked my secretary at Hethel to cable

Copp and others on the Ford VIP list to declare how much we heartily looked forward to seeing them at Zandvoort, and that itineraries were on their way . . .

On arrival at Indy we found that an engine we had brought with us from England had been severely damaged at London Airport, so one was out of commission before we had even started.

Supporting Chief Mechanic Mike Underwood were Liverpudlian Arthur ('Butty') Birchall, Irishman Eamon ('Chalky') Fullalove, Jim Pickles, Graham ('Rabbit') Bartils, and Welshman Hywel Absalom. Australian Jim Smith had departed (later we received a telephone call from a shipping company asking for his whereabout as apparently he had 'jumped ship' before joining us), and Graham Clode preferred to stay in the London area rather than move to Norfolk. As an indication of just how serious our mechanical predicament had become, Racing Manager Jim Endruweit, who had done the 1963 and '64 races as well as the ovals and numerous tests, was allocated the whole month at Indy, which did not suit him one iota:

'I was often asked by people outside Team what my favourite circuit was, but it was easier to name my least favourite – Indianapolis! All the razzmatazz suited "Laz" down to the ground, but I quite simply loathed the place, and although I could never find a good word for it there were two good reasons for this: the situation prevailing within Team, and the food.

'The American way of life never suited me, and of course what made it worse was that the vast majority of people attracted to the Speedway could never be classed as a good cross-section of the American population. Within Team there was always an enormous workload, and for the two weeks prior to leaving England unbroken all-nighters were guaranteed, and even then we never left the factory with the cars more than half completed. Absolutely exhausted, we would deliver them to the airport, have a quick wash and brush up, then leap on the next plane to follow them out.

'When you walked into the garage, there were the half-built cars and a great pile of spares, all of which you then had to rush and build into three cars for running over a period longer than a whole season of Formula 1 racing. On average our lads were there for an uninterrupted seven days a week for six weeks without a break. The track was open from 8 am to 6 pm, and when the cars came in you could very easily get a job list of work that was not simply modifications, but major re-design projects, for which we had to find local people able to help us make the bits required.

'When Colin disappeared off to another race, we would be left with enormously long job lists that usually called for complete stripping down of the cars, doing the modifications or major re-designs, rebuilding and repainting, and having them spick and span ready for running just a few days later – all this virtually locked inside swelteringly hot garages because Colin didn't want anyone to see what we were doing. Every time you emerged there would be a crowd of people all packed shoulder to shoul-

A rare cheerful moment during the '67 foray for Jim Endruweit, on the phone in the Gasoline Alley garage. It's nice to keep in touch.

der waiting to barrage you with questions.

'My appreciation of good food didn't sweeten my affair with the American Mid-West either, on the rare occasion when we did find time to eat. Being imprisoned at the track for long days meant that we had to rely on the mechanics' eating place, which was completely misnamed a "restaurant". It served the most appalling stuff, and if you starved yourself to eat back at the motel, the standard there was only marginally better. As you got nearer to the race, so the numbers of people wanting to eat grew, so the service got worse and worse. It was Indy that made me realise how fortunate those in the Formula 1 world were.'

Graham Clode: 'It was evident that Jim was not a happy fellow at Indy. Being a wine connoisseur he would order his red wine and the waitress would bring it dripping with ice. Jim would explain how it should be at normal temperature and allowed to breathe beforehand, and she would go off, only to return with it after we had finished our dessert.'

David Lazenby: 'I always liked my breakfast on a hot plate, and I remember a great hoo-ha about this at a motel in Cincinnati – we failed completely, so we picked on the mass of curlers in the waitress's hair. In the end she said either we shut up or there would be no breakfast at all.'

There were to be 87 entries for the 1967 race, 44 of them Ford-powered and just two front-engined roadsters. No fewer than 12 of the entries were to be handled by Grand Prix drivers, of whom half would not make the grade. There were 22 Offy-engined entries (19 of them supercharged or turbocharged), and the remainder were stock blocks in various configurations, as well as the highly controversial STP turbine.

With Jimmy's and Graham's wins of the previous two years, this invasion was to prompt an American request to USAC that drivers should only be allowed to enter for Indy if they ran in two other USAC events the same year. Fortunately, when it was remembered that stars such as Parnelli Jones seldom ran in USAC National Championship events other than Indy, this was rejected.

Once again Andy Granatelli's STP organisation was attracting most of the attention. Forgetting for a moment the reappearance of the new Novi V8 (this time with Roots-type blower instead of the centrifugal type), Andy was putting all his personal effort behind a turbine-engined car built in his Paxton supercharger works in Santa Monica, California. It was not the first to be seen at Indy, but it soon proved that it was much more effective than those that had gone before it. Its 'chassis' of box-girder-section aluminium alloy (called a 'Uni-Box'), with two 'Y'-shaped forks at each end, bore a resemblance to the Lotus Elan concept; the driver sat on the right-hand side of the frame, the Pratt & Whitney ST 6B-62 helicopter-style turbine on the other. Reputed to produce the equivalent of 550 bhp, it was a remarkably neat power unit; the complete car was just $12\frac{1}{2}$ feet long, weighed only 260 lbs and drove through a constant mesh gearbox (no clutch or gearchanging was required) coupled to a Ferguson 4WD system incorporating a torque-splitting mechanism to provide limited slip between front and rear wheels. Unlike previous turbine cars, it had sufficient torque to produce extraordinary acceleration, which stressed the gearbox to the extent that the car devoured four of them in practice. Braking was also unusually good, its four disc brakes assisted by an automatically operated air brake.

Jimmy had sampled the car in our end of March Firestone tyre test with '38/7', reporting quietly that it had taken a little getting used to, but omitting to say that he was lapping at over 163 mph after just 23 laps!

'It's an amazing car,' he said. 'You just sit there and drive it.'

One aspect he found strange was the virtual absence of engine noise, replaced by other sounds such as bodywork rattles, the clamping of the brake pads on to the discs, and the UJs working away – even the squealing of the tyres. As usual for Indy, the concept fuelled enormous controversy amongst drivers and team owners alike, with threats of a boycott, and it was only as the Speedway opening approached that the car was declared legal, although Parnelli had to take a 'rookie'-style test with it.

The car was to cause me personal embarrassment, which would endure for the next two years. Arriving at our chosen

motel, the Howard Johnson (Colin had gone 'up-market' briefly at the October test, staying at the Speedway Motel, but could not live with the prices or the shock of finding that he had also been charged for the rooms of both his drivers and Jackie Stewart plus anon!), I found an even longer list of people asking to meet me. It was not until I had met the first two that I realised people were convinced that I was the Mr Ferguson who had developed the four-wheel drive system! The initial reaction of those first two people was quite surprising in as much as they seemed to think that I was the instigator of some major plot to seek personal fame in an underhand manner! Unfortunately, we were to run the Ferguson system in the next two years and the misunderstandings continued.

On 27 April, as Colin and I departed for Indy, word came from BRM that an Indy H16 unit was ready for collection, but when our transport arrived to collect it our lads were sent away again because they did not have a cheque for payment. Colin was quick to respond, saying that it had not yet been demonstrated to us that the engine would deliver the promised power running with our enforced exhaust system, and that if it did, and continued to do so for more than just a few hours, we would 'rush along with cheque in hand to collect it'.

For all the declarations that we would do well with our two past Indy winners on board, it was soon apparent we would have to cope with other eventualities, most of our own making. Practice – still using our 1966 engines – saw the return of the previous year's handling problems, Graham losing the car and sliding 870 feet before brushing the wall in Turn Three. Asked by a journalist how many times he had spun, he replied, 'Cripes, I wasn't counting.' He was alternating between his Type 38 and the 42, stating a preference for the former although he would not have it for the race.

The trip to Monaco in the middle of the lead up to qualifying took five valuable days out of the programme, then came rain, intermittent but regular, and with it time-consuming track closures. (By the opening of the Speedway Jimmy had just completed 50,000 air miles since the beginning of that year.)

One morning at breakfast, as Colin and I opened our mail and discussed the phone calls and cables we had received overnight, it was patently obvious that Colin was in one of what we termed his 'quivering lower lip' moods. This signified that he had been badly upset by something and was still trying to come to terms with it, or the solution it merited. Eventually I asked him what was wrong.

'You know I don't sleep too well?' he confided. 'Well, Jimmy went out on his own last night and I went to bed early. I was woken up by him coming back to the room with some bird, and I knew it would be a long time before I went off again, but I had to pretend to be asleep, and of all things they went into the bathroom chatting away as if it was broad daylight. I couldn't believe it. They had a noisy shower together, then they both got into Jimmy's bed. By this time I was not very happy . . .

'Then she said, "What about him – won't we wake him up?",

and do you know what Jimmy said? "Don't worry about him – the silly bugger never wakes up!" Then they started thumping away – God knows what time I got to sleep ...'

Jimmy arrived for breakfast shortly afterwards, and Colin excused himself quickly by saying he had work to do. Jimmy was in good form, but I was a little surprised that he had not noticed Colin's obviously black mood. I asked him if he had had a good evening. He said he had been out for a pleasant dinner and left it at that. Later on in the month Jimmy asked me to reserve him single rooms in future; why this was I did not learn, but it was quite a break from the habit of six years.

On a couple of occasions we were joined for breakfast by two astronauts, Captains Bill Anders and Scott Carpenter, who entranced Colin and Jimmy with stories about their training programme. Imagining for some unknown reason that they would be of muscular proportions, I was surprised by what I regarded as their diminutive height – they were around the 5 ft 8 ins of Colin, Jimmy and myself. It was amusing to listen to them questioning Jimmy on the business of circulating the Speedway at high speed, then Jimmy and Colin interrogating them on their skills at looping 'choppers', their explanations almost making Colin's jaw drop!

Amusing as it was to the assembled crowd, no one amongst the relevant mechanics could have been happy to see drivers George Snider and Cale Yarborough, both aiming to be first out when the track opened, tangle in the pit lane; $25 fines were slapped upon each.

From the opening days of running Mario Andretti once again topped the speed chart in his Brabham-based look-alike, lapping at 166.8 mph, well ahead of Gurney's Eagle, which was next up with 164 mph, Jimmy working his hardest to achieve laps at 161. Quite soon four 'rookies', Chris Amon, Jochen Rindt, Richie Ginther and Pedro Rodriguez, had passed their track tests, and 54 drivers had passed their medicals. On the tyre front, Firestone announced that it was expecting the ultimate lap speeds to be around 170; the company had come well prepared, having tested 100 compounds and over 40 different tread patterns.

Jim Endruweit: '1967 was the perfect example of the rule that if you are not properly prepared, the situation will only get worse. The two Type 38 chassis were fundamentally different, inasmuch as one was asymmetric, the other symmetric, and the Type 42, having only just been hastily converted to run with a Ford, was running in this form for the very first time. Whatever was needed from the spares didn't fit, so we had to cobble things together, Colin and Maurice trying everything they could think of, and the Monroe shock absorber people modifying and changing the effect of their shock absorbers virtually every day. On top of this the drivers were never far away from the garage, so they could see quite plainly what was going on. They got more and more fraught, Colin got more and more fraught. It was quite simply a recipe for disaster ...'

Mike Underwood: 'The lads just worked themselves off their feet and on one occasion "Butty", "Chalky" and Hughie all col-

lapsed simultaneously on the floor of our third garage and fell fast asleep. We had forgotten that Colin was due back from Europe, and he suddenly walked in to find all his lads asleep. He just woke them up and in no time at all they were all back at work.'

A higher than expected fuel consumption meant hanging an extra fuel tank on the left-hand side of Graham's Type 42F after practice began in preparation for qualifying, and photographs of the car both before and after the change give a clue as to the hurried nature of the work, as the sponsor's logo is half hidden by the tank. Jimmy's Type 38 utilised the left-hand tank from the Fuji car.

Both Jimmy and Graham were naturally anxious to qualify on the first day in order to start from the all-important top grid, but Graham's car was still in a great deal of mechanical trouble, and he was unable to get either his 38 or 42F up to speed. It soon became obvious that he would have to miss Saturday's running and hope for better things the following day, and I telephoned the Mallory Park race organisers in England, where he was to drive the Formula 2 Guards Trophy race the following day, with the bad news. However, this plan also came to nought when Sunday running was washed out by rain, the first time a complete day of trials had been lost since 1950.

Mario Andretti continued to fly, breaking his own lap record with 169.779 mph, and his four-lap average with 168.982 mph. Dan Gurney took second place on the front row nearly 1½ mph slower, with Gordon Johncock third, and Parnelli Jones producing a remarkable 166.075 mph four lap average with the STP turbine to take sixth place. Although the beginning of the month had seen Jimmy working hard to overcome a repetition of the handling problems, he had slowly been dropped off by the faster cars and he could do no better than 163.213 mph in qualifying, nearly 1 mph slower than '66. Nevertheless he was the only Grand Prix driver to qualify that day, most of the 12 who had entered finding difficulty in getting over the 160 mph mark. It is also interesting to reflect that of the 25 traditional records for the race, Jimmy still retained 19, two from qualifying (one-lap and four-lap speeds) going to Mario in '67, two to Marshman in 1964 and two to Foyt, both in 1965.

However, Jimmy was down on the 16th spot on the grid, having forecast early on that Mario would take pole and Parnelli the race, in the turbine that he felt was in race trim from day one and with a considerably lower fuel consumption than any other car. Jimmy also felt that possibly a better way to ensure that there were no start-line shunts was that the traditional way of putting sometimes much faster cars at the back of the grid should be changed to the European scheme of things.

The remarkable number of 25 cars qualified on the first day, and with only eight places left to fight for, Graham was obviously going to have his work cut out.

The following week brought more aggravation. On the Wednesday Jimmy took Graham's car out in the hope that he might be able to pinpoint its inherent problems, only for its engine to blow up.

With engine changes such time-consuming affairs, that was it for the day; now we were completely devoid of engines and it was A. J. Foyt who came to our rescue when he kindly let us borrow one of his. With our list of blown engines to date, he must have seriously wondered if he was doing the right thing, especially when that one blew up as well!

Now Colin called for the 42 to be readied. On the Sunday, waiting in line for his qualifying run, water started pouring from Graham's radiator, so the car was rushed back to the garage for repairs. His final attempt in a car he was now driving for only the second time was a heart-stopper, coming literally in the closing minutes of qualifying, when he went off line to avoid a bird on the track. His run of 163.317 mph was remarkably quick considering all his traumas, quicker than Jimmy and 12 other cars; if he had qualified on the first day he would have been on row five, one place up from Jimmy. As it was he was on the 11th and last

Maintaining a sense of proportion as a delayed and last-minute Indy programme shuffles from bad to worse. Jim Clark: '163 – what's so bad about that?' Colin Chapman: 'Don't be so ——— complacent!' (Harper)

Another long night was spent changing the 38's engine, then, when Graham went out in it the following day, that one also blew up. Granatelli, with a light workload now that his car had qualified, surveyed Graham's efforts at going quickly and realised that he was employing Grand Prix methods in preference to the Indy requirement of *smoothness*, something that Andy had learned from previous Indy star Mauri Rose 20 years earlier. He asked Graham if they could have a few quiet words, and held his breath for Graham's reaction when he broached the subject. Immediately Graham's times went up 3 mph, and to Andy's astonishment Graham gave tribute to his sponsor's advice when interviewed by the press.

In Saturday morning practice for final qualifying, disaster struck Graham's Type 38 once again when another engine let go.

Colin Chapman's primary concern for 1967 – development of the brand new Cosworth-Ford DFV V8-engined Lotus 49 for Formula 1. Here's Colin in the prototype '49/1' on the damp test track at Hethel. The new car/engine combination was poised to excel upon its debut (Graham Hill pole and fastest lap, Jim Clark winning) in the Dutch Grand Prix. It simply rewrote performance standards in Formula 1. (Ford Motor Company)

Graham Hill going out to practice in the symmetrically-suspended Type 38 chassis '38/8/S', which he would set aside for the 1967 race, using the long-wheelbase special Type 42F instead. (Indianapolis Motor Speedway)

Graham standing by the Type 38 during qualifying, while Team's mechanics struggle under the direction of Jim Endruweit (left) in his red STP overalls. Standing looking on, hands in pockets and smothered in STP decals (left), is Andy's brother Joe. (Indianapolis Motor Speedway)

row of the grid, alongside Jochen Rindt.

As Colin said on that last day, 'We've tried everything in the book with Graham's car, but he just couldn't get up to speed. So I made the decision on the afternoon before final qualifying to have the Type 42F prepared. Graham only had 15 laps in the car before final qualifying, but his speed kept getting better and better. It's a tribute to Graham that he got in, and now I think about it we should be able to go a lot quicker with the car when we have had more time to tune it.'

Granatelli's advice to Graham had also played a most important part . . .

The average speed for qualifying was nearly 4 mph up on the previous year – George Snider's front-row time of 1966 was not quick enough to qualify in '67. Of the 33 cars on the grid, 24 were V8 Fords, seven were turbo Offys, one was a Super Offy one a turbine. Our pit crew was again joined by RAC timekeeper Cyril Audrey (Jabby Crombac was in the press stand), with Keith Duckworth as a guest during the final days to the DFV's first run in anger.

Highlights from my 'Lotus Running Diary' for that month of May are interesting:

May 1st – the 155 mph track limit was lifted. Jimmy running at
   162.161 mph
May 2nd – Mario out first time – did 163.5 mph
May 3rd – Graham made his last run before leaving for Monaco
   and spun Turn Three. Mario up to 166.021 mph
May 4th – Mario 166.328, McCluskey 166.1, Foyt 165.472 mph
May 5th – RAINED OFF FOR DAY AT 15.45 hrs
May 6th – RAIN ALL DAY
May 7th – RAIN IN MORNING. Pm: Mario 166.883 mph
May 8th – RAINING OFF AND ON; WIND 37 mph – only 1 hr 46
   min running
May 9th – WIND STILL HIGH – Leonard, Jones, Gurney 164.1
   mph. Rindt's 1,860-foot slide, 1,110 against the wall, severely
   damaged *Friedkin Enterprise Special*
May 10th – Mario 167.9 mph, Turbine 166.4 mph
May 11th – HIGH WINDS AGAIN – Hill lost it at Turn Three but
   didn't hit anything
May 12th – Mario 169.4, Foyt/McCluskey 167+, Lee Roy
   Yarbrough totalled his Red Ball Laycock Spec – caught fire –
   not hurt. Type 42 still not scrutinised – 85 cars at track, 72
   passed scrutineers
May 13th & 14th – Practice started 9 am, qualifying 11 am
   (10.30–11 am start-line ceremonies); Graham ran Type 38 in
   practice
May 15th – Chuck Arnold hit wall 12 times Turn Four. RAIN
   15.45 FOR REST OF DAY
May 16th – Bob Christie demolished No 82 Sheraton T Spec –
   was it a Lotus?
May 17th – Nothing special
May 18th – HIGH WINDS ALL DAY. Gary Congdon tried seven
   cars, Bobby Johns three

Thoughtful moment in the STP-Lotus garage at Indy '67 – Colin (left) and Keith Duckworth, former Lotus employee and long-time creator/supplier of Cosworth engines, first for Formula Junior, then Formulae 2 and 3, and ultimately Formula 1. (Jabby Crombac)

May 19th – HIGH WINDS. Most couldn't better 161 – Turbine did
   165 with full fuel load
May 20th & 21st – Ten cars bumped, same as 1954

Duly qualified, Graham and Colin immediately departed for England and the first test of the brand new Formula 1 Type 49, propelled by the first Cosworth DFV. Colin left one of the longest job lists ever for Jimmy's car, so long in fact that the work had still not been completed when Jimmy returned from a Formula 2 date at Zolder in Belgium, and he missed the following Friday's carburation trials, the only time he would be able to sample the car after running its 'hot' qualifying fuel and its mods before the race took place. For us Indy '67 really was turning into the disaster Jim Endruweit had forecast . . .

Graham was quite open about his problems going into and through corners correctly; he had no complaints about the engine, but as well as wondering about his driving technique he wondered if the chassis required better settings. 'You must remember,' he told the press, 'I'm a bit new here . . .'

Meanwhile the newly crowned 1967 '500 Festival Queen' was asked if she would kiss the race winner, since she had just learned from her predecessor that the milk remaining around their faces left a disgusting taste. Her predecessor doubted that anyone would match up to Graham Hill: 'He is the most Continental of them all,' she said. Graham was delighted!

For entertainment that weekend before the race, Jimmy went off to spectate at two races, the Yankee '300' at the Indianapolis Raceway Park, then the 'Little 500' at Anderson that same evening, a 500-lap sprint car race around a quarter-mile high-banked asphalt oval.

Jimmy now returned to Europe. Originally it had been planned for him to drive in the Formula 1 Syracuse Grand Prix the following weekend, but we were short of cars and he subsequently flew to Paris to pick up his own plane and fly to Belgium for the Formula 2 race at Zolder. He was at this time suffering from UK taxation problems, which greatly reduced the amount of time he could spend in England, so he was concentrating on events abroad. For some reason his on-going flight in his own aircraft went wrong, and he had to drive instead.

Bob Sparshott, one of our Formula 2 mechanics waiting at Zolder, well remembers his arrival: 'Jimmy and Graham had been entered at Zolder but Graham had to stay at Indy to qualify so we were there with two cars and an excess of lads – for us! Of the two cars, one was brand new and hadn't been tested. Jimmy arrived late into second practice having spent the night in the air, then driving himself by road from Paris; all his luggage was lost

by the airline, which included his race gear, so first he had to go around the other drivers borrowing gear. Then he leapt into the new car that he hadn't even seen before and roared off around the circuit, which he'd also never driven round before. There were only minutes left to the end of the session and we were simply staggered when he put the car on the front row of the grid just 0.2 seconds off pole time! Just like that – he had beaten McLaren, Surtees, Ickx, Brabham, the lot.'

Bob Dance: 'I remember he came in with the car after his few runs and we asked him what he needed doing. "The gear lever's a bit stiff, that's all", then, "I'm off to get some rest now," and he left. On race day, although officially he finished second overall, he really won it on elapsed time but the results were based on places in the two heats; a head gasket blew near the end and he slipped back to fourth. It was a spectacular performance ...'

Graham's Indy troubles stayed with him for the race, Jimmy being only slightly less unlucky. Thinking that he would have time to visit the lavatory before the start, Graham miscalculated both the time left to the start and the distance he would have to walk to the last row of the grid. The field was moving away as he smoothed his hair, put on his helmet and settled himself in the cockpit; then the shaft of the external starter broke!

An official spotted the lack of a car in the now fast accelerating grid, then saw Graham still motionless on the track. Confusion reigned for some minutes, as our mechanics rushed the other

1965 Indy '500' winner Jimmy Clark in '38/7' (2) poses for his 1967 '500' archive photo. Note the left-side oil tank blister built onto the new car for this season. (Indianapolis Motor Speedway)

1966 Indy '500' winner Graham Hill in the 1967 Type 42F – chassis '42/B1' – cobbled-together special, the chassis originally intended for the BRM H16-cylinder engine hastily converted with a tube-frame rear end to accept the quad-cam Ford V8. (Indianapolis Motor Speedway)

starter to the end of the grid, hindered by officials anxious to push the car into the pit lane. Eventually Graham departed down the pit road, rejoining the tail end of the grid as the field rushed by. But now, with oil blowing from the breather, he experienced a distinct lack of power that saw him dropping away from the cars in front. His 42F was so slow that he now kept his eyes on his mirrors, waiting for the field to lap him, which they soon did. It was a very embarrassing situation for the previous year's winner! Fortunately it was short-lived – rain started to fall on lap 16 and the race was stopped. Jimmy was down in 18th place, Graham 32nd, as the cars were flagged off; Graham's complete humiliation was saved slightly by Lloyd Ruby having already retired.

After the previous year's first-lap shunt, the rules now allowed work to be carried out on the cars before the restart. Graham therefore had a change of plugs, Jimmy a new ignition system. Both drivers had long conversations with Colin as to what might be done, but as the problems were merely a continuation of those suffered in practice, the outlook was positively gloomy – ignition, timing and fuel injection settings were investigated, and that was it.

Around 4.30 pm came news that the race would be run the following day, and everyone repaired to their motels. The race leader at this stage was Parnelli Jones in Granatelli's STP turbine; it had set a record-breaking pace from the outset, Parnelli already up to second place by Turn One and into the lead by the second, from where he steadily pulled away from the 'subsidiary' race,

that for piston-engine cars. He had been 15 seconds ahead when the race was stopped.

Happily Graham's sense of humour never deserted him, even in what must have appeared, even to him, a hopelessly depressing situation. From his win the year before he had latched on to the sizeable bonus available for drinking milk in the photographs taken in the winners' circle, and his catchphrase shouted at me whenever he caught sight of me during practice was a resounding, 'Oi! Where's the f—- milk?'. However, in his present lowly finishing position, he quietly told me that he thought he might desist.

One of my most vivid memories of Graham at Indy concerned his blasted dumb-bells, items he asked me to buy for him each time we went there. Despite his frequent disappearances back to Europe to take part in other races, we still had to pay the full month's cost for his room, but in most cases he would be allocated a different room on his return. In saying *au revoir* each time, Graham obviously delighted in saying that he had not found time to move his 'Andrew's-bells' to his new room, he was very worried about losing them, and would I be a good chap and collect them personally? This would involve a sometimes lengthy journey to the other end of the building complete with a motel wheelbarrow in order to carry these weighty items. The matter never ended there – usually I would also find a pile of his racing overalls for the laundry, together with a job list of other things he would like done while he was away.

The following day, Wednesday, dawned cool but sunny with a cloudless sky, an 8–15 mph wind, and rain forecast for the afternoon. The whole affair started all over again at lap 18, and by lap 22 Graham was back in for a change of plugs (4 mins 50 secs). He was to survive only nine more circuits, or 13 very slow minutes, before he was out with a holed piston. As the thoroughly dispirited team pushed his car away, Jimmy went by the pits streaming smoke; just 5 minutes after his team-mate retired, our joint No 1 was also out, oil coming from the Ford V8's trumpets after it had dropped a valve.

The STP turbine was to dominate the race until, with just three laps to go, it was out when a $5 ball-race in the transmission failed. A. J. Foyt therefore scored his third Indy '500' victory driving his Lotus 38-based Coyote, the first time a Goodyear-shod car had won since 1919. Indeed, due to a multiple shunt on his last lap A. J. was the only man classified, the first time that this had ever happened. Al Unser was second, and Joe Leonard third in another basically Lotus Type 38. Meanwhile Andretti's Indy jinx had returned early on in the second part when a wheel came off.

Although he was classified a lowly 31st, Jimmy's rewards were not insignificant. With qualifying bonus and prize money, he took home $39,572 (£16,627), with tax at 45% already deducted. In comparison, his prize and bonus monies for winning the South African Grand Prix in 1968 would be £3,064.

There was no doubt that Andy Granatelli's car had focused phenomenal attention on itself, not least by the rules committee who would soon issue restrictive regulations to ensure, they hoped, that no one else would bring a gas turbine to their hallowed Speedway . . .

To all intents and purposes our mustachioed driver turned the official prize-giving ceremony into a Graham Hill benefit. Held as usual in the Murat Temple in Indianapolis, the place was packed with crews and officials as well as a great many ticket-buying members of the public. All 33 drivers in the race received invitations and were positioned in a long line on the raised dais, Graham's bearing that of a Queen's Champion and looking quite splendid with his neatly trimmed moustache, English-style blazer and colourful tie. Even race-winner Foyt did not linger too long in a speech that held barbed comments about the turbine and Parnelli himself, although they did shake hands at the end to show that there was no animosity.

As Graham had been the previous year's winner, it was his duty to present A. J. with his race-winner's gold ring, which he did with the comment that 'we all enjoy Indianapolis', and congratulating Foyt who had driven a fine race 'in a beautifully prepared machine', no doubt a snipe at his own car. This was the third time that A. J. had received the award, and one that he said he very much appreciated, as he now had a ring for each of his three chil-

Abject failure – keeping right down on to the inside apron, blue and white smoke and steam puffing from his engine's right-hand bank exhaust megaphone, Jimmy heads '38/7' for the pits and a 35th lap retirement. A piston has been holed, and following Graham Hill's similar failure on lap 31 STP-Lotus's Indy challenge for '67 has ended. (Indianapolis Motor Speedway)

dren, which surely 'makes me a pretty good father'. When he was presented with the keys to the Pace Car, a Chevrolet Camaro, he said, 'I might trade it in for a T-Bird tomorrow,' referring to his Ford contract.

A. J. was followed by all the other drivers as they thanked their crews and sponsors. Then, after he had accepted Jimmy's and Dan Gurney's prizes on their behalf (they had left for Holland), it was Graham's turn, and he opened by thanking Lloyd Ruby, the last place finisher, for saving him from going from first to last in one swift year; he also apologised to those fans who had stood up as he went by each lap, saying 'I know him'. 'They must have been as embarrassed as I was,' he said. Then he gave a humorous discourse on Indianapolis in general, with comparisons of his winning year with the disastrous one now over. This was followed by a selection of excellent jokes, some sufficiently blue to stun the more puritan members of the essentially conservative Mid-West 'Bible Belt' audience. His performance was more a music hall turn than a speech, and when it came to an end a long time after he had got to his feet he received warm applause from those who had understood what he had been talking about. His speech had lasted 20 minutes longer than his race, and was a performance still remembered by members of the audience many, many years later.

In company with the media's reaction to the gracious Graham and his excellent sense of sportsmanship, there was also widespread comment on Jimmy's qualities, despite his low placing. His analytical approach to his new post as columnist to the local paper during the month of May had been very well received, as had his continual re-reading of the draft copy to ensure that he had written it in true Americanese. The media commented on how he had always been polite from his first appearance at the track, that his wit was first class and how he was an extremely interesting conversationalist; he was also a 'sharp dresser' who enjoyed elegant clothes and wore them well. Uppermost was their incredulity that he appreciated still being able to merge into the crowd; in other words, he was not a playboy type at all, but a real Champion who wore his honours with humility and grace.

A. J. Foyt's winning purse of $171,227 was another record. Team Lotus's income, however, reflected the result, not the effort; Graham's car earned $9,016 and Jimmy's $8,494 (race only), both sums gross!

Immediately after the race it was decided to retain temporarily chassis '38/8S', the symmetric car that Graham had valiantly tried to get up to speed throughout May, and with economies very much in mind it was dispatched by sea back to England. The two cars remaining at Indy were put up for sale initially at £3,000 each less engine (our second-hand ones £7,000) and gearbox, reduced by £250 a few months later. By October they were down to £1,750 and £4,000 respectively 'or nearest offer', Mike Underwood having been given the task of spreading the news around the teams still there. With no interest being shown, Mike finally took '42F/1' up to Canada to export it then re-import it to America, thereby saving money should it be sold in the States

Despite what should have been a totally demeaning experience, Jimmy never lost his sense of humour and his acceptance and acknowledgment of just how hard the Indy crew were working on his behalf helped make Lotus's '67 Indy effort almost bearable. (Harper)

(goods temporarily imported to the USA on a bond were charged a penalty of two hundred times the 6 per cent import duty if they were then left permanently in the country). In the meantime Mike returned all the useful spares from the garage, including the rear upright and rocking-lever jigs for the Type 42F, supposing that we needed to build the Type 42 at the factory into a similar specification. At this stage in the proceedings Colin had still not entirely dismissed the H16 engine.

In March the BRM engineers had achieved 12 hours of testing, although the engine check again showed problems with the centre power-pack bearing, as well as cracking of the camshaft lobes. The power loss had been tracked to an uncoupled lower exhaust bank, and we had supplied a Type 42 rear suspension so BRM could fabricate a coupled exhaust system to suit. At the same time they attempted to stiffen the power-pack and fitted increased capacity bearings.

In June, as the dust settled over our worst ever showing at Indy, we set plans in motion to test an H16 that September, and hopefully to race the car at that month's Trenton event, with a view to having another go, this time with BRM power, at the '500' the following year. So far engine research and development had centred on BRM unit '9601', but now unit '1/2' came into the frame, running with two-plane cranks using a coupled lower bank and a fuel mix of 40 per cent methyl-alcohol, but it produced only 500 bhp. As BRM was still conducting development on its 3-litre engine, this disappointing test convinced the engineers that they should suspend work on the Indy version until August, hoping that data gained from the smaller unit might prove useful.

In July further modifications to the power-pack castings were made, and when the new parts were fitted to the engine, by that time rebuilt to the original specification, firing as two flat-eights and running on alcohol, it gave 535 bhp. However, time was slipping by, with the new Indy project the centre of attention at Hethel, but BRM persevered and in October requested that Shell investigate fuel specifications with a view to making recommendations.

With the project nearing its close, November saw the engine rebuilt again for further tests comparing petroleum with the latest fuel formula provided by Shell. Running on the former the unit gave a reliable 510 bhp before suffering a broken piston ring. Then in January cracks in the crankcase main bearing panels were found. In view of this, together with the continued low power output and the lack of commercial value, the project was brought to a halt. It was suggested that the engine be re-run with Mark 1 crankshafts and firing order, incorporating all the later modifications including high-lift camshafts to see if the original 585 bhp could be reproduced.

Tony Rudd: 'The H16 was a bit of an orphan amongst the Matra V12s and V8s, MoD special 2-litre V8s, Chrysler hemis and turbines, regular Formula 1 engines and Lotus Twin-Cam engines and all the other oddball engines that Rubery Owen had us working on.'

Geoff Johnson: 'In hindsight it is not too surprising that the Indy H16 did not attain its anticipated performance. Being based on the Formula 1 3-litre unit, which never exceeded 400 bhp, giving 133 bhp/litre, it was unreasonable to anticipate more than 558 bhp running on petrol. The fact that the prototype gave 585 bhp, 139 bhp/litre, is creditable by itself.

'Both types of engine suffered from basic torsional vibration problems that were very destructive to various components. We improved the 3-litre unit by firstly putting additional mass on the crankshafts, then by redesigning the crankshafts to an eight-pin design. Neither of these two options was open to us on the Indy version due to the constraints of using the 3-litre unit crankcases.

'A measure of the power absorbed in the H16 engine can be judged by comparing it with the Formula 1 V12 BRM engine. In two-valve form the V12 produced 405 bhp while the 3-litre H16 struggled to achieve 400. When a four-valve head was designed for the 3-litre H16 it produced less power than the two-valve version. The same four-valve head on the 3-litre V12 saw 480 bhp (160 bhp/litre) achieved on a regular basis. Approximately 100 bhp was locked up in the four-valve H16, which dissipated itself in torsional energy within the unit and never reached the crankshaft output.'

In late June tax exile Jimmy, then in Paris, was going through his accounts in detail and wrote to me to say that he was paying for two single rooms at Indy when in fact he had been sharing a twin with Colin! Jimmy's parting comment was that he felt the expenditure 'a wee bit uneconomical to say the least – hope you can sort it out . . . PS Can't wait for your next instalment of "Guess what we owe you".'

Meanwhile once back at the factory '38/8S' was stripped down and made ready for a Firestone test at Indy at the end of August, still in its symmetric suspension form and now with a recorder/transducer 'black box' device, its numerous rolls of paper recording data that it was hoped would aid further research into suspension geometry. As Maurice Phillippe wrote at the time: 'To establish the movement of each of the four wheels we had first produced a datum calibration line, and after each run we were able to gauge from the trace exactly what the relative wheel movements were. As we had so little information regarding tyre growth there was a possibility that we might not be able to readily identify the difference in ride level due to this feature. If we could programme Jimmy to operate consistently at known rpm levels in a steady state, ie no torque, arranged at suitable intervals on successive long chutes, we could also establish the aerodynamic characteristics.'

We were very surprised at the outcome, finding that the car sat lowest when stationary. As Colin explained in an interview for *Motor* magazine: 'Even on the banking, where the extra normal load is 25 to 30 per cent of the weight of the car, it was riding above static ride level, so the aerodynamic lift was something more than that. And all these years we'd been designing the suspension so that when it really sat down on the banking it would still be all right.'

Originally scheduled to last a week, the tests were cut to only two days due to the outgoing flight carrying the car being delayed by an airline strike. Colin and Jimmy then flew to Finland for the Helsinki Formula 2 'Grand Prix' the following weekend. Four Firestone compounds were tried over the two days, and once the data had been collated the running of a Type 38 at Indy was terminated. The data was to prove a major step forward in Team Lotus design policy, as the car was found to assume previously unrealised attitudes as speeds increased; as shown by the 'wedge-shaped' Type 56 about to be built, aerodynamic design concepts were to change for ever. The test car was left in our garage with the two cars already residing there, and all three, two Ford V8 engines and a large consignment of spares were advertised in the motoring press. 'For sale by package deal or in units . . . all YOU have to do is sign up the drivers!' Was that all . . ?

Maurice Phillippe did not go to the test; instead he set out his draft project specification for the following year's Indy car, to be powered by a Cosworth DFV 2.8-litre turbo. The chassis would be the "ladder" variety arranged for a mid-wheelbase engine coupled to four-wheel drive. Fuel cells would be confined to the side sponsons, the space between the driver and engine to contain the transmission assembly, with two choices of gearbox, one three-speed, the other five.

As Team's season neared its end, there came the shattering news that Esso, our principal financial support since the 1950s, was to withdraw from racing. This brought confusion and a complete re-think of what our future plans would be. Initially I was to set up a sponsor-seeking wing within Team, producing presentation brochures for the top 200 companies. When these efforts appeared fruitless, Colin's last-ditch effort was to have me visiting the areas where Grands Prix were held three months in advance of the races to seek local one-off sponsorship combined with an advertising campaign within each country's media.

On 31 October a 1968 race programme was mapped out at Hethel by Colin, with Maurice Phillippe, Jim Endruweit and myself filling in the details. The trials and tribulations experienced by the Indy section decided Mike Underwood to leave us, and he joined the McLaren Can-Am team, although he later returned to Lotus to work with his old friend David Lazenby, then running Lotus Components. Into Mike's place moved 29-year-old Dick Scammell, then Formula 1 Chief Mechanic entering his ninth year with Team.

The minimum number of new cars required would be two for Formula 2, two for Formula 1 and three for Indy, and to ensure that the Indy cars were completed in good time in the running programme, the Formula 1 mechanics would be enlisted to help with fabrication and build. Mechanic totals would be five for each section. On the technical front, Richard Ansdale was to be invited to redesign our Formula 1 gearbox (with internals by Hewland), and my recent contact with a titanium company for sponsorship led to titanium components being supplied by them instead of money.

Although Maurice Phillippe expressed his wish to continue with the Ford V8 (in turbo-charged form) as a back-up for the forthcoming Indy race, we were already well advanced with a totally different concept . . .

The seeds of our 1968 turbine venture had been sewn as far back in 1952, courtesy of Andy Granatelli. After that year's race, in which his Grancor Wynn's car finished second driven by Jim Rathmann, Andy had a stock-block 5.4-litre (331 cu in) Cadillac engine fitted for high-speed tyre testing at Firestone's request. Some years later American Air Force General Curt LeMay, who would himself be involved with Team Lotus business in later years, arranged for a Boeing turbine to be fitted in the chassis and, with USAC Director of Competition Henry Banks driving, it ran on test at Indy without impressing.

In 1962 John Zink entered a Boeing turbine-engined car, but did not attempt to qualify it, a fact that may have been related not to its capability but to the fact that he would have to pay for his loaned engine if it took the grid. However, its appearance registered in Andy's fertile brain. He saw how it just ran and ran for thousands of miles with total reliability and fuel economy. He began a detailed investigation of gas turbines, and started to formulate plans.

Now it was a question of a suitable transmission. When Andy first met Stirling Moss in the early 1960s, the Englishman had waxed lyrical about the Ferguson 4WD system, with which he had won a Formula 1 race in 1961, and its tremendous improvement in traction. Stirling's enthusiasm had so fired Andy that in August 1962 he paid for that car – the Ferguson-Climax P99 – to be demonstrated at Indy, driven by Jack Fairman and Bobby Marshman. The latter had taken to the car in a flash, lapping at 141 mph without once lifting his foot. Andy booked a flight to England to investigate further.

The concept of four-wheel drive was not revolutionary, as the Dutch-built Spijker six-cylinder racing car of 1902 had employed such a system, as had Bugatti and Harry Miller around 1932. But the Ferguson system was unique in achieving balanced drive to all four wheels.

The story of Ferguson Research is rooted deep in motor racing history, originating with the famous English motor cycle and car ace Freddie Dixon. While in Belfast for the Tourist Trophy, Freddie had prepared his car in a garage owned by Harry Ferguson, and the two had immediately struck up what became a lifelong friendship. They talked of producing a lightweight road car, then in 1937 Freddie evolved plans for a Land Speed Record car utilising four-wheel drive. He was unable to finance the idea, so it floundered.

However, a year later racing driver A. P. R. (Tony) Rolt (of Jaguar fame) came to prominence driving an ERA, and he asked Freddie to tune the car. Then the war intervened, and Rolt was captured at Dunkirk to become an inmate at Colditz Castle. After the war the two co-operated again in preparing and racing the Alfa-Aitken (née Bimotore Alfa Romeo). Rolt had friends who also enthused over four-wheel drive, and the group built a two-seater 4WD experimental road car on a limited budget.

In 1946 Harry Ferguson took Ford America to court for infringement of patent rights on his tractor designs, winning £3 million in damages. After a great many unconnected developments involving the three principals, they came together when Harry Ferguson Research Ltd was formed in 1950, another member of the group being former Aston Martin designer Claude Hill, another 4WD devotee.

The company concentrated on research and development for the motor industry, but Ferguson and Rolt (Dixon had left in 1952 following a policy disagreement) continued their basic interest in motor racing. In 1959 Ferguson suggested that they should build a 4WD racing car incorporating many other new ideas to run in 2½-litre Formula 1 during 1960; it was actually ready for the new 1½-litre Formula in 1961, but also ran in 2½-litre InterContinental Formula form. Employing a Coventry-

Climax engine, construction of the car, known as Project 99, began in 1960, and was complete in only seven months. For team management expertise Rolt had turned to his friend, private Formula 1 entrant Rob Walker, whose principal driver was Stirling Moss. Stirling drove the controversial car in the minor Oulton Park Gold Cup race and won handsomely, securing not only the last Formula 1 race win for a front-engined car, but also the only one ever to feature four-wheel drive, hence his words of praise to Andy Granatelli.

After Andy's visit to Ferguson, he took Rolt back to Studebaker, initially to investigate using 4WD for all its production designs. This idea fell by the wayside, but Andy and Rolt scored a success when Studebaker proposed that the system be used on the all-powerful Novi V8, and that it would sponsor both engineering programmes.

What Andy claimed at the time to be the most expensive racing car ever to run at Indy, arrived there on 26 March 1964 from Ferguson's plant in England. Five days later it was very seriously damaged in a garage fire at the Speedway, but after a feverish rebuild programme it returned restored for the month of May. Due to lack of time, driver Bobby Unser qualified it on the second weekend in 22nd position at just on 155 mph; only three other cars had lapped faster. Sadly it was taken out in the fiery first-lap accident that killed Sachs and MacDonald.

In 1965 the 4WD Novi, its engine boasting 775 bhp at 10,000 rpm and again driven by Bobby Unser, was running the day before first qualifying, clocking comfortable laps at 160 mph when another car spun in front of it and it was demolished. The previous year's car was made ready and Unser qualified at 157.467 mph for a third-row slot.

Again misfortune struck on race day, the car going out on only lap 69 when a fitting on an oil-line broke off the supercharger. In 1966 the car was wrecked at a Phoenix tyre test; it was rebuilt but wrecked yet again at Indy just prior to qualifying.

Meanwhile, following Zink's 1962 appearance, Andy Granatelli had been studying gas turbine power. In 1963 he approached Studebaker to sponsor a turbine-powered car with Ferguson 4WD, but the response had been to take things one step at a time, and the 4WD concept had been chosen for Novi power. Both turbines had been legal under USAC regulations since 1955, and in 1965 Andy set up a turbine R&D division led by Englishman Ken Wallis.

Wallis, a 37-year-old resident of Palos Verdes, California, had wide experience of aircraft design. He had worked with General Electric and Vickers Armstrong in England as a design engineer and pilot, was now with Douglas Aircraft and had been associated with the Supersonic Combustion Ram-Jet project. While working with Andy's brothers Vince and Joe, he had fathered much of the design of the STP Paxton Turbocar, powered by the Pratt & Whitney turbine, which had run so convincingly in Parnelli's hands in the 1967 Indy '500'.

One of Andy's principal delights with the gas engine was its economy; its purchase price was $30,000 compared to the Ford V8's $26,000, but its life between overhauls was 1,200 hours, or, as Andy reckoned it, 12 years of USAC races! Even the racing Ford's remarkable 6-10 hours between overhauls – at $7,000 to $9,000 a throw – began to look hideously expensive. The turbine also scored on the safety aspect – with no water and only a little over 2 gallons of oil required, and an engine requiring no maintenance, the crews could concentrate on every aspect of the chassis.

The Turbocar was entered for the 1966 race as No 59, but an outside contractor's serious mistake during preparation saw the entry cancelled. The Granatellis then found their hands full with Novi disasters, but Andy told USAC of his plans to run the turbine car again the following year. However, in January 1967, as it was made ready for its press launch, the board put a new size limit on gas turbines, reducing their permissible annulus, or air intake area, to 23.999 square inches, a cut of 25 per cent. But the laugh was on them temporarily, as Andy's turbine had a still smaller air intake.

Then came a ruling that the engine must have a substantial protective shield around it to safeguard fuel tanks, and possibly spectators, if the turbine flew apart, this for an aircraft engine! Although most observers reckoned that a shield estimated to weigh around 300 lbs would provide all the handicap necessary, Andy came up with a titanium equivalent weighing just 40 lbs. Later USAC called in experts from both the automotive and turbine worlds to settle the power equivalency formula between turbine and piston engines. The final assertion was that the former produced 550 hp, the arguing was halted, temporarily, and what Andy termed his 'space age car' was allowed to enter the 1967 race.

However, the controversy sparked back into life immediately the car was unveiled, and at Indy Foyt called it an aeroplane: 'It ain't no car and it just don't belong here'. Some drivers claimed that its raised air brake flap hid their view of the track, to which the counter was that those running Fords with spoilers on their megaphone exhausts offered even higher obstruction. Others complained of the smell the turbine created, while some claimed that running close behind it caused their engine temperatures to soar . . .

On Memorial Day 1967 the car was leading the race comfortably when a $5 ball bearing failed with just 10 of the 500 miles to go.

Five days later USAC again sat down to discuss the car and its future. Now the annulus area was reduced by a further 25 per cent, to 15.999 square inches, reducing its horsepower to an estimated 480 compared to the 700-750 of some of the piston engines. The only answer to this was to produce a vehicle that would go through the corners very much quicker than its rivals.

In July USAC outlawed the side-by-side driver/engine concept employed by Andy's car; in August air brakes were also banned. If Andy had any trace of a persecution complex, he would then have given up on the Speedway, but there was more to come. He attended August's Formula 1 Canadian Grand Prix with Pratt &

Whitney's senior engineer, Fred Cowley. Fred, who was soon to be known by our crew as 'Flame-Out' Fred, had joined United Aircraft ten years earlier and was well versed in turbine installation and field operation; as such his duties included customer liaison. He had worked closely with Andy in the build and running of the 1967 STP Paxton car and was then preparing a paper on turbine power at Indianapolis to present to the Society of Automotive Engineers. Fred spent the weekend constructing an agreement with Andy for the supply of turbines to suit the new regulations, and their evenings were spent with Colin, Jimmy and Graham.

Fred Cowley: 'My wife still remembers those very entertaining dinners, and she recalls that Jimmy was the best dancer. At the end of the weekend Andy and I signed the deal; although there was to be some controversy within UA about the project, our company President was solidly behind the venture and I believe that it became a positive programme that publicised a relatively new engine product.'

In January 1968 came a ban on wide tyres for all four wheels (the layout employed by the 4WD system); they could now only be used on the rear wheels. Later this was modified to decree that 4WD systems had to run the smaller front wheel tyres all round, with a further regulation that two-wheel-drive cars could have 14-inch rim widths on the rear. Andy contacted Richard Nixon's law firm and proceeded to take USAC to court.

Through July and August 1967 it was apparent that Andy would be continuing STP's support of Team Lotus, and the attention of both parties was focused on Phillippe's four-wheel-drive Cosworth-engined car, the 2.8-litre V8 unit destined at that time to be supercharged by Andy's Paxton organisation. Andy visited the Mexican Grand Prix in October and he and Colin agreed the final draft of the contract over a relaxed breakfast (Andy and his wife Dolly experiencing one of Colin's 'I'll just have a coffee'-style breakfasts of considerable proportions).

Early in December Andy telephoned Colin to say, 'We go turbine one more time.' He had again contracted P&W for a turbine to suit the new regulations, and had decided to take a gamble. Hardly had Colin put the phone down than our shipping agents in London were telling me that an aircraft turbine had arrived at London Airport!

For 1968 USAC brought in three mandatory pit stops, at each of which fuel had to be added. The club's officials were always most helpful in supplying us with news of their thoughts and advice on which way they thought events would take us: Henry Banks, Director of Competition, Harlan Fengler, Chief Steward (whom Jochen Rindt called 'Harlan Finger'), Paul Johnson, Steward, and Harry Hartz, Vice-Chairman of the Technical Committee. The Public Relations Director, the blob-shaped Jim Smith, was also always around to advise on sticky moments. They all shared an enormous Speedway history between them; Banks had driven six times in the classic, Fengler back in 1923 (he raced against Christian Lautenschlager, for goodness sake, past winner for Mercedes of the 1908 and 1914 Grands Prix of

France!), and Hartz on six occasions, taking three second places and two fourths. I worked with all of them, but day-to-day liaison was mainly with Clarence Cagle, Superintendent of the Track; it was he who presented me at a USAC function with black-and-white chequered socks and bow-tie to 'welcome me into the Speedway family'. Even the man honoured as the 'first spectator in line', Larry Bisceglia, had been parking his camper on West 16th Street at the beginning of May since 1948! Of the girls, June Swango and Edna Ragsdale in the USAC office were enormously helpful, while the medical director, Dr Tom Hannah, managed to bring a touch of humour to even the most embarrassing ailments, the number of drivers treated for VD each month of May being marked up on his statistical scoreboard.

Maurice Phillippe's concept for the 1968 contender, which had started off in August with Cosworth power, was soon adapted for the turbine, although there was no assurance at this stage that the new regulations would allow sufficient power to be generated. In order to comply with the compressor inlet regulations, P&W removed the first two axial stages of the compressor and reduced the blade length of the third stage. At the same time a considerable programme of wind tunnel testing continued.

Unlike the Cosworth unit, which was stressed to accept chassis loads, the turbine had to remain flexibly mounted at three points, with sufficient clearance for it to expand. For instance, running at full power the internal heat generated increased its length by $3/16$ inch, its width by $1/16$ inch. Working closely with 'Flame-Out' Fred Cowley, Maurice made the left-hand forward mounting rigid to up, down and sideways loading, the mounting opposite it being telescopic and designed to accommodate up, down, and fore-and-aft loads. The third mounting, at the rear of the turbine, incorporated a ball joint working in a fore-and-aft slot, which allowed free expansion in length yet also prevented the unit twisting due to torsional deflection in the chassis.

As the internal shafts ran at very high speeds, at 40,000 rpm efficient bearing lubrication was critical, as also was Maurice's and Fred's concern that bearings and shafts were not distorted out of line by way of external loadings, as had caused failures with the Howmet gas turbine endurance racing coupe.

Maurice Phillippe: 'Due to the high turning speed of turbine shafts, high gyroscopic forces are generated, which could have affected the handling of the car; in this respect we were fortunate that the Pratt & Whitney unit's power and gas generator shafts turned in opposite directions, thereby cancelling out any gyroscopic forces . . .'

Quite apart from Andy Granatelli's connections with Ferguson Research, it was logical that they would be the most experienced organisation to work with in the production of an efficient four-wheel-drive system.

Maurice: 'No overhung loads were permissible on the turbine's output shaft, so we had to find an alternative way to transfer the drive to the side-mounted drive-line. Ferguson's initial proposal was that this should be by 3-inch Morse chain; although not fully accepting this suggestion (Ferguson was to investigate four different configurations), we eventually conceded that it was the best.'

Although Morse had no previous experience of its chains operating at such high speeds, the company was keen to help at all stages.

An engineer who had long experience of transmissions, and 4WD in particular, as well as a motor racing background, was Englishman Derek Gardner, the Ferguson Research representative working with us throughout the project. Derek had first joined Hobbs Transmissions in 1956, working on its automatic gearbox systems, and had joined Ferguson as a transmission designer four years later.

He recalled the excellence of the Morse product: 'After a set mileage at Indy we would take off the chains and I would rush off to the Morse people in Ithaca, New York State; there they would check them for wear and I would then fly back to Indy with them. After a modicum of stretch initially, wear was negligible. I think I was more liable to wear, as to have four of those heavy chains in a case was quite tiring! But I have to say the Morse people were extremely good and full of enthusiasm.'

As Maurice wrote later: 'We took responsibility for failures that might occur, but in practice chain performance proved exceptional. The outer sprocket contained a compound system of planetary gears to provide different torques front and rear. Overall gear ratios could be readily effected by a change of sprocket size, as could those of the axles, but this was by no means a trackside operation. In the drive-lines themselves, torsional twisting of the shafts absorbed vibration in the system. The axles I schemed and presented to ZF for design and manufacture had crown-wheels and pinions of spiral-bevel type.'

With its weight distribution and drive characteristics at 50/50, Maurice went for virtually identical suspensions front and rear, the top wishbones extended inboard to provide rocker arms for spring and damper units mounted beyond the extremities of the 'tub'.

Maurice: 'With inboard disc brakes, suspension units and driver's legs taking up all the available space in the front, the steering layout presented a problem. The solution here was to mount the rack immediately behind the top wishbone, but this meant that the tie rods were angled well forwards and this brought high bending loads on the rack-end bushes; to reduce frictional loading the rack was run on bobbins with miniature ball bearings.'

The engine installation also had to take into account the efficiency requirement that it only receive cold air, and that it be fully insulated from 'leaks' of hot air from other sources. An increase of only 1°F in intake air temperature reduced the engine output power by 3 per cent.

Maurice: 'The intake zone had to be built into a pressure-tight plenum chamber so that the full effects of ram pressure could be utilised. Air entered the intake at car speed, but for the engine to remain efficient this speed was not to exceed 100 feet per second, or 68 mph. As the speed of the car could exceed 200 mph, or 300 feet per second, the intake duct had to diverge to three times the intake area to reduce air speed to the required figure.'

This called for the hot zones within the car to be adequately ventilated, and it was arranged that hot air would exit through the exhaust duct behind the driver. It would be driven upwards behind the driver's back, through the engine oil cooler and thence past the transfer drive into the hot zone, then out. The exhaust tract design played an important part in engine efficiency, having to turn the gas flow through 15 degrees by means of three aerofoil-type deflectors. Its 50 lbs of residual thrust thus helped to keep the nose of the car down while at the same time promoting some forward thrust. The ducts were made by Chinn of Coventry to Rolls-Royce specification at a cost of £285 each, with tooling of £250 amortised.

Maurice: 'Air intake and exhausting was studied during wind tunnel testing with quarter-scale models. We wanted to eliminate all lift at the front of the car and overall to produce download; because of the engine's intake location the ducts in the body were well back on the car and the important requirement here was to ensure a clean flow of air to them. The flush intake had to be on a positive pressure surface and was not to be affected by crosswinds, and the deep sides to the cockpit ensured clean and straight flow to the intakes. Dirty air coming from the front suspension did not reach the top surface of the body as the sharpness of the body radius separated turbulent and clean air. A long tail would have been more efficient, but as the regulations laid down the maximum length of the car, we settled for the flat concave shape.'

The electrical power required for the starter to crank the gas generator compressor and turbine to 19,500 rpm was considerable.

Maurice: 'Fortunately the turbine was so light that I was able to have two 24-volt batteries weighing 80 lbs right in the nose of the car, all of which provided us with a useful balancing weight and we were still well under the minimum weight level.'

Albert Adams's department (he has been with Lotus for 36 years) made all the fibreglass Team bodies. When the Type 56 turbine came along he added an ingredient to make the bodies more durable to the excess heat he thought would occur, an idea with which Colin agreed. 'I'm proud to have been a part of Colin's working life and that's it as far as I'm concerned . . .'

Because of the length of the engine, the rear axle had to be as close to the engine case as possible, and to ensure this the fuel-control unit was mounted further back in the car to allow the axle to pass within half an inch of the fuel pump drive.

Maurice: 'Due to the requirements of the engine diameter and the need for the driveshaft to pass alongside it, it was necessary to mount this 2 inches to the right-hand side. From a weight point of view this proved advantageous, as it balanced exactly the concentration of weight in the drive-line on the left-hand side of the centre-line.'

Despite USAC regulations forbidding ballast, Maurice was soon

Hastily converted, unsuccessful and, post-race, unwanted though Graham Hill's 1967 '500' Lotus 42F might have been, what Colin described as its 'preposterously long wheelbase' set him and his designer Maurice Phillippe thinking seriously, since Graham ultimately reported that the car handled extremely well. The longer wheelbase offered better controlled pitch-change for more consistent aerodynamic performance, and this train of thought led to the wedge-form Type 56s for the following year. Here, with engine removed, the 42F's multi-tubular engine bay frame is visible. That monocoque had been intended to unite with a fully-stressed BRM H16-cylinder engine whose castings alone would have provided the rear part of the chassis. (Indianapolis Motor Speedway)

to resort to adding strip lead when he discovered that his creation was some 100 lbs underweight. To enable easy insertion into the left-hand front and rear tank bays, this lead took the form of two layers each 3/16 inch thick by 7½ inches wide, totalling 86 inches in length, bolted to the tank bay floors. The lead had to be rolled for insertion through the relatively small tank access holes, then unrolled in situ.

Maurice's design pad also saw mechanic's tool trays complete with cork roller feet designed to prevent chassis paint being damaged when work was in progress.

One of Pratt & Whitney's recommendations was that the car's

gearbox should be lubricated with the same type of oil as that used in the engine, to counter the effects of a different gearbox oil finding its way past the appropriate seal.

The cost of building the four Lotus 56 4WD turbine cars, less power units, showed a predictable increase over their predecessors, but was nothing abnormal. Design and jig construction accounted for $2,750, the Ferguson transfer drive $4,750, assembly and build labour $6,000. A bare 'tub' with bodywork came to $3,624, ancillary items $3,000 and component parts $17,000, a grand total net cost of some $38,000 per vehicle.

CHAPTER NINE

1968:
Tragedy Upon Tragedy

At the beginning of 1968 I made a concerted effort to alert possible buyers of our 1967 Indy team cars about the opportunity that was passing them by! From Georges Filipinetti in Switzerland to Moises Solana in Mexico, and Lindsey Hopkins and George Bryant in the USA, I tried my best, but to no avail. The Type 42 'tub' we had left in the factory, chassis '42B/2', was sold to Lotus Components, the associated company run by David Lazenby.

Racing driver Robs Lamplough: 'I made one of my frequent visits to Hethel to see what was going on, and on this occasion David showed me the Type 42 "tub", still in its STP livery, which I bought, then sold on to Canadian Bill Brack who was planning to go Formula 5000 and Formula A racing. All the BRM bits had gone back to Bourne, and Bill got mechanic Barry Sullivan to put in a Chevvy V8 unit. Designer Jo Marquart, who had worked with Maurice in Team Lotus, designed uprights for it and other bits and pieces.'

The Chevrolet 5-litre stock-block V8 dry-sump engine was prepared by Landon Engines in Detroit, and Brack secured Castrol sponsorship, this hybrid car being called the Lotus GTX, a suffix that appeared on its Marquart-designed uprights. Later, at the Lime Rock, Connecticut, race in August 1969, Brack suffered a tremendous shunt in it.

Lamplough: 'The accident really was enormous; I know because I was following. His car just went end-over-end at the end of the main straight, finishing up as scrap. I remember that Bill took the remains back to his base at Toronto.'

In January 1968, meanwhile, I learned that the type of electronic timing equipment we wanted at Indy would cost £2,000. So, with all the seating areas essential to our plan reserved until goodness knew when, we dropped the idea.

As the New Year opened Colin and Maurice were at ZF discussing Team's requirements for Indy. Colin wanted five car sets of axles, ten in all, complete with four ratio changes. He wanted the crown-wheels and pinions to be multi-purpose, ie capable of use at front or rear. He was careful to point out that as the front units would always carry the lighter load of the two, he wanted the units cut so that the helix angle always suited the rear axle,

the unit under the most load. He carefully set out the required programme dates for casing pattern completion, machining times as well as assembly and signing-off dates. Commencement of testing depended entirely on ZF getting these dates right. Colin repeated ZF's welcome arrangement of past years whereby it only looked to Team Lotus for 40 per cent of the cost, the residue being set against 'the development and prestige activities' of the British-based team.

Our initial international race programme showed Monaco clashing with the second qualifying weekend at Indy, but Firestone came to my rescue with the offer of its quickest company plane available to fill in for non-existent scheduled airline flights.

On 1 February Andy Granatelli and United Aircraft's 'Flame-Out' Fred Cowley came to Hethel to agree final arrangements. Andy wanted a grandly publicised test at Indy in March, and time, as always, was running short. I always looked forward to meeting Andy; no doubt his invitation to work for him when I left Chapman provided a reassuring note that was absent from other business relationships. He and his brothers and son were straight out of the movies in their pronunciation and actions, and everything was go, go, go from the outset and stayed that way.

Unfortunately Colin did not view Andy with the same affection. Like Graham Hill, Andy was his own man in the fullest sense, and did not measure his words in order to please Chapman, although there was never a hint of cynicism or criticism implied. Andy, it could be said, loved Colin; he was always enthralled by the Englishman's approach to his motor racing, and in that way they were very similar.

But Andy, like Graham, could make comments guaranteed not to go down well with the Old Man. On this visit lunch was at the Lansdown Hotel in Norwich, transport there in Colin's American Ford Galaxie. While passing through the village of East Carleton, with Andy sitting in the front, a group of farmers armed with guns and enjoying a shoot suddenly appeared on the road ahead.

'Jesus Christ!' gasped the STP boss, sufficiently agile despite his enormous size to go flat on the seat and slide below dashboard level. Everyone laughed as Andy commented that he had surely

A quiet March moment in the Indy pit lane provided time for yet another publicity photograph, this now rare image capturing what could have been a supreme team: Parnelli Jones in STP's Wallis-built 'Silent Sam' Turbocar, the robbed heroine of the 1967 '500'; Big Andy and Colin themselves; and the latest Lotus-Pratt & Whitney 56 with double-World Champion Jim Clark on board. Jimmy was in the last month of his life . . . (Indianapolis Motor Speedway)

not come all this way only to be rubbed out by the Norfolk Mafia; then, not for the first time, he made a comment that stung Chapman's well-developed self-esteem: 'Still, at least if you die with me, Colin, it will make you famous!' My Guv'nor's response was a muted one . . .

Neither did Andy's generous intake of food sit well with Colin. At that particular meal Andy ordered lasagne for his starter; when the waiter returned to take orders for the main course, Andy ordered soup.

'But that's a starter, sir,' said the waiter.

'Yes, I know it is,' said Andy, 'but I'd like to try it.'

After the soup Andy then had another helping of lasagne, while Colin, always tense about his own weight, looked on helplessly,

1965 Indy '500' winner Jim Clark before going out to test the last Indycar he would ever experience, '56/1', in March 1968. (G. Crombac)

● 1968: TRAGEDY UPON TRAGEDY

still waiting to order his main course.

The memory of the 1968 season always comes back to me whenever people ask me if a season about to open is going to be a good one. The line-up for Indy as that year began was a manager's dream. Names such as Jim Clark, Graham Hill, Parnelli Jones, Jackie Stewart, Mike Spence, Mario Andretti, Lloyd Ruby all flashed through the media mills. It was a start to a season that I shall never forget, as one tragedy after another fell upon us.

Indeed, it promised to be an exceptionally exciting and rewarding season. We had two World Champions and Indy winners as joint No 1s, and both were down to drive our new 4WD gas turbine cars at Indianapolis, while Andy had the star talent of Indy-winner Parnelli Jones signed to drive his 1967 turbine again, this time, hopefully, with more expensive bearings in its gearbox . . ! While Andy was at Hethel we composed press releases that would ensure worldwide coverage.

Our agreement confirmed that two Type 56s, together with a quantity of designated spares, such as gear ratios, wheels and transfer boxes, and suspension components, would become Andy's property in exchange for two turbines suitable for Formula 1 regulations, on condition that Team Lotus (or Worldwide Racing as it was now known for overseas events) held exclusive rights for the use of such engines from Pratt &

By 1968 Jackie Stewart was fast becoming Jimmy Clark's closest rival in Formula 1, he also shone upon his Indy debut in John Mecom's American Red Ball Special Lola-Ford, and had almost won the 1966 '500'. His team-mate Graham Hill won instead.

Whitney. This arrangement was dependent upon STP continuing to participate in this international programme.

Andy's crew would prepare their two cars, and Team those for Jimmy and Graham, the latter to be paid retainers of $22,500 and $15,000 respectively. Team would pay its own 'month of May' costs as well as those for the construction of all four chassis, while STP would pay for all turbines. Although the percentage paid to mechanics for pole and race prize money would be paid in respect of their own two cars, no one could foresee the problems that this would bring upon us.

However, Colin was seeking increased income from the STP contract because 'the cars are working out very much more expensive than I had at first thought'. As he pointed out, this was due to the cost of the Ferguson and ZF equipment, although it was to turn out that overall the total cost of the cars was only a little more than the 1966/67 versions.

In mid-January Colin and Maurice attended a meeting at Ferguson Research to finalise their design parameters; with all drawings completed three days later, Ferguson was to provide the new equipment, including production of patterns, castings, machining and assembly just 34 days later.

The first 'live' gas turbine arrived at London Airport in the middle of February, and it took two days to clear customs despite frantic negotiation. Then at the end of that month ZF informed us of a delay in delivering the five car sets of axles. Although the delay was only four days and was due to late arrival of driveshaft tubes, which we were having made in England, they were deeply apologetic. What was of most interest was that to date ZF's design staff had put in a total of 500 hours of work.

For some reason the import of aircraft-style turbines en route to a car company caused Customs & Excise indigestion, and only several meetings later did we evolve an acceptable bonding scheme. Additionally, freighting movements for the engines had to be watched as they were ultra-sensitive to vibration; special pallets with a shock-absorbing structure between the pallet and chassis of each car were used when they were completed and shipped to America.

The Customs situation in the States was no better. Although America and Canada had an 'understanding' whereby car components moving from one country to the other attracted no duty, in our case the Canadian product was entering America from England. Even if we shipped the cars to Canada first prior to entering America, no one was able to tell us if a turbine in a car chassis would be accepted as a car component. Not only was there the possibility of an extremely high duty to be paid, it was also odds on that there would be long delays unacceptable to a tense test and race programme in which every day was crucial.

In early March I was off to America. We had three court cases to attend to in Indianapolis, a visit to Hollywood for a film, and meetings in New York with Grand Prix Models Corporation, a company set up to administer royalty payments to a number of race car constructors worldwide.

Two of the court cases, in Marion County Court, Indianapolis, saw me as plaintiff, the other as defendant. The latter was another case of Colin's anxiety to prove that he could walk on water, but Clarence Cagle of the Speedway was also named in our writ, and this caused him some agitation. Granatelli was also involved in court action with a suit against USAC on six counts, a lengthy affair lasting 21 days in which he sought 'injunctions to halt USAC's discriminations'. Under focus were a number of contentious points, of which the most serious was USAC's move to withhold STP's renewal of its corporate membership. It was an action based on the club's assertion that for the 1967 race STP had not followed its requirement that accessory companies notify it which cars in the race are using their products. Other subjects for legal debate concerned USAC's sudden rule changes, contravening the accepted time-scale for regulation modifications and effectively placing heavy restrictions on turbine-powered and four-wheel-drive cars. As Andy was to comment later, 'I won just about everything but the final judgement.' On the judge's advice, USAC reinstated STP's membership.

Not long after, Andy was on a Chicago–Indy flight when the plane had to turn back for an emergency landing. Andy was heard to comment, 'Kee-rist, I've lived by the turbine and now it looks as if I'll die by it.'

I had circulated all the Lotus dealers worldwide in my quest to sell the two Type 38s and the 42F still residing in our garages at the track, and Jim Spencer, the American Mid-West dealer (who had taken Whitmore's Lotus-Cortina seat in the Marlboro race) had picked up on this almost immediately. He soon found a customer who viewed the cars and asked us to supply a quote for symmetric suspension, a task that due to our other work would have to be delayed. The decision was made to purchase both Type 38s and relevant spares, and a cheque for $12,000 was handed over to Spencer on 21 February.

In the meantime our New York broker signalled that due to a slip by the Customs officer present at the time of the Type 42F's original importation into America, we had paid permanent import duty on it, while one of the Type 38s was shown as having passed into the States on a temporary basis, the very opposite of our instruction. Believing that the Type 42F had entered on a temporary basis, we had, as already described, then exported it to Canada and re-imported it into America, paying the full duty, so that it could be sold without let or hindrance.

The would-be purchaser was naturally not overjoyed at the delay, but another fly was about to land in the ointment. Colin, without reference to anyone, had sold the cars from under me! His customer was a flying enthusiast who dealt in planes and also liked Lotus road products; he wanted all three race cars, two engines, spares and two Elan +2s, the race cars going for $36,000 total. There was no way I could persuade Colin that my deal had come first, and broke the news to Spencer by cable, who in turn relayed it to his customer. Back came the reply: 'Customer reaction violent'. Colin tried appeasement, offering the would-be customer his sincere apologies and offering to build new versions. The response was swift, in the form of a court summons . . . We

lost the case and the last of our Type 38s were soon gone.

I didn't do too well in the other two cases, either. One, suing an American party who had received our Mount Fuji appearance monies from 1966, became a payment on a never-never scheme that promised much until well into 1970, then petered out. The other case concerned a purchaser of Indy spares, whose pleas of desperation for a quick delivery resulted in his cheque bouncing. Again the action eventually slowed and stopped.

From Indy I returned to New York and the offices of Grand Prix Models Corporation on Hudson Street. (These were a block or two away from the 'Half Note' jazz club, an excellent rendezvous and lunch spot for a jazz enthusiast like myself. Lunchtimes would find what to me were legendary names rehearsing their evening performance or merely visiting for a relaxed time on the stand with their friends. One could listen to Zoot Simms rehearsing, and Tony Bennett's pianist John Bunch letting his hair down.)

GPMC was a group of American entrepreneurs, all but one heavily engaged with their main businesses, who had invited four constructors, Cooper, Brabham, BRM and ourselves, to a wildly extravagant weekend in New York in 1965, following which the British group had received $100,000 to set up its own company in London to safeguard its part of the deal. The ultimate aim was for all race car constructors worldwide to band together to safeguard their interests and to enjoy royalty income from other people's use of their trademarks and trade names, designs and related items of personal property.

The boss of GPMC's New York HQ was the former master of ceremonies at the famed Minsky's nightspot, Eli Tockar. His fellow Vice-Presidents included Major-General Perry Housington II, of Executive-Jet Corporation, and millionaire J. Elroy McCaw, one of whose projects had been to provide New York with cable TV. Elroy had commuted weekly from his home in Seattle for many years, initially by 'sleeper' Stratocruiser, the early 'upstairs-downstairs' aircraft. Also involved was former President Eisenhower's Secretary of the Treasury, Robert B. Anderson, and General Curtis E. LeMay, famed as 'Bombs Away with Curt LeMay' for the part he played in the Second World War, in particular his planning and personal involvement in the atomic bombing of Japan. As Secretary of the British company and liaison man for both concerns, I was in New York to attend the toy fair and meet various manufacturers there.

Two days later I was in Hollywood, staying at the Continental Hyatt on Sunset Boulevard, to discuss a projected film about Team Lotus. One of our guests at the 1967 Indy '500' had been film director Roman Polanski, whose attendance had been engineered by the promotions man at Grand Prix Models, keen to generate income for both parties.

My opposite number in the American side of GPMC was Californian Reeve Whitson who, apart from his extraordinary entrepreneurial skills (sadly diminished by the fact that he never followed up on his initial successes), had an operatic voice of some note and was a famed 'bird-puller'. When he phoned me in

New York to check my time of arrival, he asked me to define my choice of 'company'. Although a fan of the opposite sex, I always found the American approach to such matters a trifle teasing; I merely said something to the effect that I didn't bother about such company when I was working, to which Reeve's response was, 'Save the worry – how about Miss Universe?'

Amazingly, at the airport Reeve greeted me with a fabulously attractive Swedish blonde on each arm, one Miss Universe, the other her sister Ulla-Lena. You can guess from the fact that I remember her sister's name rather than hers, that Miss Universe was Reeve's own 'special'!

It was not long before I realised that Polanski had far more important things on his agenda than to make a film about Team Lotus, although in true American fashion no one came out and said so! When I arrived at Paramount Studios he was in post-production for his film *Rosemary's Baby* starring Mia Farrow. He invited me to an afternoon's sound dubbing wherein one of the actors – it may have been Farrow – merely had to say the single word 'goodbye' to a couple outside a hotel in New York. We all sat in almost total darkness while Roman willed the actor to get the tone he wanted, the piece of film being run over and over again. After no more than an hour of these proceedings, I decided that film-making was not my cup of tea. I was thoroughly bored and later almost as frustrated as the celebrated director when he finally shouted 'That's it!', only to discover that the sound man had not recorded that particular attempt.

Nonetheless, we had several good and entertaining dinners with Roman and his producer friend and fellow Pole Gene Gutowski, as well as lunches at the studio with Roman's glamorous wife Sharon Tate and actor Karl Malden. Not long afterwards Sharon fell tragic victim to the Charles Manson gang.

An invitation from J. C. Agajanian to be his guest at the 200-mile USAC race that he promoted at the Hanford 1½-mile track some 200 miles north of Los Angeles provided a welcome return to reality. J. C.'s hospitality was, as usual, outstanding, saddened only by his car, traditionally numbered '98' and driven by Billy Vukovich, becoming the first retirement. Gordon Johncock won at 122 mph, ahead of Al Unser and Lloyd Ruby.

One eye-opening GPMC-related episode followed a meeting with the toy manufacturer, Mattel Corporation, which was then sweeping the toy world with the 'Hot Wheels' model car range. Company Vice-President of Research and Design, and instigator of nearly 40 of America's best-selling toys, including the Barbie doll, was the effervescent 42-year-old Jack Ryan, one-time designer of the Sparrow and Hawk missiles and various NASA projects, and whose fifth and last wife would be his next door neighbour, Zsa Zsa Gabor.

With more than 1,000 world-wide patents to his name, Ryan had an enormous mock-Tudor home in Bel-Air, and I could tell that it would be no ordinary occasion when I arrived mid-afternoon and found two very young, attractive and scantily dressed twin girls twirling and gyrating to rock music and laser lighting in the heavily curtained front hall. The whole place was controlled by the telephone system – anyone knowing the code could switch on, dim or switch off the tennis court, swimming pool or garden lights, or tune in to bugged bedrooms anywhere in the house. The ornately decorated main guest room, 'for the cutest chick of the evening' as Jack explained, had a 'dumb waiter' positioned immediately behind the king-and-queen-sized headboard, and when he showed me how breakfast was delivered I remarked how enormous the breakfasts must be to merit such a huge contraption.

'That's because I deliver it personally,' was the reply.

Jack was very proud of the extra floor of the house he had commissioned, and took me outside to view the project. I looked skywards at the top floor, but Jack directed my gaze to eye level.

'To add to the top would have made it quite hideous, so I had the whole place jacked up and a new ground floor built,' he explained. 'D'you like it?'

The building was cross-shaped in plan, with four enormous wings emanating from a central point; as Jack explained, he lived in one, visiting guests another, while his wife and girlfriend had one each.

Dinner was for ten or so, and when it was over Jack asked his chauffeur to bring 'the red one' round to the front door. Immediately we were all ushered into a room full of firemen's uniforms and asked to choose capes, trousers and bright yellow firemen's helmets.

The 'red one' was a very large 1920s-style fire engine of the type seen in movies, the crew sitting back-to-back down the centre. Once we were safely on board, a long, brightly polished brass restraining bar was fastened at waist level, the huge engine was started and the stereo, playing a Frank Sinatra song, sprang automatically to life and we were soon rumbling along at commendably high speed towards our night club destination. This was a renowned niterie know as 'The Factory', which was literally just that, its outside appearance giving no clue as to what it contained. Its acre-sized goods lift was still functioning and it seemed as though hundreds of guests piled in with us to be taken up to the action.

I found it amusing that the cloakroom staff did not bat an eyelid when 14 'firemen' and 'firewomen' handed in their capes and yellow helmets. The surroundings were unchanged since the building's period as a warehouse, and a number of film stars known even to me were enjoying themselves on the dance floor, including Tony Curtis and his young wife.

When the time drew near to leave, Jack asked his chauffeur to bring the fire engine round. Shortly afterwards came news that its gearbox was playing up, so Jack ordered 'the cars' to be used; these turned out to be three identical Facel-Vegas, left at the club for such emergencies!

Also on my visiting list was a meeting with General LeMay who also lived in Bel-Air, his magnificent house and gardens commanding outstanding views of the area, and resplendent with oil paintings and water colours of wartime scenes. The cigar-chewing 'Old Ironpants', as he was known in the services, was a formidable figure and was about to stand as Vice-President on George Wallace's ticket in what would be for LeMay a disastrous episode. Then 61 years of age and an extremely busy person, he was always keen to know the latest news of Team Lotus, and of Jimmy in particular. He was Chairman of Networks Electronics Corporation and gave me a variety of ball joints for use on our cars, which we soon fitted as standard. I stayed overnight, enjoying the warm hospitality of his lovely wife, Helen, and watching him devour thick cigars one after the other. When I left on a visit to a nearby shopping centre, LeMay requested I bring him back a box of cigars, and I caught my breath at the thought of how much they would cost.

'Whatever you do, Andy, don't go over 15 cents [about sixpence] each,' he advised me, 'and try haggling ...'

When I returned to Paramount it became obvious that I was wasting my time hanging around, so I telephoned Colin to say that I was about to depart. His response was that I must be having such a good time that I needed to come home for some rest, but I countered this by saying that I had been locked away in dark places for so long that I needed fresh air ...

That evening Reeve gave me a farewell party at Cyrano's on Sunset, a restaurant frequented both by well-known stars and those climbing the arduous ladder. It was a superb evening and we were well looked after by the maître d', Gio (Giovanni) Casara. He was a sailing enthusiast like myself, and as my plane did not take off until the following evening he invited me for a sail on his yacht to Catalina Island, some 20 miles off Los Angeles. It was a glorious sail and, having a skin that quickly colours under the sun, my appearance soon resembled that of a typical beach bum!

My return to England was interrupted by a stop-over in New York; staying at the ultra-costly St Regis Sheraton on Fifth Avenue – Grand Prix Models spared no expense! I had another meeting with Customs & Excise officials at JFK, and was present when the first turbine arrived en route to Indy for its first test. I also had a meeting with our trade mark agent in New York, Michael Salter; his office was on Fifth Avenue, and as I strolled along to meet him there was Colin coming the other way! He was on his way to Indy and had stopped off in NY. His clipped 'Hi' heralded a cool approach. He looked me over, no doubt finding a hair to remove from my jacket, and taking in my bright tan.

'You look like you've had a rough time,' he said. 'No wonder you need rest at home.'

Our chat was a hurried one; no explanation would have sufficed, and Colin was obviously in no mood for banter. Soon we had parted.

Meanwhile Andy was really milking the media with turbine publicity, securing TV personality Johnny Carson's presence at Indy to drive the Paxton car before a TV crew. Parnelli Jones was on hand with advice, telling Carson to 'straighten out the turns as much as possible, making sure to be down on the white line in the centre of the short chutes, then accelerating easy out to the wall on exit.' Carson's drive was a spirited one; with just a few

laps practice he was clocked at 168 mph on the straights, and averaged 135 mph!

That night in my hotel, the telephone rang.

'Hallo, father!' came a familiar Scottish voice. It was Jimmy, now in Indy to test the Type 56 (chassis '56/2'). He had been away on the Tasman series, so we had not spoken for nearly two months, the last occasion being frantic discussions about the politics of the new Gold Leaf tobacco livery that had appeared on our cars for the first time at Christchurch on 20 January.

'I've decided I won't want your job after all,' Jimmy joked, and he went on to recall the hassles he had endured with the race organisers and others when, as acting team manager, he had fought to have the new regulations concerning livery displays accepted.

'And you're lucky they didn't bring me home in a box,' he joked. He explained how he was having problems with a misfiring engine in pouring rain at Teretonga, then, jabbing his foot up and down on the throttle, it had suddenly come to life over a bump doing 150 mph. 'I knocked down everything in sight,' he recounted. The car had leapt over a ditch into an orchard, hitting a tree only after the car lost momentum.

The conversation was unusual in that it was over an hour long before I noticed. Suddenly it occurred to me that for Jimmy to talk this long was not in character.

'Is this a collect call?' I asked.

There was laughter at the other end.

Promotable future – Andy Granatelli counselling TV personality Johnny Carson before his admirably quick laps at the Speedway in 'Silent Sam', the Ken Wallis-designed Pratt & Whitney gas turbine-powered STP Turbocar, which so overshadowed Lotus by nearly winning the '67 '500'. Parnelli Jones looks on (left), with Joe Granatelli (centre). (Indianapolis Motor Speedway)

wanted to drive; for example, he had taken part in the stock car race at Rockingham the previous October, an event Colin would never have agreed to a year or two earlier, as he regarded his No 1 as being far too valuable to risk in other people's cars. But Jimmy had quickly dismissed the Brands seat.

'Mann's lot promised to keep me in touch while I was doing the Tasman,' he said, 'and I haven't heard a dicky-bird. I'll do Hockenheim instead.'

The conversation drifted on as we discussed everything that had happened since we had last met. Graham had driven '56/2', now at Indy, at Hethel on 20 March – the day before it had left England. He had run there for 2 hours, frequently at full race power, which translated into 180 mph down Hethel's test-track runway, and he had also practised full-power standing starts.

After Hockenheim was scheduled a two-day test at Zandvoort of the Formula 2 Type '57' De Dion car, which would leave Hethel on the evening of Sunday 7 April. After Zandvoort Jimmy would fly back to Hethel, where we could sit down and sort out the rest of the year's plans.

Eventually we said cheerio, and that was the last time I was to speak to Jimmy Clark . . .

Meanwhile, in the Longueuil, Quebec, plant of Pratt & Whitney development work was under way, featuring Jim 'high idle' Pickles.

Fred Cowley: 'The March Indy test showed that we needed an improvement in engine acceleration response; I asked Bendix in South Bend to modify the fuel control unit metering valve to increase the "gain", thereby allowing more fuel for a given travel, much as you would change the needle in an SU carburettor, and Little Vince took all our units along.

'The so-called "high idle" was a device that increased the engine's idle speed, thereby improving the response time. However, I believe that when the drivers learned to modulate the throttle instead of taking their foot full off, much as you would do with a piston engine, the lag problem was resolved. Graham told me some time after that he only used the high idle a time or two, but it was a bit frightening and he quickly learned how to drive without it.'

Jim's 'high idle' tag had come about as a result of his solving what could have been a lengthy procedure in setting the turbine's idling limit. A 'T'-handle on the dash panel was connected by a push-pull Morse cable to a quadrant lever at the lower left-hand rear corner of the turbine, which could be altered to provide a pre-determined amount of rpm. The mechanism was hidden within the car, and to eradicate the need to remove the body, and being of a slim build, Jim was able to insert himself under the rear of the body of the car, complete with cranked 3/16-inch spanners he had altered to facilitate the task.

Arthur Birchall was with Chief Mechanic Dick Scammell at Indy to look after the first Indy running of our Type 56s: 'I can still remember Andy Granatelli insisting that Jimmy sand-bag on times; he had a court case against USAC going on down in the town and he wanted us to play it very easy so as not to get anyone's backs up. All Jimmy said was "It's fantastic!" I was called

Executive jet-set – (left to right) Perry Housington, Jack Brabham, Jimmy, Colin and Mike Spence arriving at Indianapolis '68 in a Learjet publicity shot. Each year an enormous slice of corporate America rode the Indy bandwagon . . . (Publicity Photographers)

'No, I'm just feeling generous,' he said, then after a long pause, 'Actually it's on the Indy garage bill so you'll pay for it in the end!' he chuckled.

We started talking about immediate plans. There were two Formula 2 races coming up, Barcelona at the end of the week and Hockenheim a week later. Jimmy was already entered for the Spanish race, but there was a question mark over Hockenheim; he had already told me earlier in the year that he had been offered an Alan Mann Ford team drive in the BOAC '500' sports car race at Brands that same day.

Certain pundits have since intimated that Jimmy had no choice but to drive where Team Lotus told him to, but this is a complete falsehood. He had attained sufficient authority within Team Lotus and with Colin some years before to state exactly where he down to the court room as a witness and just sat there waiting to be called. I can't remember if I gave evidence or not, so I presume I was too tired to slot it into my memory!'

The test, even if run at reduced speeds (Jimmy's best was 161 mph), was deemed a success by Andy's promotional machine; Firestone was there in force utilising twelve electronic speed traps around the 2½-mile track.

At a Hethel debrief on 2 April, Colin presented a 54-item job list, part of the meeting being conducted around the car that had returned from Indy just two days after running had ended. The list ranged from the massive task of increasing the internal width of the cockpit, via a Girling/Ferodo redesign of the braking system, to provision of a chain-stretch indicator. The lining of the seat required remodelling to suit Jimmy, and modifications were needed in order that Graham's longer legs would fit comfortably.

Colin was critical of the untidy nature of the external oil plumbing, a matter he wanted drawn to the attention of Ferguson Research, along with the provision of more efficient lubrication of the differential planet gears. The instrument panel needed to be moved forward by 9 inches, together with a re-grouping of the instruments themselves, with the addition of a torque meter and fuel-pressure gauge. Pedal positions were to be changed and location pins on body fittings improved. Suspension springs needed a thorough analysis; perhaps modified Formula 1 springs could be

utilised? The fuel system needed revision as well as an increase in capacity; also two more catch tanks needed to be fitted, one for the fuel dump valve, the other for the transfer case.

Standardisation of pipe union threads to American spec was required, and for body-side fasteners Colin recommended the Mark 7 style. As to the dreaded question of illegal ballast, Colin wanted the car weighed on two different sets of scales to establish exactly what the amount required should be.

Almost the last item on the list was the provision of more steering lock. One decision concerned the wheels we would run; although we had acquired a large stock of both 15-inch and 16-inch wheels (80 in all), it was decided to stay with the former, the remainder being sold to Firestone.

As construction of the other three cars was well progressed, all the items on the modifications list applied to them as well. Graham Hill demonstrated '56/1' to the press at Hethel three weeks later, and all four cars were air-freighted to Indy at the end of April, two to be run by Granatelli's team.

But before that came the fateful Hockenheim race on Sunday 7 April 1968. I was at Brands Hatch overseeing the Type 47 Europa for John Miles and Jackie Oliver in the BOAC '500', a 6-hour endurance race, while Colin was having a rare break from racing, on holiday in Switzerland.

My lasting memory is of turning, during the race, to see tears

Press photo call team portrait at Hethel before the four-wheel-drive Type 56 turbine cars were flown out to Indy – Graham Hill, Maurice Phillippe, Dick Scammell and Colin with the cars. There was evidently some difference of opinion on where to place the assorted 'Lotus', 'STP', 'Amoco' and 'Firestone' decals . . . (Phipps Photographic)

'56/1' during that same shoot at Hethel, demonstrating its midship-mounted Pratt & Whitney STN6-74 gas turbine engine with raked front-end exhaust funnel, 'bathtub'-type monocoque chassis, inboard-mounted co-axial coilspring/dampers, chunky ventilated brake discs, and crush-resistant FPT oil tanks. (Lotus)

Graham whooshes '56/1' past the factory, nose-up under power on the Hethel test track, showing the car's extraordinary door-stop shape. Has there ever been a cleaner profile for any major-Formula open-wheeler . . ? (Motoring News)

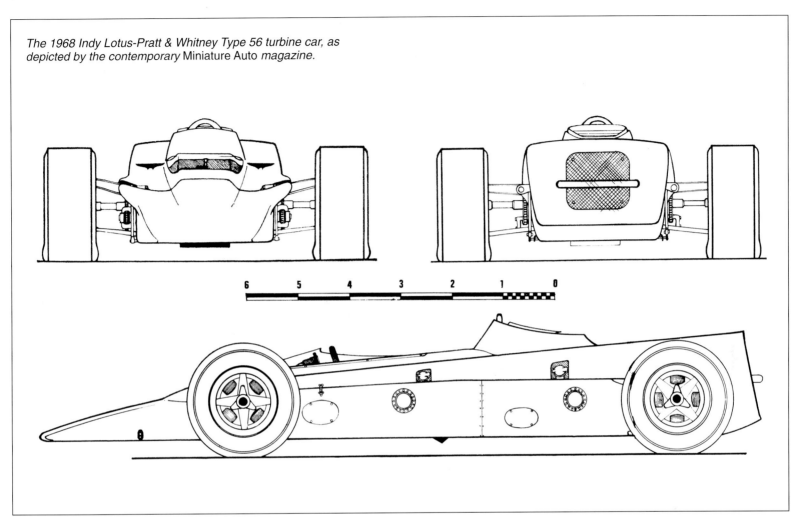

The 1968 Indy Lotus-Pratt & Whitney Type 56 turbine car, as depicted by the contemporary Miniature Auto *magazine.*

rolling down Jabby Crombac's face in great profusion and someone saying, 'It's Jim.'

My first thought was indicative of our false sense of security about the legendary Scotsman. 'My God, what's happened to Endruweit?' flashed through my brain, but I quickly discovered the truth. At Hockenheim Jimmy had crashed his F2 Type 48. He was dead.

It was left to me to decide if we should withdraw our Type 47, but I quickly dismissed that thought; it went on to win its class four laps clear and 10th overall.

It was not until late in the evening that I broke down and wept uncontrollably for what seemed like hours. I was simply exhausted by the enormity of the tragedy.

Later came reports that Jimmy had remained gloomy and pensive throughout that weekend at Hockenheim, due it was said to worry about the car he was to drive, as if a mechanical failure was on the cards. In practice he had, like his team-mate Graham, been plagued by metering unit problems, which had afflicted other cars and which in Jimmy's case had proved so troublesome to fix that he had missed one practice session altogether.

As to the gloom, Stefan Weibach, to this day a German fan of Jimmy's, recently sent me photographs of the Scotsman thoroughly enjoying himself with a beer the night before the race, attending a function at a local vineyard to which he had been invited by his friend and fellow racing driver, Kurt Ahrens, who was to race a Brabham. Jimmy had thanked Kurt with a handwritten note saying 'Wishing Kurt the second-best luck tomorrow'.

Andy Granatelli, like so many, was heartbroken; immediately following a cable of condolence he telephoned to say that whatever Colin now wished to do regarding Indy he would go along with.

My first meeting with Colin in his office at Hethel was another occasion for tears from us both. He looked, and sounded, absolutely ghastly. On top of this were all the wild stories being cabled and telexed amongst the mass of messages of condolence that Jim's crash had been caused by a person or people on the track – some said children running across in front of him had caused the accident.

The funeral was held on the Wednesday, and I flew to Scotland with Colin and Hazel in the company plane. The whole occasion remains a blur and I cannot remember who else was with us. I can remember Colin watching Dennis Austin (then Managing Director of Lotus Cars) who was flying another company plane with Colin's children on board, take off downwind from Hethel, and Colin shouting loudly through the floor-to-ceiling glass wall of his office for Dennis to abort take-off.

Considering that I had known Jimmy for over seven years, I find it quite astonishing on reflection that I had never before met his mother, father or sisters. He had talked of his family, mainly his father, but he had never asked me for a race ticket for them. The house was filled with racing drivers, mechanics and other racing personalities, and the family were all remarkably stoic, and gave us all a warm greeting.

In the years that followed I grew closer to Jimmy's family, but it was as if Jimmy had kept the two parts of his life – farming and international motor racing – completely separate. Certainly the family did not appear to understand fully just how extraordinary Jimmy's talents and exploits had been, and perhaps this lack of inside knowledge stemmed from his carefully orchestrated desire never to cause then undue worry.

We flew back that evening, and the next day Peter Jowitt, of the Farnborough aircraft accident investigation department, an RAC scrutineer, examined the wreckage of Jimmy's car in our race shop at Hethel. During the day Colin suddenly took me to one side.

'I'd like you to have a break,' he said. 'I've got the air tickets here for you and Phyllis to take the family to Ibiza tomorrow. I'll see you Monday week.'

Colin had a villa there overlooking the Mediterranean, and it was a super place to be, although his huge volume of neatly handwritten instructions as to what *not* to do was a little daunting. To save water, Colin advised his guests to wait to use the toilet until they visited a restaurant nearly a mile away. I remarked to his wife Hazel later that it must be a worry being on the bone for water, to which she replied, 'Yes I don't know why Colin does that, the villa is built on a huge storage tank holding over three tons of the stuff.'

Regarding 'Phyllis', Colin always had a problem remembering names. My wife's name was Sylvia.

I returned to Hethel the day that Graham demonstrated '56/1' to the press, and the news was announced that Jackie Stewart would be his team-mate at Indy. Just a few days later the cars, spares and crew left for the States.

However, moves were afoot to add another driver, and Colin spoke to Granatelli about BRM driver – ex-Lotus – Mike Spence. Andy's response was immediately affirmative. He cabled: 'I think we ought to bring Mike Spence to the Speedway. I feel that if we pay his expenses and provide him with a driver's test he should be well satisfied. Drivers are extremely scarce, and in fact there aren't 33 qualified drivers to drive the 33 cars that will eventually make the programme and it is obvious that for every car we get into the programme we will have one less competitor, plus the fact that even 33rd position pays $1,000.'

In the week leading to Silverstone's International Trophy race meeting on 27 April, the Northamptonshire circuit saw a further Type 56 test, both Graham and Mike Spence driving the car. Here Colin and I approached BRM's Tony Rudd (they were also testing) for permission to borrow Mike for a test drive at Indy. The American timetable did not clash with any Formula 1 date, and Tony called Mike into the conversation to finalise the deal.

Immediately after BRM's approval I gave Mike a letter setting out the arrangement. His Indy tests in our car would end with his departure to the Spanish Grand Prix on Wednesday 8 May, and during this period it would be up to Andy Granatelli to appraise how he took to the Speedway. Travel and hotel costs and reasonable out-of-pocket expenses would all be STP's responsibility. If all went well, immediately after Mike's return from Spain, there would be a Team Lotus Worldwide Racing agreement for him, on the understanding that he might be seconded to the STP section of the programme.

Mike Spence was a really lovely fellow, quiet and unassuming, completely devoid of politics and without an axe to grind in any direction. Thirty-one years old, he had started racing at the age of 19 and combined an increasingly fast style with sensitivity and intelligence. I had first met him at Cooper in 1960, when the family firm, Coburn Engineers, had acquired a Formula Junior Cooper for him. We had met again in 1962 when he had joined Ian Walker driving a Lotus 22, and in 1963 he had signed with Ron Harris-Team Lotus, also for Formula Junior. From there he had graduated to our Formula 1 section, taking a full-time role after Peter Arundell's horrific crash at Rheims, winning at Brands after Jimmy's crash in 1965 and the World Championship South African Grand Prix in 1966.

He had then left us to join the '2nd XI' BRM team of Tim Parnell, but when Graham returned to us for 1967, Mike had been elevated to No 2 slot alongside Jackie Stewart. He had brought home the infamous H16-engined car six times, a sure mark of his delicacy of touch.

Now with a thriving Lotus dealership a short distance west of London, Mike was also involved in investing his surplus monies, and from the time we left for Indianapolis he tried the soft-sell on me for shares in some Australian timber country. He had a very appealing smile, and after a run in the car and a debrief with Colin, his face would break into a grin, then the chat about buying timber would continue.

At this time the atmosphere between Andy and Colin was deteriorating quite noticeably. In February Colin had written to Andy coupling our Indy programme and finances to a similar deal for Formula 1, with equally large sums of money added to the original agreement. Andy had needed time to think about this proposal and also the best way to present it to his board; he was entitled to seek time, but Colin had lost patience after a month had passed and telephoned him stipulating that unless he agreed the proposal we would not ship the Indy cars. As the press launch had already taken place, this sudden turn by Colin

Such a thoroughly nice bloke, and a very fine racing driver – Mike Spence. (Geoffrey Goddard)

promised to be highly embarrassing to all concerned, particularly so for STP's President.

In response Andy had composed an account of all that had gone before, registering his hurt and dismay that Colin should question his integrity and honesty. The relationship to date had been good and sound, Andy continued, and only once had their voices been raised at each other, and that merely because a fuel filter had been omitted from the Type 56 used in the March test.

Colin had also strongly complained about what he saw as extraordinarily large STP decals on the cars, but as Andy gently pointed out, he was paying for the exercise, he was the sponsor and 'the whole world knows the name of the cars'. (Colin was to respond to this by having extremely large Lotus decals made for positioning in front of the windscreen.) Andy also reminded

Colin that the Englishman had failed to support Andy's court case by substantiating that the power of the Ford engines exceeded that of the turbines; Colin had physically only been a short step away from the courtroom, yet had failed to appear or even to provide a letter or telegram in STP's assistance. Andy felt that this inaction had negated his defence. Additionally, the magazine *Sports Illustrated* had sent a photographer all the way to Hethel to take photographs required for an article, but had been turned away at the gates.

Colin had also publicised how much money he was spending on the project, but Andy took him to task on this by setting out the main points of the combined budget. With Firestone and petroleum monies alone, Colin was due to realise a maximum of $200,000, a sum that Andy pointed out should pay our expenses 'lock, stock and barrel, with money left over'. For his part, Andy had already seen $150,000-$200,000 washed down the drain by the lawsuit, and an additional $500,000 was still to be spent on the turbines, drivers' fees, mechanics and overheads. Colin had also broken the agreement by not providing STP with its two cars early in March as he had promised.

Andy's tone continued to be soft and understanding, and he ended by saying, 'I have said my piece and this does not require an answer. Let's make racing fun from here on in.'

At the end of April came the Spanish Formula 2 European Championship race at Jarama, Madrid, and the Formula 1 International Trophy race at Silverstone. Graham Hill was entered in both, leaving after Saturday's British event and practising at Jarama on race morning, his Gold Leaf Team Lotus Formula 2 appearance in Spain being the first since Jimmy's accident. Jackie Stewart, now an overseas resident, concentrated on the Spanish event in his Matra, but after recording pole position he left the road on his last practice lap, finishing up in the catch fencing with a wrist damaged badly enough to prevent him from starting. After medical attention he left to join us at Indy.

Being Jackie, he had already arranged a courtesy Cadillac with the Cleverley Cadillac agency in Indianapolis, but when he collected it Jim Cleverley offered him three of the enormous vehicles! When he returned to the motel he jokingly explained his plan; he and Graham would have one each and I would have the third. We would all park in a space furthest away from the Motel entrance, and thus leave Colin to continue using his 'compact'. The mental strain became immense!

On arrival at the Howard Johnson Motel a great stack of mail awaited each of us, the majority being messages of commiseration for Jimmy's loss, poems, some of them many pages long, letters of condolence from church groups and others, most containing details of the special services they had arranged, and appearing a little bizarre to English eyes. Someone had actually produced a record called 'The Ballad of Jimmy Clark', and we turned down their request to 'authorise' it.

Not long after his arrival, Colin was stopped for speeding. Asked for his driving licence, he had immediately put a hand to his back pocket, but suspecting that he was about to draw a gun, the police had immediately spreadeagled him across the bonnet (hood) of his car, which Colin did not appreciate one little bit!

Indy's fifth largest entry of 77 cars had been listed for the '500' by the time the track opened, with seven Grand Prix drivers named. The entries of three turbine-engined cars in 1962, '66 and '67 had now grown to nine, four of them Lotus Type 56, the STP entry of the previous year and three of Carroll Shelby's 'Botany 500' cars powered by General Electric units, two of them entered for Bruce McLaren and Denny Hulme to drive. These had been designed by former Granatelli designer Ken Wallis, who had produced 1967's 'Silent Sam' that Parnelli had driven, but who had left Andy the previous year, allegedly taking some of Andy's staff with him. The story went that Goodyear's support had run into the megabucks area, but the car's appearance was remarkably similar to Wallis's first turbine for Andy, its publicity giving assurances that it would attain speeds in excess of 170 mph.

The ninth entry was the Jack Adams Wynn-Storm car fitted with an Allison 250-C18 turbine mounted at the front of car, which, unlike the other cars regulated to an inlet annulus area of 15.9 square inches, was down to just 12 square inches. It was the brainchild of Glenn Bryant, whose previous projects included experimental aircraft. It was said to be so aerodynamically stable that it would self-correct itself if it got out of shape in a corner. It incorporated De Dion suspension with a Watts linkage system, but it was withdrawn before practice.

In the Ford camp, Lou Meyer was now providing a turbocharged version of the V8 quad-cam, complete with a kit that would reduce the 255 cubic inches to 168. Sadly, Mario Andretti's car owner, the friendly Al Dean, had just recently succumbed to cancer, and Mario had acquired the team, lock stock and barrel; his car was the first monocoque built by the famed Eddie Kuzma of Los Angeles. Of all the entries, just one was a roadster, the Mallard turbocharged Offy of the heroic Jim Hurtubise.

The month of May opened with us in very good order. All four of the cars were in pristine shape, and besides this I had already purchased Graham's required set of dumb-bells!

Graham ('56/3') and Mike ('56/1') were out on the first day of running, Graham establishing fastest lap of the day at over 154 mph, the track stewards initially imposing a 155 mph limit. The next day Mike, still acclimatising himself, successfully passed his 140–145 mph after a reward for running initially an 155 mph. Strange as it may sound, Graham confided to me that he was finding it extremely hard to acclimatise to two-pedal operation.

'I've got no problems at all driving American road cars, but I can't transfer it to here without concentrating the whole time,' he told me, adding, 'but don't tell anyone otherwise I'll be in big trouble!'

Pundits were soon applauding the fine handling of our cars, especially after they had recorded the highest ever speeds through Turn One. The previous record holder, Mario Andretti, had clocked an average speed through the quarter-mile-long turn at 154 mph, whereas all the drivers in our cars, whether regulars or those merely sampling, were consistently running at Mario's speeds; Graham was regularly up to 156 mph and once topped 158, such details being spewed out daily on the track's information sheets. Unfortunately, although these speeds were 5–8 mph quicker than the average driver, the cars were topping out at around 197 mph on the straights with virtually no grunt left to pass other cars.

Graham was doing an incredible job bringing all of us out of the stupor caused by Hockenheim. I really cannot praise him enough for his spirit and enormous effort to keep us all in top pitch; after all, in Jimmy he had also lost a very close friend, but his character in blotting the affair from both his and our minds was extraordinary.

The speed limit was removed on 3 May and Mike soon completed his 'rookie' test, later in the day clocking second fastest time of the day at 160.915 mph to McCluskey's fastest of 161 mph-plus. The same day Parnelli Jones stepped out of the STP Paxton car for good. He explained that he had had a hard enough job the previous year to take sixth place on the grid, and now with the regulatory cut of one-third of its potency he felt his task was hopeless.

'If I can't get a shot at the front row, I don't want to race,' he said. Andy's men parked the turbine in their garage and the indefatigable STP boss went hunting for drivers . . .

A day later (5 May) Graham was back in front with 165.411 mph with Mike just a smidgen under 165 mph. As the press put it, he was picking up friends as fast as speeds; they liked his ready smile, his ability to laugh when kidded and his ability to kid back. In short, one wrote, he was winning over the speedway both on and off the track. Gurney's Olsonite Eagles were third and fourth at over 163 mph.

One day Reeve Whitson of Grand Prix Models arrived in our garage asking whoever would listen to him who they thought was the greatest General in history. Immediately the shout went up 'Montgomery'; when this was not approved, 'Wellington'. After mentions of Napoleon, Reeve looked around disapprovingly and said it was 'LeMay', which was a name unfamiliar to an Englishman's ears. A few minutes later, the General himself walked into the garage carrying some parts he had ordered from his Californian company. He was introduced to Graham Hill with a typical and seemingly endless American flourish from Reeve, Graham quite unperturbed. Eventually the praises came to an end, and Graham looked the venerable General straight in the eye.

'Ever done any flying, General?' he asked.

Art Pollard was the next driver to sample No 40, the turbine discarded by Parnelli. Art, a 41-year-old from Oregon, had been racing for 13 years, the past three in Championship cars. He was an immensely popular personality who really endeared himself to our crew. His first appearance outside our garage early one morning was also memorable.

Mechanic Doug Garner: 'I didn't recognise this chap standing outside our garage and I asked if I could help him. Art said he wanted to speak to Colin and I asked him why – he could have been a supplier or something. He said, "Yes, I'd like a drive." I burst out laughing and said, "You must be joking – *everyone* wants to drive our cars. Shouldn't you be the other side of the fence?" Then he burst out laughing, and we always considered that first meeting a huge joke.

'When he came into the garage he turned up his nose at our doughnuts that we'd got from the mechanics' restaurant. "I'll get you some real ones," he said, and off he went. Do you know, he was gone half an hour, driving out of the track to get them, and from then on he always kept us supplied with doughnuts . . . he was a really nice guy and had a super family whom he made sure we all met . . .'

Art had been entered initially in another car, but soon after driving Andy's turbine he was up to 163 mph, and not long after was just under 166 mph. Then Joe Leonard tried it, and was soon into Art's times. Both were full of praise for the car, Leonard now having changed his stance on turbines voiced the previous year. Both drivers still drove the cars they had been entered in, but both kept coming back for more.

On the Sunday evening Graham took Colin, Jackie, Maurice Phillippe, Mike and myself out for dinner to a restaurant where, in a State that was non-alcoholic on the Sabbath, they were already used to catering for him. Obviously our table's requirement was for only a small intake of wine, which was served in coffee cups, a scheme that worked well until a change of waitress, when a very young girl, unaware of what we wanted, poured coffee into our wine. A simple change of cups would have sufficed, but Graham, taking a swig of coffee mixed with wine, gave the girl what was really a sweet rebuke, but which appeared to devastate her. After she had taken the cups away I in turn rebuked Graham.

'Where were you brought up Graham?' I said. 'Anyone would think you went to Orange Hill Grammar School!'

Graham burst out laughing. 'How did you know I went there?' he asked.

'I didn't – it was my school.'

We had indeed gone to the same school, but Graham had been three years ahead of me. I reminded him of a girl from a nearby school who for a penny, or perhaps tuppence, from each of her highly appreciative audience of schoolboys would take her knickers down in one of our air raid shelters. She must have made a small fortune from her enterprise, and Graham claimed to have known of her. From then on the evening hinged around said girl's exploits, the legend greatly enhanced by Graham's keen sense of imagination . . .

Colin had been keen to sign Mario Andretti ever since 1965, and now he asked me to invite the American ace to drive one of our Formula 1 cars at Monza and in the American Grand Prix at Watkins Glen. Mario suggested that we have dinner at the 'Cove', a popular niterie just across from the Speedway, and I was amazed to discover that he was a racing driver who actually *drank alcohol*! Although it was only a minute amount, after Jimmy's very occasional beer, Graham's odd sip of wine and

Colin's single vodka Martini, I was quite taken aback . . .

The deal done, there was need for a further chat the next day.

'Don't call me real early,' said Mario. 'Make it around ten.'

At breakfast, discussing the need for a special test session at Monza for Mario, Colin said he'd phone our new driver. When I told him to make it around ten, his face fell.

'Is that the time he gets up?' said a visibly perturbed Colin.

'No, it's just that I said I'd phone him at ten,' I replied.

'He's not on the . . ?' asked Colin, his hand tracing the arc of someone having a drink.

'Good Lord, no!' I replied.

'Well I hope not,' said Colin. 'Remind me when it's ten.'

My secretary had cabled me on 1 May to say that Jimmy's lawyers wanted rooms at Indy for two nights. They wanted to outline the plans for the Jim Clark Foundation being set up in his memory, although why the subject could not wait until we were all back in England no one knew. As Colin succinctly put it, 'Jimmy's only been gone three weeks and the legal beagles already have their fingers in the honey-pot!'

Present at the meeting was Colin, Jackie Stewart, Graham and myself, and after the 'Scottish bullocks' (as Colin and I had described them since the early 1960s) had left, the four of us discussed the plan's good and bad points. Eventually they asked me to write to the lawyers saying that we already had plenty of experience in organising similar arrangements, and could think of no one else with the experience, time or knowledge to do the thing properly. As I was asked to phrase it, 'it is essential to have a vital and snappy set-up and not a tottering giant overburdened with politics and very hard to define guidelines. Its aim of increasing safety worldwide would be hard to clarify, and we hope we can have further discussions on the subject with you when we return home.'

The following day Dan Gurney shook the establishment (and us!) with a 167 mph-plus in his *stock-block*-engined Eagle, and over 165 mph in his Ford-engined version. The place was definitely warming up.

On Tuesday 7 May Mike Spence drew the plaudits of the increasingly interested pundits with a lap at 169.555 mph, less than 1/2 mph below Mario and the track record. He had run 10 laps at more than 168 mph and four over 169 mph without fuss. Graham recorded 169.045 mph, both runs in strong winds and running with full fuel loads.

Mike was understandably thrilled with his times. 'I think there's more to come,' he told the press.

Of the 28 cars practising, none were near our team's times, only Mario Andretti having gone faster the previous year at 169.779 mph when setting pole position. Later came reports that a race steward had confided to Mike that he was running too low through the Turns.

As work continued on the cars that morning, Colin gave an interview to a journalist, quietly explaining his feelings at the loss of Jimmy and how in the subsequent three weeks he had wanted to quit the sport and close down Team Lotus. But thoughts of his contractual obligations and the Team staff he employed had eventually brought him round. He then talked of his early days in racing, and his natural bounce began to return. In the middle of the interview Graham and Mike carried a large cake into the garage, bearing a card inscribed 'Good luck to Colin, Graham, Mike, etc.'

Graham laughed. 'Young Fergie's got a mention, then. See, they've put "etc" on it!'

Around 4.30 pm, with our running finished for the day, I left our exuberant crew to visit the nearby bank on business. I returned about an hour later, and as I parked a friend leaned into the car and asked how Mike was.

'Oh, he's over the moon – very happy,' I said.

'Haven't you heard?' my friend said. 'He's been taken to the hospital – he had a shunt.'

'No, he can't have!' I replied, 'We've finished running.'

My friend shook his head. 'Nope, he was running OK, but he hit the wall on One.'

I hurried to our garage, where the lads said that Colin wanted me at the Methodist Hospital as soon as possible; they did not know how Mike was.

The only STP car that had run (chassis '56/2') had 24-year-old

Problems – a brainstorming session in the pit lane as 'Little Vince' Granatelli examines, Greg Weld frets over his poor times, Andy Granatelli sympathises. Perhaps Mike Spence should take out the car to demonstrate that the car is not the problem . . .

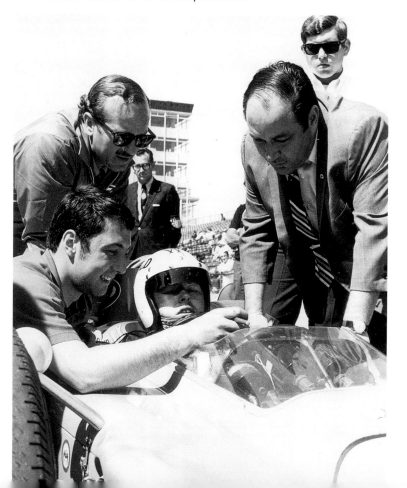

Greg Weld at the wheel; he had passed his driver's refresher test only the previous day, so had not approached our own cars' times. This had given rise to the age-old question of whether it was due to the car or its driver, and Colin had been asked if Mike could evaluate the car, but had refused. That afternoon he had been asked again, and relented.

The accident happened just minutes after Mike had set off, but he was already lapping at 163 mph. Experienced observers reported that he had gone higher than usual on entry to Turn One on his first lap and higher still as he approached it the second time. In fact, Chief Observer Walt Myers had switched on the yellow lights even before Mike had hit the wall.

The car slid 300 feet then hit the wall at 45 degrees. The impact tore off its right-side wheels, but otherwise there was little visible damage, and it continued for nearly 400 feet along the wall, sliding another 240 feet back into the middle of the track before coming to rest, its turbine still whining. When the right-front wheel had been torn off it had been restrained by a track rod, swinging back round like a slingshot through a radius to impact violently against Mike's head, tearing off his helmet and leaving black tyre marks across it, its strap still fastened.

Mike was unconscious when the rescue crew lifted him from the car, and he was rushed to Methodist Hospital. There I met an ashen-faced Colin being consoled by Jackie Stewart, as hospital staff explained that Mike had very serious head injuries and was critically ill in intensive care. He had sustained no other injuries.

Ferguson's Derek Gardner arrived at Indy that same day. Asked if the STP car was any different mechanically, as a possible factor in Mike's accident, he confirmed that all the cars had been fitted with the Type A differential giving 50/50 front/rear torque distribution. Only later did some drivers report that this gave too much understeer, and the Type B differential was made available to provide 5 per cent more torque to the rear wheels. In Derek's opinion, the accident had resulted purely from Mike entering Turn One on too high a line.

Colin slowly pulled round, and we compiled the telephone numbers to be called, initially those of neuro-surgeons. We were advised that the best was in Washington, and here Firestone immediately came to our rescue with an offer of a company jet to fly to Dulles Airport straight away. We spoke to the surgeon, who said that he would be able to join the aircraft on its arrival, and to air traffic control there to explain the emergency and ask them to expedite the plane's departure.

The hospital then informed us that an eminent surgeon from Chicago, Dr Paul Bucy, was already in the hospital, and that he was currently attending Mike. Colin bravely took on the task of telephoning Mike's wife Lynn, and his parents. I was allotted Mike's business associate, David Porter, BRM's Tony Rudd and others, while Jackie phoned Louis Stanley of BRM, who always excelled in such emergencies. Meanwhile the hospital staff consoled us as best they could, with constant supplies of coffee, advice and visits from Speedway doctor Tom Hannah.

At around 9 pm the hospital staff told us that they were con-

Mike is happy to give it a go. Colin, thoughtful as ever, strides up in the background just before Mike's fatal run.

templating therapy prior to conducting brain surgery, in an attempt to reduce the shock to Mike's system. Then at 9.45 pm we were told that Mike had passed away.

There followed the distressing task of once more calling those we had telephoned earlier – Colin was able to abort the Washington take-off – and when this had been done Colin and Jackie left the hospital while I stayed on to attend to the necessary heart-breaking arrangements. The Speedway funeral home was operational 24 hours a day, so I was able to make the arrangements almost immediately, after which I returned to the Motel, where I packed Mike's gear into the cases that we had only just carried out with us. Then the front desk called to say that some mail had just been delivered.

It was a press statement from Carroll Shelby's organisation withdrawing its two Goodyear-backed 'Botany 500' turbines scheduled to be driven by Denny Hulme and Bruce McLaren. Considering the events of the past few hours, the wording was singularly inappropriate. It read: 'After complete and intensive testing it is felt that at the present time it is impossible to make a turbine-powered car competitive with a reasonable degree of safety. Therefore the Shelby Racing Co turbines are being withdrawn.' No mention was made of the fact that these Ken Wallis creations had been unable to get over 161 mph, nor comment on the reports there were problems with chassis flexure.

I finally climbed sadly into bed in the early hours, then early the next morning Colin called me to his room. His packed cases were just inside the door, and he was writing a press statement that he wanted issued as soon as possible.

'I'm leaving and won't be back,' he said. 'I'm not going to Spain. Read this and see if any changes should be made. I've told Andy he is to work with you. There's my briefcase – everything is in

there you'll need. Don't try to contact me – I'll see you back in England.' And with that he was gone.

I ordered breakfast in Colin's room and went though his briefcase to see what he had left me. We all used company-issue leather briefcases that opened at the top, and as usual Colin's was packed to the gunwales. I typed out Colin's press statement and a letter to Granatelli in which Colin delegated administrative duties to myself and technical decisions to Dick Scammell. He made it clear that he did not approve of Greg Weld driving STP's 56, and asked Andy 'to find a thoroughly experienced Indy driver for it'. If Greg drove it Colin would disassociate himself from any responsibility or liability for accident damage. He also stipulated that Jackie Stewart would drive car No 60 ('56/1'), the Team Lotus entry to be prepared by Team Lotus mechanics. I then drove the couple of miles to the Speedway after settling the bills for Mike's and Colin's rooms.

I pinned the Old Man's statement up in the press room. It read: 'I am filled with grief at the loss of my long-time friend and associate, Jimmy Clark, and the additional loss, just a month later to the day, of Mike Spence. As an understandable result, I want nothing more to do with the 1968 Indianapolis race. I just do not have the heart for it. I thank my good friend, Andy Granatelli, for taking over in my stead and allowing me to carry out my decision. As entrant and owner of these cars, Andy will have an added burden and responsibility since things must go on. I appreciate his action.'

Colin went on to say that the withdrawal of two 'competitive' turbines by another owner, being associated with the death of Mike Spence, was regrettable.

Time to go.

'Both Andy and I agreed,' his statement continued, 'that the combination of 4WD and turbine power provides the safest kind of racing vehicles, and this combination is here to stay. It should be obvious that the tragic accident which took Mike Spence had nothing to do with the design, power source or construction of his car, as has been further confirmed by the action today of Chief Steward Harlan Fengler in releasing these cars for further running, and the USAC Technical Committee has found no mechanical failure.'

The funeral home suggested that a short memorial service be held in the chapel that evening; they would post notices at the track inviting anyone wished to attend. There was not a single empty seat, and I was taken aback to see the senior level of those attending from other teams, undoubtedly due to them having been so taken by Mike's sheer quality in the few days that he had been at the Speedway.

The documentation needed to take Mike back to England seemed immense, most of it highly personal, and I had to telephone his friends in England to acquire details and to liaise with what Lynn wanted. Additionally the press was calling from all over the world wanting an insight into what had occurred, what our plans were and how Colin was taking it. Time flashed by, as did the opportunity for meals. I had given up cigarettes some four and a half years earlier, smoking only small cigars since then, but I suddenly had a longing for a cigarette to curb my hunger, and I purchased a pack of Viceroys in the mechanics' restaurant. The first one was horrible, the second only fractionally less so. By the 20th I was hooked again, and have remained so to this day.

Later that day I received Andy Granatelli's letter in reply to Colin's. He wanted Colin to cable acceptance that he, Andy, was in overall charge, and that Colin's reference to Dick Scammell's responsibilities only concerned those normally under the control of a chief mechanic; in other words, Andy was to remain in charge of policy decisions. Andy also wanted Colin to cable power of attorney for me to handle and sign all documents. Finally, he asked Colin if he wanted to sell the whole Indy section lock, stock and barrel, adding the condition that Team Lotus crew members should stay on in the States.

It was accepted that car No 70 ('56/3') would be Graham's. Andy proposed that the quickest of the four cars, Mike Spence's original chassis '56/1' (race No 60), be parked in STP's garage until a 'top American driver was obtained', and that No 20 ('56/4'), officially entered for Jackie Stewart, be prepared by our Team crew for Jackie to run when he was able. Jackie soon got wind of this and indicated both his concern and displeasure; it had to be car 60 he drove or he would consider withdrawal. Joe Leonard continued to practise his 'Vel's Parnelli Jones Ford' and Art Pollard his *Thermo-King Special* entered by Don Gerhardt.

Meanwhile, Derek Gardner, having found the transmission oil pumps not man enough for the task, was busy sketching a new increased-capacity unit complete with revised oil pump drive.

Derek: 'I left the manufacture to Joe Baber's engineering shop nearby, and they produced an excellent unit. The pump rotor people quickly arrived with lots of bits and pieces, and from then on everything proved more than adequate.'

Five days after the accident Mike's time still remained unbeaten.

CHAPTER TEN

1968:
Turbocar Twilight

Colin was back in his office at Hethel on 9 May, preparing himself for another emotionally draining funeral, that of Mike Spence, the following Tuesday in Bray church, near Maidenhead. Meanwhile Jim Endruweit led the Formula 1 crew to Spain to attend to Graham Hill's sole Type 49 entry; although a new 49 to 'B' specification had been taken, Colin gave orders that it was not to be run, so Graham had to make do with '49/1'. But once again he pulled the rabbit from the hat, cheering everyone with a great win, his first Grand Prix victory ever in a Lotus!

Then came an internal problem within Team. Making a telephone call to Jim Endruweit, I was informed that he no longer worked for us! As he had been a stalwart member of Team Lotus for the past ten very long years, this came as a considerable shock, and it was not until I returned to England over a month later that I discovered what had taken place.

In the week following the Spanish race he was called into Colin's office to face both the Old Man and Fred Bushell. Colin explained that he desperately wanted someone of quality, knowledge and experience to run Lotus Cars' service department; it had hitherto been run by a director who had proved totally incapable and was now in a desperate state trying to cope with a spate of production car problems. Colin gave Jim the weekend to think it over; when Jim asked if he had an alternative, Colin replied, 'Not really – I advise you to take it!'

It seemed to Jim as if Colin really had 'walked away from racing', as he had stated publicly, and it was obvious that he was in a serious quandary about Team's future; therefore with the possibility of the organisation seriously contracting its activities, he accepted his new post.

Later, Colin would take the changes further, promoting Dick Scammell to the post of Racing Manager. He went to great lengths to explain that we were both in line to become directors, titles, however, that failed to attract either of us. Such 'promotions' merely meant an unchanged level of income with an even greater work load, and it was not long before we could see that the proposals were a concoction without foundation . . .

Back at Indy the technical scrutineers' inspection of car No 30 in which Mike had crashed ended on 8 May. They indicated offi-cially that there had been no failure, but as the cars were a new product they would be 'held off the track until their investigation was completed'. However, approval to run again came later that afternoon, although we would hear more from the Technical Committee. In the meantime, anticipating possible trouble, Maurice requested that the British Steel Corporation supply official confirmation that the material they had supplied to us was to the American requirement.

By 8 May there had been 53 interruptions to running for various reasons, or 15 per cent of possible running time. Then Southerner Lee Roy Yarbrough walked into our garage. Rumoured to have started his career driving souped-up cars for bootleggers in his home state of South Carolina, I was initially told that he was first and foremost a 'sedan driver' of the NASCAR fraternity, and a feeling of apprehension closed over me! I had met saloon car drivers, both before and after their single-seater accidents. Thirty-year-old Lee Roy had first appeared at the Speedway in 1965, but had not completed his 'rookie' test until the following year.

During his first run in the turbine I was surprised each time he safely crossed the start/finish line, although there was no good reason for such pessimism. He had not told me that he was a winner of Grand National NASCAR events and had held the Daytona lap record twice, the second time at over 183 mph. Then again, he had wiped out two Indy cars in 1967, one in a collision, and in 1969 would break the Speedway's record for a 'moving accident' with 1 1/4 miles accomplished after hitting the wall leaving Turn Four and losing a wheel, but not coming to a halt until Turn Two! Later he qualified 8th, so perhaps my agitation was merited.

When he came into the pits I asked him how he had got on.

'I tell ya, I'm used to sitting inside these things,' he said, 'and I find it funny having the wind in my face!'

In the evening we were chatting in the garage when a telephone call came through for him.

'Oh my Lord,' I heard him say, then he cupped his hand over the mouthpiece and told me, 'Ma house is on fire.'

Lee Roy remained cool and calm as he listened to the dreadful tale of woe from his neighbour. Then he asked the neighbour if he thought he could get into the roof area without anyone noticing to rescue some boxes he wanted, but the chance seemed slim. When he put the phone down he said, 'I've got a whole stack of race cash up there – sure hope he can do something!' He did not reappear, so I never heard the outcome ...

Outside, our garage area looked like a used car lot, with our old Type 42F standing forlorn and slightly rusty with a large 'For Sale' notice on it and with crates of spares alongside, including our remaining two- and five-speed ZF gearboxes. Because of shortage of space in the garage, I had arranged some months earlier to store the car with Betty Packard, the widow of a former racing driver who lived just outside the Speedway on West 15th. Unfortunately the move was made at dead of night, and I hadn't noticed large holes in her garage roof. Consequently, when we retrieved the car its cockpit was full of water, it was rusty and the crew had to waste time bulling it up for sale. Now it was on display, its sign assuring that the lucky buyer could also have two Ford V8s, spares *and* a race entry; STP had six for five cars, so Andy agreed to throw in the spare to complete a nice package. But there was hardly a rush to buy, despite the local press doing some rather jokey articles about it, describing it as the car in which 'Graham Whatsisname drove 23 laps'. It was for sale at £1,750 ($4,000), but there were no takers ...

Rumours were abroad of another Mount Fuji race early in 1969, news that again had fired up Colin before he had left. I cabled and telephoned Hubert Schroeder at the FIA in Paris to register our strongest protest. At the same time Bobby Johns, our 1965 driver, was still trying to obtain a credit on the tax that had been deducted from his purse (by reason of the gross being taxed for a foreign team), so I visited the revenue offices in Indianapolis to try to resolve the problem.

On Friday and Saturday 9–10 May rain caused considerable disruption, but fortunately not to us as Graham was racing in Spain. Then on the Sunday we were hit by a broadside from the Technical Committee. In a letter simultaneously released to the press, Harlan Fengler drew our attention to certain Type 56 components that did not comply with USAC requirements, adding that there was no evidence of deficiencies in our cars but that new parts would have to be made and fitted. The ruling covered steering and suspension parts, which, although covered by British certificates of manufacture confirming their equivalency or better in material strengths, did not satisfy the Committee. We would be allowed to qualify on the original components, but new ones would be required for the race.

Rather than run the risk of the same thing happening with new parts made from British material, we immediately purchased the American materials specified by USAC and shipped them back to the factory for four new car sets to be made.

Late on 11 May came word that STP would wheel out Mike's original car No 60 for Mario Andretti to sample the next day; if the outcome was successful, there would have to be agreement on the sum of compensation to be paid to Mario's principal spon-

sor. Both Mario and Lloyd Ruby sampled the car, although their current contracts soon dispelled any thoughts of their jumping ship. Mario lapped at 168.4, Lloyd at 166.5.

Mario wrote later: 'Andy had been romancing me heavily to try one of his turbines. So I took a whack at it, and received a jolt. Within a few laps I had hit 168.4 mph, which was considerably faster than I had travelled in my turbo Ford. While I kept some reservations about turbines, I was amazed by its handling characteristics. It was by far the best-balanced and easiest-handling car I had ever tried. I was positive that, with a few days' practice, I could push it over 170 with no trouble at all ...'

Although a deal with STP could have been signed on the spot, Mario was not going to dump both his hard-working crew and his good friends and sponsors, Overseas National Airways, so any romance between him and the STP-Lotus turbines ended there. However, there would be another development in the story before that happened.

The next day Art Pollard was back for another run in the '67 STP Paxton turbine. After he had whistled round at 168 mph he returned to the pits to find Joe Leonard awaiting his turn. Joe, a soft-spoken 33-year-old Californian, had began racing on motor cycles 18 years previously, winning three National Championships and being runner-up in four. His score of 27 victories in major motor cycle races was a record. He had started driving midget cars in 1958, then stock cars, before turning in a USAC Championship ride, appearing at the Speedway in '65 driving for Dan Gurney's All American Racers, then A. J. Foyt's organisation, when he qualified fifth and finished third in 1967. In the turbine he was soon up to 167 mph, only for the car to get away from him in Turn One. He smacked the wall hard. He was OK, but the car certainly was not ...

Andy Granatelli didn't mince his words: 'If we had a red-hot driver signed we'd rebuild later. But we haven't and we won't. Next year it will be outclassed so we'll put it in a museum some place.'

The possible controversy over who would drive which car petered out when Jackie Stewart got the thumbs down at his next meeting with the medics; with a brittle bone structure, the scaphoid bone in his wrist was now found to have suffered a hairline crack in his Formula 2 accident, and his recovery period would encompass both qualifying weekends. His forced withdrawal meant that Graham now held the fort alone, while Andy scouted round for suitable (and available) drivers ...

Then on 15 May Colin returned to the Speedway. This was completely unheralded, and he merely gave his customary 'Hi', picked up his briefcase and proceeded as if nothing had occurred.

Later that day I put out a press release saying that the Technical Committee's requirement for new parts, together with Stewart's enforced withdrawal, had served to alter Colin's earlier decision not to participate. 'I thought Mike and Jimmy would want me back here, so it's only right that I return to Indianapolis.'

Meanwhile, the track's statistics office continued to issue a

STP-Lotus recruits for the 1968 '500' – Joe Leonard and Art Pollard. (Both Indianapolis Motor Speedway)

mass of information, including news that the yellow lights had gone on when a turtle had been found circulating the track . . .

Thursday 16 May saw Joe Leonard welcomed on board, and he started his acclimatisation runs in No 60 with over 36 hours left before qualifying. Bobby Unser (Eagle Turbo Offy) had just become the first driver to break the 170 mph barrier (170.778 mph) when Joe began working up to speed. Two hours after Unser's record lap, and on a day plagued by gusting winds, Joe suddenly clocked 170.422 mph, a remarkable achievement. He waxed lyrical about the car; in his opinion a piston-engined car was no match for a turbine. 'It's like comparing a Mustang with a Thunderbird, or a Chevvy with a Cadillac . . .' he said.

Art Pollard also jumped ship from his initially designated team, and he was now circulating in No 20.

The next day was the last before qualifying, but it was rained off just over an hour after the track had opened (28 hours of practice had been wiped out by rain), so Joe and Art were to qualify with only minimum running experience. There were 84 entries for the race, of which 42 were to attempt qualifying.

Meanwhile Pratt & Whitney's 'Flame-Out Fred' Cowley was monitoring the running of his turbines. Contrary to some accounts, alleging that we had switched from kerosene to gasoline to achieve higher speeds, both the STP and Team Lotus turbines had run on AMOCO (American Oil Corporation) pure ISO 100 octane lead-free gasoline from the very beginning of tests and continued to do so during May practice. With the fuel was mixed a quantity of STP fuel additive to provide fuel pump lubrication.

During Colin's absence a situation crept up on us that was to cause much animosity – the question of who was our Chief Mechanic. From the outset Team Lotus's Dick Scammell had been responsible for building and testing these cars, and his crew consisted of Arthur 'Butty' Birchall, Jim 'High Idle' Pickles, Douggie Garner, Scotsman Bill 'Willie' Cowe and Hywel 'Hughie' Absalom, all of whom had worked long and hard to produce our four magnificent cars. But soon after arrival at Indy the newspapers and other media were soon crediting 'Big Vince' Granatelli as our 'chief spanner', and he was soon explaining how he had engineered and built our cars. At first Dick and his colleagues laughed this off as a bad joke, but as the days passed the indignation grew. The STP propaganda mill was churning out statements about its design and construction of the cars, and it became clear that I would have to do something about it . . .

A solution had to be found. Fortunately Dick was willing to forsake the abused title of Chief Mechanic without any strings attached, so I approached Andy purely to resolve the split of monies earned. I argued that the total prize monies due to the mechanics, plus the cash equivalents of 'gifts in kind', should be split 20 per cent to the STP men, who had only just appeared on the scene, and 80 per cent to our Team Lotus lads.

Andy turned this down flat, and when Colin returned he told me that he was fed up to the back teeth with such haggling, and that we would make up the difference.

Soon after, Colin resumed writing letters to Andy. Both were frequently tied up with press gatherings and sponsor and trade meetings, and their paths seemed only to cross at distracting functions. In our case, Colin always preferred to put his feelings on paper to save time later explaining a situation to lawyers!

He opened his first letter on an admonitory note: 'You now have a disillusioned friend and if things are not settled very quickly you may have an extremely bitter associate.' He described how he had submerged his Team's identity beneath the red paint and STP banner for the two previous years, and he would be happy to continue that way; but now he wanted nothing of the 'partnership' or 'co-operative deal' that the relationship had grown into because of the strains imposed. Another point concerned the crash damage to car No 30; Colin regarded this as an STP-owned vehicle and wanted Andy to accept the repair costs in writing. Finally, he pointed out that he had signed the STP agreement with which Andy had presented him in Mexico only as a result of Andy's requirement to have something on paper for his board; now Colin wanted ratified the agreement that he had presented to Andy earlier in 1968.

I presented this letter to Andy, but although Colin waited around for a presumed meeting nothing happened. The next morning Colin wrote again, saying that time was definitely running out and that unless something was agreed before midnight the following day (on the eve of qualifying) he 'would have to take whatever steps are necessary to protect my interests and to restrain the cars from running henceforth.' He feared that unless he took such a stand nothing would ever be achieved . . .

At the eleventh hour a deal was finally thrashed out: the agreement between the two organisations would revert to that of previous years – put simply, STP would run their show and we would run ours.

Around 260,000 spectators attended qualifying on 18 May. Amid all the noise of the fanfares it was a delight to stand beside our cars as they whistled away at high rpm with no strain on the eardrums – for this reason alone I had been a turbine devotee from the start.

In the draw for qualifying start position I drew a 3 for Graham (which was good, as he could then run early and make a relaxed departure for Europe) and 17 for Art Pollard (which was not so good as it would fall in the hottest part of the day).

We could not have asked more from Graham. His first timed lap was 171.887 mph (52.36 seconds for the 2$\frac{1}{2}$ miles), his second 0.2 seconds slower, the next .07 down, his last a fraction quicker; one-tenth of a second equalled 0.32 mph average speed. His four-lap qualifying average was therefore a scintillating 171.208 mph, and as he rolled into the pit lane for the customary interview Colin actually broke down and cried, while Andy planted a wet kiss on Graham's grimacing face. Bobby Unser's run in his Eagle Turbo Offy averaged 169.507 mph, and by the time the American's run ended Graham was on his way to the airport, he and us secure in the knowledge that he had taken pole.

Later in the day came Joe Leonard in Mike Spence's original (and very fast) car. With only the minimum of experience in the Type 56 (Andy was to say later that Joe had done a mere 20 laps) he set off. His first lap was exactly the same as Graham's, causing the spectators to go wild. His second lap was fractionally quicker – the fastest ever known at the Speedway – and the crowd went wild again. His final two laps were slightly slower, but still fractionally faster than Graham's. All four laps averaged over 171 mph, his average being 171.559 mph, and his elapsed time for them 3.29.84 to Graham's 3.30.27. It was a record-breaking run that clinched pole position, with Graham second, the first time in 19 years that team-mates had qualified 1st and 2nd for the Indy '500'. Part of Joe's substantial pole prize was a cheque for $6,000 from Coca-Cola, the first time that the drinks company featured monetarily at a motor race.

Art's run came later in the day after a mere six laps in his car, and he set 11th fastest time at 166.297 mph for a place on row four. While our jubilant crew tidied the garage before enjoying a celebratory dinner, Andy scratched out an agreement to suit Colin. STP would pay $80,000 for the option of purchasing prior to 8 June any or all three of the remaining race cars at $40,000 each (less engines) plus a full complement of spares, value not to exceed $10,000 per car. The essential components required were listed, and interestingly these included fuel bladders, which would increase each car's capacity to maximum.

Additionally, STP would be responsible for Art Pollard's fees; the agreement called for signature within three days, after which it would be null and void. Colin signed it back in England and immediately requested payment before the race.

As time drew near for Colin and Hazel to return to Europe the rain simply hissed down. I arranged a helicopter for their departure, but predictably the pilot's designated landing spot was not near enough for Colin; he had brought three heavy suitcases as well as his excessively heavy briefcase. When I reminded him of the chopper, he turned on Hazel and myself and said, 'Come on you two – let's get a move on!'

So saying he left the garage, empty handed, and plunged into the deluge outside. Hazel picked up one suitcase and his briefcase, I the two remaining suitcases. I was wearing a sweat-inducing plastic raincoat, and we followed our 'genius', still unencumbered by any luggage, slipping and sliding in the quagmire, in the general direction of the chopper. He roared off ahead, leaving us loaded to the gunwales and both mumbling loud but unheard protests. Fortunately the roar of the helicopter drowned out my loud shout of 'Whoopee!' as it staggered into the air . . . The Old Man had gone, and we could relax again.

Our winning of pole position was to rub fresh salt into our Team Lotus crew's wounds. 'Big Vince' was wildly feted and interviewed, and more was to come at the pole position extravaganza at the Murat Temple the following Wednesday, the invitations being plastered with Vince's name. The only reason our crew attended was to keep score of the numerous prizes and monetary awards. The only physical awards items to find their way to England were the four road tyres awarded by Firestone and the 500 gallons of fuel awarded by Humble Oil and arranged through Esso Petroleum, the tools, equipment, suits and mass of other goodies being translated into money.

Only Jochen Rindt qualified on the second day before rain washed out the proceedings. The following day of normal practice was similarly interrupted, although Pollard was now lapping nearly 2 mph faster than he had qualified. On 22 May Leonard, encumbered with a full fuel load, was lapping consistently at over 169 mph.

Rain, plus the usual accidents, played a major part in the week preceding second qualifying; Sunday was delayed by a wet track until an hour after the usual closing time, Monday then being scheduled for the remaining cars to qualify. The infield was reduced to a quagmire, and light aircraft owners were advised to leave the sodden Weir Cook airport and use outlying airports, with aircraft over 12,500 lbs guaranteed hard standing. One car was initially disqualified for being underweight, but later reinstated when the scales were found inaccurate. The Chief Mechanic, Wally Meskowski, called in the Weights & Measures Bureau and the scales were found to be off by 6, 10, 15 and 19 lbs using 2,000 lb weights. Wally's enthusiasm earned him a $100

Qualifying weekend saw the Speedway grandstands packed – as usual – providing a noisy background to the STP-Lotus crew lined up behind Graham's 56. (Indianapolis Motor Speedway)

Easy-going, immensely popular – and quick enough – Art Pollard & Co with STP's 56. (Indianapolis Motor Speedway)

fine for improper conduct! Another serious crash left 'rookie' Bob Hurt paralysed when he broke his neck in Turn One.

Ferguson's Derek Gardner was finding his hours constantly extended as the transmission systems were closely scrutinised and torque splits discussed: 'Checking the differential clearances was a lengthy business, as to gain access the fore-and-aft drive systems and many other components had to be removed. If the crew started at 5 pm it would be around midnight before they finished. From the initial 50/50 (front/rear) torque split, I had a 30/70 sent out from England early in the month, then tried a 32/68. At one stage I spent two days locked up in my motel room designing a new one . . . There were eventually six or seven variations.'

'All four cars suffered from vibration at high speeds; I think Joe Leonard's tunnel vision somehow proved a compensation, but Art reported that it was so bad his eyeballs were going into a flutter until the tears caused by it blurred his vision. This was not a serious problem for the short practice runs, but we obviously had to correct it for the race. At first we thought the transmission

system was the cause, but then we discovered significant variations in the tyres so we carefully matched them into car sets. In fact, the transmission systems proved trouble-free throughout practice and the race.'

Contrary to media reports made at the time and inevitably repeated since, the first two grid positions had not been achieved by switching between kerosene and gasoline.

Fred Cowley: 'As far as I know there were no changes made to the Team Lotus or STP engines. I was responsible for all the adjustments made for qualification and either performed them personally or watched while they were done. Despite working the engines hard we suffered no internal engine fault during the month of May. We did have one at Far Hills oval where I warned Andy of the inevitable consequences; also in the Hockenheim Formula 1 race that would follow in 1971, in which the oil system was over-serviced, but even then we repaired the engine, shipping it back and returning it to Europe in the space of one week.

'I must say I enjoyed the race programme thoroughly and in all my extensive dealings with Colin Chapman our relationship remained excellent, both on and off the track. I have many personal memories of dealing with both him and Hazel, and flying with Colin on occasion.'

Sunday's final qualifying was rained off and only completed on the Monday. Only 'Carburation Day' on the Tuesday allowed final pre-race running; our new suspension parts had been fitted and running was vital to set up the cars. Due to the 20 days of rain that had afflicted practice, assembly and final preparation of the pit fuel bowsers was late, and the drivers were warned to exert special care in the pit road. Even the three hours allotted for running were rain-dampened, and after only a half an hour the period was halted with another promised for the following morning.

All three of our cars ran in this aborted first session; Joe Leonard's car now sported a 'Day-glo' 'chartreuse' nose to distinguish it, and he was fastest at close on 167 mph, Pollard second at 164.8 mph, and Graham unable to crack 160 mph.

The weather was more favourable for the elaborate '500' Festival Parade in the city that evening; over 250,000 spectators cheering the vintage cars, blaring bands, race drivers, dancing girls, clowns, squads of drum majorettes and garishly coloured floats. The road in front of the reviewing stand was covered by a 37,000-square-foot chequered carpet!

Graham's amazing ability to keep pulling rabbits from hats continued at Monaco, where his second consecutive win in the Type 49 marked Team's third victory in the year's opening three Championship races, and the crew's spirits continued to rise. From the Principality the usual hurried return was made to the Speedway for the '500' the following Thursday. While he was away Joe Leonard ran consistent laps at over 169 mph on a full fuel load.

At this time I formed an association with a girl named 'Siggy', a German naturalised American. She was dynamite, with a voice to match. As Dick Scammell remarked, she was 'the only woman I know who can drown out 33 cars on a starting grid by yelling good luck to me.' Siggy's driving matched her explosive character, and taking me home after a late night she jumped some lights, and I was thrown out of the passenger door onto the road in the resulting 'T-bone' collision with another car. Fortunately I survived the experience with only severe shock.

The month saw me invited in an official capacity to two interesting events. The first was as an honorary guest at the Indianapolis heat for the Soap Box Derby Championship for boys aged 11 to 15. Sponsored by Chevrolet in conjunction with radio and TV stations, major tyre companies, newspapers, and civic groups across America, there were 50,000 entrants overall. Each boy had to build his own car within a set of regulations, and most had gone out and obtained their own sponsorship. As one entrant, a school in Cleveland, ran its soapbox as *The Jim Clark Special – Team Lotus*, I was asked by the organisers to attend as a member of Team. I thoroughly enjoyed it, but sadly I was back in England by the time 'our' entry ran and never did hear the result.

I then had to present a prize at a figure-of-eight race meeting, which I soon decided was public suicide! Each driver had to make a lightning decision at each crossover (there being nothing so cissy as a bridge) whether to aim behind or ahead of the car crossing his path, and with the fastest qualifiers starting from the back of the field, all hell was let loose when the starter dropped his flag. Held in the late evening, there were families and very young children in the packed spectator enclosures. At the end of the programme I was shown to the podium, but nobody showed up for their prizes so I followed some officials down to the race paddock, where our entry was barred by some large guards. We were told we would have to wait as there was a race car owners' meeting going on.

Suddenly there came the sound of shouting and scuffling accompanied by some loud thumps, and a group of owners and drivers burst into view in an enormous free-for-all punch-up. As it seemed that the 'meeting' would not end happily, I bade farewell to the officials and made my exit ...

Although Colin and Andy's latest agreement had been an unusually short one-page document, Colin had warned me that he was expecting an even longer addendum, and sure enough one was delivered to our Howard Johnson Motel in the small hours of race morning, shortly after Colin and I had left STP's race-eve cocktail and dinner party. Two and a half pages long, Colin merely passed it to me at breakfast to arrange a meeting with our Indianapolis lawyers some time after the race. By this time we had on the books three individual legal practices.

Every meeting with Andy was an event to relish. He always stayed in the same suite at the back of the Speedway Motel, complete with office and sitting room for his many business meetings. Another office adjoined for his delightful and highly efficient secretary, Mrs Ange Green, who regardless of the traumas surrounding her always had a smile on her face. It was said that Andy only slept two or three hours a night and spent most of his waking hours at work. Certainly his enormous output bore testimony to this.

When we were working at STP in Des Plaines one Saturday, Andy had suggested we continue the following day. 'I'll be in the office usual time,' he said. On arrival, I found him surrounded by fellow Italians from all walks of life to whom Andy introduced me, but whether they were family or friends I never discovered.

Race morning, 30 May, saw us having our usual early morning breakfast at the motel. Graham, Colin and I were joined by timekeeper Cyril Audrey and Jabby Crombac. Earlier in the month I had befriended the weather bureau staff at Weir Cook Airport to ensure quality forecasts. The day promised showers at one-third race distance, with the sun returning for the afternoon.

Timekeeper Cyril Audrey devised a plan to assist us with our inefficient lap scoring arrangements. Basically this was to have a person sited in the back row of the Tower Terrace stand immediately behind the pits, a relatively high vantage point, armed with a two-way radio. The operator there could establish the positions of every car in the field by viewing them down the back straight.

```
INDIANAPOLIS.....
CLIMATIC DATA FOR MAY 30TH... 1871 TO 1967  FOR INDIANAPOLIS INDIANA

TEMPERATURES.......
MAXIMUM...HIGHEST 94 IN 1859  LOWEST 58 IN 1915   NORMAL 77
MINIMUM...LOWEST   37 IN 1889 AND 1947.  HIGHEST 74 IN 1874 AND 1942
          NORMAL  55.

PRECIPITATION ...
1871 TO 1967   36  DAYS WITH MEASUREABLE AMOUNTS.


FOR THE PERIOD  1956 TO 1967
TEMPERATURES MAXIMUM 85 IN 1956
MINIMUM 42 IN 1961.

PRECIPITATION .....
1956 TO 1967   5 DAYS .... 42  PERCENT .. WITH MEASUREABLE AMOUNTS.

YEAR     PRECIPITATION    APPROXIMATE TIME OF OCCURRENCE
1956        0.24         2AM TO 3.AM AND 6PM TO MIDNIGHT
 57         0.49         4.30PM TO 9PM
 58         TRACE        11PM TO 11.30PM
 59         TRACE        MIDNIGHT TO 2AM AND 10AM TO 12.30PM
 60         0.26         1AM TO 5AM
 61         NONE
 62         0.17         2AM TO 7.30AM
 63         NONE
 64         NONE
 65         TRACE        MIDNIGHT TO 12.08AM
 66         NONE
 67         .21          11AM TO 3.30PM  4PM TO MIDNIGHT.
```

'Climatic data for May 30th 1871 to 1967 . . .' One of the services provided by the author's new friends in the Weir Cook weather bureau. (Author's collection)

It was also essential that the radio system should cut out the race noises, and coupled to this was the need for an accurate electronic lap scorer as a back-up. I went to Pye for the radio and Golay, the Swiss watch manufacturer, for Breitling timing equipment, then Cathodeon Electronics for ancillary items. The position of the seat for the observer was absolutely crucial due to various items interrupting his view, and when I contacted the Speedway's ticket office, whose staff were always extremely helpful, I found that all the vital seats had been reserved for many years in advance. Then, on the pretext that the local press from Norwich, England, were planning to attend the race, I applied for press stand tickets, but all to no avail.

A poll of the racing press considered Graham favourite to win with odds of 5–3, our three cars being reckoned to turn the event into a two-part affair with the piston-engined cars suffering from reduced race performance. Granatelli, asked for his opinion, reckoned 'his' cars would have lapped the field by the 100-mile mark. Also heavily backed was Al Unser's *Retzloff Chemical Special*, which was the only other 4WD entry, a Lola with a turbo Ford V8 engine.

We were at the garages by 6.30 am, and proceedings began at 8.30 when the cars were pushed to the pit lane. Right on schedule the loudspeakers boomed out track-owner Tony Hulman's famous exhortation: 'Gentlemen – start your engines'. As thousands of balloons floated into the sky, 300,000 spectators saw the pack move off with William Ford, grandson of Henry, piloting the Ford Torino Pace Car with an astronaut alongside him handling radio contact and former driver Duke Nalon in its back seat. Their orders were to run at 75 to 80 mph down the back straight, then accelerate out of the fourth turn to 100 mph. If the grid was in correct formation the Pace Car would then dive into the pit entrance and the race would be on.

Fortunately all went to plan and, as the green flag waved, Joe Leonard took the lead followed by Bobby Unser and Mario Andretti, Graham sixth and Pollard eleventh. Mario only covered a lap and a bit before his Brawner-Brabham-Ford holed a piston and his team's second car was called in for him to take over. Again a piston failed, and Andretti was out for good by lap 25.

On lap 8, to the great delight of the enormous crowd, Bobby Unser roared past Leonard and started to extend his lead, breaking the previous record average for the first 50 miles at 162.997 mph, with Graham fifth and Pollard 10th. By this time Leonard was closely tailing Unser, but when the two encountered traffic, Joe dropped back to a 4-second margin. Hill was now fifth, Pollard 11th 14 seconds behind him. Turbine power was lacking the necessary grunt to pass piston-engined cars easily, Leonard saying later that he was 30 bhp short of qualifying power for reliability.

Lap 40 and Pollard headed for the pits, the first of our cars to refuel, a stop lasting 19 seconds. At the same time Bobby Unser's brother, Al, became the eighth retirement when he hit the wall in Turn One, taking two wheels off his 4WD Lola; wreckage from his accident hit Gary Bettenhausen's following car, injuring one of his legs so badly that he was forced to retire. Another car hit one of the loose wheels.

The cautionary yellow lights saw many cars stop for fuel, including the two leaders, Lloyd Ruby, by dint of a quicker car, assuming the advantage. It was lap 90 before Unser retook the lead at a record race average of 159.033 mph. Leonard tailed Ruby before retaking second place five laps later, then it was Graham trailing Ruby, Pollard circulating ninth. Gurney (Eagle) and Foyt (Coyote) enjoyed a classic battle that regularly saw them just a second apart over 160 miles, but it ended when Foyt encountered engine failure.

At half distance our three cars were circulating in the first nine, the first three in the race covered by just 5 seconds. Then on lap 110 came disaster. Graham lost a right-front wheel and hit the wall leaving Turn Two, sliding along it for 200 feet.

Mechanic Doug Garner: 'Some front suspension components on the 56 were a tight fit, especially around the top rocking arm pivot bearing, which took most of the load at that corner. The pin locating the pivot bearing was secured by a solid bush, which was welded into a two-legged plate riveted to the chassis, and the way everything was laid out meant that we had to grind away a section of the bush as well as the chassis to get sufficient clearance. There was a slight variation between the individual chassis; Graham's car needed more grinding than the others, and this was the point where it tore out, sending him into the wall.'

'Butty' Birchall: 'I remember the night before the race we had a confab about the weakness in the steel of the chassis at that point, and we stole back into the garage around 4 am on race morning to add some weld there . . .'

Under the yellow Unser made another fuel stop, leaving the lead to Leonard until he, too, pitted and Bobby retook the lead. Lap 140 and only 2 seconds covered the first three, Leonard (third) hampered by that lack of 30 bhp. After his second stop, Pollard held ninth place before gaining on the cars ahead. By lap 130 he was seventh and still gaining.

By lap 150 (three-quarter distance) Unser still led but was closely followed by Ruby, Leonard adrift by 5 seconds and slipping further back as he stopped for more fuel on lap 156, 16 seconds being enough to take on the amount required for the final 44 laps to the finish. But Ruby also stopped for fuel, so they were now only 1 second apart.

When Unser made his third and final stop for fuel on lap 167, he led by almost a lap, but his stop took 26 seconds while Ruby and Leonard inherited first and second places. Unser also had a gearbox problem and only just managed to get away in top gear.

Ruby's inherited lead lasted for only eight laps before a misfire set in and he made a long stop. Leonard, then running just 4 seconds adrift, assumed first place. He led Unser by 8 seconds,

Pollard was now seventh and the hearts of our crew picked up a beat.

On lap 183, 42 miles from the chequered flag, a car hit the wall, taking out much brickwork and catching fire. The first two of the safety crew's fire extinguishers failed to operate and the blaze was a lengthy one, as was the accompanying yellow-light period, which allowed everyone to close up upon race-leader Leonard.

The yellow lights were extinguished just nine laps from the finish, when the loud pedals were pressed, and as they went down so did Leonard's turbine. Joe held up his hand as the car lost speed on the main straight watched by an astonished crowd. The fuel pump shaft had sheared. Then, heartbreakingly, just a lap later Pollard's car followed suit – his fuel pump shaft had also sheared.

The Offy enthusiasts were well rewarded by Unser's victorious drive, seeing their favoured engine in an American Eagle chassis back in the limelight after a lapse of four years and a month of 'turbine fever'. Just five cars completed the 200 laps, with 11 still

Race day 1968 – Joe Leonard shimmers away from his last pit stop. A tense Andy Granatelli wills on the car and driver alike. (Indianapolis Motor Speedway)

running. Unser's race average was a new record of 152.882 mph, despite the race having been slowed by the yellows for a total of 47 minutes. He had led for 127 laps, Ruby 42, Leonard 31, the trio dominating the race throughout.

When Derek Gardner inspected the transmission of Leonard's car he discovered what he described as a 'quite unbelievable' sight. 'There was just a charred mess of a greatly overheated system that was virtually wrecked, the heat having even warped the casing; the oil had carbonised and there was what appeared to be coal dust everywhere. When I looked further I found that the oil pipes sited under the car had been flattened from what I presume was Joe making an excursion. It had obviously run in this condition for a long time and I've no reason to think that it would finally have failed over those last few miles. Overall, it said a lot for the transmission that it had survived so long!'

Following that 1968 race various reasons were put forward for the failure of the two fuel pump shafts. The most popular reason was that we had switched from kerosene to gasoline just before the race, and that the lack of kerosene's natural lubrication had been the cause. However, as Fred Cowley recalled: 'The reason for the failure of the two shafts at the same time was never discovered, although the same pumps were used in the Milwaukee race ten days later. I believe that a combination of several laps of yellow when pump cooling would have been severely affected and the lower lubrication quality of the fuel may have been the combination that caused momentary seizure of the vane pumps. But we will probably never know. It was certainly not clear that a steel shaft would have fared any better. I had ordered the phosphor-bronze shafts to be fitted because they were developed with the engine, in spite of the rather well-made shafts Colin Chapman had prepared. I may have been motivated by a preference to run bronze against the steel engine and pump drives, rather than steel-on-steel, since lubrication was not all that good.'

He was sure that all three cars ran phosphor-bronze pump shafts, but the story has persisted that a stronger steel shaft had been fitted in Graham's crashed car. 'Butty' Birchall recalled a conversation he had with Chapman the day before the race, in which they discussed fuel pump drives. Worried about what he felt was a frail bronze drive, 'Butty' had plumped for the steel quill-shaft equivalent for Graham's car, and the Old Man's response had been 'go ahead and fit it just as long as you're sure it will last'. 'Flame out' Fred obviously was not let in on the secret.

Granatelli, after his two near misses at victory in almost a year, was not keen to discuss the reason for failure. 'Does it really matter what went wrong?' he said. 'It wasn't my time. Now let's see if they [USAC] ban turbines. There weren't any Offenhausers out there that couldn't blow us off the track. We were running 420 to 450 hp and they were running 620 to 650. In traffic it was evident that they could slaughter us. The turbines didn't have the horsepower to pass.'

Prize-giving was held the following evening at the Murat Temple, Colin assiduously noting in his usual small and neat handwriting every sum of money announced, nudging me every

time a large sum was cited. The total prize and accessory money for the race was $712,269, Unser's share being $177,523. Leonard was classified 12th, Pollard 13th and Graham 19th, their gross prize monies $37,403, $12,833 and $13.693 respectively, Graham's income boosted by his second place on the starting grid. Team Lotus's share from all three cars totalled $13,000 (gross).

While the Team Lotus crew packed for home, STP prepared for its next race at Milwaukee the following weekend. Our contract called for ownership of all four Type 56s to pass to STP for its ongoing programme of racing turbines for the remainder of the USAC Championship trail. Andy wanted the two turbines damaged in the Spence/Hill accidents ('56/2' and '56/3' respectively) to be returned to Hethel for immediate repairs. While such arrangements were being activated, Colin and I spent whatever time Granatelli had spare tying up the loose ends of the contract and re-examining its specified spares lists, as well as detailing those that STP wanted delivered from England quickly. Also, after the failure of Graham's car, Andy wanted the front frames of his two current cars strengthened, and Colin explained the modifications to our remaining mechanics. Of most importance were the discussions concerning a suitable 3-litre equivalent suitable turbine for Formula 1. With Leonard's transmission cooked beyond repair, Derek Gardner fitted the prototype aluminium unit that Ferguson had produced prior to manufacture in magnesium.

Team Lotus mechanic Doug Garner had been seconded to the STP camp at their request early in the month and had been delighted to hear that they all finished work promptly at lunchtime, eating in a pleasant restaurant outside the track. They again stopped work at 6 pm, and Doug thought that he had gone to heaven until he discovered that such liberal living would not apply to him.

Doug: 'The day after the race I watched "Little Vince" unpacking and listing all the various spares we had and ticking each off his lists. After some time he turned to Andrew Ferguson and said, "Some of these spares have been used." When Andrew replied that there was nothing in the contract specifying that they should be new, there was a deathly silence and I thought, "My God, we're going to be done in our beds, horse's heads and all that." Our lads always jokingly reckoned STP was a Mafia organisation, so it all figured!'

The clearing-up process continued for the next two days, and on the Sunday evening Colin took our crew (Graham had already returned to England for a Formula 2 race that Monday) to a dinner at the Lamplighter Inn, a popular venue with live entertainment. I arrived late – just in time to have the bill handed to me! As I surveyed the sum, the maitre d' told me that the Speedway's senior doctor, Dr Hannah, was present and had supplied Colin's table with champagne with his compliments. It was an event that would have a far-reaching effect on my future with Team Lotus ...

On 2 June Colin and Andy signed another agreement. In this Andy laid down the requirements for Colin to provide the modification to the front frame sections in time for Milwaukee the next weekend. Also, of the mechanics seconded from Team Lotus, there had to be one 'with the capability of adjusting the chassis as required to make it handle', itself a confession that 'Big Vince's' title of Chief Mechanic was a sham. Andy also stressed that he wanted personally to select the spares comprising the $10,000 of components for each of the four cars, a fact that riled Colin, who saw no reason for not charging for spares that he had received free of charge from our trade support companies!

Colin left for England the next day, en route to the Belgian Grand Prix, as the USAC Rules Committee met in closed session to discuss the future of turbines. The committee members were all 'establishment' comprising piston-engined car entrants, their drivers and chief mechanics, and a short and sharp decision was quickly reached: turbines should be outlawed from 1 January 1969. This decision was then passed to the USAC Board for ratification, another body composed entirely of 'establishment' figures; senior member J. C. Agajanian commented before they met that he saw no reason for them decide to reach any other conclusion.

Although, when asked his opinion, 'Big Vince' Granatelli expressed his feeling that the Board would surely not want to be seen to be taking a backward step, Andy was more pragmatic, harbouring serious doubts as to the final outcome. He deeply regretted the news, especially as 'the 15-inch turbine formula has produced the most competitive "500" in decades'. Of that there was no doubt, Unser, Leonard and Ruby having been in contention for the victor's laurels for nearly 480 miles. The final decision was left for a Board meeting scheduled for early July, and although they did not follow the recommendation to the letter, they went so close as to make no odds.

From January 1970 turbines used in racing would have to be of the 'automotive' type (there were none), pending which the equivalency formula would be re-examined for the 1969 race. As to 4WD, all USAC cars from January 1970 would be restricted to two-wheel drive only, the USAC statement calling the 4WD system 'extremely expensive', a comment that stung Ferguson Research sufficiently to trigger a press release calling the USAC statement 'so lame as to be laughable', and claiming that the comment was merely a pretext for the ban.

The result of the meeting caused Granatelli to rethink his ownership of four 4WD turbine-engined cars bound to become redundant, although this must previously have seemed highly likely. He immediately wrote to Colin, asking that Team leave the two damaged cars untouched at Hethel until the final USAC decision be made. He also wanted Colin's confirmation that Ford V8 engines could replace the turbines in the 56s (setting a conversion cost limit of $10,000 per car), and that Team Lotus would continue to supply STP with car spares. Regarding Colin's Formula 1 turbine requirement, Andy confirmed that he had two Indy power units surplus to his requirements, which United Aircraft could convert accordingly for £10,000 each. Eventually Colin suggested swapping the Type 56s at Hethel (repaired) for

the Formula 1 modified turbines, but this idea was itself later dropped.

When the equivalency survey for the 1969 USAC season was announced in August, it put the last nails in the turbines' coffin. The air inlet area was further reduced, despite its 33 per cent cut after the 1967 race, by another 25 per cent, bringing the 23.999-square-inch allowance of 1967 right down to 11.999 square inches. Turbocharged engines were also reduced in capacity, from 2.8 litres to 2.65, but as this amounted to a mere 5.3 per cent it could simply be offset by an increase in boost pressure, the governing body's hostility towards gas turbine power (if any proof was needed) being writ large for the last time.

Additionally, for 1969, the last season of 4WD, such cars were limited to a maximum rim width of 10 inches, which suited us but restricted the Al Unser Lola, which had run 14-inch rear and 10-inch fronts. As the tyre engineers pointed out, they could easily change their tyre contours to bring the previous 'shoe' contact back to what it had been.

Along with mechanics 'Butty' Birchall, Doug Garner and 'High Idle' Pickles, seconded to STP to assist with preparation of the cars for Milwaukee, plus Fred Cowley and Derek Gardner, I was to stay in the States for the next two weeks, paying several visits to STP's HQ in Des Plaines as Team's Indy association with turbines slowly reached its conclusion and Colin focused more on obtaining similar power for his Formula 1 section.

I went to Milwaukee on a race-team charter flight, and as someone never entirely happy with flying, my mind was not put at rest by discovering that we were to travel on an ancient DC3 Dakota. The outward flight was acceptable, but when we boarded the aircraft for the return trip we found two crates of empty beer cans outside the flight crew's door, which suddenly opened to reveal a scruffy figure wearing a modicum of crew insignia topped by a bright-red face; giving us a glazed grin, he failing to notice the crates, tripped and accelerated past us down the tail-wheeled airliner's tilted aisle.

'Oh well,' someone said. 'At least we know the pilot's on board ...'

For the Milwaukee race, over 150 laps of the 1-mile oval, Ferguson Research engineer Derek Gardner found that a radical alteration had been made to STP's cars: 'In just the few days since the "500", somebody had modified the cars so they now had both inboard and outboard brakes. It was obvious that this had been done by STP personnel as the standard of workmanship could only be classified as "rude engineering", certainly not up to Team Lotus quality.'

Sadly the race disappointed after reassuring practice times. Pollard (115.861 mph) and Leonard (115.533 mph) qualified third and fourth respectively behind pole man Roger McCluskey, (116.204 mph) and Indy winner Bobby Unser, but neither lasted long, Leonard crashing on lap 38 and Pollard being black-flagged on lap 61 after visibly losing fuel.

Even more tragic was the terrible and fiery three-car accident on lap 3 that took race driver Ronnie Duman's life, seriously burned Norm Brown and inflicted lesser burns on Bay Darnell. I had got to know Ronnie's family very well during the month of May; his wife Betty came to my rescue when I was unable to find someone to sew and re-sew the cloth sponsor patches on driver and mechanic uniforms, as our trade support picture changed almost on a daily basis. Ronnie had finished sixth in the '500', an apparent change of fortune for this hard-working and enthusiastic driver, who had been burned badly in the 1964 Indy disaster. Consequently his death – following those of Jimmy and Mike – again hit me badly.

On the following Tuesday STP announced that it had sold Leonard's now bent Indy turbine (chassis '56/1') to Parnelli Jones to run under the long-winded name of *The Parnelli Jones Firestone-STP Special* in the remaining USAC races of 1968. Parnelli, according to the blurb, was keen to 'do all I can to continue pioneering this new idea in auto racing', and Andy also announced that he would make available other gas turbine engines to members of the racing fraternity. As he pointed out, a non-blown Ford race engine cost $27,000, a turbo version $40,000 and a turbo-Offy, which had made the Ford engines virtually obsolete at that time, $22,000. A gas turbine then cost $30,000, but with more customers would cost less, while its servicing costs over a season would be virtually nil ...

The USAC road race at Mosport, Canada, took place on the weekend after Milwaukee, and with his road-racing experience Graham Hill replaced Art Pollard, Parnelli Jones's ex-Leonard car a non-starter as it was still being repaired after its Milwaukee accident. Graham shunted his Type 56 in practice after hitting a patch of oil – he left the road, cleared a ditch and flew through the air for 30 feet before graunching along the rough for 200 feet – but not before showing its obvious potential by earning a place on the front row of the grid. His best time had been 1.22.35 compared to Denny Hulme's Can-Am record time of 1.20.7 and Jim Clark's previous best Formula 1 practice lap of 1.22.4.

Graham emerged unscathed, but the damage was sufficiently severe to make the 56 a non-starter. UA's Fred Cowley was on hand to inspect the chassis and his photographs, showing both ends torn around the suspension, were hurriedly air-mailed to Maurice Phillippe to assist him in making the necessary chassis changes and arranging for new parts to be flown out.

Graham reported that he had been pleasantly surprised by the car's handling on a road circuit, but that the throttle response had been poor.

Sadly, the promise of a new turbine era was not to be. Of the 12 remaining races, Leonard's result at Hanford was best, starting from pole to finish fourth, the next best Pollard's fifth at Castle Rock. Leonard had been running second in the closing stages when a half shaft broke, while Pollard had been third 5 miles from the finish when his throttle broke.

At August's Milwaukee '200' both cars ran 1st and 2nd well ahead of the field; on lap 122 Leonard had an inner joint break up, and 16 laps later Pollard's brake fluid had boiled away. Both cars broke both track and distance/speed records.

There were four races the cars did not enter, the only other event of note being December's 'musical chairs' race at Riverside where Mario Andretti and Bobby Unser, chasing the USAC Championship title down to the last race for all they were worth, both made pre-race plans to drive the 'back-up' cars. Mario only needed to finish fifth to gain the title, and, already sidelined in his *Overseas National Airways Special* Ford-engined car, hopped into Leonard's turbine, not knowing it was out of brakes, only to wreck it after his second lap when he collided with Pollard's similar car (in third), which also retired. He then relieved Lloyd Ruby and finished third, but having to share his race points it was all to no avail, Bobby Unser taking the title with 4330 points, just 11 more than Mario. If Mario had forsaken the turbine drive and taken Ruby's car he would have taken the title. It had been the closest National Championship finish in USAC history.

At Hethel the two Type 56s damaged at Indy were nearing completion by the end of July, awaiting turbines or perhaps piston engines from STP. Both had required new 'tubs' and suspension parts, and after completion the Team's fabricators carried on to build a slightly modified, but outwardly similar, version for Formula 1.

Mid-June saw the Colin/Andy love-hate relationship flare up again. A copy of the *Toronto Star* newspaper had been sent to Colin, detailing Andy's post-accident comments in which he had said of the turbine cars, 'Colin Chapman built them all right, but he built what I told him to build.'

Colin's initial indignation was quickly followed by an express air-mail letter to Granatelli. He wrote: 'Not only myself but my entire design staff are sick and tired of you personally continuing to claim not only a large slice but almost the entire responsibility for the design of our Type 56 turbine car. This you know to be manifestly untrue, as until February, when you visited us in England, you knew nothing of the car's general configuration. I allowed you to take a model away on the firm personal promise that it would not be used for publicity, but again this was one of the Granatelli promises that have been broken.

'The last straw came with the enclosed newspaper cutting, which I am afraid is just one more nail in the coffin of our relationship.

'Please, Andy, try to take even a halfway look at the position and desist from this totally erroneous impression you are trying to create. The only alternative would be, of course, for me to call a worldwide press conference and acquaint them with the true facts ...'

Colin personally detailed to Grand Prix Models his 1968 commemorative gift to our crew, senior trade support companies and others, selecting a 7-inch-long matt black wheel-less model of a Type 56 mounted complete with an inscription. On Andy Granatelli's he inscribed, 'To my very dear friend Andy, from Colin.'

On the same day that he wrote to Andy, Colin also wrote to Ford America's Jacque Passino. He assumed that Passino had heard from Firestone that Team Lotus was already engaged in producing a piston-powered version of the 4WD 'wedge' car for the

Road racing the turbocars – Granatelli and Parnelli Jones ran their Type 56s in some post-Indy events including the year's USAC finale, the Rex Mays '300' here at Riverside Raceway, California, on 1 December. Art Pollard shimmers through Turn Six in No 20, and Joe Leonard heels into the apex of Turn Seven in No 60. Throttle lag and additional brake demand inherent with the gas turbine engine thanks to its lack of over-run retardation rendered the Lotus door-stops far from ideal for road racing use. Regardless, Colin believed that such problems could be overcome and he planned a full team of 3-litre equivalent Formula 1 Lotus turbocars for '69 . . . (Both Bob Tronolone)

The author's moulded Type 56 bodyform trophy presented by Colin to Team members as a memento of Indy '68. The inscription reads 'For a wonderful effort – Indianapolis 1968'. (Focalpoint, Norwich)

following year's Indy '500', and that he, Colin, would like 'to review the possibility of installing a turbo-supercharged Ford V8'. He intimated that Ford's engine and Lotus's new chassis would be fully sorted simultaneously, but that without Ford's firm backing, he would 'find it impossible to utilise Ford engines and may have to look elsewhere ...'

Ford's 1968 effort at the Speedway had initially been acclaimed as the 'main counter-attack' in the fight against the turbines, but

Turbocar era postscript 1: At the 1980s/90s height of the boom-and-bust historic car market, the ex-Graham Hill Lotus 56 – '56/3' – is offered at auction in Las Vegas beside an unsuccessful earlier rear-engined Indy car, the Rounds Rocket *of 1949.*

events had shown them to be third best, even behind the turbocharged Offies; 16 of them had qualified, one had taken victory and another eight had finished in the first 11.

Of the naturally aspirated Fords, nine had qualified, one (Dan Gurney's 5-litre stock-block version with Weslake heads) had taken second place, and the standard quad-cam unit in his second car, driven by Denny Hulme, fourth. The next best Ford was in McElreath's 14th-place car.

Ford's turbocharged unit, built in a collaboration between Ford, Louis Meyer and Bendix (fuel injection), had only powered four cars in the race; Andretti's had expired on lap 2 (holed piston), the remaining three retiring for reasons not connected with the engine. Although it had been rumoured to have virtually no limit to its power, the time available for research and reliability had run out. The grapevine had it that the Meyers, father and son, had seen nearly 800 hp on the dyno at half throttle, but it had been achieved in leaps and bounds, 500 hp alleged to come in suddenly within a band of only 500 rpm!

Andy Granatelli, accompanied by Firestone's Bill McCrary, arrived at Hethel over the second weekend of July. At this stage no final decision regarding turbines had been announced by USAC, so the lengthy meeting covered both types of propulsion. Andy also ordered a convertible Special Equipment Elan, resplendent in STP rocket red, for his wife Dolly, Colin personally issuing the order to his sales department with the strict instruction that he would carry out the extensive road test himself.

A deal was agreed whereby Colin would go ahead with a turbine in Formula 1 providing that they had a much improved throttle response, better fuel consumption and a minimum output of 500 bhp. Colin professed to have become 'hooked on turbine power', but was seriously worried about the finance required, and he gave Andy a budget proposal.

Shortly after Granatelli's return home he cabled news of the further restriction on turbines, together with a request for a quote for piston-engined cars for 1969. On 26 July came Andy's draft of an agreement for the new year's race and his confirmation that STP was already investigating various forms of piston power. Additionally he wanted the two repaired Type 56s returned as back-ups for his current programme, and confirmed that he would have a modified Pratt & Whitney turbine suitable for Formula 1 races ready to air-freight in two weeks.

Shortly after Andy's departure from Hethel, Jacque Passino arrived in Norfolk. Colin put it to him that the latest version of the Lotus 16-valve 2-litre engine (the LV 220, the prefix standing for 'Lotus Vauxhall') had proved even better than he had dared hope initially, and it was now producing a reliable 250 hp on gasoline, with Colin prophesying that 270 hp was on the cards. Not only that, Colin explained, but from the outset the design concept had been capable of expansion into a quad-cam 32-valve V8 weighing close to 375 lbs and using common cylinder heads and other components, plus a possible increase in stroke, which would provide a unit of 4.2-litre capacity giving 500 bhp on gasoline or 600 bhp on alcohol.

Turbocar era postscript 2: The ex-Joe Leonard Lotus 56 – '56/1' – carefully chocked up on display in the lobby of the First Brands (STP) HQ in Connecticut, September 1993. (Courtesy Fred Cowley)

Colin confirmed that Lotus could commence production of such an engine immediately, promising that a sufficient number for Indianapolis 1969 could be produced and race-tested with time to spare. Moreover, Colin continued, if Ford America provided the development costs of $100,000, plus a further $100,000 to cover the cost of the first five engines, they could be called Fords. Further examples, he said, could be supplied at $17,500 each. Stressing the need for an early decision, Colin bade farewell to Jacque, promising to fly to Dearborn to discuss the matter further if required.

Colin also wrote to Granatelli repeating the suggestion that he had put to Jacque, adding, 'I really do feel this is a better way to go rather than play around with the current Ford engine, so inadequately designed in so many respects that it would be better to work with something designed as a proper racing engine from the outset and which is capable of producing very much higher outputs than the current Ford engine will ever be capable of.'

Then Colin added a note of caution: 'If Ford decides not to go ahead with this project, could you think of anyone else in the States interested in putting up $200,000? In return we would be prepared to dedicate the engine to them, cast their name on the cam box, etc . . .'

A month later came Ford's decision. As Don Wahrman of Ford's Product Development Group wrote to Colin, 'USAC's rules have left the turbo-charged Indy engine at 161 CID. We feel with this displacement this engine should have the best possibilities. Thank you for your offer of a new 4.2-litre engine, but we do not intend to pursue this area.'

CHAPTER ELEVEN

1969:
Out of Time

Andy persevered with his turbine car programme right through to the last race of 1968, continuing to send regular purchase orders to Team Lotus for both car and transmission spares. But by August Colin had lost interest in turbines, preferring instead to concentrate on his new car for 1969, later to be designated the Type 64.

The two rebuilt Type 56 cars remained at Cheshunt throughout September, and it was only after another plea to STP to supply piston or turbine engines for installation that a dummy turbine arrived. Eventually the cars were signed off and air-freighted to Andy in October, with only one major snag. I had cabled him for payment of $80,000 in advance before shipping the two cars, to which his cabled reply read: 'If you don't trust me by now, then keep the cars.' Negotiation ended with Andy arranging for c.o.d. payments at Los Angeles airport.

To provide Team with another top driver, Colin was planning to sign Jochen Rindt, and with Colin's assurance that only constructive discussion with the Austrian was required, I went off to chat to Jochen during a tyre test.

When he noticed my approach in the paddock he greeted me with an aggressively loud, 'Do you want to kill me then?' When I asked him to explain, he continued, 'You don't really expect me to get in a Lotus do you? I don't want to die, so if you've come to see me you've wasted your journey!'

Nothing I said to Jochen appeared even half likely to induce constructive discussion, and eventually I returned to Hethel. I explained the situation to Colin, who to my surprise seemed quite unmoved.

'You'd better find someone else then,' he said. 'Try Ickx.'

Soon afterwards Jacky Ickx and I met at the Westbury Hotel in Conduit Street, London, the Belgian driver accompanied by journalist Bernard Cahier and some friends. Then with Ferrari, Jacky had given Enzo his only Grand Prix win of the year, and I had met him the previous season when he drove our works Lotus-Cortina. It was a good meeting; Jacky was a quiet and reasonable fellow, and we left it that I would quickly answer his queries.

Two weeks later Colin suddenly appeared at my desk.

'Quick,' he said, 'we have to announce our new driver today,

within the hour if you can; there can't be any delay.'

'You've spoken to Jacky then?'

'Jacky? Jacky? Jacky who? I'm talking about Jochen. He's just about to issue a press release in Vienna.'

And with that Colin was gone . . .

Poor Ickx. The news of Jochen Rindt's move to Lotus was out before we could contact the Belgian, and that would have been the first he had heard it.

In November Colin was tying up all the loose strings for the following year's race. He had heard from Firestone that Ford America was interested in close co-operation with one or two teams, and with Mario Andretti's signature on a Team Lotus Indy contract (alongside those of Graham and Jochen Rindt), and Mario's interest in running a Type 64 for the remainder of the USAC season, Colin could see this as the perfect link. As he put it to Jacque Passino, Team Lotus might be the only organisation with full Firestone backing at Indy, and he was looking for Ford support as he did not relish merely 'buying Ford engines from the "corner store"'. The American entrants would have gained experience in running such engines regularly, whereas Team Lotus would only have the one crack of the whip, so to his mind factory support was crucial.

Colin suggested that Ford might like to loan fully competitive engines for Indy, following which they could be sold to Mario's sponsor. Either this, said Colin, or he would look to turbo-Offies as motive power. Ford reacted quickly and a dummy turbocharged V8 unit arrived at Hethel in November.

In a letter to Andy in that month, Colin outlined his plans to run turbo-Fords at Indy if Firestone agreed a contract (Firestone had announced its withdrawal from Formula 1), and that being the case he would like a straight sponsorship deal as in 1967. Also, as the Team's new Formula 1 turbine car was three-quarters built, perhaps Andy would provide a suitable turbine for it as a straight swop for his Formula 1 sponsorship revenue.

The news of Jochen joining us sent a guarded ripple of anticipation through our crew members; they knew full well his capabilities, but also his inability to suffer fools gladly. In our Indy section there was already a great deal of respect for his courage, and appreciation of his humour. He had first appeared at Indy in a tyre test in 1966, immediately expressing his dislike of the place. In his first Indy race of 1967 he had again publicly criticised the whole extravaganza, complaining loudly about all the sitting about, as he put it, 'for days on end', and the long delays in fitting tyres. He was also not impressed by the continual stoppages for spots of rain and any debris on the track, and wondered, again publicly, what the outcome would be if there were as many pigeons in residence at Indy as there were in Trafalgar Square. And he called Chief Steward Harlan Fengler, 'Harlan Finger'.

These were all statements guaranteed to go down well with mechanics! He had waited a week for his car to be made ready, then almost immediately had survived an enormous accident, arriving at Turn One at 190 mph with his throttle stuck wide open. Aiming the car to achieve what he called only a glancing blow, he saw in his mirrors the rear of his car on fire, so quickly released his harness and stood up ready to abandon ship. All ended well, but the ambulance driver who insisted on taking Jochen to the medical centre was visibly unnerved by what he

Stylish recruit – Team Lotus's new signing for '69, the mercurial Austrian Jochen Rindt, is interviewed for local television at the Hethel factory. (S. J. Brown)

had seen, and Jochen offered *him* a cigarette to calm *his* nerves, then later climbed from the ambulance to open the security gates into the paddock.

In the race, after two attempts at qualifying in different cars, the Austrian had retired on lap 108, classified 24th. Happier in 1968 to be driving Jack Brabham's Repco Brabham, he posted the second retirement on lap 9.

Maurice Phillippe penned another 'bathtub' car, this one the longest Team Lotus Indy car ever; at 15 ft 4 ins long it was 14 inches longer than the gas turbine Type 56 and 1 foot longer than the extended Type 42, but 2 ft 3 ins longer than the last Type 38.

For its four-wheel-drive transmission Colin and Maurice worked closely with both Hewland and ZF, the British company supplying the gearbox and transfer drive casings, gear ratios, and numerous internal components, and ZF providing differential housings, driveshafts front and rear, crown-wheels and pinions, planet bevel gears and associated parts.

After admirably fulfilling his task as Chief Mechanic of the Indy section in 1968, Dick Scammell was now promoted to Racing Manager (Engineering), responsible for all Team's categories of racing. As already mentioned, although Colin had spoken to both of us about his plans to put us on the board of Team Lotus, neither of us felt inclined to welcome the change; in fact, we both regarded the whole thing as a dangling carrot that would dangle for ever.

One of the first things that Dick produced was a 'Mechanics' Information Booklet' detailing all the mechanics' tasks from loading the transporter at the factory, to all the items that needed constant attention at the circuit. An addendum listed all the mechanical failures due to human error in the past year, complete with future rectification instructions.

The 1969 agreement signed by Colin and Andy did in fact follow Colin's requirement that it should follow the '67 arrangement, ie that the two companies be independent contractors and not, as in 1968, running a joint venture. As in previous years, STP would purchase each of three cars, provided that they started in the race, this year at $25,000 per car. In addition there were bonuses of considerable sums covering pole position, record-breaking one- and four-lap averages, as well as winning the race.

As 1968 came to an end I was still seeking additional sponsorship, with approaches to fuel companies such as Humble, American Oil, Gulf and others; in most cases I found that the STP connection frightened them off, and later, when Humble announced its withdrawal from racing, came news that everyone was in trouble with their respective oil companies, who were suddenly switching en masse to a programme of race bonus payments only. Andy was keen to cajole American Oil (AMOCO) to join us regardless of the reduced monies, as he felt that they had suffered badly at the hands of the world's press after our turbines had retired due to fuel deficiencies and the subsequent pump failure. Additionally, AMOCO had not been best pleased in 1968 when our mechanics had used the old-style pit boards with Humble's name all over them . . .

Other organisations I approached included TIA and Sears

An STP publicity shot captioned 'Champion innovators – Anthony (Andy) Granatelli, president of STP Corporation, and Colin Chapman, president of Lotus Cars Ltd, conclude agreement for their fourth annual association in racing STP-Lotus team cars at Indianapolis Motor Speedway on Memorial Day, 1969. Chapman has built four new 1969 STP-Lotus wedge design racers which will run as STP-Lotus Specials, powered with turbocharged Ford V8 racing engines.' Four brand mentions in two sentences for both STP and Lotus – was someone already aware of Colin's growing jealousies . . ? (STP Corporation)

Roebuck. The offer was for them to either concentrate solely upon Indianapolis (I also supplied background details of the Indianapolis race cinema shows), or to take in our remaining worldwide programme. With Mario Andretti now on the strength, I also prepared a brochure for his USAC sponsor, Overseas National Airways; our cars then wore John Player Gold Leaf livery, and when I suggested that perhaps we might carry the initials 'ONA' prominently, Players vetoed the idea because in the UK those initials were associated with contraceptives!

Part of the suggested overall deal was that Team Lotus would arrange 'dramatic occasions' to publicise the sponsor's involvement at both outward and incoming airports, and free-of-charge interviewing periods with Colin and our drivers whenever requested.

At the first of the 'trial board meetings' for Dick and myself, we asked Colin to define the practical measures to be taken where cars might be in short supply for our three allegedly 'equal No 1 drivers'. Colin's answer was that Graham would have first choice, Jochen second and Mario third . . . Another point was that Colin

still hankered after building a big sports car, and he added the production of a Can-Am budget for 1969.

In January the first live Ford engine arrived at Hethel, live that is apart from exhausts and turbo, which arrived a week later with Danny Jones of Ford to help with installation. All this was confirmed to Mario, who in answer to our plea to USAC for more information plus regulations for the forthcoming race, had handed them a useful rocket. Additionally, Mario said that he would send us copies of everything he received from USAC so that nothing was missed. He was also seeking sponsorship for us, working with Indy promotions agent Chuck Barnes in company with lawyer Dave Lockton, while also keeping tabs on Firestone and Ford on our behalf.

At the end of January came news that the substantial Firestone support for Mario's Type 64 programme was being withdrawn, Andy Granatelli's STP filling the breach. In telling us of the new situation, Andy announced that he was installing Plymouth engines in his remaining Type 56 turbine chassis, and asked us to quote for two new bare 'tubs', complete with bodywork, able to accept the Plymouth units and all his current stock of running gear; the package was to be at Los Angeles airport not later than 15 March. He also confirmed the titles of our Type 64s as *STP Oil Treatment Specials*; after yet another exchange with Colin, the 'Lotus' prefix was later added!

As for the Formula 1 turbine, Andy requested that he also run this as an *STP Oil Treatment Special*, for which he would give financial support to all our other racing sections on the proviso that Lotus Cars and all dealerships recommend STP products, a plan for which he would pay a support figure of $100,000.

Poor Mario must have wondered what was going on when, early in February, he received a cable from Colin reading, 'Please, for the benefit of all concerned, will you refrain from doing a definite deal with Granatelli until you clear this with us, because we are still arguing with him over last year, and until this is resolved we will not do a deal with him for 1969 . . .'

As can be imagined, the many invoices and charge details for building cars and authorising the build of transmissions in 1968 was an accountant's nightmare but, undeterred, Andy was personally trying to unravel every item, and his discoveries drove Colin close to apoplexy. On top of that, the re-import of Canadian-built turbines into America with the rebuilt chassis under the enforced c.o.d. arrangement had puzzled US Customs. We had shown Customs the value of the cars at £1,500 each, but STP had unnecessarily quoted Customs our c.o.d. requirement of $40,000 per car. Now Andy was looking to us for help in retrieving the large amount of duty he had been forced to pay, but Colin's patience was fast running out! The solution he put forward was for Andy to tell Customs it had all been a typist's error, and reminded him that since he was always referring on radio and TV to how expensive these cars were, he was largely to blame. 'This disastrous problem can be laid entirely at your feet,' he declared.

Additionally, Andy had gone to press with the announcement of his Plymouth-engined cars for 1969, and Colin had once again been infuriated to find that the converted Type 56 chassis had been described as 'STP-built', with no mention of Lotus. This straw almost broke the English camel's back!

Now Colin wanted complete charge of the 1969 Type 64 programme, both publicly and behind the scenes, and wanted Andy to slow any possible deal with AMOCO as he was busy firming up a contract with BP Sinclair, the British/American association. However, Andy terminated such thoughts by emphasising that his 1968 deal had included a first option for 1969.

Furthermore, although Andy had secured a similar fuel retainer for Graham, Jochen's was just a sixth of that. As Andy put it, 'When Jochin (sic) becomes World Champion, wins the "500" and speaks English adequately to be a good public relations man, I'll increase it.' As for retainer and sponsor sums paid to Team, Andy's comment was simply 'the honeymoon is over'.

In mid-February came a letter from Ford confirming that its renewed interest in and support for Team Lotus was entirely due to Mario being part of our plans. The company would 'supply the engines and technical competence to run them at Indianapolis providing Mario's Type 64 (identical in specification to the other cars) be sold to him so he could run it as a separate operation from the "500" through to the end of the year, and that during the month of May it be part of the overall Team Lotus operation.'

By this time Andy's list of components required for his own cars had grown considerably, one order alone calling for 36 15-inch-diameter wheels (the rim width changed from 9 inches to 10 inches due to new USAC regulations and with the extra inch spread equally but with an offset identical to that of the Type 56), complete steering gear assemblies, new differentials (as Type 64), four car sets of wheel nuts, 33 anti-roll bars and numerous other items, the majority required by 14 March. On 3 March the vexed agreement with STP was finally signed, having been altered considerably from its initial draft.

As the first car neared completion, Mario finalised his deal with Granatelli. But possible testing time at the Speedway was running short (only two days were allowed), so focus turned to the 1-mile Hanford Speedway in California, Mario supplying us with detailed tyre diameters coupled to appropriate gear ratios.

Chief Mechanic Arthur 'Butty' Birchall piloted chassis '64/1' round Hethel for its shakedown and immediately encountered a problem: 'We couldn't work out what was causing an enormous vibration as it accelerated down the straight at Hethel. Eventually we discovered it was wheel-spin that was coming in even at high speeds. The power was simply phenomenal, and whereas we had been expecting 700–800 bhp it was giving around 1,000 bhp, Ford's Danny Jones later telling me that they had regularly seen 1,025 on their dyno. I can tell you it gave me a shock and I found it very difficult to drive, even comparatively slowly. There was around a 3-second throttle lag on the turbo coming in, and when it did the kick in the back was indescribable! At Hethel's hairpin it was impossible to steer it under power, and I felt that anyone signed to drive it was welcome to it!'

After an all-nighter the first car was finally completed on the

In the Formula 1 pits at Kyalami during the 1969 South African Grand Prix meeting, diminutive newcomer Mario Andretti (second left) shares a joke with Jochen, Colin and Graham.

morning of Thursday 27 March; after an initial design registration photo session, Graham Hill took it out for a run on the factory test-track. The next two days were scheduled for Silverstone Formula 1 practice, but further tests of the Type 64 were required, and the Formula 1 section missed out on Friday's first practice day (Jochen growling to the press at Silverstone that he was ready but his team wasn't). Graham spent both days running the Type 64, on the Saturday hopping in his plane back and forth to Silverstone. All the time Colin, oblivious to the restricted running time, kept issuing orders for the car to be air-freighted immediately to Indianapolis, an order ignored for its sheer impracticality. Then BOAC staff walked out on strike, and any chance of a trip to Indy was gone; for the first time in my life I was exhilarated to learn of major industrial action!

The Monday after the Silverstone race (in which a revitalised Jochen finished in second place after an inspired 'man of the race' drive behind Jack Brabham), Graham was back at Hethel for further tests. The gearbox had been prone to overheating, even at Hethel, so a gearbox oil cooler was fitted. On Wednesday evening the car was prepared to be air-freighted, and at midnight was at London Airport ready for departure to Los Angeles, together with five large boxes of spares. After two days of tests, the car was air-freighted back to Hethel with an enormous job list to be incorporated in all four cars – a formidable task.

On a typically chill and frosty Norfolk March morning the most complicated Indy Lotus ever conceived – the four-wheel-drive, turbocharged V8 '64/1' – is prepared for its initial shakedown run in Graham's hands at Hethel. (All David Phipps)

Since the Monaco Grand Prix date fell as usual on the same weekend as first qualifying at Indy, we applied to the CSI for their jurisdiction on the rule whereby a driver could not take part in an international event if he had competed in another race less than 24 hours earlier. Both we and BRM had fallen foul of the ruling at the previous year's Italian Grand Prix, where transatlantic trips for Bobby Unser and Mario Andretti had been to no avail, but these had concerned two races and not, as now, qualifying and a race. If the CSI turned the scheme down, Graham and Jochen would forsake the all-important first qualifying weekend, going to Monaco instead, while Mario would sort out the Type 64 at Indy.

Eventually the CSI confirmed that the transatlantic hops, skips and jumps would be acceptable, and we set in motion a wild number of airline movements to ensure Graham's and Jochen's four transatlantic trips in six days, with Indy and Monaco practice, Indy qualifying and the Monaco race in between. They would leave Indy on the Wednesday afternoon and undertake 14 hours of travel on three airlines to arrive in time for Thursday afternoon practice in Monaco. They would stay over to Friday, practice in the morning, then depart for another three different airline connections – and a longer journey this time of 16 hours – to arrive back in Indy at 9 pm on Friday night.

Saturday would see qualifying, and if all went well our drivers would be back in the air a little after 5 pm, arriving in Nice at lunchtime on Sunday, landing an hour and a half before the start of the Grand Prix – this time a mere 13-hour hop. On Sunday night after the race they would enjoy the luxury of a bed, then hot-foot it back to Indy at 9.35 the next morning. Without allowances for delays or intermediate travel, they would spend over 61 hours in the air.

The build programme of these highly complicated cars had proved more time-consuming than the most pessimistic forecasts. The first two sets of completed transmissions arrived on 23 April, just two days before the shipping date, when in a sensible programme the completed cars would have been departing the factory for London Airport. Team's fabrication shop was equally hard pressed in having to make revised suspension components, the first set of which was not ready until 25 April, the first body nearing completion a day later.

As with previous Indy races, the timetable was becoming a nightmare, but amazingly chassis '64/4', Mario's race car, left for the States on 30 April and was receiving the attention of his Indy mechanics two days later as they prepared it for its first run.

The participation of Graham and Jochen in the Formula 1 Spanish Grand Prix on 4 May, with the Speedway opening on the 1st, gave our Indy crew a little leeway, but Graham's car ('64/2') did not leave England until race day in Spain, Jochen's ('64/3') did not arrive at Indy until as late as 8 May, while the spare car (Mario's Hanford test car, chassis '64/1') arrived on 11 May, like the others that had preceded it by no means complete.

But in Spain we suffered the disaster of losing both our Formula 1 cars on Barcelona's Montjuich circuit. Starting from

The 1969 STP-Lotus-Ford 64 was an imposing box of tricks. STP's press release photo of the car in the Indy pit lane is breathlessly captioned: 'Mario's mount – high angle distorts wild design of newest STP-Lotus to come to Indianapolis. This machine, of modified wedge design, has advantage of four-wheel drive and is powered by newest series turbocharged Ford double-overhead-camshaft V8 racing engine and is assigned to Mario Andretti one of four top drivers on STP racing team for 1969.' This is the car that took Mario so heavily into the wall during practice for the '500'. (STP Corporation)

the front row (Jochen on pole), both cars had been smashed by enormous impact against the armco crash barriers when their spindly rear wings had both collapsed as the cars breasted a hump in a 150 mph bend. Fortunately Graham was shaken but unhurt, while Jochen, surviving a worse impact by reason of his car hitting Graham's wreck and cartwheeling over it to finish upside down, suffered severe concussion, a broken nose and cheekbone, and cuts to his face. Now the programme needed drastic alteration.

Jochen went off to his doctor for a fuller assessment, while we anticipated the worst, fearing a substantial convalescence period. Graham, meanwhile, merely brushed himself down in trouper fashion and set off for Indy. I was already there, and Colin, with his hands full at the factory, phoned me to say 'choose someone else for Monaco'. I approached Richard Attwood, who would be an excellent back-up for Graham, and so he proved. As for Indy, we would await Jochen's decision; if he was declared unfit, we would leave Andy to decide the best man to fill his shoes …

In leaving Hethel for Indy at the end of April, I had had my usual last-minute chat with Colin to bring us both up to date with events. We spent remarkably little time together, a fact that Colin declared proved that Team Lotus was constantly pointing in the right direction. As I left his office, he called me back.

'You remember the singer at the Lamplighter party last year?'

'No I don't,' I replied. 'I only got there in time to pay the bill.'

Colin laughed. 'Oh yes, I remember now. Do you have her phone number?'

'No, but I'll get it for you.'

On my way out of the race shop I met Chief Mechanic Arthur Birchall, standing in the midst of a pile of components and half-finished cars and also anxious to be on his way.

'Do you remember the singer at the Lamplighter last year?' I asked.

'Yes, I do.'

'Would you have her address or phone number?'

'I'll have it at Indy,' he said, then smiled. 'And why do you want it?'

'I don't,' I said. 'I'll see you at Indy.'

My reason for leaving before the rest of the crew was to meet up with Mario to sort out the background details to the Type 64, the supply of components for the remainder of his USAC season and to finalise our Formula 1 programme together. He suggested that we have dinner at the Cove, the bar-cum-restaurant across from the Speedway frequented by most of the racing fraternity from senior management to mechanics, and seemingly devoid of fans anxious to waste time or interrupt conversations. It was modestly priced, boasted live musicians and had a good feel to it.

As Mario and I brought each other up to date with events, suddenly there came a feminine 'Hi!', and an attractive girl appeared at the table. Mario got to his feet.

'Andrew, this is Moss. She's a really nice girl, not one of the bunch around here. Moss, this is Andrew.'

It was immediately obvious that she was not 'one of the bunch' around the Speedway. When she heard my accent she told me that she was second-generation American with English roots. It was a conversation I had heard many times before. She didn't stay long, then as she went to leave she said, 'You're always welcome at my home; come around and tell me about England and your good old Queen! If you're up early enough just drop in for breakfast. I'm a draughtsman, or even a draughtswoman, and I leave for work at eight.'

I made a note of her address.

'She's real nice,' said Mario. 'You won't get into trouble with her …'

A couple of days later I remembered the invitation. Anything was better than sitting in a HoJo Motel eating breakfast on my own. Moss's home was 5 minutes drive away.

What I would call a civilised table complete with chat far removed from racing was a godsend. Moss lived with her sister Anita and brother and really was a draughtswoman, supplement-ing her income with modelling for fashion houses. She had just finished a session for 'Terry's of California', and there was a pile of photographic proofs of her in a selection of clothes and with three or four wigs.

'Here, take one,' she said, scribbling on it 'Thanks for dropping by'.

Back at the Speedway Mario was over the moon with his re-vamped Type 64. He wrote later, 'Chapman had made the suggested changes and added a few wrinkles of his own. Man, it was a gorgeous car. For the first few days I just wanted to stand around and look at it.'

Chief of Mario's crew was veteran mechanic Clint Brawner, who had been hooked on racing for 41 years, first building midget racers back in 1932, then coming to the Speedway in 1952. Cars prepared by him had taken 43 victories, 21 of them by Mario who had secured two of Clint's five national titles. Co-crew chief was 31-year-old Jim McGee, whose initial bout as a race mechanic had been interrupted by Army service. He had first arrived at Indy in 1963, but after three weeks' fruitless search for a job had returned the following year. Clint had signed him up and they were still together.

On his first shakedown run, Mario was even more impressed by the 64. Its steering problems had been corrected, and it ran so smoothly that it was like taking a Sunday drive. 'I hit a 160.5 mph cruising speed on a few laps,' he wrote. Three days later he was up to 166.451 mph, and three days after that (11 May) he clocked 168 mph. Fastest at that time was Foyt at 169.237 mph, but Mario was not perturbed.

'I hadn't turned my critter loose yet,' he said.

All this had been accomplished in a relaxed and confident manner, Mario's crew, like him, content to go one easy step at a time, but the mood in our own garages was very different …

It took three days after its arrival to get Graham's car nearly completed, and on the Sunday that saw Mario running over 168 mph, Colin produced a 19-item job list for completion before Graham set forth. Among the items listed was rigging the chassis, altering the cockpit and windscreen to give clearance for Graham's knuckles, repositioning switches, and flushing off all bolts projecting below the undertray. Later the same day, the car was officially weighed, which after deduction of the fuel load gave a reading of 1,516 lbs, some 166 lbs over-weight. At the same time Colin recorded the 64's authentic fuel capacity as 73.4 US gallons.

The car ran for the first time the next day, Monday 12 May, Graham slowly returning to report that the engine would not run. The spark plugs were changed, but still it refused to run, and was returned to our garage for a 3-hour investigation. Graham eventually managed nine consecutive laps, his fastest a lowly 150.7 mph, nearly 19 mph slower than Mario. Colin noted that the steering was heavy, the throttle settings brought in high power too early, and the engine was, according to Graham, coughing once on the front straight, twice on the back straight.

That night Colin provided 'Butty' Birchall with a 21-item job list, which included fitting new heat shields below the blower, gear lever alterations to ensure easier second gear selection and yet more changes to the cockpit/windscreen to clear Graham's knuckles.

With the regulations banning moveable airflow attachments or devices, the large rear 'wings' of the Type 64 posed a time-consuming problem for our mechanics.

'Butty': 'If the old man wanted a 1-degree change of angle it meant a long process of removing the rear wing from the bodywork, repairing the tears in the fibreglass, then resetting the wings to the new angle. Once everything was re-attached, the bodywork had to be made good and resprayed in time for running again the next morning.

One evening Colin visited me in my motel room for a chat. As he sat down, he abruptly pointed to the photograph that Moss had given me, which I had propped up on my table amongst the innumerable job lists and phone call information.

'Has she been here?' he asked.

'No, I had it given to me,' I replied, taken aback by his question.

'I don't think that's funny,' he said, and immediately left the room.

I was nonplussed by this reaction, but gave it some thought. Later, when I met Moss again, I asked if she had ever been a singer . . .

'Oh yes,' she said. 'That's another one of my activities I haven't told you about. I've been singing for some time and last month I sang with the Duke Ellington band opening a new hotel in Indy. Last year I was singing at the Lamplighter when your crew was having a party. Weren't you there?'

Immediately the penny dropped. I could see what Colin had thought about my actions prior to his arrival . . .

I asked Moss if I could give Colin her telephone number.

'Good Lord, no! I'm not into fellows phoning me like that,' she said. 'To be honest, I'm not very keen on the race fraternity, with only a very few exceptions.'

From then on my relationship with Colin deteriorated fast. I had always prided myself on the fact that, having seen numerous other management staff come and go during my eight years in a Lotus hot seat, once it happened to me I would take my leave. From then on Colin insisted on my going to dinner with him every evening, usually in company with Maurice Phillippe; sadly, Maurice allied himself to Colin's criticism of my organisation of Team Lotus.

One evening during dinner at Weir Cook airport, I could restrain myself no longer and told them both what I thought of them, telling them that I considered they had too much to rectify at the Speedway without advising me on areas of which they had no knowledge.

For once Colin quickly paid the bill and we returned to our HoJo Motel. As Maurice left us, Colin followed me to my room.

Once inside, he asked what I now planned.

'Within the next minute or two I shall be driving to Indy,' I replied.

Speedway supremo Tony Hulman, Kirk Douglas and Andrew Ferguson with the lovely draughtswoman/singer/model Moss, whose presence unwittingly triggered such tensions within Team's hierarchy at Indy. (Steve Rosenbaum Photography)

'No you won't,' he said. 'I want you in bed and ready for tomorrow, bushy tailed,' he said.

'Balls,' I said. 'When it gets to 11 or 12 at night I reckon that's my time, not yours, and I go off to enjoy some jazz. Make of that what you like . . .'

'I'm going to lock your room,' said Colin (he always had a duplicate set of room keys). 'What will you do about that?'

'Easy,' I replied. 'Same as before – watch.'

I quickly slid aside the patio window and stepped outside.

'Like this.'

When I peered back into the room, Colin had gone. I drove into town, calling first at the '19th Hole', a jazz rendezvous that was special for me and at which I was the only white participant. My friend behind the bar had one arm missing from the elbow, and in between numbers I was always fascinated by his ability to collect up numerous glasses with his stump.

It was a great place, its groups far beyond any others I knew for quality.

After visiting two or three such venues I returned to the hotel. Waiting at the desk was a letter from Peter Warr. His slot-racing business had failed some time previously and now he was looking for a job in motor racing. He had enjoyed an interview with

John Surtees but had not fancied the environment – did I know of anything better? I hurried a note off to him. Yes, my job was now vacant – how about that?

Unexpectedly – for me anyway – Peter could not believe his eyes when he read my letter and sadly lacking decorum rushed off to Colin to announce that I was leaving. Uncivilised as both my letter and Warr's action was, Colin and I had a down-to-earth chat and he accepted the news that Warr had announced in advance . . .

The same day as Graham had slowly rumbled round the Speedway, Mario was well into his stride but harbouring doubts – perhaps he was just a sniff away from disaster? Had he been taken in by the smooth running of his new 4WD car and engine, and was he being lulled to sleep? He determined to be even more attentive, and slow to evoke any changes.

On 12 May he warmed up the car slowly, then put his foot down. The clocks registered a 170.197 mph lap; the very next day he was up to 171.474 mph. On Wednesday 14th he was clocking 171.657 mph, 2 mph better than Foyt's time, and just a smidgen under Leonard's previous record 1968 time of 171.953 mph.

By this time Jochen's car (chassis '64/3') had arrived from Hethel and our very tired crew had launched into preparing it for first running. One late evening the telephone in our garage rang. I answered it to be greeted by the dulcet tones of Dale Porteous a former Team mechanic, enquiring as to the state of play; he was in New York.

'How about coming to help us?' I suggested. 'We're in it up to our necks. When could you get here?'

True Team man that he was, Dale arrived next morning. Everyone was truly delighted to see him again, regardless of the work schedule. The British/Colonial staff of Team Lotus through the 1960s provided an admirable mix, one that Derek Gardner would look back on with affection: 'I found that Team always had a good working atmosphere completely devoid of politics or petty jealousies. Everyone worked for Team or Colin without fear or favour.'

Dale was to stay with us for the next four weeks . . .

After a prodigious survey of Graham's engine and car and a change of gear ratios to try and establish its problems, lunchtime on Tuesday 13 May saw Graham again encountering a misfire. After 15 laps he clocked 161.8 mph, just as Mario turned in 171.474 mph; then in Turn Four Graham spun, fortunately without hitting anything. That night's job list centred around the engine and fuel system, with the fuel filter element under close scrutiny, together with a chat with Ford's Danny Jones about fuel pressure settings.

By now the decision had been taken for Graham to forsake Indy running and drive in all the Monaco practice sessions and race; it was a decision that was to work well for us as the rains returned to Indy in full measure and washed out both days of first qualifying. Before he departed, Graham tried his Speedway car again. After seven laps he was up to 159.8 mph, then after a stop for damper changes dropped to 155 before clocking 158.1

mph. The fuel mixture was enriched and 161.6 mph was registered . . . Then a run just prior to Graham's departure saw his engine blow. Now 'Butty' and his lads had a 54-item job list to contend with, plus an engine change.

On Monday Graham was back in the air returning to the States (he had won at Monaco for a record-setting fifth time, with Attwood fourth), but Mario was encountering problems. With qualifying washed out, his crew had turned to tuning the chassis under full-fuel-load running, and quite soon the American ace was turning in consistent speeds in the mid-167 mph range with several laps over 169 mph. Then his right rear universal joint broke, as it had at the Hanford test, the lack of drive causing his engine to blow.

Tuesday therefore found Mario's crew repairing his car, while our lads were still attempting to complete the long job list on Graham's, who was not to get out on the track until Wednesday afternoon, when he managed a best of 157.07 mph. He reporting that the car displayed a tendency to turn right in all four left-hand corners! Colin noted that the engine was coughing badly and that oil was leaking from the rear differential.

It was around this time that Mario suffered an almighty accident in Turn Four. His crew had taken great care in restoring their Type 64, and on Wednesday morning Mario went out for a shakedown run which showed that the car was back in fine shape. In the afternoon he went out again for a high-speed run. He covered two relatively slow laps and in the short chute between Turns Three and Four put his foot down in order to achieve maximum speed down the main straight. As he entered Turn Four he heard a noise that heralded a breakage, and the car went into a high-speed spin, during which he saw what turned out to be his right-rear wheel in the air.

Enormous impact loads as he hit the wall backwards completely demolished the car, with parts and debris flying high into the air as the wreck simultaneously burst into a ball of fire. As Mario remarked later, he was lucky not to be stunned. Sensing the heat of the enveloping fire through his overalls, his face exposed to great pain and fully alert to the need to vacate the car without delay, Mario snapped open his harness and baled out while the wreck was still moving.

Mario had just passed Art Pollard in his STP car and amazingly Pollard managed to steer safely through the wreckage of what others later described as reminiscent of an aircraft accident. He hurriedly stopped his car to render assistance.

What was truly remarkable was Mario's cool, calm demeanour when we met him back in his garage after a quick visit to the medical centre. Considering the fire that had enveloped him, his facial burns, which clearly showed where his goggles had been, appeared remarkably light, but must have been very painful. Before long he was discussing a programme for preparing another car, this time the latest of his Brawner Hawk 'home-built' cars, which he had already raced twice. What seriously perturbed him was the fact that all the Lotus's suspension parts had been put through the regulatory safety requirement of magnafluxing

Mario at high speed in '64/1' shortly before that right-rear hub let go . . . (Indianapolis Motor Speedway)

Failed investment – the shattered, foam-coated remains of Mario's 64 are swung clear of the track by the USAC wrecker truck's crane jib. While the monocoque has been crushed and twisted abaft the engine-bay bulkhead, by some miracle the nose oil and water radiators have emerged unscathed and still attached. Note the Type 64's inboard ventilated disc brakes on the front driveshafts and eccentric steering gear. Mario was lucky to escape with minor – although still painful – burns. (Indianapolis Motor Speedway)

that same morning without pinpointing the imperfection of the car's right-rear hub.

Colin offered him Jochen's car, but Mario declined. He knew that our two cars were nowhere near ready, the Austrian's least of all. After its tardy arrival on 12 May, just before the cancelled first qualifying weekend, the initial job list for completing the car amounted to 61 items, Colin adding the reminder that so far it had taken around 4 hours merely to start an engine! He wanted to put four batteries on the engine-start trolley, hopeful that the additional juice would help reduce the problem. 'Butty' added item 62: 'New set of mechanics'.

Colin had made a delayed dash to Monaco at the last moment, and at the airport had scribbled detailed instructions for action during his absence, suggesting that we take up Mario's offer to give Jochen's car an initial run. Colin anticipated that the car would suffer from oversteer and listed all the changes that should be made, detailing everything from roll-bar changes to tyre pressure alterations. At this stage the car had neither sponsor display nor race numbers, so the signwriter had to do his lengthy job before Jochen could take his first run, scheduled for 19 May now that the medics had cleared him fit to drive. Again, our ten-man crew set to work.

Jochen arrived on the 19th, and although obviously not completely fit, he was happy to think that he would only be at what he called 'the dreaded Indy' for a few days before departing again. As to the chaos in our garages, he made little comment, his facial expression saying it all.

The preparatory work on his car was still in progress on 20 May, and he was not to have his first shakedown laps until lunchtime on the Wednesday, the day of Mario's accident. He managed 12 laps, his fastest a sniff under 145 mph. This dismal showing was followed by a fault rectification report, detailing that the clutch would not free, water temperature was sky high, steering too heavy – on top of this, Jochen's run had been ended by fuel starvation. Less driver and fuel and without a body, the car weighed in at 1,652 lbs, 302 lbs over the minimum limit.

On Wednesday evening a fraught meeting in the Team garages set in motion a programme to produce uprights man enough for their task. There were now just two days left before the one and only qualifying weekend. While Colin and Maurice busily calculated and sketched, as well as producing closely detailed explanatory notes (Mario's hub failure had its origin in incorrect machining, and drawings were produced to avoid any repetition), we sounded the alarm bells around the various engineering shops in the vicinity that we would soon invade. The items down for replacement were hubs, outboard driveshafts, yoke ends, outboard driveshaft plugs and bearing spacer sleeves.

The first person we approached for help was Eddie Kuzma, considered one of the best metal men in American racing. His expertise, dating back to before the war, was second to none. He had already rebuilt the Lotus 34s of Parnelli Jones and A. J. Foyt, had built Mario's Brabham replica and helped with the construction of Foyt's Coyotes. He agreed to fabricate the rear upright

replacements to Maurice's drawings.

While Maurice talked to the Speedway Machine Tool company, State Gear, Joe Baker and Industrial Heat Treatment, I was following them up, discussing time schedules and collection times. Fortunately all the companies accepted all-night working as a matter of course, and I drew up a programme schedule of what I would collect from whom at a selected time for onward delivery to another company; three car sets of all items had been ordered. Ted Halibrand also threw in his lot with us, loaning State Gear the only spline hobbing cutters in the vicinity.

I explained that I would be asleep in my car outside each establishment until woken up with the first pair of anything; for example, I would rush machined intermediate driveshaft blanks ready for splining at both ends from Speedway Machine Tool to State Gear, and from there to Industrial Heat Treatment for hardening to Rockwell 'C' specification, then glass beading treatment.

After a thorough examination of our two cars, practice running recommenced. In the free practice period prior to the start of qualifying, Graham went out only to encounter an engine flat spot. The plugs were changed but the problem persisted. Later he went out again for just six laps, his best time 57.54 seconds or a speed of 156.52 mph. It was to be his last ever run on the track.

Jochen also went out, but his engine was rough and prone to cut out, and the throttle was sticking. His best time over 12 laps was 58.10 (154.90 mph). His second run was no better, and with the engine persisting with its intermittent coughing its timing was checked. Next time out he was up to 158.4 mph, but then a yellow light brought him in. When he went out again his engine was appreciably worse. A further five-lap spell saw him up to 161 mph, but on the next lap he spun. His tyres were changed and he went out for another seven laps, but it was a fruitless effort. His best time was 58.34 (154.3 mph) and he brought the car in …

The hours dragged by in the production of the new parts, but everything appeared to be going to plan. Then, as dawn broke outside State Gear, someone woke me to say that there had been a sudden power-cut, their machines had gone berserk and the threads on our new hubs had been chewed to oblivion.

'Butty': 'I got this telephone call from Andrew in the small hours and knew that all had been lost. The 1969 Indy race, for us, had passed into the record books.'

Next on the agenda was a serious confab with Colin, who, even prior to breakfast, was remarkably controlled, or perhaps relieved. We quietly set out the wording for a press release, told Graham and Jochen the news, and pinned up the release in the press room:

'May 23rd 1969
PRESS STATEMENT
Detailed investigations have shown that the reason for the accident last Wednesday to Mario Andretti's car No 2 was a fault in the manufacture of the right rear hub, which caused it to fail under load and allow the right rear wheel to come off.

These hubs were not of our own manufacture, but were provided to us by an outside supplier. The failure was clearly due to improper heat treating of the metal to obtain the proper degree of hardness.

In view of this and that there has been insufficient time to manufacture and fit new parts which would allow the drivers to qualify and race with adequate safety, we have decided in co-operation with our primary sponsors STP and FIRESTONE that the entries No 70 and 80 to be driven by HILL and RINDT are being withdrawn.

We have been plagued by this shortage of time through our entire program of preparation for Indianapolis this year because of impending rule changes which could affect design coming as late as the January 11 USAC meeting. Thus we could not make our usual March testing date at which time such problems would have been evident.'

At the press gathering that followed several journalists suggested that there was more to the story than our statement indicated. Was not the fact that our two cars for Hill and Rindt had failed to get above 161 mph the real contributory factor?

I explained that the problems we had faced were manifold. Our schedule had called for fitting the new hubs, a 5-hour task, as of 5.30 am that morning, but the machining problem had ruled that out. In addition, the weather forecast had predicted rain in the afternoon (the last day of qualifying), so the odds remained against us. Also, if we had been successful, very little running time would have been left for us to set up the cars in the period left before the race.

Colin: 'We could have had the parts made inside two days, but that would have been two days too late. We'll be back though – you can't quit when you're down, can you?'

We were asked why our two drivers had not been allowed to drive other cars under the circumstances, and I pointed out that Jochen had been invited to drive a Goodyear-shod car (we were all contracted to Firestone) and that in any case there just was not enough time remaining. In Graham's case he had already stated that he had not even considered another drive.

'If Team Lotus is withdrawing I reckon I am too. Knowing the effort that has been put in, I think it is tragic, but I agree 100 per cent with Colin's decision.'

It was then that I put the fly in the ointment. Asked if there were any further reasons, I replied that if USAC could speed up its act and not leave its final regulatory decisions until as late as January we could all be in with a better chance.

USAC's Charlie Brockman immediately made his opinions known. 'I don't know the full reasons for their withdrawal but their reference to the lateness of our rules is totally absurd and poppycock,' he said.

Brockman's statement brought Andy into the act with a counter-charge, saying that as USAC had changed the rules for the '68 race in January of that year, the threat that further changes might be made for the '69 race in the preceding January were all too apparent.

The press decided to sit on the fence, saying that USAC's rule changes should be announced two years in advance, but adding that even if the race was held in July each year, some drivers and car owners would still not be ready to run …

As it was, Indy 1969 had seen us run 113 laps with Graham's car and 58 with Jochen's, while the spare had run only at Hanford in the Andretti test.

As soon as the news was released and the press conference over, our lads started packing for home. But the drama had another act yet to run …

Team Lotus agreements had always included the words 'we will use our best endeavours', without a thought that one day maybe we would not start a race. Now we had to face the fact that this dreaded, unthinkable event had occurred.

Monday 26 May, just four days before the race, was scheduled for the final settlement meeting between Colin and Andy at the Speedway Motel. I was a couple of minutes late and as I walked towards Andy's room I heard a car in the car park opposite the line of rooms revving wildly before the 'clunk' as the driver engaged reverse. The projectile, travelling tail-first, nearly caught me, but my jump for life found me alongside an infuriated Colin at the wheel.

'How many lawyers have you got here?' he bellowed through the tiny top gap in the car window.

'Four,' I replied.

'Right, alert them all,' said Colin, thrusting the gear knob into drive. 'We're not selling him the cars. Hide them!'

With that there was a scream of tyres and he was gone.

I walked into Andy's room. Both he, in his huge black rocking chair, enormous handkerchief at his brow, and his secretary, Ange Green, were obviously bemused.

'What was that all about?' he asked. 'All I did was question the cost of some spares and he lit off. Remember, you haven't even attempted qualifying, you've withdrawn the cars, so they are all junk. Let's sort this thing out. Wanna coffee?'

I knew in my heart that whatever Andy suggested would fall on deaf ears. When I got back to the Motel Colin wanted to see me.

'I'm off,' he said. 'The STP agreement is defunct. I think I have a deal [I always caught my breath at Colin's suggestion that he might have any deal] with Firestone and I'll settle for selling them the three cars for $75,000 with spares. You stay here to sort it out, but only deal with Mario or Firestone direct, not STP.

'Sort out the rear-hub modifications for the three cars, but if you can manage it only modify the rear of the spare car and leave the rest of it as is. Try not to get into installing an engine. That's the hubs, Hookes joints, and shafts for the *rear* only. Leave the existing modified hubs and joints for the front …

'You keep "Butty" plus two mechanics to go to Milwaukee, but only race one car. I've told the rest to go home. Once "Butty" and his lads have finished, they're to come home as well. Only modify one car and don't do any work in overtime and get a quote first. While you're sitting about, try and firm up a 1970 deal for sponsorship and send Maurice home with the modified original rear hubs for our Formula 1 cars. Oh yes, and send the tubular roll-bars with him. Pack up all the spares, apart from those you sell, or which are part of the agreement, and send the rest home by air. One final thing, only accept Mario's or Firestone's signature. I will not accept any promise from STP or anyone connected with it . . .'

As usual Colin had written the gist of this chat out so there could be no misunderstanding, and he handed me his neatly written notes.

'Supposing Andy does give you a cheque for the full amount,' Colin added as an afterthought, 'get it in the bank immediately and wait for it to be credited before you do anything, and keep me posted at every stage.'

Re-reading our agreement once more, and anxious to keep ourselves covered if a cheque was not received by the deadline of 1 June, Colin suggested that we sit down and compose a letter to be given to Andy on that date.

Meanwhile qualifying saw A. J. Foyt take pole with a four-lap average of 170.568 mph, the plucky Mario second at 170.455 mph driving the Hawk. Third spot on the front row, as in 1968, went to Bobby Unser, all three powered by turbocharged Fords. A. J. had set his sights on breaking Leonard's Type 56 turbine pole time of the previous year, but a sticking waste-gate on his turbo put paid to that; as A. J. himself put it, he considered himself fortunate even to have completed his run, his engine coughing and spluttering from the second of his four laps.

Of the 33 cars on the grid, 19 were Offy-engined and 11 Ford-powered, all 30 turbocharged. The remainder were the two naturally aspirated Repco V8s in the Jack Braham and Peter Revson cars, Gurney staying with his stock-block Ford. One of the many interesting facts to emerge from the Indy statistics office was that the average age of the 33 drivers was 36!

I was to enjoy the relaxed position of spectator on race day, and along with nearly 300,000 others saw a thoroughly well-deserved and convincing win for Mario. He had endured a horrendous shunt only to be out first thing the following day in his Hawk as if nothing had happened, and had carried on from there, almost immediately up to A. J.'s times.

Mario led for 114 of the 200 laps of the race, finishing 5 miles ahead of second-man Dan Gurney, the winning total purse being over $200,000.

And Andy? After 23 years of trying he had finally achieved his lifelong ambition, and he told the crowd of press men surrounding him, 'Now I only want to win as many times as I've lost.' Then, pausing for a moment, he returned to his old love: 'Regardless of winning with a piston engine, I'd still love to come back with a turbine.' At the prize-giving he jokingly accused Mario of ruining his 23-year image as a 'loser'.

Our letter to Andy, outlining our plans for the disposal of the

The morning after – Victory pose at the Speedway for Andretti, Granatelli and their winning Hawk-Ford, raced following Colin Chapman's withdrawal of the Lotus-Ford 64s. (Indianapolis Motor Speedway)

TEAM LOTUS: THE INDIANAPOLIS YEARS •

three remaining cars, drew attention to the fact that under the terms of our agreement we had now fulfilled the requirement of providing modified parts to render the cars competitive.

Andy's response was immediate, reminding us that the cars had been withdrawn as unsafe; they 'did not establish ability to run in competition', which was the pre-condition of the STP purchase obligation. Andy also went on to caution us that STP had a vested interest in the vehicles, plus considerable losses in goodwill, prestige, advertising value, etc, and that if we sold the cars without STP's consent they would look to us for damages. He suggested I visit him in Des Plaines to try and find a solution. He retained a jovial outlook on the affair, remarking how bemused he was at the lengths to which Colin would go just to sell spares at inflated prices!

I phoned Colin later, but he absolutely refused to budge, his theme being that we had not guaranteed results, only effort. 'You go back to Indy and I'll call you later at the motel,' he said.

His call came in the middle of the night, Colin asking me to return to Andy at Des Plaines first thing in the morning with a new proposal. This proved unacceptable to Andy, and I phoned Colin to tell him.

'I'm worried about STP seizing the cars,' Colin announced. 'Fly back to Indy immediately and hide them where they can't find them.'

To find lock-ups capable of taking three cars plus an enormous amount of spares proved impossible; additionally it was against Indiana law to work on cars in such premises. I mentioned my problem to Wanda, a secretary with our freight agents at the airport.

'My husband would be thrilled to help you,' she said. 'I'll get him to clear out our garage right away.'

Our remaining crew, Arthur Birchall, Hughie Absalom and Dale Porteous quickly acquired a trailer and the long process of ferrying all our equipment began. When he saw the mass of items in his pristine garage, Wanda's husband did not appear as thrilled as she had suggested he might, but eventually everything was locked away and we returned to Indianapolis. Bill Brack of Lotus Canada was there to collect the Type 42 that had haunted us since 1967, and the process of sorting through the spares he wanted kept us busy.

Meanwhile Colin kept changing his mind, and the revised proposals kept me back and forth to Chicago; each afternoon I would phone him with a report, after which he would ask me to return to Indy. Bored and not a little wary of all the jets on which I was commuting, I chose a friendly commercial service flying four- and sometimes six-seater piston-engined planes to and from Chicago. For his part Andy thought the protracted negotiations were a riot!

One morning Arthur Birchall phoned me from his motel, his voice hushed.

'I'm in the lobby,' he said quietly, 'and there are some legal-looking fellows at the desk asking for you. What shall we do?'

Anxious that no proceedings be taken against our crew, and

Mario with his wife Dee Ann and sons Jeff, 5, and Michael, 6, enjoy the civic reception parade that home-town Nazareth, Pennsylvania, accorded the Indy winner. (Bill Sauro)

Having been instructed by Colin to hide all the cars and ensure that Granatelli did not get them, the author managed to house them in the home garage of Lotus's shipping agent's secretary at Indianapolis Airport. One of the 64s is being loaded back on to the hastily rented trailer by 'Butty' and Dale Porteous. Here was an epic in the making . . .

now firm in the belief that STP had opened the offensive, we arranged a rendezvous to discuss our plans. Throughout the day I phoned my motel to check if anyone had arrived there, but there was only a message to call Ford. Eventually it transpired that the legal beagles were representing Ford, their comptrollers convinced that I was attempting to steal their engines! By 13 June they had been removed from the cars and were safely delivered to Lou Meyer's shop.

It soon became obvious that my frequent meetings with Andy were not progressing the situation, and my hopes that each time Colin asked me to return to Indy meant that I would soon be homeward-bound were beginning to fade. Eventually Colin terminated the negotiations, issuing his now famous announcement: 'Bring the cars back to Hethel where I will *personally* hacksaw them in half, *personally* dig a big hole and *personally* bury them.' As it turned out, it would have saved Colin a lot of further aggravation if he had done just that!

Wanda asked me how I would like the cars packed. I chose the best tarred, reinforced cardboard wrapping and good quality crates and bid my charges goodbye, never dreaming that I would ever see them again. On 28 June I arrived home, my nine-week sojourn over.

Colin expressed surprise at my appearance. 'Are you sure I said come home?' he asked. 'You could have tried another deal . . .'

Events surrounding the Type 64s were to continue for some time, unknown to me, and I left Team Lotus as planned at the end of the 1969 season.

In 1976 I rejoined the company, and in December of the following year, without being given any clues as to what I was about to see, I was asked to identify the contents of some crates stored in a three-quarters-open barn. To say I was surprised at the sight that met my eyes is a mild understatement. The crates were those I had last seen eight and a half years earlier, the tarred paper acquired at some expense being unravelled to reveal three Type 64s.

1969 postscript – More than eight years after the race, 19 December 1977, this was the author's amazing moment in one of the Hethel storage hangars as those expensive oiled-paper-lined packing cases were broken open to reveal the engineless, unraced, unloved Type 64s just as they had left Indy for the last time. (Focalpoint, Norwich)

'64/3', with body panels re-attached, in the Directors' Garage at Hethel awaiting a potential customer . . . (Focalpoint, Norwich)

The three surviving Type 64s on parade and available for private sale absolutely dwarf the 'little' 3-litre Cosworth-powered Formula 1 Type 63 (second from right). (Focalpoint, Norwich)

It transpired that in November 1971 Colin had come across the crates, Indy spares and two Formula 1 cars in the factory and had issued the instruction to get rid of them. With Colin it was always best to leave matters until he saw the items again in order to establish that he had not changed his mind, but on this occasion someone had carried out his order immediately; a buyer had been found and a deposit paid.

As in times gone by, as soon as Colin discovered what was happening he brought proceedings to an abrupt halt. The prospective buyer initiated legal action, which was to drag on over the years until Team Lotus eventually lost the case; the cars were now scheduled to be prepared and made ready for collection.

The Type 64 project had been a costly affair from beginning to end . . .

POSTSCRIPT

1984-85

After the demise of the STP-Lotus Indianapolis programme in 1969, Colin Chapman and Team never seriously contemplated a return to the American speedway classic.

Times were changing. Under the dynamic and unwaveringly profit-minded direction of new Formula 1 Constructors' Association supremo Bernie Ecclestone, the annual World Championship series of Grand Prix races attracted ever-expanding worldwide media interest as commercial sponsorship ballooned beyond our wildest dreams. Progressively the supposed

Three of the design team which helped bring Team Lotus back to competitiveness in Formula 1, in their office at Ketteringham Hall, the company's palatial headquarters in rural Norfolk, and a stone's throw from Hethel. David Senior (left), Gerard Ducarouge and Jerry Booen. (Focalpoint, Norwich)

financial bonanza offered by the Indy '500' looked less attractive as the rewards of Formula 1 grew rapidly, the proportion changing in Formula 1's favour with every passing season.

In the early 1970s Colin Chapman and Team Lotus remained at the forefront of World Championship Grand Prix racing. The Maurice Phillippe-designed Lotus 72 – with its torsion-bar suspension and 'door-stop' profile – became one of the most durable of all Formula 1 designs, surviving no fewer than six seasons in front-line competition. During that period Type 72s won no fewer than 20 World Championship-qualifying Grands Prix and three Formula 1 Constructors' world titles.

Team Lotus struggled in 1975–76, then Mario Andretti drove a new Type 77 car to victory in the Japanese Grand Prix, held at the scene of Colin's former *bête noire* Indy car outing, the Mount Fuji Raceway. Then through 1977 and '78 Colin prompted the design revolution that saw aerodynamicist Peter Wright become instrumental in introducing to Formula 1 the under-body 'ground effect' aerodynamics technology that would see Team Lotus again re-write the record books.

Mario and Colin built a relationship of mutual respect and trust in which constructor and driver worked together more closely than at any time since Jimmy Clark's death. Mario won the Formula 1 Driver's World Championship title at a canter in 1978, but thereafter Team's fortunes nose-dived as Colin became increasingly distracted by the problems of ensuring mere survival for what had become the diverse Group of Lotus companies.

The 1979 Lotus Type 80 Formula 1 car proved itself an untameable disaster, and in 1980–81 Colin's last great celebrated attempt to drive a coach and horses through the small print of Formula 1 regulations foundered on the rocks of combined Formula 1 Constructors' Association opposition and a new and vociferously disciplinarian governing body.

Slowly Team began to recover in Formula 1, but then, in the small hours of 16 December 1982, after spending the previous day in Paris before flying home, Colin Chapman suffered a massive heart attack and died. He was only 54. He had always fought a battle with his weight, but had seemed very fit, as his successful annual private pilot's medicals had demonstrated.

Group Lotus and Team Lotus rode this massive shock and survived. Former team manager Peter Warr took over as Chief Executive of Team Lotus, and soon Frenchman Gerard Ducarouge – an ex-Matra, Ligier and Alfa Romeo engineer – was appointed to take technical charge of Team as it embarked upon a post-Chapman career, with turbocharged 1.5-litre Renault V6 Formula 1 engines replacing the age-old – and so successful – Cosworth-Ford V8s.

Then in 1984 Team Lotus was approached by English-born American businessman Roy Winkelmann, who proposed a Lotus return to Indianapolis-style competition in America, for which he would find suitable sponsorship. Roy had raced his own Cooper-Bristol sports during the 1950s before really making his name on the international motor racing scene with his British-based Formula 2 team of Brabham cars, based at Slough in Buckinghamshire, where he owned and ran a large bowling and leisure centre and other interests including a security company. Former Team Lotus Formula Junior driver Alan Rees ran Winkelmann Racing's activities, doubling for several seasons as player manager and from 1965 team-mate to its great star, contemporary King of Formula 2 racing, Jochen Rindt.

Everything about the Winkelmann Racing operation spelled care, forethought and quality, characteristics that tall, rangy Roy – who liked to portray himself as something of a mystery man, ex-CIA, a 'spook' – demanded in all his activities.

In 1969 the team abruptly broke up, some of its personnel (led by Alan Rees) forming the core of March Engineering. Roy found himself effectively abandoned by those who had formerly run his racing team for him, and he was left with no active racing link other than his continuing relationship with Rindt, whom he advised on business matters. But September 1970 saw the fatal accident of the Austrian World Champion-to-be in practice at Monza . . .

Roy thereafter stayed away from racing for many years, while developing his extraordinary mixture of security, counter-intelligence and night club businesses. But he never completely lost the itch to return to racing.

Meanwhile, during the long period of Lotus's absence from Indianapolis-style racing, the old traditional governing body of National Championship speedway racing in America – USAC – was effectively deposed by a confederation of team owners led prominently by Roger Penske and Dan Gurney, who formed a rival and effective replacement body entitled 'Championship Auto Racing Teams' (CART).

Ultimately this body assumed control of what was formally re-titled 'Indycar' racing, and while the Indianapolis 500-Miles classic remained the jewel in each year's 'Championship Trail' crown, it became the only qualifying round still under USAC's control and was run to what were in detail often significantly different regulations.

By 1984 Roy Winkelmann believed that he was seeing a blossoming international interest in American CART racing, and perceived enormous commercial sponsorship potential. At that time

The slender moulded carbon-composite chassis nacelle for Roy Winkelmann's new-generation Indy Lotus Type 96 carried separate detachable body panels to provide its aerodynamic outer skin. Here in the load-bearing 'tub', function was everything, finish was irrelevant. (Focalpoint, Norwich)

Lotus made up the carbon-composite chassis from a grooved, folded and bonded flat sheet, the major joints then being sealed with bonding tape and finally cured. Inserted inner skin sections then provided full-length torsion boxes on each side, with access apertures for maintenance and fuel bag insertion. Radiators were outrigged on each side, to be enclosed in underwing side-pod panelling. (Focalpoint, Norwich)

CART racing was dominated by the British-built 2.65-litre turbocharged DFX version of the magnificent 3-litre Formula Cosworth DFV/DFY family of V8 engines. Roy Winkelmann knew both Keith Duckworth and Mike Costin of Cosworth Engineering, and he appreciated that nobody in CART competition had their engines prepared first-hand by the Northampton company itself. Instead they used engines commonly built and rebuilt by Stateside specialists from imported kits of parts.

Having obtained some assurance from Cosworth Engineering that it would be prepared to build 'works' engines for a Winkelmann Racing CART operation, Roy then looked to Lotus to provide him with a tailor-made 'works' chassis rather than the off-the-peg, made-down-to-a-price proprietary cars readily avail-

able at that time from March or Lola, and commissioned a Ducarouge-designed Lotus Indycar to be built for the 1985 season.

This was an interesting project for the Ketteringham crew, and while Winkelmann announced his intention to return to motor racing with a three-year CART programme under the name 'Winkelmann Team Lotus', running Lotus chassis, Cosworth engines and supported by as yet unspecified commercial sponsorship, his representatives were combing the US to arrange suitable big-business backing.

Ducarouge flew out to the CART Championship round in New York's new Meadowlands road circuit before setting down thoughts for a chassis concept derived from the 1985 Lotus Type

The underwing floor of the Type 96, front end to the right, in this shot on Team Lotus's 1980s race-shop floor at Ketteringham Hall, near Hethel. The underwing venturi sections rise up on each side of the engine-bay undertray section to the left. The up-curled leading edges on each side at the right will provide the lower lips of the side-pod radiator intakes. (Focalpoint, Norwich)

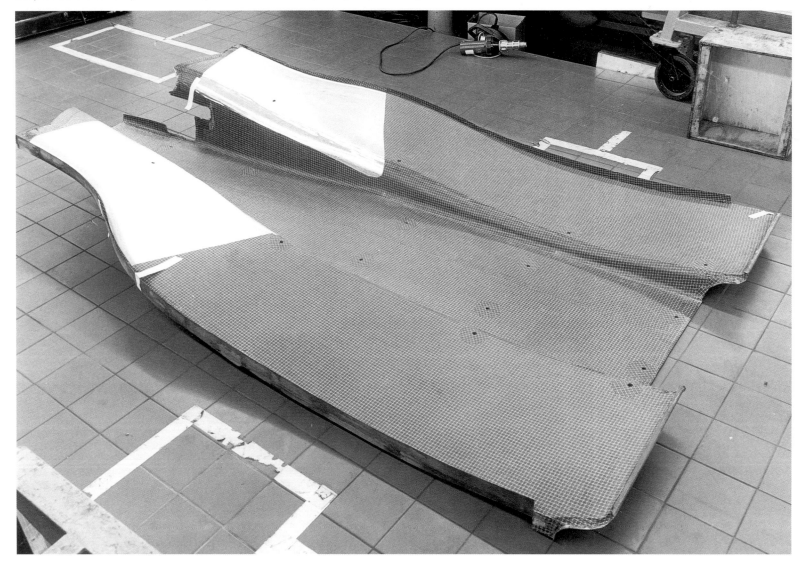

The most important aspect of the Type 96 that no competitor ever got to see – note the slender transaxle flanked by twin onboard jack cylinders, and broad underwing 'ground effect' venturis with air exit as unobstructed as was then thought possible by suspension links and driveshafts. (Focalpoint, Norwich)

95T carbon-composite moulded chassis design, but now to comply with CART racing regulations. The new chassis 'tub' was to be moulded generally to the same method as the 95T, but was to feature much thicker and stronger laminations because, as Gerard put it, '. . . it was possible that the car could 'it a concrete wall at 320 kilometres an hour'!

The new car used the basic carbon/Kevlar composite sandwich skins, pre-impregnated with resin, that had been Lotus's Formula 1 practice, but to gain extra shear-strength the original void-filling Nomex paper-foil honeycomb was replaced by a lightweight aluminium-foil honeycomb. This material required far more delicate and sensitive handling, but it proved far stronger when bent. In this respect the new Type 96 Indycar marked a new beginning, as Lotus's subsequent Formula 1 'tubs' would also employ aluminium honeycomb filling in place of the Nomex used in the Types 88 to 95T of 1981–84.

One prototype Type 96 Indycar was completed, but even before it was finished it became abundantly apparent to all Team's people at Ketteringham Hall that poor Winkelmann and his aides were facing an American CART establishment that was not at all enthusiastic about the prospect of a Winkelmann Team

Lotus, running 'works' engines, breaking into their kind of racing.

Amid much behind-the-scenes manoeuvring, Roy's prime sponsorship scout, Ekrem Sami, was unable to secure the sponsorship demanded to support such an ambitious scheme, while Peter Warr became increasingly alarmed at the capital outlay that Lotus had incurred in building the prototype car, and for which no payment appeared to be forthcoming. Available driver talent also seemed more attracted to the known-quantity 'comfort factor' provided by teams offering customer Lola or March chassis to face what was really the only factory team in Indycar contention, Penske.

After long weeks of uncertainty, unfulfilled promises, claim and counter-claim, the whole Type 96 project stuttered to a halt. In effect, Roy Winkelmann retired hurt, vacating the motor racing scene once more in one direction, while Lotus's management put it down to an awful miscalculation and went off in another – to concentrate once more upon pure-bred Formula 1.

The Team was left with a very expensive CART racing prototype Indycar standing in one corner of its race shop, where it remained silent, unwanted and unloved through the 1985 season in which it had been intended to compete.

By 1986 this handsome British Racing Green-liveried one-off was

All dressed up, but nowhere to go – Unraced, unloved and ultimately unwanted, the sole completed Type 96 poses for the local industrial photographer's camera in the rain outside Ketteringham Hall. Without adequate sponsorship the mid-'80s Indy Lotus programme proved a costly gamble, on which Team Lotus lost heavily. (Focalpoint, Norwich)

no longer eligible under altered American Indycar Championship regulations, so like the 1969 Type 64s it was fated to become merely a fascinating show car – an interesting reminder of what might have been. Sadly, however, it was one Indy Lotus that never even got as far as running under its own power.

In retrospect this was a very sad postscript to the once dazzling story of what in their respective days, and in their respective classes, had been two great teams of immense stature and achievement – Team Lotus and Winkelmann Racing. *Sic transit gloria* ...

Technical Specifications

Editor's Note: What follows are essentially Andrew Ferguson's painstaking Indy Lotus notes,
tables and musings upon the history of the cars and the personnel, as at the time of his passing.

LOTUS-FORD TYPE 29 – 1963

Chassis
Twin-tube 'ladder-frame' stressed skin riveted structure of various gauges but mainly 16g aluminium-alloy sheet with front and rear steel sub-frames.

Power unit
Ford 260 Fairlane based 90 degree V8 pushrod.
Aluminium crankcase, block and heads.
Capacity – 4195 cc (255 cu in)
Weight – 357 lbs*
Bore & stroke – 3.76 inches x 2.87 inches
Gasoline octane rating – 103.5.
376 bhp @ 7200 rpm*
Compression ratio – 12.5:1
Carbs – Weber 4 twin-choke 58 mm (Indy)* – 48 mm (Ovals)*
Ignition – Magnetic-trigger transistorized
Spark plugs – Autolite
Battery – Varley 6 cell 12v 26 amp

Transmission
Type 37A Colotti 4 speed gearbox. 3 plate 7^{1}/2 inch Borg & Beck clutch.
Saginaw recirculating ball bearing spline drive shafts with Hookes type universal joints each end. Provision for separate 1 Imp gallon (1.2 US) oil tank left-hand side of gearbox.
Gearlever r/h side of cockpit. 2 piece linkage.

Fuel tanks
42 Imperial gallons (50 US). Five compartments within chassis containing FPT (Fireproof Tanks, Portsmouth) rubberised rupture proof bag tanks, four in side sponsons, one behind driver seat bulkhead; sixth in g.r.p. encased aluminium tank behind instrument panel (over driver's legs). 'Filler-cap' in this tank acted as air vent when refuelling through a valve on left-hand side of car.
All tanks inter-connected with non-return valves to prevent fuel surge on corners and braking. Rearward surge allowed to fuel off-takes.
Three electric Bendix fuel pumps under driver's legs.

Oil tank
4 Imperial gallons (4.8 US)

Brakes
Girling 10^{1}/2 inch (as used) or 11^{1}/2 inch discs 2 master cylinders. Independent front/rear operation. Ferodo/Raybestos pads interchanged.

Wheels
Specially manufactured Dunlop peg-drive light alloy perforated disc with knock-off hubs.
Front – 15 inch diameter – Rim width 6 inches
Rear – 15 or 16 inch – Rim width 8 inches
(in race car ran Halibrand rear wheels 15 inch diameter 9 inch rim width)

Tyres
Front – 5.50/6.00/6.50 x 15 inch
Rear – 7.00 x 16 or 8.25 x 15/16 inch
Dunlop tyres fitted for initial testing. Firestone in 500 race. Dunlops on 1 mile ovals.

Front suspension
Chassis offset of 2^{3}/8 inches to left by means of longer suspension links on right-hand side to reduce weight transfer and improve tyre wear and cornering. Welded up cantilever top rocking arms operating inboard coil spring/Armstrong co-axial damper unit with lower wishbone. Magnesium/zirconium cast vertical links.

Rear suspension
Single top arm and reversed lower wishbone with single chassis mounting. Unequal length twin parallel radius arms. Anti-roll bar. Outboard coil spring/Armstrong damper unit. Both wishbones and top arms equal length with chassis off-set effected by extended chassis pick-up points on right-hand side. Magnesium/zirconium cast vertical links. Utilising equal length rocking arms at front and second set of attachment points at rear of chassis, car could be run in symmetrical/asymmetrical form as required.

Steering
Lotus rack-and-pinion with adjustable column, 12 inch 3 spoke light alloy Springall steering wheel. 2^{1}/4 turns lock to lock.

Cooling
Ducts incorporated in nose fed cooling air to suspension and cockpit. Combined oil/water radiator in nose, sited in front of 'V' shaped (to deflect air) oil tank. Water and oil pipes (the latter concentric), with clutch and

brake plumbing located in 'V' shaped channel incorporated in underside of chassis, with insulated water return pipe on top of sponson alongside driver.

Body
GRP detachable one piece nose cowling/cockpit surround/perspex windscreen. Engine cover and gearbox fairing.

Dimensions
Wheelbase	96 inches
Front track	56 inches
Rear track	56 inches
Overall length	12 feet 6 inches
Overall width (body)	28 inches
Overall width	65 inches
Overall height	$30^{1}/_{2}$ inches
Ground clearance	$3^{3}/_{4}$ inches
Weight	1130 lbs with oil/water
Weight distribution	40% front 60% rear (with driver and half fuel load)

Colours (Indy 500)
Jim Clark – BR green with yellow stripe topside and around nose cowling.
Dan Gurney – white with blue stripe topside and around nose cowling.

Race/chassis numbers
Practice
JC: ch no 29/3 Race: 92; DG: ch no 29/2 Race: 91; Spare: 29/1 Race: 93
Qualifying & race
JC: ch no 29/3 Race 92; DG: ch no 29/1 Race 93; Spare: Badly damaged.

*Data Ford America

TYPE 29 CHASSIS RECORD 1963
(three cars)

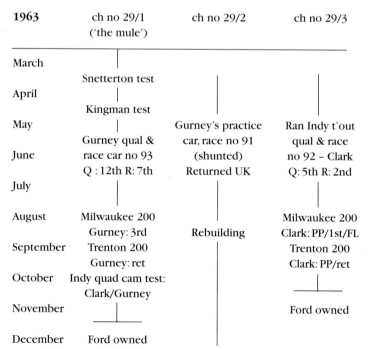

1963	ch no 29/1 ('the mule')	ch no 29/2	ch no 29/3
March			
April	Snetterton test		
	Kingman test		
May		Gurney's practice car, race no 91 (shunted)	Ran Indy t'out qual & race
June	Gurney qual & race car no 93 Q : 12th R: 7th	Returned UK	no 92 – Clark Q: 5th R: 2nd
July			
August	Milwaukee 200 Gurney: 3rd	Rebuilding	Milwaukee 200 Clark: PP/1st/FL
September	Trenton 200 Gurney: ret		Trenton 200 Clark: PP/ret
October	Indy quad cam test: Clark/Gurney		
November			Ford owned
December	Ford owned		

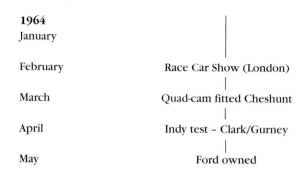

1964	
January	
February	Race Car Show (London)
March	Quad-cam fitted Cheshunt
April	Indy test – Clark/Gurney
May	Ford owned

HISTORICAL SUMMARY
Team Lotus chassis allocation was never a set procedure; in other words, Jimmy did not always drive a particular chassis from the date of build and it is most fortunate that Jim Endruweit's notes, listing chassis movements in 1963, still exist.

The chart reliably details events of that year, but following Ford's ownership and like most cars when sold, the trail disappeared. Ford's engine reference in paperwork related only to a car's race number, e.g. 'engine from car number 93'.

Reports and articles written in the intervening years have speculated upon the routes the three cars followed, but it is impossible to endorse these as Team Lotus frequently changed chassis plates around to suit the travel documentation in existence at the time. Such changes were not illegal and were actioned merely to hasten customs clearance.

Possibly the earliest attempt to trace Lotus-Indy chassis movements was instigated by Jabby Crombac in 1965 when he interviewed me at Cheshunt for an article he wrote for his magazine, *Sport-Auto*. Jabby recorded that of the 29s that actually *raced* in the 1963 Indy 500, the Clark and Gurney cars were 'destroyed by Marshman', Dan's shunted car, that had been rebuilt, shown as sold to Jerry Alderman Ford for its driver Al Miller. Publisher, Floyd Clymer agreed with this, but also reported that the latter car had previously been driven by Marshman in the 1964 race. This I find hard to believe as the car had only just been rebuilt by Team immediately prior to the race and Marshman had already chalked up a considerable test mileage in another Type 29, or perhaps both 29s still in America.

According to the Indianapolis Speedway Museum, chassis 29/1 (the 'mule' prototype) was on site in 1992, displayed as the Jim Clark car he drove at Indy in 1963, a suggestion that does not accord with its chassis number. Also, it has Goodyear tyres, (the car ran Firestone in the 500, Dunlop elsewhere), makeshift back 'plates' to the front wheels and a deep Dan Gurney style windscreen. It has no badge or 'Lotus powered by Ford' lettering on the nose, there is no yellow pinstripe on the cockpit sides and the exhaust pipes are out of true. It was also reported last year that the chassis plate is taped over.

These criticisms, apart from the chassis number, are minor errors of livery and therefore unimportant, but if we assume the car is a genuine Type 29, it leaves two cars to account for.

Over the 1963-64 winter, we know Marshman drove both green and white cars in testing. We also know, contrary to popular belief, that Dan's shunted car (29/2) was not in Ford's or Hopkins' hands at the tail end of 1963 because it remained in England until April 1964. Marshman had two or three (perhaps more), major accidents in Type 29s before the one that proved fatal and on two occasions the wrecked cars returned to Cheshunt for rebuilding.

Another fallacy that has crept in over the years, is that Marshman's fatal accident was in a Type 34 (see Type 34 summary).

Team Lotus supplied Type 29 components to American owners over quite a long period in the 'sixties, so perhaps one or two replicas were produced. The Type 29 that Al Miller drove for Jerry Alderman, a Ford dealer in Indianapolis, ran in the 1965 500 (finished fourth), and 1966, when it was damaged in the first lap accident. It was commonly referred to as the ex-Hopkins-Firebird car, so perhaps it was indeed one of them.

LOTUS INDIANAPOLIS PERSONNEL

Team Lotus

				Others at Indy
1963	Endruweit	Laz	Riley	Fowler/Phipps
				Forrest Hughes
Ovals:	Endruweit	Laz	Riley	Jim Gardner
1964	Endruweit	Laz	Riley	Gardner
	Underwood	Clode	Duxberry	Forrest Hughes
	Smith (Jim)			(drowned)
Ovals:	Laz	Dance	Sparshott	Alan Moffat
	Bob Davies (Cortina)	R. Parsons		
	Riley (contracted back)	John 'Gear'		
1965	Laz	U'wood	Clode	Randy Singer (big!)
	Smith (J.)	Butty		Russ Brandenberg
	John 'Gear'			(small American)
Disaster temps:				?????
	Dance	Sparshott		(tall, thin American)
				Peter Jackson
Hill climbs:	Laz	Clode		Alan Moffat
				Jim Gardner
1966	Laz	U'wood	Clode	
	Butty	McCall (Cortinas)		
Fuji:	U'wood	Butty		
1967	Endruweit	U'wood	Butty	Californians:
	Pickles	Rabbit	Chalky	J. Martinez &
	McCall	Absalom		R. Berry
1968	Scammell	Butty	Absalom	Fred Cowley
	Pickles	Garner	Cowe	Derek Gardner
				'Claude Monolok'
1969	Butty	Chalky	Garner	Brawner/McGee
	Mower (J.90)	Absalom	Rabbit	Derek Gardner
	Smith (R.)	Pickles		Dale Porteous
	Dance			(came from New
				York – May
				14–June 21)

LOTUS-FORD TYPE 34 – 1964

Chassis
Twin-tube 'ladder-frame' stressed skin riveted structure of various gauges but mainly 16g aluminium-alloy sheet with front and rear steel sub-frames.

Power-unit
Ford 90 degree V8 d.o.h.c. (quad cam) 32 valve. Cams driven by fourteen straight toothed spur gears. Aluminium crankcase, block and heads.
Capacity – 4195 cc (255 cu ins)
Weight – 396 lbs*
Bore & stroke – 3.76 inches x 2.87 inches
Fuel injection – Hilborn-Ford (mechanical pump driven by inlet camshaft).
Compression ratio – 14.1
Oil filter – Frame
425 bhp @ 8000 rpm (gasoline)*
475 bhp @ 8250 rpm (methanol)*
Fuel consumption (gasoline) – 3.5-4.5 mpg (Imperial).
Ignition – Ford breakerless transistorised.
Spark plugs – Autolite
Battery – Varley 6 cell 12v 26 amp

Transmission
ZF 2 DS 20 – 2 speed gearbox (derived from the 5 speed version fitted to Lotus Type 30). 3 plate $7^1/2$ inch Borg & Beck clutch
Saginaw recirculating ball spline drive shafts with Hookes type universal joints each end.
Gearlever r/h side of cockpit.

Fuel tanks
42 Imperial gallons (50.4 US). Five compartments within chassis containing FPT rubberised rupture-proof bag tanks. Four in side sponsons, one behind driver seat bulkhead sixth in g.r.p. encased aluminium tank behind instrument panel (over driver's legs). Aircraft style 'air vent' for refuelling.
All tanks inter-connected with non-return valves to prevent fuel surge on corners and braking. Rearward surge allowed to fuel off-takes. Hilborn-Ford mechanical fuel pump.

Oil tank
4 Imperial gallons (4.8 U.S.). For short ovals a $2/2^1/2$ Imperial gallon (2.4/3 US) oil tank was attached to outside left-hand side of tub alongside driver.

Brakes
Vented $10^1/2$ inch Girling disc with Raybestos pads. 2 master cylinders. Independent front/rear operation.

Wheels
Lotus 4 spoke cast magnesium with knock-off hubs.
Front – 15 inch diameter – Rim width 6 inches
Rear – 15 or 16 inch – Rim width 8 inches

Tyres
Indy 500 – Dunlop; Ovals – Firestone
Front – 6.50 x 15 inch
Rear – 8.25 x 15 or 16 inch

Front suspension

Chassis offset of 2³/8 inches to left by means of longer suspension links on right-hand side to reduce weight transfer and improve tyre wear and cornering. Welded-up cantilever top rocking arms operating inboard coil spring/Monroe co-axial damper unit with lower wishbone. Magnesium/zirconium cast vertical links.

Rear suspension

Single top arm and reversed lower wishbone with single chassis mounting. Unequal length twin radius arms. Anti-roll bar. Outboard coil spring/Monroe damper unit. Both wishbones and top arms equal length with chassis offset effected by extended chassis pick-up points on right-hand side. Magnesium/zirconium cast vertical links. Team Lotus ran this car in asymmetrical form only.

Steering

Lotus rack-and-pinion with adjustable column. 12 inch 3 spoke Springall light alloy steering wheel. 2¹/4 turns lock to lock.

Cooling

Ducts incorporated in nose fed cooling air to suspension and cockpit. Combined oil/water radiator in nose, sited in front of the 4 Imp gall (4.8 US) oil tank 'V' shaped to deflect air. Water and oil pipes (the latter concentric) with clutch and brake plumbing located in 'V' shaped channel incorporated in underside of chassis with insulated water return pipe on top of sponson alongside driver.

Body

GRP detachable one piece nose cowling/cockpit surround/perspex windscreen. Engine cover and gearbox fairing.

Dimensions

Wheelbase	96 inches
Front track	56 inches
Rear track	56 inches
Overall length	12 feet 6 inches
Overall width (body)	28 inches
Overall width	65/66 inches
Overall height	31 inches
Ground clearance	3³/4 inches
Weight	1200 pounds
Weight distribution	40% front 60% rear

Colours (Indy 500)

Jim Clark – BR green with yellow stripe topside and around nose cowling.
Dan Gurney – white with blue stripe topside and around nose cowling.

Race/chassis numbers

Practice and race numbers (chassis numbers not recorded).
JC: 6 ; DG: 12; Spare car: 36 (not used)

*Data Ford America

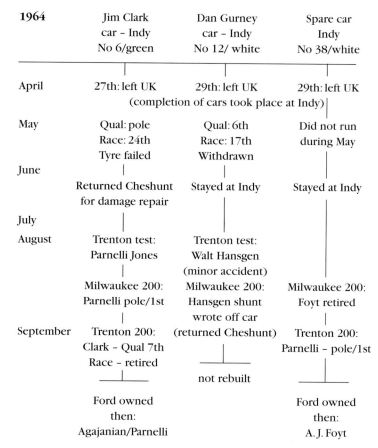

TYPE 34 CHASSIS RECORD 1964*
(three cars)

1964	Jim Clark car – Indy No 6/green	Dan Gurney car – Indy No 12/ white	Spare car Indy No 38/white
April	27th: left UK	29th: left UK	29th: left UK
		(completion of cars took place at Indy)	
May	Qual: pole Race: 24th Tyre failed	Qual: 6th Race: 17th Withdrawn	Did not run during May
June	Returned Cheshunt for damage repair	Stayed at Indy	Stayed at Indy
July			
August	Trenton test: Parnelli Jones	Trenton test: Walt Hansgen (minor accident)	
	Milwaukee 200: Parnelli pole/1st	Milwaukee 200: Hansgen shunt wrote off car (returned Cheshunt)	Milwaukee 200: Foyt retired
September	Trenton 200: Clark – Qual 7th Race – retired	not rebuilt	Trenton 200: Parnelli – pole/1st
	Ford owned then: Agajanian/Parnelli		Ford owned then: A. J. Foyt

*there is no reliable contemporary evidence as to chassis number cum driver

HISTORICAL SUMMARY

In the absence of chassis number records, I have identified the cars by their driver names and race numbers as of the Indianapolis 500 of 1964. Unlike the majority of race entry requirements in those days, the Indianapolis authorities did not require a chassis number and so another source of definition was lost. Entry forms and fees, (closing date mid-April) were acknowledged by notification of the car's race number, the latter being the reference by which the car was known from then on, e.g, 'Clark car, number 6'.

The overwhelming handicap for Team Lotus that year was a much delayed construction programme. There was no time for prototype testing, and even Jimmy commented to the media that all three cars had left Cheshunt unfinished and with a great deal of work to be done in our Speedway garages. This would account for our spare car remaining unused during May as it would have taken too much time to prepare to race standard.

After Dan Gurney's enforced withdrawal from the race, his car, (race number 12), remained in America until the Trenton test, August 17th/18th. I have assumed it was this car and not the spare as running data would have already accumulated. Also, with Hansgen's weight closer to Dan's than Jimmy's, (185 pounds) and his height some 2¹/2 inches taller than the Scotsman, cockpit fitting and driver comfort would have been more easily achieved.

At the end of the day in which Hansgen's first accident occurred the Team moved onto Milwaukee, where damage to the car was rectified. Bob Dance recorded that the crew's 'out of bed' hours for the three days, including driving the transporter and rebuilding the car, totalled 59 out of a possible 72 hours.

Walt's second shunt (at Milwaukee) that followed the rebuild was far more serious. Bob Dance's diary shows that work continued straight through for 26 hours, but whereas he remembers rebuilding the car, our records show the wreckage was returned to Cheshunt where it became the subject of much discussion and correspondence between Ford and Lotus. It was not rebuilt and finally disappeared from our records when the salvageable parts were shipped to Dearborn.

Perhaps due to excessive fatigue, Bob's 'rebuild' described the interchange of parts and preparation of the spare car that had not run in May and which would have required preparation to race standard.

Jim Clark's damaged car, (race number 6), returned to Cheshunt for repairs in mid-June. Parnelli Jones drove it at the Trenton test, (August 17th/18th) and when its steering broke, Parnelli skilfully restricted damage by merely 'kissing' the wall, and photographs show that he raced the car at Milwaukee with its slightly marked nose. He took pole position and won the race, complete with fastest lap, the car numbered with Parnelli's personal '98' but still in British racing green.

Jimmy was back in the car for the September Trenton 200 race, displaying his Indy race number 6; unusually, the engine was down on power and eventually he retired. After the race, the car passed into Ford ownership. It is not known if J. C. Agajanian acquired it from Ford immediately, but his driver, Parnelli Jones drove it at Phoenix November 22nd that year, still in its Team colours of green and yellow, a fact that may point to recent acquisition. Jones started from pole but retired in the race.

It would follow that this is the car Parnelli drove at Indy in 1965, labelled the *Agajanian Hurst Gear Shift Special*, the car reputed to remain in Parnelli's ownership to this day. Floyd Clymer's *1965 Indy Yearbook* suggested this was so, the car itself known as a Kuzma-Lotus after being 'completely re-designed and modified by Eddie Kuzma'.

The spare car, (race no 36), that did not run during May 1964, is assumed to be the chassis that first saw action at Milwaukee following Hansgen's accident and which called for an all-nighter of preparation. As it can be accepted it was initially built to suit Jimmy's dimensions, no doubt some considerable time was spent 'enlarging' it to suit A. J. Foyt, who was 25 pounds heavier and three inches taller than the Scot. In the Milwaukee race, A. J. retired it (needlessly as it transpired), virtually before the race got underway, whilst at Trenton, with Jimmy back in his green car, Parnelli drove it. He started from pole and won the race, one lap clear.

After Trenton the car went to Ford and it is pure supposition that it became Foyt's for the 1965 Indy 500, running as the *Sheraton-Thompson Special*; Clymer's yearbook states this was the case. Once again, the race publicity reported it had been completely rebuilt and modified, this time by Lujie Lesovsky; the latter was a very popular and skilled figure at the Speedway and was a most accomplished freelance sheet metal fabricator who assisted Team Lotus on many occasions.

Regardless of Messrs Kuzma and Lesovsky's undoubted skills, one is left to ponder Chapman's feelings when he surveyed the American press releases! Of Marshman's fatal accident in 1964, several scribes later suggested he

had been driving, a Type 34. However, as we know the spare car had been reduced to wreckage we must look to the other two cars for clues. A few days after the tragic event we received a simple mechanical enquiry about the Agajanian car from Ford; Foyt had also acquired his Type 34 by this time, but no request came for spares or rebuilding advice so it seems most unlikely A. J.'s car had been involved in the accident. Also, A. J. was very much a Goodyear contracted driver, Marshman with Firestone, though he tested both.

LOTUS-FORD TYPE 38 – 1965

Chassis
Full monocoque fabricated from sheet aluminium alloy and sheet metal of various gauges, but mainly 16g, incorporating longitudinal and lateral diaphragms that formed the fuel tank bays as well as providing additional strength and stiffness. Front and rear steel sub-frames carried suspension, steering and pedal mountings.

Power unit
Ford 90 degree V8 d.o.h.c. (quad-cam) 32 valve. Cams driven by 14 straight toothed spur gears. Aluminium crankcase, block and heads.
Capacity – 4195 cc. (255 cu ins)
Weight – 396 lbs
Bore & stroke – 3.76 inches x 2.87 inches
Fuel injection – Hilborn-Ford mechanical pump driven by inlet camshaft
Oil filter – Fram aircraft type
495 bhp @ 8800 rpm (methanol)
Compression ratio – 12.5:1
Fuel consumption range – 2–4 mpg (Imperial) 1.66–3.33 mpg (US)
Ignition – Ford breakerless transistorised
Spark Plugs – Autolite
Battery – Autolite 6 cell 12v 26 amp
The unit's lubrication system had been revised since 1964 and major moving parts reworked.

Transmission
ZF 2 DS 20 – 2 speed gearbox with separate oil pump and radiator. Twin plate diaphragm $8^{1}/2$ inch Borg & Beck clutch. Limited slip differential, spiral bevel crown wheel and pinion. Detroit sliding universal joints with BRD half shafts. Gearlever r/h side of cockpit

Fuel tanks
48.3 Imperial gallons (58 US). Three cells within chassis (one full length each side of the car, one behind the driver's seat) containing FPT hycatrol rubberised bag tanks, foam filled to prevent surge and for safety in event of an accident. Fuel fed through non-return valve to a gravity reservoir at rear of car. Aeroquip flexible hose lines. Hilborn Ford fuel pump. (Additional 2 Imperial gallon (2.40 US) reserve fuel tank was fitted during practice for the race.)

Oil tank
Main and supplementary 'birdbath' reservoir. Total capacity 7 Imperial (8.4 US) gallons. Aeroquip flexible hose lines

Brakes
Ventilated $12^{1}/2$ inch Girling discs and calipers/Raybestos pads. Two master cylinders. Independent front/rear operation.

Wheels

Lotus 4 spoke peg drive cast magnesium with knock-off hubs.
Front – 15 inch diameter – Rim width 8¹/2 inches
Rear – 15/16 inch diameter – Rim width 9¹/2 inches

Tyres

Firestone (Goodyear tried in practice)
Front – 9.20 x 15 inch
Rear – 12.00 x 15 or 16 inch

Front suspension

Chassis off-set of 3 inches to left by means of longer suspension links and bulkhead extension 'ears' for top rocking arms on right-hand side to reduce weight transfer and improve tyre wear and cornering. Welded up cantilever top rocking arms operating inboard coil spring/Monroe co-axial damper unit with lower wishbone. Magnesium/zirconium cast vertical links.

Rear suspension

Single top arm and reversed lower wishbone with single chassis mounting. Unequal length twin radius arms. Anti-roll bar. Outboard coil spring/Monroe co-axial damper unit. Magnesium/zirconium cast vertical links. Unlike Types 29 & 34, chassis off-set was effected by longer top link and lower wishbone on right-hand side i.e. chassis pick-up points both front and rear were equidistant from centre line of car, although later variations occurred.

Steering

Lotus rack-and-pinion with adjustable column. 12 inch 3 spoke light alloy Springall steering wheel. 2¹/4 turns lock to lock.

Cooling

Ducts incorporated in nose fed cooling air to suspension and cockpit, an exterior scoop for additional cockpit cooling fitted on top of nose in-line with the front bulkhead added during practice at Indy. Combined oil/water Serck radiator, fully ducted, in nose of car sited in front of the 3 Imp gall (3.6 US), primary oil tank, the latter 'V' shaped to deflect air. Oil and water pipes contained within two 'V' shaped channels incorporated in underside of chassis.

Body

GRP detachable nose cowling to front bulkhead, engine cover and two air intakes, gearbox fairing. Two piece perspex windscreen incorporating 'slot', although prototype employed one piece windscreen

Dimensions

Wheelbase	96 inches
Front track	60 inches
Rear track	60 inches
Overall length	13 feet
Overall width (body)	28 inches
Overall width	73 inches
Overall height	31 inches
Ground clearance	3¹/2 inches
Dry weight (1965)	1250 pounds
Weight distribution	40% front 60% rear

* The Ford V8 engine ran consistently to 9,100 rpm and even 9,300 rpm during initial trials; one engine covered nearly 1,500 miles before a routine inspection.

** Fuel tanks were originally designed along the 5 tank principle employed previously, but the regulation change enforcing gravity refuelling called for a redesign.

TYPE 38 CHASSIS RECORD 1965
(five cars)
* second car built (chassis 38/3) sold to Dan Gurney and not recorded here

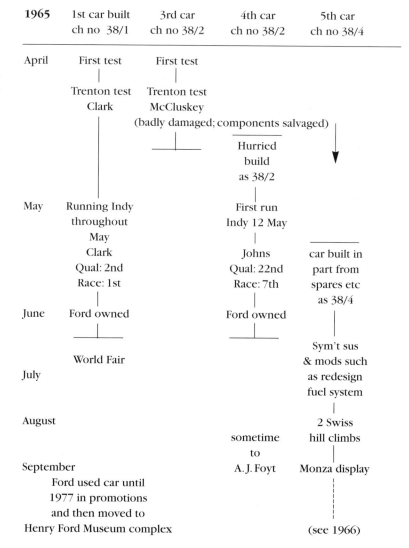

1965	1st car built ch no 38/1	3rd car ch no 38/2	4th car ch no 38/2	5th car ch no 38/4
April	First test — Trenton test — Clark	First test — Trenton test — McCluskey (badly damaged; components salvaged)	Hurried build as 38/2	
May	Running Indy throughout May — Clark Qual: 2nd Race: 1st		First run Indy 12 May — Johns Qual: 22nd Race: 7th	car built in part from spares etc as 38/4
June	Ford owned		Ford owned	
	World Fair			Sym't sus & mods such as redesign fuel system
July				
August			sometime to	2 Swiss hill climbs
September	Ford used car until 1977 in promotions and then moved to Henry Ford Museum complex		A. J. Foyt	Monza display (see 1966)

LOTUS-FORD TYPE 38 – 1966

For 1966 the Type 38 was to be superseded by the Type 42 of designer Maurice Phillippe, but subsequent events were to find modified versions of the 38 used as the team's mainstay in 1966 and 1967.

Numerous detail changes were made to suspension geometry and chassis pick-up points to cope with both increased engine power and changes in wheel designs brought about by developments in tyre constructions and profiles.

The first and most substantial design changes to the Type 38 came after the 1965 Indy 500 when, without a defined Formula 1 programme for the following year, the sole and newly built Type 38 (chassis 38/4), at Cheshunt became a general test vehicle. The car embodied symmetric suspension, ran in two Swiss hill-climbs, appeared in various displays and tested multi-tubular De Dion rear suspension.

Both the symmetrical and De Dion layouts saw design changes to uprights, (vertical links), wishbones, brakes and calipers for tests which included roll centre experimentation. When the H16 BRM engines failed to materialise for the 1966 race and the Type 42's were temporarily shelved, 38/4 was converted to asymmetric suspension and along with the 'soft alloy' chassis no 38/7, hurriedly prepared and air freighted to Indianapolis.

Both cars were given the suffix 'B' in Team Lotus and STP publicity, no doubt to emphasise they were not merely year old cars. From Maurice Phillippe's notes of the period and those of Ford America, the following is the list of what were relatively minor changes to cars and engines, the relevant data for the previous year shown in brackets.

Power-unit

Updates on the specification for the 1966 race included a more efficient oil pump and oil gland together with a redesign that enabled oil lines to be routed fore or aft as required. The engines, now designated 'C' series, cost $22,000 ($15,000), the update kit for 1965 engines costing $1,200.

The 1966 engines produced 525 bhp @ 9000 rpm (495 bhp @ 9000 rpm), the 1965 and 1966 engines both methanol burners.

Fuel tanks

Total capacity increased by 2 gallons (Imperial) 2.4 (US) by enlarged reserve/collector tank.
Side tanks – 2 x 22 Imperial gallons (26.4 US)
Seat tank – 3 Imperial gallons (3.6 US)
Reserve and collector tank – 3 Imperial (3.6 US)

Brakes

Ventilated 12 inch Girling disc front and rear ($12^1/_2$ inch)

Wheels

Halibrand on rear. (Lotus 4-spoke)

Dimensions

Overall length	13 feet 1 inch (13 feet)
Overall width (body)	30 inches (28 inches)
Overall width (incl. wheels)	72 inches (73 inches)
Ground clearance	3 inches laden – 3.75 inches unladen ($3^1/_2$ inches)
Dry weight	1350 pounds (1250 pounds) (regulation change)

By June 1966, the Type 38 badly damaged in Unser's race accident was the only car retained by Team Lotus. Insurance broker approval to rebuild the car was delayed and the last in the Type 38 line, chassis 38/8, or /8S as it was referred to on many occasions, was constructed. The 'S' suffix related to its symmetrical suspension which it retained up to the time of its sale and Team supplied drawings to its owner to enable him to convert it to asymmetric.

TYPE 38 CHASSIS RECORD 1966

(five cars)
*One car from 1965, three 'soft alloy' and one regular car built, Team Lotus and STP publicity termed the Type 38s as 38B

1966	from 1965 ch no 38/4 (5th car)	'soft alloy' 38/5 (6th car)	Components/Team 38/6 (7th car)	38/7 (8th car)	Team car 38/8 (10th car)
January	Race Show (London)				
February	Snetterton test				
March	De Dion test Goodwood (discarded)	Team's Indy section assisting with build & assembly			
April		Shipped Dean Van Lines (Mario Andretti)	Shipped A.J. Foyt		
May	Running Indy throughout May Clark Qual: 2nd Race: 2nd			Running Indy throughout May Unser Qual: 23rd Race: 12th (crashed) Badly damaged	
June	Sold A.J. Foyt accident Mil'kee Team rebuild			Insurance broker approval	38/8 (or 38S) built
July				Rebuilt (virtually	
August	Returned A.J.			new car)	test
September					Fuji trip Indy test
					Both cars retained for 1967

LOTUS-FORD TYPE 38 – 1967

That the damage to Unser's car in the 1966 Indy 500 was severe is substantiated by the fact an almost completely new vehicle was required to replace it. Including this car and the one involved in the Trenton accident of April 1965, it can be seen that a total of ten Type 38s were built in the two years 1965 and 1966.

Of these, eight were built with asymmetric suspension, chassis 38/4 ran in both symmetric and asymmetric form, 38/8 remaining symmetric throughout its life with Team Lotus.

The 1967 Indy race found Team Lotus in even more chaos than the previous year, Chapman persisting with his assumption that the BRM H16 engines would eventually be delivered. Former Indy chief mechanic David Lazenby had become general manager of Lotus Components and Mike Underwood took his place at Indy. Lazenby later described his transfer as 'the biggest mistake of my life', a sentiment not too far from Underwood's thoughts as he surveyed the scene in our Indy garages.

Recently joined Graham Hill stayed with his symmetric 38/8 most of the month of May, but he failed to get up to speed and he fell back on the Type 42 that had been hurriedly converted to take a Ford V8.

Jim Clark stayed with his Type 38, (38/7), but both drivers must have pondered why the Team had not given Indy 1967 a miss; Jimmy qualified 16th and finished 31st in the race.

Testing continued with the cars after the race and were then advertised for sale, their swansong coming in a Marion County courtroom early the following year.

It marked a sad conclusion to one of Team's most remarkable models.

TYPE 38 CHASSIS RECORD 1967

(two cars)

*1967 was the second year planned for the introduction of the Type 42

1967	from 1966 ch 38/7	from 1966 38.8 or 38S
March	Car left UK for Indy test (Clark)	
April		Car left UK for Indy
May	Running at Indy throughout May (Clark) Qual: 16th Race: 31st (burned piston)	Used in practice by Graham Hill (race no 80) but he raced the 42F
June	Remained Indy garage	Returned UK by sea
August		Firestone Indy test
November	Both cars advertised for sale	
1968 February	court case	

LOTUS-BRM TYPE 42 – 1966–1967

Chassis

A monocoque fabricated from sheet aluminium alloy and steel of various gauges, mainly 16g, incorporating longitudinal and lateral diaphragms forming the fuel tank bays. Front and rear steel sub-frames carried suspension, steering and pedal mountings. Unlike its Indianapolis predecessor, the monocoque terminated in a bulkhead immediately behind the driver's seat. The load bearing BRM H16 engine was attached to the bulkhead by steel channel support plates, its BRM gearbox carrying the rear sub-frame with its suspension pick-up points, only the radius arms being attached to the tub. The latter was considerably stiffer torsionally than any previous Lotus single-seater and weighed only 80 pounds.

Power-unit*

BRM H16, best described as an 'H' lying on its side, was an enlarged version of BRM's 3-litre F1 horizontally opposed unit. Based on two V8 $1^1/2$ litre engines, with the 'V's flattened and mounted one on top of the other. Two nitrided flat crankshafts set 90 degrees to each other, linked by three spur gears. Light alloy crankcase and cylinder heads with steel liners. Two camshafts per bank, (8 total) operating 32 valves.
Weight – 565 pounds (F1 version 546 pounds)
Capacity – 4.2 litre (4198 cc) 255 cu ins
Bore & stroke – 2.938 inches x 2.362 inches
Fuel injection – Lucas – 2 metering units driven via internal toothed rubber belt front upper camshaft drive.
Spark plugs – Champion
BHP – Initially reported as 566 bhp @ 9,750 rpm running on gasoline. (see summary)
Ignition – 2 Lucas distributors driven from upper crankshaft by skew gears. Lucas transistorised ignition to 16 spark-plugs.
Battery – Varley 6 cell 12 v 26 amp (components unique to the 4.2 litre engine were crankshafts, con-rods, liners, piston and power-pack assemblies and camshafts).

Transmission

BRM 3-speed gearbox with alloy casing. Borg and Beck twin-plate diaphragm $8^1/2$ inch diameter clutch. Limited slip differential, hypoid crown wheel and pinion. Sliding spline half-shafts. Right-hand gearlever operating a Teleflex cable.

Fuel tanks

48.3 Imperial (58 US), gallons carried in three flexible FPT hycatrol rubberised bag tanks, one of 19 Imperial gallons (22.8 US) each side of car, and one of 10.3 Imperial gallons, (12.4 US), behind the driver's seat. Foam filled to prevent surge and increase safety. Fuel fed through non-return valve to reservoir tank at rear of car, pumped by Lucas 'bomb' to Lucas fuel injection system. The 'bomb' was mounted in front of the radiator for maximum cooling unlike the BRM F1 scheme where it was situated under the driver's legs.

Oil tank

Main tank of 3 Imperial gallons, (3.6 US), and supplementary 'birdbath' reservoir; total capacity 7 Imperial gallons (8.4 US). 'Both' engines comprising the H16 were lubricated by one system, the lower crankshaft operating the oil pump by gears. The main pump was a three gear scavenge

228

type, with two smaller pumps fitted to and retrieving oil from, the lower camboxes. Aeroquip flexible hose lines.

Brakes
Girling ventilated 12 inch diameter disc brakes and calipers. Raybestos pads. Two master cylinders and independent front/rear operation.

Wheels
Lotus four spoke peg drive cast magnesium with knock-off hubs.
Front – 15 inch diameter – Rim width: $8^1/_2$ inches
Rear – 15 inch diameter – Rim width: $9^1/_2$ inches

Tyres
Firestone
Front – 9.20 x 15
Rear – 12.00 x 15

Front suspension
Chassis off-set of 3 inches to left by means of longer suspension links and bulkhead extension 'ears' for top rocking arms for right-hand side. Welded up cantilever top rocking arms operating inboard coil spring/Monroe co-axial damper units with wide based lower wishbones. Magnesium/zirconium cast vertical links.

Rear suspension
Single top arm and reversed lower wishbone with single chassis mounting. Unequal length track control arms. Anti-roll bar. Outboard coil-spring/Monroe co-axial damper units. Magnesium/zirconium cast vertical links.

Steering
Lotus rack-and-pinion with adjustable column. 13 inch 3 spoke light alloy Springall steering wheel. $2^1/_4$ turns lock to lock.

Cooling
Ducts incorporated in side of car's nose fed cooling air to shock absorbers. A duct forward of the windscreen supplied cool air to the cockpit. Combined oil/water radiator by Serck, fully ducted, in nose of car in front of the primary oil tank 'V' shape to deflect air. Oil and water pipes formed part of the exterior body contours at lower edges of monocoque. The two BRM water pumps (one for each bank) were driven by a train of gears at the front of the engine.

Body
GRP detachable nose cowling to front bulkhead, engine cover and gearbox/tail fairing. Two piece perspex windscreen incorporating 'slot'.

Dimensions
Wheelbase	96 inches
Front track	60 inches
Rear track	60 inches
Overall length	13 feet 6 inches
Overall body width (at engine bulkhead)	30 inches
Overall width	73 inches
Overall height	30.5 inches
Ground clearance	3.5 inches
Dry weight	1350 pounds

LOTUS-BRM/FORD TYPE 42 – 1966–1967

Two Type 42 chassis were built at Cheshunt over the winter of 1965/66, numbers 42B/1 and /2, the 'B' relating to the Indy version of the BRM H16 engine for which the cars were designed. The cars were the first major item on newly joined designer Maurice Phillippe's job list, his parameters governed by the Team's programme of cost cutting. He was to design mirror image cars for F1 (Type 43) and Indy, (Type 42) utilising components left from Types' 38, 33 (F1), 30 and 40 (big sports cars).

Very late into the programme Chapman had to accept that the BRM H16 engines would not materialise and the cars were put to one side and Type 38s hurriedly prepared.

The incomplete cars went to Norfolk when the factory moved from Cheshunt and when the H16s were promised for the 1967 race, the cars were dusted down and updated. There were new Firestone compounds available in four different configurations and for these the 15 inch wheels were succeeded by 16 inch (front and rear). These were designed in December 1966, but by March there had been a return to 15 inch wheels further modified from original. In tandem with these changes, came regular reappraisals of suspension components and geometry, the 16 inch specification taken to Indy for trials in practice.

Team Lotus and STP announced to the press that the H16 would be seen at Indianapolis, repeating BRM's claim that the unit was producing 650 bhp at 9,750 rpm on the dyno. In fact, over the whole period of development the engine had registered between 453 bhp and 588 bhp, not necessarily in a progressive order.

This time an engine did materialise and a car was tested at Snetterton in March 1967; it lasted five laps before a serious mechanical malfunction occurred. Although we didn't know at the time, it was to mark the end of a project termed 'that mechanical sandwich' by Andy Granatelli.

When, just three weeks away from departure to America, it was confirmed there would be no BRM engine for the race, one car was quickly converted to take an Indy Ford V8 as preparation went ahead to get the two Type 38s into shape. As the BRM engine was load bearing and the Ford was not, a tubular space frame was attached to the tub's rear bulkhead.

In anticipating Bourne's forthcoming problem, Maurice and fellow 'pencil', Geoff Ferris had designed the frame as a fail-safe measure as early as January, but the suspension modifications had forestalled the scheme. It was not signed off until April 7th, a date by which test running should have long been completed.

The Ford V8 was considerably longer than the BRM unit and so the wheelbase of the 1967 car grew from 95 inches to 106 inches, the overall length of the car now 14 feet 4 inches instead of the original 13 feet 6 inches. Overall width was narrowed to $71^1/_2$ inches (from 73 inches) and ground clearance went to 3 inches from $3^1/_2$ inches.

Both 42s had been entered for the race, listing BRM motive power, 42B/1 (later F/1) given the race number 81 and 42B/2 race number 30; the former entry was later withdrawn. Chassis plate 42B/1 had the 'B' roughly overstamped with an 'F' and was flown to Indy, the second chassis, 42B/2 remaining in the factory. It is interesting to reflect that several historians have since insisted both cars were despatched to Indy, even supplying photographs that they feel sure proves their point; sadly, such evidence merely underlines the fact there were so many changes made to the one car from day to day running anyone could be forgiven for assuming there were two cars involved!

Graham Hill, like Jimmy preferred his Type 38 (38/8S) in practice; whether it was due to its symmetric suspension we shall never know, but Graham was unable to get up to speed and the sole Type 42 was dragged out in desperation, but eventual success in qualifying. The month of May must also have been extremely galling for poor Maurice. The Type 42, his first car for Team Lotus, had first been shelved for a year and then hastily butchered to take another power-unit; also he had been forced to update another designer's car two years in a row …

After the Team's poor showing the car was advertised for sale; it had been temporarily imported and so to ease sale in the 'States the car was taken over the border to Canada, and then re-imported on a permanent basis. It was to remain at Indy until sold to Canadian, Bill Brack in January 1969 but was not collected until June, some two years after its last race. Brack sold the car to race driver Robs Lamplough in 1970 who displayed the car at the Saarbrucken Show the same year. Later he sold it to a private collector, who it is believed retains it to this day.

Team Lotus sold the second car (42B/2) to Lotus Components in December 1967, from where it passed to Robs Lamplough along with the two Type 43 'mirror image' F1 cars.

Robs took all three cars to engineer Ken Nicholls for conversion to F5000/Formula A specification and Ken remembers the project well.

Ken: 'I took the front bulkhead out of the Indy car, (42B/2) to rework it from asymmetric to symmetric. I'm pretty sure I didn't make a new bulkhead; remember I had the two Type 43 F1 cars to copy from so it wasn't a difficult task.'

Robs then sold the car to Brack and Jo Marquart, assistant to Maurice Phillippe, designed new front uprights for it. Lotus Canada mechanic, Barry Sullivan installed a 5-litre dry-sump Chevvy V8 reputed to produce 500 bhp and built by Landon Engines of Detroit. Sullivan converted the car at Hethel and it was renamed the 'Castrol Lotus GTX' for Brack to campaign in the F5000/Formula A races of 1969.

At the Lime Rock event in August, Brack suffered an enormous accident at the end of the main straight, coincidentally right in front of Lamplough; Robs reported recently that it was 'positively a skip job' and that Brack took the wreck back to Toronto where he sold it for scrap. Robs also remembered the 'ears' on the front box for the off-set suspension although, of course, Brack ran it in symmetric form.

The car is now believed to be in a private collection in America.

TYPE 42 CHASSIS RECORD (1966–1967)
(two cars)

1966	ch no 42B/1	ch no 42B/2
	(the 'B' suffix was for BRM)	

January	Both monocoques were built at this time, but when the H16
February	engines did not materialise the tubs were put to one side
March	and Type 38 Ford engined cars took their place

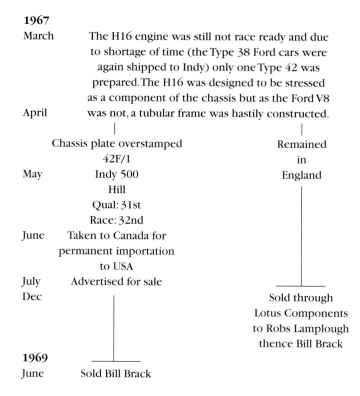

1967		
March	The H16 engine was still not race ready and due to shortage of time (the Type 38 Ford cars were again shipped to Indy) only one Type 42 was prepared. The H16 was designed to be stressed as a component of the chassis but as the Ford V8	
April	was not, a tubular frame was hastily constructed.	
	Chassis plate overstamped 42F/1	Remained in
May	Indy 500 Hill Qual: 31st Race: 32nd	England
June	Taken to Canada for permanent importation to USA	
July	Advertised for sale	
Dec		Sold through Lotus Components to Robs Lamplough thence Bill Brack
1969		
June	Sold Bill Brack	

LOTUS-PRATT & WHITNEY TYPE 56 – 1968

Chassis
Twin-tube 'ladder-frame' stressed skin riveted structure of various gauges, but mainly 16-gauge aluminium-alloy sheet with front and rear bulkhead structures, suspension pick-ups etc, in steel.

Power-unit
Pratt & Whitney STN6B-74 gas turbine with three-stage axial compressor and 15.999-square inches intake annulus area compared to five-stage compressor and 24-square inches intake annulus area of the 1967 STP-Paxton Turbocar unit also by Pratt & Whitney. A single-stage centrifugal compressor then fed air into a reverse-flow annular combustion chamber. Burning aviation kerosene fuel gas generator turbine separate from power output turbine revving respectively to 20,000 and 38,000rpm. Nominal power output burning aviation kerosene 430bhp at 6,230rpm at sea-level, at 69degs Fahrenheit ambient temperature – power diminishing to c.400bhp at 80F – output torque c.790ft/lb at stall, diminishing with speed – burning alternative gasoline fuel power output 500bhp-plus but raised turbine blade temperature from c. 1,650 to c.1,850degsF – with 80 per cent idle setting throttle lag from full over-run to maximum torque 0.2-second against 0.5 second at 60 per cent idle speed – engine length, 60-inches – engine weight 260lbs bare.

Transmission
Power unit was offset c.2-inches to the right to accommodate front and rear propeller shafts passing along left-side of tub. Output shaft at front-end of gas turbine drove via 3-inch Morse chain into Ferguson Formula compound centre differential situated behind left-rear of cockpit – fore-and-aft drive

from solid steel torsion shafts powering ZF spiral-bevel limited-slip final-drive units on front and rear axle lines, Hardy-Spicer jointed drive-shafts then powering road wheels – compound differential stressed to accommodate c.700bhp. Standard 'Type A' centre-differential provided 50:50 torque split to front and rear drive systems – alternative 'Type B' provided 45:55 rearward torque bias

Fuel tanks

89 gallons of aviation kerosene or alternative gasoline, accommodated in four main FPT rubberised rupture-proof bag tanks within the 'monocoque' chassis bays – filling via aeronautical-standard Avery-Hardoll non-drip spring-loaded pressure couplings situated in the chassis flanks, one per cell. All tanks inter-connected with non-return valves to prevent fuel surge on corners and under braking. Rearward surge allowed to fuel off-takes.

Oil tank

Large capacity rupture-proof membrane protected outboard reservoir slung from rear face of rear bulkhead in tail of car – flanked by smaller-capacity catch tank of similar construction

Brakes

Girling $10^1/4$ inch diameter x $1^1/8$ inch thick ventilated discs with underslung (bottom-mounted) calipers – the assemblies each mounted inboard upon the transmission half-shafts at front and rear – two master cylinders and independent front/rear operation. Ferodo/Raybestos pads interchanged.

Wheels

Specially-manufactured Lotus peg-drive magnesium-alloy four-spoke castings retained by three-eared knock-off centre-lock spinners. 15-inch diameter x 9.5-inch wide rims front and rear.

Tyres

Firestone tyres
Front – 9.20 x 15 inch
Rear – 9.20 x 15 inch

Front suspension

Fabricated unequal-length upper and lower wishbones – front element of top wishbone extending inboard into bell-crank to actuate inboard-mounted co-axial coilspring/damper – cast magnesium Lotus upright/hub carrier uses common design for both front and rear and both sides, featuring duplicate steering arms front and rear, only rearward arm on front suspension attached to steering track rods.

Rear suspension

Fabricated unequal-length upper and lower wishbones – front element of top wishbone extending inboard into bell-crank to actuate inboard-mounted co-axial coilspring/damper – only lower wishbone differs in design from front suspension. Cast magnesium Lotus upright/hub carrier uses common design for both front and rear and both sides, featuring duplicate steering arms front and rear, both being locked-off via tie-bars to top wishbone arms for directional stability and adjustment.

Steering

Lotus rack-and-pinion with adjustable column, rack mounting and track-rods situated behind the front-axle line – 12-inch three-spoke light-alloy steering wheel with padded leather rim.

Cooling

Gas turbine engine self-cooling/heat resistant – transmission oil cooling – brake ducts and chimneys provided for inboard discs front and rear.

Body

GRP detachable 'chisel'-section nose cowling, separate GRP detachable one-piece cockpit surround/windscreen/engine bay/tail cowling.

Dimensions

Wheelbase	102 inches (8ft 6ins)
Maximum track width	$62^1/2$ inches (5ft $2^1/2$ ins)
Overall height	32 inches (2ft 8ins)
Overall length	174 inches (14ft 2ins)
Overall width	75 inches (6ft 3ins)
Ground clearance	$3^1/4$ inches
Weight	c.1,350lbs
Weight distribution	c. 43% front: 57% rear
Colours	STP dayglo flame vermilion

LOTUS-FORD TYPE 64 – 1969

Chassis

Twin-tube 'ladder-frame' stressed-skin riveted structure of various gauges derived from preceding year's Type 56 design, mainly 16-gauge aluminium-alloy sheet with front and rear bulkhead structures, suspension pick-ups etc, in steel.

Power-unit

159-cubic inch – 2.65-litre – Ford 'quad-cam' 90-degree alloy V8 with Garrett AiResearch turbocharger and Hilborn fuel injection – mounted 'about-face' in rear bay to place clutch/output face immediately behind rear cockpit bulkhead, powering specially-designed Lotus-Hewland gearbox, central torque-split and outputs to ZF final-drive/differential units on front and rear axle lines. Power output in excess of 700bhp at 10,000rpm.

Transmission

Power unit installation arranged to accommodate Lotus-designed ZF- and Hewland-made 4-wheel drive system incorporating Ferguson Formula components – front and rear propeller shafts passing along left-side of tub. Output shaft at front-end of gas turbine drove via 3-inch Morse chain into Ferguson Formula compound centre differential situated behind left-rear of cockpit – fore-and-aft drive from solid steel torsion shafts powering ZF spiral-bevel limited-slip final-drive units on front and rear axle lines, Hardy-Spicer jointed drive-shafts then powering road wheels – compound differential stressed to accommodate c.850bhp.

Fuel tanks

75 gallons of alcohol fuel, accommodated in four main FPT rubberised rupture-proof bag tanks within the 'monocoque' chassis bays – filling via aeronautical-standard Avery-Hardoll non-drip spring-loaded pressure couplings. All tanks inter-connected with non-return valves to prevent fuel surge on corners and under braking. Rearward surge allowed to fuel off-takes.

Oil tank

Large capacity rupture-proof membrane protected outboard reservoir slung from rear face of rear bulkhead in tail of car – flanked by smaller-capacity catch tank of similar construction

Brakes

Girling ventilated discs mounted inboard upon the transmission half-shafts at front and rear – two master cylinders and independent front/rear operation. Ferodo/Raybestos pads interchanged.

Wheels

Specially-manufactured Lotus peg-drive magnesium-alloy four-spoke castings retained by three-eared knock-off centre-lock spinners. 15-inch diameter x 10.0-inch wide rims front and rear.

Tyres

Firestone tyres
Front – 9.20 x 15 inch
Rear – 9.20 x 15 inch

Front suspension

Fabricated unequal-length upper and lower wishbones – front element of top wishbone extending inboard into bell-crank to actuate inboard-mounted co-axial coilspring/damper – cast magnesium Lotus upright/hub carrier uses common design for both front and rear and both sides, featuring duplicate steering arms front and rear, only rearward arm on front suspension attached to steering.

Rear suspension

Fabricated unequal-length upper and lower wishbones – front element of top wishbone extending inboard into bell-crank to actuate inboard-mounted co-axial coilspring/damper – only lower wishbone differs in design from front suspension. Cast magnesium Lotus upright/hub carrier uses common design for both front and rear and both sides, featuring duplicate steering arms front and rear, both being locked-off via tie-bars to top wishbone arms for directional stability and adjustment.

Steering

Lotus/Cam Gears rack-and-pinion with adjustable column, swinging rack mounting and track-rods situated ahead of the front-axle line – 12-inch three-spoke light-alloy steering wheel with padded leather rim.

Cooling

Nose-mounted water cooling radiator/oil cooling matrices in conventional nose duct – expended radiator airflow exhausted through front suspension cut-outs each side of body – transmission oil cooling – brake ducts and chimneys provided for inboard discs front and rear.

Body

GRP detachable 'chisel'-section nose cowling, separate GRP detachable cockpit surround/windscreen and also a third separate engine bay/tail cowl moulding incorporating vast 'duck tail' aerodynamic empennage since USAC regulations specifically prohibited road-race/Formula 1-style strutted rear wings permitting free airflow licking undersurface. Rear ducktail effect trimmed out by low aspect-ratio front canard surfaces each side of nose-cone.

Dimensions

Wheelbase	100 inches (8ft 4ins)
Maximum track width	$62^{1}/_{2}$ inches (5ft $2^{1}/_{2}$ ins)
Overall height	32 inches (2ft 8ins)
Overall length	160 inches (13ft 4ins)
Overall width	75 inches (6ft 3 ins)
Ground clearance	$3^{1}/_{4}$ inches
Weight	c. 1,400lbs
Weight distribution	c. 47% front: 53% rear
Colours	STP dayglo flame vermilion

APPENDIX 2

Major event race record of USAC Lotuses 1963–1969

30 MAY 1963 – INDIANAPOLIS 500-MILES

92	Jim Clark	29-Ford '29/3'	Q.5th – 149.750mph **F. SECOND – 142.752mph**
93	Dan Gurney	29-Ford '29/1'	Q. 12th – 149.019mph F. 7th – 140.071mph
91	Dan Gurney	29-Ford '29/2'	Wrecked in qualifying crash

18 AUGUST 1963 – MILWAUKEE 200-MILES

| 92 | Jim Clark | 29-Ford '29/3' | **Q. POLE – 109.307mph** **F. FIRST – 104.48mph** |
| 93 | Dan Gurney | 29-Ford '29/1' | **Q. SECOND – 108.781mph** F. 3rd – flagged, 199 laps |

22 SEPTEMBER 1963 – TRENTON 200-MILES

| 92 | Jim Clark | 29-Ford '29/3' | **Q. POLE – 109.356mph** C. 21st – Rtd, oil pipe, **LED** |
| 93 | Dan Gurney | 29-Ford '29/1' | **Q. SECOND – 109.025mph** C. 16th – Rtd, oil pipe, **LED** |

30 MAY 1964 – INDIANAPOLIS 500-MILES

12	Dan Gurney	34-Ford '34/1'*	Q.6th – 154.487mph C. 17th – withdrawn at 110 laps
6	Jim Clark	34-Ford '34/3'*	**Q. POLE – 158.828mph** C. 24th – Rtd, tyre, 47 laps – **LED**
51	Bobby Marshman	29-Ford '29/2'	**Q. 2nd – 157.857mph** C. 25th – Rtd oil pipe, 39 laps – **LED**
36	Team spare car	34-Ford '34/2'*	Not used for race

23 AUGUST 1964 – MILWAUKEE 200-MILES

98	Parnelli Jones	34-Ford '34/3'	**Q. POLE – 111.012mph** **F. FIRST – 104.48mph**
1	A.J.Foyt	34-Ford '34/2'	Q. 3rd – 109.900mph Disqualified – 1 lap
51	Bobby Marshman	29-Ford '29/3'?	Q.7th – 107.223mph C. 24th – flagged, 37 laps

27 SEPTEMBER 1964 – TRENTON 200-MILES

| 98 | Parnelli Jones | 34-Ford '34/2' | **Q. POLE – 114.140mph** **F. FIRST – 96.415mph** |
| 6 | Jim Clark | 34-Ford '34/3' | Q.7th – 109.923mph Rtd – mechanical, 96 laps |

31 MAY 1965 – INDIANAPOLIS 500-MILES

82	Jim Clark	38-Ford '38/1'	**Q. 2nd – 160.729mph** **F. FIRST – 150.686mph**
98	Parnelli Jones	34-Ford '34/3'	Q. 5th – 158.625mph **F. 2nd – 149.200mph**
74	Al Miller	29-Ford '29/2'	Q. 7th – 157.805mph F. 4th – 146.581mph
83	Bobby Johns	38-Ford '38/2'(2)	Q. 22nd – 155.481mph F. 7th – flagged, 197 laps
1	A.J.Foyt	34-Ford '34/2'	**Q. POLE – 161.233mph** C. 15th – drop gears, 115 laps
17	Dan Gurney	38-Ford '38/3'	**Q. 3rd – 158.898mph** C. 26th – timing gears, 42 laps

Believed correct Type 34 chassis numbers

30 MAY 1966 – INDIANAPOLIS 500-MILES

19	Jim Clark	38-Ford '38/4'	Q. 2nd – 164.114mph F. 2nd – 143.843mph
18	Al Unser	38-Ford '38/7'	Q. 23rd – 162.372mph C. 12th – crash, 161 laps
2	A.J.Foyt	38-Ford '38/6'	Q. 18th – 161.355mph C. 26th – collision, 0 laps
75	Al Miller	29-Ford '29/2'	Q. 30th – 158.681mph C. 30th – collision, 0 laps
1	Mario Andretti	38-Ford '38/5'	Used in practice but unraced

30 MAY 1967 – INDIANAPOLIS 500-MILES

22	Larry Dickson	38-Ford '38/3'	Q. 21st – 162.543mph C. 15th – spun out, 180 laps
31	Jim Clark	38-Ford '38/7'(2)	Q. 16th – 163.213mph C. 31st – piston, 35 laps
81	Graham Hill	42F-Ford '42/B1'	Q. 31st – 163.317mph C. 32nd – piston, 23 laps
80	Graham Hill	38-Ford '38/8/S'	Originally assigned car set aside during qualifying

30 MAY 1968 – INDIANAPOLIS 500-MILES

60	Joe Leonard	56-P&W '56/1'	*Q. POLE – 171.599mph* C. 12th – fuel pump shaft, 191 laps – *LED*
20	Art Pollard	56-P&W '56/4'	Q. 11th – 166.297mph C. 13th – fuel pump shaft, 188 laps
70	Graham Hill	56-P&W '56/3'	Q. 2nd – 171.208mph C. 19th – crashed, 110 laps
30	Greg Weld	56-P&W '56/2'	Damaged in Mike Spence's fatal practice crash

30 MAY 1969 – INDIANAPOLIS 500-MILES

64	Mario Andretti	64-Ford '64/4'	Wrecked in practice crash due to hub failure
70	Graham Hill	64-Ford '64/2'	Withdrawn after delays caused by above
80	Jochen Rindt	64-Ford '64/3'	Withdrawn as above
60	Team spare car	64-Ford '64/1'	Spare car duties ended by team withdrawal above

Chassis Register, 1963–1996

CHASSIS SUMMARY

Between 1963 and 1969, Team Lotus and Lotus Components manufactured a total of 26 single-seater racing cars to compete at Indianapolis and in other USAC Championship races.

These comprised three 1963-series Type 29s, three 1964-series Type 34s, ten 1965–66 Type 38s, two 1966–67 Type 42s, four 1968 gas turbine Type 56s and four turbocharged Ford V8-engined 1969 Type 64s.

The solitary, stillborn Lotus Type 96 prototype was manufactured by Team Lotus for CART/Indycar racing in 1984.

The following list includes three American-built quad-cam Ford V8-powered USAC cars which were based by manufacturer Carroll Horton upon the Lotus Type 29 design and practise, which used some contemporary Lotus components, and which have subsequently been sometimes confused with the British-built genuine article.

Any further information from readers concerning the history of any of the cars on these pages – and particularly photographic coverage of the cars in the 1966 Mt Fuji event or other minor USAC Championship events – would be gratefully received ...

1963 PROGRAMME

LOTUS-FORD TYPE 29
Three cars built new at Cheshunt, England, 1963

Chassis '29/1'
Pushrod Ford V8 engine – 1963 USAC/Indianapolis race entry number '93' – 'The Mule' prototype and Indy '500' team spare car – painted green and yellow – repainted white and blue and driven by Dan Gurney in 1963 '500' after he had damaged his assigned '29/2' – finished SEVENTH – Milwaukee '200' – driver Gurney – finished 3rd – Trenton '200' Gurney retired – from Team Lotus to Ford Motor Company and converted to quad-cam Ford V8 power as test hack for 1964 programme – *subsequently preserved in the Indianapolis Speedway Museum, presented as Jim Clark's 1963 2nd-place car, which it is not – and retained 1996.*

Chassis '29/2'
Pushrod Ford V8 engine – 1963 USAC/Indianapolis race entry number '91' – Dan Gurney's assigned 1963 race car – painted white and blue – severely damaged in Dan's qualifying crash – returned to Cheshunt for tub repair – converted to quad-cam Ford V8 power for 1964 – one of the Type 29s provided by Ford to Lindsey Hopkins for Bobby Marshman to drive as 1964 USAC/Indianapolis race entry number '51' – the *'Pure Firebird Special'* – painted red and white – led race before retirement in 1964 '500' – damaged in Marshman's race accident at Milwaukee week following Indy – subsequently from Ford Dearborn with suspension parts of a second Type 29 to Carroll Horton for entrant Jerry Alderman and driver Al Miller as *'Jerry Alderman Special'* – painted white-and-blue – 1965 USAC/Indianapolis race entry number '74' – finished FOURTH in 1965 '500' – retained 1966 USAC/Indianapolis race entry number '75' – involved in multiple collision on startline of 1966 '500' but survived with moderate damage – rebuilt by Carroll Horton as show car for Stewart-Warner company use during 1967 – to Nelson Carr for *Formule Libre* – sold by his uncle Scott Carr to Jim Toensing, California – to Tom Candlish/Chris Mann and UK ownership syndicate – *beautifully restored by Sid Hoole Racing, with Mathwall Engineering pushrod Ford V8 engine, England, 1993–96 – to Brooks auction sale, Goodwood Festival of Speed, June 1996 ...*

Chassis '29/3'
Pushrod Ford V8 engine – 1963 USAC/Indianapolis race entry number '92' – Jim Clark's assigned 1963 race car – painted green and yellow – qualified 5th, finished SECOND – Milwaukee '200' qualified on POLE, finished FIRST, driver Clark – Trenton '200' – qualified on POLE, retired, driver Clark – taken over by Ford Dearborn – converted to quad-cam Ford V8 engine and supplied to Lindsey Hopkins team as *'Pure Firebird Special'* replacement for damaged '29/2' post-Milwaukee 1964 – inheriting Hopkins team's 1964-season USAC/Indianapolis race entry number '91' – painted white and red – we believe this was definitely the *'Pure Firebird Special'* Type 29 destroyed in Bobby Marshman's fatal accident while testing at Phoenix, Arizona, November 1964. *According to most accounts destroyed by fire after heavy impact – some suggest rear end of tub survived but not useable – WRITTEN-OFF.*

THE CARROLL HORTON 'TYPE 29 REPLICAS':
From the ex-Ford float of Lotus Type 29 components, it appears that during 1965–67 Carroll Horton also assembled three further cars around new-made chassis tubs:

This trio may be identified as follows:

'The Green Car': *Quad-cam Ford V8 engine – Lotus-based design modi-*

fied to offer enlarged fuel capacity for 1966 Indy '500' but subsequently found still to be short on capacity – finished too late for the event, subsequently unraced – ran during filming of the Paul Newman movie 'Winning' in 1968 – subsequently to Tom Acker – to William Wonder/Tom Powers, USA – believed retained 1996.

'The Silver Car': *Quad-cam Ford V8 engine – One of an effectively identical pair (see 'Gold Car' below) assembled as a Type 29-based USAC car design with new enlarged race-tankage stressed-skin tub labelled as having been manufactured by* 'AlCraft Bodies, Madison Heights, Michigan' – *1967 USAC/Indianapolis race number '11' – the* 'Autoteria Car Wash Manufacturers Special' *entered by Diana Horton – driver Al Smith not amongst qualifiers for the '500' – repainted white as 1968 USAC/Indianapolis race number '71' – the* 'Stewart-Warner Special', *driver Jerry Titus not amongst qualifiers for the '500' – reappeared under same USAC/Indianapolis race number '71', same car title, at Indianapolis – subsequently to Tom Acker in company with 'Green Car' above – retaining white livery* – to anonymous owner resident in USA, and retained 1996.

'The Gold Car': *Quad-cam Ford V8 engine – As above – entered by Diana Horton with 1967 USAC/Indianapolis race number '75' as the* "Ashland Oil Special' *– driver Ronnie Bucknum failed to qualify for the '500' – car believed to have been used in several unsuccessful qualifying attempts at Indianapolis – damaged in final attempt 1969* – subsequent fate unknown – *possibly surplus to requirements and* WRITTEN-OFF?

1964 PROGRAMME

LOTUS-FORD TYPE 34
Three cars built new at Cheshunt, England, 1964 – individual chassis number assignations cannot be confirmed, and these three individual cars may in fact have swopped plate identities at various times during their careers – each car's individual history is, however, believed correct irrespective of number notionally applied

Chassis '34/1'
Quad-cam Ford V8 engine – Believed to have been 1964 USAC/Indianapolis race entry number '12' – Dan Gurney's assigned race car, 1964 '500' – painted white and blue – qualified 6th, withdrawn after tyre failures – severely damaged in Walt Hansgen's testing accident, Milwaukee, 1964 – *WRITTEN-OFF.*

Chassis '34/2'
Quad-cam Ford V8 engine – 1964 USAC/Indianapolis race entry number '36' – painted white and blue – Team spare car through May 1964 – to A. J. Foyt 1964 USAC race entry number '1' at Milwaukee '200' (23-8-64) – believed to have been Parnelli Jones's 1964 USAC race entry number '98' at Trenton '200' (27-9-64) – POLE and FIRST – reworked by Lujie Lesovsky as Ansted-Thompson Racing's 1965 *Sheraton Thompson Special* for A. J. Foyt – painted pearl, red and blue – 1965 USAC/Indianapolis race number '1' – pole position at Indianapolis for the 1965 '500', driver Foyt – retired – subsequently retained by Ansted-Thompson Racing/Foyt Enterprises – sold in the Foyt Collection auction at Indianapolis 1994 – *to Pat Ryan, USA, and retained 1996.*

Chassis '34/3'
Quad-cam Ford V8 engine – 1964 USAC/Indianapolis race entry number '6' – Believed to have been Jim Clark's assigned race car, 1964 '500' – painted green and yellow – qualified on POLE – retired from '500', tyre failure, driver Clark – run as J. C. Agajanian/Parnelli Jones USAC race entry number '98' in Milwaukee '200' (23-8-64) driven by Jones – POLE and FIRST – believed used by Clark race number '6' at Trenton '200' 1964 – qualified 7th/retired – then to Agajanian/Jones as '98' in Phoenix '200' (22-11-64) – car modified by Eddie Kuzma as *'Agajanian Hurst Special'* – painted ivory and gold, for Jones – 1965 USAC/Indianapolis race entry number '98' – SECOND – car preserved by Jones – *subsequently to Vel's Parnelli Jones, Los Angeles, USA, and retained 1996.*

1965 PROGRAMME

LOTUS-FORD TYPE 38
Ten cars built new at Cheshunt/Abbey Panels/Hethel, England, 1965–67 – five in 1965 – four in 1966 – one in 1967 as follows:

Chassis '38/1'
Quad-cam Ford V8 engine – 1965 USAC/Indianapolis race entry number '82' – Jim Clark's assigned race car, 1965 '500' – painted green and yellow – qualified SECOND and RACE WINNER – taken over by Ford immediately after the event – consigned to the Ford Museum, generally neglected and abused *circa* 1969 to 1989 and permitted to deteriorate into a damaged and disgusting state – *Ford Museum, Greenfield Village, Detroit, Michigan, USA, and retained 1996.*

Chassis '38/2'
Quad-cam Ford V8 engine – 1965 USAC/Indianapolis race entry number '83' – original '38/2' very badly damaged by Roger McCluskey in Trenton testing accident – painted green and yellow – replaced by new car rebuilt around new monocoque including some salvaged components from original wreck – thus '38/2' (1) here is believed to have been *WRITTEN-OFF.*

Chassis '38/2' (2)
Quad-cam Ford V8 engine – Chronologically the fourth Type 38 to be built, replacing the McCluskey write-off but taking its chassis serial for Customs purposes and also its 1965 USAC/Indianapolis race entry number '83' – Bobby Johns' assigned race car for 1965 '500' – qualified 22nd, finished SEVENTH – from Team Lotus post-Indy to Ford Motor Company – believed used as show car carrying race-winning car number '82' and masquerading as victorious '38/1' – subsequently to Ansted-Thompson Racing Inc/Foyt Enterprises for A. J. Foyt – modified by Eddie Kuzma and reappeared with new Foyt Enterprises 'Coyote' top tub skin for 1966 '500' as Coyote-Ford *Sheraton-Thompson Special* – painted white, red and blue – for George Snider – 1966 USAC/Indianapolis race entry number '82' – qualified third on front row 1966 '500' – crashed – salvaged parts combined with Foyt's own '38/6' wreck from same race to create new car for 1967 season retaining USAC/Indianapolis race entry number '82' – believed to have been the car severely damaged in Bob Christie's 1967 qualifying crash – see '38/6' – *WRITTEN-OFF.*

Chassis '38/3'
Quad-cam Ford V8 engine – 1965 USAC/Indianapolis race entry number '17'

- supplied to Dan Gurney's All-American Racers Inc. as his private entry for 1965 '500' but retired from race – to Gordon Van Liew for driver Larry Dickson and modified by Eddie Kuzma as *'Vita Fresh Orange Juice Special'* – 1967 USAC/Indianapolis race entry number '22' – retired from 1967 '500', driver Dickson – to Ansted-Thompson Racing/Foyt Enterprises – to Dick Smothers – on loan to Cunningham Museum – subsequently to Harrah Museum – sold by auction – *little since heard of car, believed to anonymous ownership and retained 1996.*

Chassis '38/4'

Quad-cam Ford V8 engine – Built-up post-Indy '65 including some McCluskey car (first '38/2') components – painted green and yellow – debut Jim Clark Ste Ursanne les Rangiers and Ollon–Villars mountain-climb events, Switzerland, August 1965 – tested briefly with De Dion rear suspension – STP-Team Lotus 1966 USAC/Indianapolis race entry number '19' – painted STP dayglo red and white – Jim Clark's assigned race car – qualified SECOND, finished SECOND in 1966 '500' – to Ansted-Thompson Racing Inc/Foyt Enterprises – crashed at Milwaukee – rebuilt by Lotus in the UK – *(N.B. before rebuild this car had asymmetric suspension only, post-rebuild it seems to have been fitted with alternative pick-ups for both symmetric and asymmetric suspension; this car has distinctive gearchange clearance pocket which former Team mechanic 'Chalky' Fullalove swears was put in for Clark pre-Fuji '66, inferring this car may have been taken over by Team Lotus as Clark's Japanese race entry [did not start after engine failure during qualifying warm-up] but see '38/8/S')* – returned to Foyt – subsequently to mechanic/driver Crockey Peterson for Formula 5000 – to Chuck Haines – *to Jim Jaeger, USA, and retained 1996.*

1966 PROGRAMME

Chassis '38/5'

Quad-cam Ford V8 engine – 1966 Abbey Panels-built so-called 'Soft-Alloy Special' – supplied via Lotus Components Ltd to Dean Van Lines/Mario Andretti as 1966 *'Dean Van Lines Special'* – painted white and blue – USAC/Indianapolis race entry number '1' – used in practice but unraced in 1966 '500' – to Gene White 1967 for driver Lloyd Ruby as *'American Red Ball Special'* – painted white, red and gold – USAC entry number '25' (interchanged by White team with similarly-numbered Mongoose-Offy turbo) – successful season included qualifying 4th/finishing 2nd Milwaukee 150 – 2nd/1st Langhorne 100 – 2nd/4th Mosport 100 – 4th/4th second Mosport 100 – pole/16th Indianapolis 150 – 4th/4th Ste Jovite 100, 4th/3rd in second Ste Jovite 100 – 11th/4th Riverside 300 – to Paul Wells – to Chuck Haines – to Steve Forrestal/John Mecom – *to anonymous owner resident in USA, and retained 1996.*

Chassis '38/6'

Quad-cam Ford V8 engine – 1966 Abbey Panels-built so-called 'Soft-Alloy Special' – supplied via Lotus Components Ltd to Ansted-Thompson Racing Inc/Foyt Racing Enterprises as *'Sheraton-Thompson Special'* – painted white, blue and red – initially as Foyt's back-up 1966 USAC/Indianapolis race entry number '45' then renumbered '2' as A. J.'s race car for 1966 '500' – severely damaged in startline collision – *see '38/2' (2)* – WRITTEN-OFF.

Chassis '38/7'

Quad-cam Ford V8 engine – 1966 Abbey Panels-built so-called 'Soft-Alloy Special' – taken over by STP-Team Lotus as 1966 USAC/Indianapolis race entry number '18' – painted STP dayglo red and white – Al Unser's assigned car – qualified 23rd, classified 12th – crashed during 1966 '500' – left-front severely crushed and monocoque discarded after inspection at Hethel, England, to be replaced by new under same identity – *thus '38/7'(1)WRITTEN-OFF.*

Chassis '38/8/S'

Quad-cam Ford V8 engine – 1966 Team-built symmetrical suspension Type 38 – *(Team records indicate this car was completed during the Autumn of 1966 and was that taken to 1966 Fuji Raceway USAC event, Japan, for Jim Clark – did not start after qualifying warm-up engine failure – but other vestigial conflicting Team evidence suggests this car was not in fact built until following year. In this case Clark's Mt Fuji car may have been '38/4' – see opposite)* – in any case '38/8/S' here became 1967 USAC/Indianapolis race entry number '80' – Graham Hill's assigned back-up car for 1967 '500' – failed to achieve competitive speed despite much practice – ultimately set aside as unraced spare – subsequently to Frank Eggers/Wayne Koch/Art Leers partnership – to Jerry Grew – to Jim Haynes – subject of uncharacteristically misleading feature in *'Automobile Quarterly'* portraying this car as Clark's 'real' 1965 Indy '500' winner, which claim was such demonstrable tosh as to be laughable – subsequently to Sam Foster – *to anonymous collector resident in USA, and retained 1996.*
NB – *Two Type 42 cars built this season were held over until 1967 due to non-delivery of BRM H16-cylinder engines, see below.*

1967 PROGRAMME

Chassis '38/7' (2)

Quad-cam Ford V8 engine – As above – car rebuilt around new monocoque at Hethel, England – retained by STP/Team Lotus as 1967 USAC/Indianapolis race entry number '31' – painted STP dayglo red and white – driven by Jim Clark in 1967 '500' – qualified 16th, classified 31st, retired – to Frank Eggers/Wayne Koch/Art Leers partnership – to Bill Lough – to Chuck Haines – *via Steve Forrestal to Japan – with Japanese collector, 1996.*

LOTUS-BRM TYPE 42 (LATER CONVERTED TO FORD V8 POWER)

Two cars built new at Hethel, England, 1966 – only one later converted to quad-cam Ford V8 power for 1967 Indianapolis '500' as Type 42F.

Chassis '42/B1'

Chassis originally intended for 4.2-litre USAC variant BRM H16-cylinder engine in 1966 – 1967 USAC/Indianapolis race entry number '81' – painted STP dayglo red-and-white – modified by Team Lotus to accept quad-cam Ford V8 engine as unique Type 42F – chassis plate over-stamped '42F/1' – for Graham Hill in 1967 '500' – qualified 31st, classified 32nd, retired – car remained with STP/Team Lotus unsold through 1969 – eventually to Bill Brack, Canada – painted in Castrol livery as a show car with dummy Chevrolet V8 engine to match his Formula 5000 '42/B2' conversion below – *subsequently to anonymous UK collector and retained 1996.*

Chassis '42/B2'

Second chassis originally intended for 4.2-litre USAC variant BRM H16-cylinder engine - painted STP dayglo red and white - remained engineless at Hethel factory 1967 - eventually sold via Robs Lamplough to Bill Brack, Canada, as basis of Castrol GTX-Ford Formula 5000 car - overturned in race accident at Lime Rock, USA, 1968, in spectacular incident which damaged suspension corners but which monocoque tub survived relatively little damaged - to unknown private owner in Toronto - to Alan Secrest, Ohio, USA - to Chuck Haines - *to anonymous collector resident in USA, and retained 1996.*

1968 PROGRAMME

LOTUS-PRATT & WHITNEY TYPE 56
Four cars built new at Hethel, 1968.

Chassis '56/1'
Pratt & Whitney gas turbine engine/Ferguson Formula 4-wheel drive system - 1968 USAC/Indianapolis race entry number '60' - painted STP dayglo red - test-driven by Graham Hill at Hethel - STP/Team Lotus practice spare car for 1968 '500' - assigned to Joe Leonard - pole position and led 1968 Indianapolis '500' - retired in closing stages - subsequently to Parnelli Jones - *to Vel's-Parnelli Jones, Los Angeles, USA with complete Pratt & Whitney engine and retained 1996.*

Chassis '56/2'
Pratt & Whitney gas turbine engine/Ferguson Formula 4-wheel drive system - 1968 USAC/Indianapolis race entry number '30' - painted STP dayglo red - STP/Team Lotus assigned to Greg Weld for 1968 '500' - test-driven by Mike Spence during Indy practice, crashed fatally - car repaired, returned to Hethel and became basis of unique Lotus-Pratt & Whitney Type 56B - chassis '56B/1' - painted John Player Gold Leaf brand red, white and gold - later John Player gold and black - 3-litre equivalent Formula 1 car raced during 1971 - *1996 with John Player Ltd, displayed at The Donington Collection of Single-Seater Racing Cars, Derby, England and retained 1996.*

Chassis '56/3'
Pratt & Whitney gas turbine engine/Ferguson Formula 4-wheel drive system - 1968 USAC/Indianapolis race entry number '70' - painted STP dayglo red - STP/Team Lotus - assigned to Graham Hill for 1968 '500' - crashed during race - repaired and retained by STP - preserved by Vince Granatelli - loaned to Harrah Automobile Museum - to Jim Williams - *with complete Pratt & Whitney engine donated to Indianapolis Speedway Museum and retained 1996.*

Chassis '56/4'
Pratt & Whitney gas turbine engine/Ferguson Formula 4-wheel drive system - 1968 USAC/Indianapolis race entry number '20' - painted STP dayglo red - STP/Team Lotus - assigned to Art Pollard for 1968 '500' - cannibalised for spares by STP - monocoque retained and reassembled with running-gear parts but without a 'live round' engine as STP show car - Vince Granatelli retains runnable Pratt & Whitney engine - *car displayed by STP's successor company - First Brands Corporation, Danbury, Connecticut, USA - and retained 1996.*

NB - It is often considered, and I have recorded in print, that these Type 56 cars were 'converted' by STP c.1969 to Offenhauser and Plymouth piston-engined configuration for 1969-70 USAC racing. Vince Granatelli assures us - August 1996 - that the 1968 Lotus 56 gas turbine cars as above were in fact preserved intact - "...the piston-engined versions were built all new by us, perfect Lotus copies - chassis, running gear, diffs, everything identical - to accept the conventional engines". Their fates? "They were all crashed, smashed, crushed and junked...they just got used up - they weren't important...". ...Doug Nye

1969 PROGRAMME

LOTUS-FORD TURBO TYPE 64
Four cars built new at Hethel, 1969.

Chassis '64/1'
Quad-cam turbocharged Ford V8 engine/Ferguson Formula 4-wheel drive system - 1969 USAC/Indianapolis race entry number '60' - painted STP dayglo red - STP/Team Lotus - test-driven by Graham Hill at Hethel - team spare car for 1969 '500' - via Robs Lamplough 1970s to Peter Briggs, for York Motor Museum, Western Australia - *subsequently to Glen Waters, UK, and retained, 1996.*

Chassis '64/2'
Quad-cam turbocharged Ford V8 engine/Ferguson Formula 4-wheel drive system - 1969 USAC/Indianapolis race entry number '70' - painted STP dayglo red - STP/Team Lotus - assigned to Graham Hill for 1969 '500' - with Robs Lamplough 1970-80s - *to anonymous British collector and retained, 1996.*

Chassis '64/3'
Quad-cam turbocharged Ford V8 engine/Ferguson Formula 4-wheel drive system - 1969 USAC/Indianapolis race entry number '80' - painted STP dayglo red - STP/Team Lotus - assigned to Jochen Rindt for 1969 '500' - both car and driver survived enormous high-speed spin during Indy practice in this car - with Robs Lamplough 1970-80s - *to anonymous collector resident in USA and retained, 1996.*

Chassis '64/4'
Quad-cam turbocharged Ford V8 engine/Ferguson Formula 4-wheel drive system - painted STP dayglo red - 1969 USAC/Indianapolis race entry number '2' - STP/Team Lotus - assigned to Mario Andretti for 1969 '500' - crashed during practice due to rear hub failure, destroyed by impact and fire - *WRITTEN-OFF.*

LOTUS-COSWORTH FORD DFX TYPE 96
One prototype built new by Team Lotus at Ketteringham Hall, 1984, for prospective private owner/team sponsor Roy Winkelmann.

Chassis '96T/1'
Intended for turbocharged Cosworth-Ford DFX V8 engine - never ran - *retained by Team Lotus/Historic Team Lotus, UK, 1996*

Index

Page numbers in *italics* indicate illustrations

Absalom, Hywel 152, 154, 187, 213
Adams, Albert 166
Agajanian, J. C. ('Aggie') 16, 49, 50, 53, 53, 87, 97, 103, 104, 133, 172, 195
Alderman, Jerry – see Ford
Amon, Chris 154
Anderson, Robert B. 171
Andretti, Mario 127, 128, 133, 146, 181, 203, 206; 1965 '500' 104, 108; 1966 '500' 135, 135, 136, 138, 143, 143; 1967 '500' 154, 160; 1968 '500' 170, 180, 181, 186, 192; 1969 '500' 200, 202, 208, 209, 210, 212, 212, 213; 1975-6 216
Arundell, Peter 66, 178
Attwood, Richard 205, 208
Audrey, Cyril, RAC timekeeper 50, 51, 80, 82, 142, 157, 191

Banks, Henry 165
Barry, Mick 100
Bartils, Graham 152
'Bath-tub' chassis, origin of term 28-29, 36, 63
Beebe, Leo 86, 87, 89, 90, 91, 97, 126, 132, 134, 150
Belgian GP 1966 149
Bignotti, George 103, 106, 110
Birchall, Arthur 134, 136, 137, 142, 146, 147, 152, 154, 174, 187, 192, 195, 203, 206, 208, 211, 213, 213
Booen, Jerry 216
Brabham, Jack 15, 16, 19, 50, 174
Brack, Bill 168
Brawner, Clint 206
British Racing Green, attitudes to at Indy 46
BRM H16 engine for Indy 129ff, 146, 147, 149, 150, 151, 151, 153, 162
Broadley, Eric, and Lola Cars 56, 64, 65
Brown, Norm 195
Bushell, Fred 30, 69, 86, 185
'Butty' – see Arthur Birchall

Cagle, Clarence 165, 171
Carson, Johnny 173, 173
'Chalky' – see Eamon Fullalove
Chapman, Colin 6, 10, 29, 40, 45, 47, 49, 51, 71, 82, 97, 98, 105, 110, 121, 122, 123, 136, 142, 155, 157, 169, 174, 175, 183, 202, 203; death of 216-217; character 20, 32,

42-43, 44, 56, 59, 64, 65, 66, 76, 103, 137, 141-142, 147, 153-154, 188
Chappell, Ron 100
'Chins, Charlie' – see Mike Underwood
Clark, Jim 6; contracts with Lotus 69; relations with Chapman 72, 154; 1962 World Championship 20, 23, 29, 30, 31; 1963 '500' 22-24, 29, 29, 37, 40, 40, 41, 43, 45, 52, 66, 109; 1963 International Trophy, Silverstone 46; 1963 Monaco GP 50; 1963 Milwaukee '200' 57ff; 1963 Italian GP 59; 1963 Trenton '200' 59ff; 1963 Mexican GP 61; 1963 South African GP 63; testing quad-cam engine 61; 1964 Silverstone 71; 1964 Monaco GP 75; 1964 Dutch GP 80; 1964 '500' 75, 78ff, 82, 85, 110; 1964 Trenton '200' 91; 1965 Trenton 99; 1965 '500' 104, 105, 106ff, 112, 121, 122, 123; 1965 Swiss hill-climbs 127; 1966 Monaco GP 139; 1966 '500' 115, 136, 138, 142, 143, 145; 1966 US GP 146; 1966 Italian GP 149-150; 1966 US GP 150; 1967 '500' 116, 155, 158, 160, 161; 1968 '500' 169, 173-174, 174; death at Hockenheim 177; funeral 177-178; Jim Clark Foundation set up 181; character 30, 31, 54, 130, 161
Clode, Graham 70, 99, 105, 106, 123, 124, 127, 128, 136, 141, 142, 142, 152
Colotti gearboxes 28, 32, 34, 35, 36
Cooper, John 16, 73
Copp, Harley 14, 151
Costin, Mike 17, 27, 64, 65, 130, 218
Cosworth DFV V8 engine 14, 129, 155, 155, 163, 165, 218
Cowe, Bill 187
Cowley, Fred 165, 168, 174, 187, 190, 194, 195
Crosthwaite, John 19

Dance, Bob 32, 42, 88, 89, 100, 126, 127, 158
Darnell, Bay 195
Davies, John 88
Dean, Al (Dean Van Lines team) 127, 180
De Tomaso, Alejandro 130
Dickson, Larry 117
Dixon, Freddie 163

Ducarouge, Gerard 216, 217, 218
Duckworth, Keith 157, 157, 218
Duman, Ronnie 82, 195-196
Dutch Grand Prix, Zandvoort: 1962 18; 1964 80
Duxberry, John 70

Ecclestone, Bernie 216
Endruweit, Jim 17, 23-24, 26, 31-32, 37, 39, 45, 49, 51, 52, 59, 70, 84, 95, 98, 116, 129, 146, 151, 152, 152, 154, 156, 163, 185
English Ford Line Association (EFLO) 65, 66, 70, 87, 123, 132
Evans, Dave 15, 16, 86, 104

Farmer, George 34
Fengler, Harlan 53, 165, 184, 186, 201
Ferguson, Andrew 8, 98, 207; Lotus Competitions Manager 27, 73; accounting duties 27, 66, 202; office at Lotus 30; making travel arrangements 59; at Indy 72, 82, 142; founding of Formula 1 Constructors' Assoc 65; and company aviation 65; 'nursemaiding' Chapman 73; seeking sponsorship 201-202; leaves Lotus 207-208, 214
Ferguson Research 57, 163-164, 165, 166, 170, 175, 195
four-wheel-drive system 57, 153, 163
Ferrari, association with Ford 56
Ferris, Geoff 134
Fisher, Carl G. 11

Ford engines
First V8 engines 13-14
PR V8 for 1963 '500' 21ff, 24ff, 34, 34ff, 35, 37, 39, 39, 40-42, 46, 55; to replace turbines in 56s 195
Quad-cam for 1964 '500' 16, 56, 60ff, 67, 67, 68, 69, 71
for 1965 '500' 94, 95, 126
for 1966 '500' 133, 141
for 1967 '500' 150, 151
Turbo-supercharged V8 for 1969 198, 202, 212
Lotus LV 220 offered to Ford for 1969 198

Ford, Jerry Alderman 151
Fowler, Bill 45, 48, 95, 99, 106
Foyt, A. J. 1963 '500' 45; 1963

Milwaukee '200' 57; 1963 Trenton '200' 59; 1964 '500' 75, 79, 84; 1964 Trenton '200' 89; 1965 '500' 101ff, 106, 113, 121; 1965 Milwaukee '200' 126; 1966 '500' 116, 135, 136, 138, 142, 146; 1966 Milwaukee '200' 145; 1967 '500' 157, 160; 1968 '500' 192; 1969 '500' 212
Franks, Roy 66, 100
French Grand Prix: 1962 20
Frey, Donald 15, 16, 21, 86, 122, 124
Fuels, comparisons between 22, 25, 47, 85, 94, 95, 142
fuel bags/tanks 32, 94, 133
Fullalove, Eamon 152, 154
'Funny cars' 16

Gardner, 'Big Jim' 52
Gardner, Derek 166, 182, 184, 190, 194, 195, 208
Garner, Doug 180, 187, 192, 194, 195
Gas turbine-engined cars (see also Pratt & Whitney, Paxton Turbocar, Lotus Type 56) 153, 159, 160, 164, 165, 195, 196, 197, 198, 200
Gay, William (Bill) H. 15, 25, 28, 35, 39, 50, 55, 62
Ginther, Richie 154
Granatelli, Anthony 'Andy' (see also STP and Team Lotus) 11, 57, 104, 118, 127, 130, 131, 137, 142, 144, 155, 163, 164, 168, 169, 171, 173, 177, 178, 182, 183, 184, 186, 188, 191, 192, 193, 194, 195, 198, 199, 200, 202, 212, 212, 214
Granatelli, 'Big Vince' 130, 131, 187-188, 189, 195
Granatelli, 'Little Vince' 130, 137, 182, 194
Granatelli, Joe 130, 156, 173
Grand Prix Models Corporation 170, 171, 180, 196
Gregory, Masten 74, 74, 127
Group Lotus, move to Hethel 148
Gulf Oil Corporation 138
Gurney, Dan 18-20; character 54; French GP, 1962 20; 1963 '500' 26-27, 29, 38, 40, 40, 46, 48, crash 48, 48, 50, 54, 109; 1963 Monaco GP 50; 1963 Milwaukee '200' 57; testing quad-cam engine 61; 1964 Sebring 12-Hours 70; 1964 Silverstone 71; 1964 Dutch GP 80; 1964 '500' 75, 83

All-American Racers 68, 95, 124; 1965 '500' 97, 99, 104, 106, 106ff, 108, 113, 121; 1966 133; 1967 '500' 154; 1968 '500' 180, 181, 192; 1969 '500' 212
Championship Auto Racing Teams (CART) 217

Halibrand, Ted 45, 133
wheels 46, 48
Hall, Norm 82
Hannah, Dr Tom 165, 182
Hansgen, Walt 87, 89
Hartz, Harry 165
Hawker, Colin 100
Hayes, Walter 134
Hefty, Bob 87
Hethel, Norfolk, Group Lotus HQ 148, 175, 176
Hickman, Ron 17
Hilborn, Stuart 14
Hilborn fuel injection system 60
Hill, Graham 137; 1963 '500' 45; 1966 '500' 136, 142, 143; 1967 '500' 116, 148, 155ff, 156, 158, 159; 1968 '500' 170, 175, 175, 180, 181, 188, 191, 192, 194; 1968 Spanish GP 185; 1968 Monaco GP 191; 1968 Mosport 196; 1969 Spanish GP 205; 1969 Monaco GP 208; 1969 '500' 200, 202, 203, 203, 206, 208; character 159, 161
Hill-climbs, Switzerland 1965 127
Holdaway, George 34
Holt, Vic 95
Honda, Soichiro 71
Hopkins, Lindsey 16, 62, 63, 68, 79, 110, 128
Housington, Maj-Gen Perry 171, 174
Howard Johnson Motel, Indianapolis 153
Hughes, Forrest 80
Hulman, Anton (Tony) Jnr 12, 137-138, 145, 207
Hulme, Denny 180, 183
Hurtubise, Jim 51, 93, 104, 180

Iacocca, Lee 15, 56, 78, 85, 91
Ickx, Jacky 200

Indianapolis Motor Speedway
'Brickyard', origin of name 11
Garages ('Gasoline Alley') 8, 12, 14, 44, 51, 71, 74, 121, 142, 152, 152; toilets 137-138